2015 MINUTES OF THE GENERAL ASSEMBLY CUMBERLAND PRESBYTERIAN CHURCH

Office of the General Assembly

Cumberland Presbyterian Church

September 2015

8207 Traditional Place
Cordova (Memphis), Tennessee 38016

©2015 Office of the General Assembly, CPC

All Rights Reserved. No part of this book may be reproduced or transmitted in any form or by any means, electronic or mechanical, including photocopying, recording, or by any information storage or retrieval system, without permission in writing from the publisher. For information address Office of the General Assembly, Cumberland Presbyterian Center, 8207 Traditional Place, Cordova (Memphis), Tennessee, 38016-7414.

Published and distributed by The Discipleship Ministry Team, CPC Memphis, Tennessee

The Discipleship Ministry Team of the Ministry Council of the Cumberland Presbyterian Church is the successor organization to the Board of Christian Education of the Cumberland Presbyterian Church.

Funded, in part, by your contributions to Our United Outreach.

First Edition 2015

Revised to correct printing errors, September 15, 2016

ISBN-13: 978-0692540640
ISBN-10: 0692540644

OUR UNITED OUTREACH
Made Possible In Part By Your Tithe To Our United Outreach

Vision of Ministry

Biblically-based and Christ-centered
    born out of a specifi sense of mission,
    the Cumberland Presbyterian Church strives to be true to its heritage:
    to be open to God's reforming spirit,
    to work cooperatively with the larger Body of Christ,
    and to nurture the connectional bonds that make us one.
The Cumberland Presbyterian Church seeks—to be the hands and feet of Christ in witness and service to the world and, above all, the Cumberland Presbyterian Church lives out the love of God to the glory of Jesus Christ.

TABLE OF CONTENTS

Vision of Ministry 1
Program 3
Commissioners 5
Youth Advisory Delegates 6
Committees and Abbreviations 6
Committee Meeting Rooms 6
Committee Assignments 7
Assembly Meetings and Officer 8
By Laws of General Assembly Corporation 11
Memorial Roll of Ministers 21
Living General Assembly Moderators 22
Membership of Boards and Agencies 23

Reports
    Moderator 31
    Stated Clerk 32
    Ministry Council Report One 38
    Board of Stewardship, Foundation and Benefit 60
    Board of the Historical Foundation 71
    Board of Trustees of Memphis Theological Seminary 86
    OUO Committee 104
    Commission on Chaplains and Military Personnel 106
    Permanent Judiciary Committee 108
    Nominating Committee 109
    Place of Meeting Committee 111
    Unifie Committee on Theology and Social Concerns 113
    Unificatio Task Force 123
    Board of Trustees of Bethel University 124
    Board of Trustees of the Cumberland Presbyterian Children's Home 127

Memorial 133

Agency Budgets 135

General Assembly Minutes 143

Audits 154

Appendices 289

Church Calendar 306

THE CUMBERLAND PRESBYTERIAN CHURCH

PROGRAM SCHEDULE

Assembly Meetings: Colegio Americano, Cali, Colombia
General Assembly Office: Technology Building, firs floo
Women's Ministry Office: Technology Building, firs floo
Retiring Moderator: The Reverend Lisa Anderson, West Tennessee Presbytery
Host: Andes and Cauca Valley Presbyteries
Joint Host Committee Chair: Mr. Jairo Lopez, Cauca Valley Presbytery
Worship Directors The Reverend Jairo Rodreguez and Reverend Boyce Wallace, Cauca Valley Presbytery
Pianist: Ms. Jaivel Snelling, Wildersville, Tennessee

FIRST DAY - SATURDAY, JUNE 20, 2015

Location	Time	Event
Colesium	8:00 a.m.	Children's Festival
Bldg 9 Classroom F	8:00 a.m.	Orientation for GA Committee Chairs/Co-Chairs
Bldg 9 Classroom G		Orientation for Youth Advisory Delegates (YADs)
Chapel	9:00 a.m.	General Orientation for Everyone
Technology Bldg.	9:30 a.m.	Women's Ministry Convention Meets
Chapel	9:30 a.m.	Orientation for Commissioners and Youth Advisory Delegates
Bldg. 9 Classrooms	10:00 a.m.	Committees Meet
Cafeteria		Lunch Break (see meal schedule for service times)
		Committees Meet following lunch (till 2:00 p.m.)
Chapel	3:00 p.m.	Welcome, Pastor Host, Local Official
	3:30 p.m.	Opening Worship
		The Retiring Moderator: The Reverend Lisa Anderson, W. TN. Presbytery
		Worship Director: The Reverend Jairo Rodreguez, Cauca Valley Presbytery
	4:30 p.m.	Break for Commissioners and YAD's to move to Commissioners Section for business session
	4:45 p.m.	Constitution of the General Assembly
		Adoption of the Agenda
		Report of the Credentials Committee
		Election of Moderator
		Election of Vice-Moderator
		Presentation by the Stated Clerk, Mike Sharpe
		Communications
		Greetings from CPCA - Mr. Leon Cole, Moderator
		Presentation by the Program of Alternate Studies - Michael Qualls
		Corrections to preliminary minutes
		Commissioner Resolutions
		Committee Appointments and Referrals to Committees
	5:30 p.m.	Break for Dinner (see meal schedule for service times)

EVENING PROGRAM

Cafeteria	6:00 p.m.	Light Dinner Reception (*finger foods*) honoring the Moderator and Vice-Moderator of the General Assembly, the Immediate Past Moderator, the President-Elect and the President of the Cumberland Presbyterian Women's Convention
Bldg 9 Classrooms	7:00 p.m.	Committees Meet (till 8:30 p.m.)

SECOND DAY - SUNDAY, JUNE 21, 2015

Location	Time	Event
See Schedule /Assignments		Worship with Local Churches in Cauca Valley Presbytery
		Lunch With Host Church
		Dinner on your own
Chapel	4:00 p.m.	Missionaries/Former Missionaries/Families Reunion (by invitation)
Cafeteria	5:00 p.m.	Clergy Women Gathering (by invitation)

EVENING PROGRAM

Chapel	6:30 p.m.	A Night of Memories/Sharing by Former Missionaries to Colombia and their Family Members

THIRD DAY - MONDAY, JUNE 22, 2015

Location	Time	Event
Chapel	8:00 a.m.	Devotional, Ms. Noriko Matsumoto, Japan Presbytery
	8:45 a.m.	General Assembly business session (if needed)
		Adjourn for Committee Meetings
		Committee Meetings (till 5:00 p.m.)
Technology.Bldg	8:45 a.m.	Women's Ministry Convention
Convention Center	12:00 p.m.	Lunch Break (see meal schedule for service times)
Bldg 9 Classrooms	1:30 p.m.	Committee Meetings (till 5:00 p.m.) **(see location listing)**
	2:00 p.m.	Convention Field Trips
Technology Bldg.	2:00 p.m.	Concert by Bethel University Quartet
	4:00 p.m.	Unification (CPC/CPCA) Presentation/Q & A
Cafeteria	5:30 p.m.	Break for Dinner (see meal schedule for service times)

EVENING PROGRAM

Location	Time	Event
Chapel	7:00 p.m.	"Celebrating 90 years of Mission and Ministry in Colombia" (*A Service of Worship/Holy Communion/Offering for "Set Them Free"*)
Chapel	8:30 p.m.	Cake & Ice Cream Reception following worship service

FOURTH DAY - TUESDAY, JUNE 23, 2015

Location	Time	Event
Chapel	8:00 a.m.	Devotional, Mr. Caleb Rhodes, Youth Advisory Delegate, Missouri Presbytery
	8:45 a.m.	General Assembly Business
Technology Bldg.	9:00 a.m.	Women's Ministry Convention
Cafeteria	12:00 noon	Lunch Break (see meal schedule for service times)
	2:00 p.m.	General Assembly Business
Cafeteria	5:00 p.m.	Dinner Break (see meal schedule for service times)

EVENING PROGRAM

Location	Time	Event
Coliseum	7:00 p.m.	Colombian Cultural Celebration

FIFTH DAY - WEDNESDAY, JUNE 24, 2015

Location	Time	Event
See Tour Schedule		Sight-Seeing Day (optional tours)

SIXTH DAY - THURSDAY, JUNE 25, 2015

Location	Time	Event
See Tour Schedule		Sight-Seeing Day (optional tours)

EVENING PROGRAM

Location	Time	Event
Chapel	6:30 p.m.	Closing Worship

THE CUMBERLAND PRESBYTERIAN CHURCH

COMMISSIONERS
to the
ONE HUNDRED EIGHTY-FIFTH GENERAL ASSEMBLY

PRESBYTERY	MINISTER	COMMITTEE	ELDER	COMMITTEE
Andes (2)	Juan Castano	S/E	Rene Porras	C/M/P
	Michele Gentry	HE	Cecilia Taborda	MC/C/D
Arkansas (2)	Jason Chambers	C/M/P	Donald Hogue	HE
	Duawn Mearns	TSC	Mickey Shell	J
Cauca Valley (3)	Luciria Aguirre	HE	Jesus Maria Garcia	C/M/P
	Fabiola Ariza	TSC	Martha Rodriguez	CPCH/HF
	Wilfrido Quinonez	C/M/P	Julio Cesar Urrutia	S/E
Choctaw (1)	Virginia Espinoza	J	Dean Dancer	TSC
Columbia (2)	Jimmy Miller	C/M/P	Jerry Bowers	HE
	Bob Mullenix	MC/C/D	John Koelz	S/E
Covenant (3)	Kenneth Richards	MC/C/D	Marty Heim	HE
	Terra Sisco	MC/C/D	Jon Pendergrass	C/M/P
	Jesse Thornton	TSC	Baker Thompson	S/E
Cumberland (2)	Freddie Norris	J	Jennifer Curtis	S/E
	Dennis Preston	MC/C/D		
Cumberland East Coast (1)	John Ko	HE		
Del Cristo (1)	George Estes	HE		
East Tennessee (3)	Chris Franklin	J	Nancy Franklin	J
	TJ Malinoski	S/E	Ernst Jean	C/M/P
			Gloria Ortiz	TSC
Grace (3)	Sam Foreman	J	Ben Ingram	MC/C/D
	Keith Mariott	TSC	Donald Ratchford	CPCH/HF
	Lynn Thomas	CPCH/HF		
Hong Kong (2)	Ella Hung	MC/C/D		
	So Li Wong	MC/C/D		
Hope (1)	Susan Parker	CPCH/HF	Leigh Prosser	TSC
Japan (1)	Takehiko Miyai	C/M/P	Takeshi Yohena	C/M/P
Missouri (1)	Linda Rodden	C/M/P	Judith Steffen-Drake	J
Murfreesboro (4)	Joseph Butler	J	Bonnie Gamble	CPCH/HF
	Charles McCaskey	C/M/P	Rusty Mangrum	MC/C/D
	Tommy Jobe	MC/C/D	Mac Nolen	C/M/P
	Brent Wills	CPCH/HF	Naomi Smith	TSC
Nashville (4)	Ted Bane	HE	Mac Holland	MC/C/D
	Fred Polacek	S/E	Mike Salyer	C/M/P
	Kip Rush	TSC	Mike Tuttle	J
	Rob Truitt	CPCH/HF	Susan Wyatt	HE
North Central (2)	Jeff Biggs	C/M/P	Adam McReynolds	S/E
	Edward Montoya	S/E	Sandra Stence	CPCH/HF
Red River (3)	Stephanie Brown	CPCH/HF	Mikel Davis	MC/C/D
	Rich Shugert	TSC	Sheri Kuykendall	S/E
	Cassandra Thomas	S/E	Kathy Lofton	HE
Robert Donnell (1)	Keith Lorick	TSC	Kathy McMurry	J
Tenn./Georgia (3)	Glenn Brister	S/E	James Condra	HE
	Jimmy Byrd	CPCH/HF	Sylvia Hall	CPCH/HF
	Tom Martin	J	Randy Miller	TSC
Trinity (2)	Toby Davis	J	Marvin Terrell	MC/C/D
	Fredy Diaz	S/E	Charelle Webb	CPCH/HF
West Tennessee (3)	Lisa Anderson	TSC	Andrew Castleman	TSC
	Corey Cummings	CPCH/HF	Thomas Keenan	J
	Doy Daniels	HE		

YOUTH ADVISORY DELEGATES
to the
ONE HUNDRED EIGHTY-FOURTH GENERAL ASSEMBLY
(Each Presbytery is eligible to send two Youth Advisory Delegates)

PRESBYTERY	DELEGATE	COMMITTEE
Arkansas	Miles Bray	S/E
Choctaw	(no youth)	
Columbia	(no youth)	
Covenant	Kelsey Hayes	TSC
	Haley Weatherford	J
Cumberland	Tanner Lindsey	TSC
del Cristo	(no youth)	
East Tennessee	(no youth)	
Grace	(no youth)	
Hope	(no youth)	
Japan	Fumika Satoh	M/M/C
Missouri	Caleb Rhodes	HE
Murfreesboro	William Moss	TSC
	Arianna Whaley	S/E
Nashville	Jessica Bane	M/M/C
	Wendy Keiser	CPCH/HF
North Central	Charli Uhlrich	CPCH/HF
Red River	Jacob Perkey	CPCH/HF
	Logan Reed	J
Robert Donnell	John Lorick	MC/C/D
Tennessee Georgia	(no youth)	
Trinity	Benjamin Diaz	M/M/C
	Davis Webb	MC/C/D
West Tennessee	Hunter Webster	HE

COMMITTEES ABBREVIATIONS AND MEETING ROOMS

Colegio Americano
All committees will meet in Building 9.
(see Campus Map of Colegio)

ABBREV.	COMMITTEE	MEETING ROOMS
C/M/P	Chaplains/Missions/Pastoral Development	G
CPCH/HF	Children's Home/Historial Foundation	F
HE	Higher Education	E
J	Judiciary	D
MC/C/D	Ministry Council/Communications/Discipleship	C
S/E	Stewardship/Elected Officers	B
TSC	Theology/Social Concerns	A

COMMITTEE ASSIGNMENTS

1. **CHAPLAINS/MISSIONS/PASTORAL DEVELOPMENT (Bldg 9 room G)**
   Chair: Rev. Charles McCaskey **Co-Chair:** Rev. Linda Rodden
   Ministers: Jeff Biggs, Jason Chambers, Jimmy Miller, Takehiko Miyai, Wilfrido Quinonez
   Elders: Jesus Maria Garcia, Ernst Jean, Mac Nolen, Jon Pendergrass, Rene Porras, Mike Sayler, Takeshi Yohena
   Youth Advisory Delegates: Jessica Bane, Benjamin Diaz, Fumika Satoh

2. **CHILDREN'S HOME/HISTORICAL FOUNDATION (Bldg 9 room F)**
   Chair: Rev. Susan Parker **Co-Chair:** Rev. Rob Truitt
   Ministers: Stephanie Brown, Jimmy Byrd, Corey Cummings, Lynn Thomas, Brent Wills
   Elders: Bonnie Gamble, Sylvia Hall, Donald Ratchford, Martha Rodriguez, Sandra Stence, Charelle Webb
   Youth Advisory Delegates: Wendy Keiser, Jacob Perkey, Charli Uhlrich

3. **HIGHER EDUCATION (Bldg 9 room E)**
   Chair: Rev. George Estes **Co-Chair:** Rev. Doy Daniels
   Ministers: Lucira Aguirre, Ted Bane, Chris Franklin, Michele Gentry, John Ko
   Elders: Jerry Bowers, James Condra, Martin Heim, Donald Hogue, Kathy Lofton, Susan Wyatt
   Youth Advisory Delegates: Caleb Rhodes, Hunter Webster

4. **JUDICIARY (Bldg 9 room D)**
   Chair: Rev. Virginia Espinoza **Co-Chair:** Rev. Joe Butler
   Ministers: Toby Davis, Sam Foreman, Tom Martin, Freddie Norris
   Elders: Nancy Franklin, Thomas Keenan, Kathy McMurry, Mickey Shell, Judith Steffen-Drake, Mike Tuttle
   Youth Advisory Delegates: Logan Reed, Haley Weatherford

5. **MINISTRY COUNCIL/COMMUNICATIONS/DISCIPLESHIP (Bldg 9 room C)**
   Chair: Elder Mikel Davis **Co-Chair:** Rev. Terra Sisco
   Ministers: Ella Hung, Tommy Jobe, Robert Mullenix, Dennis Preston, Ken Richards, So Li Wong
   Elders: Mac Holland, Ben Ingram, Rusty Mangrum, Cecilia Taborda, Marvin Terrell
   Youth Advisory Delegates: John Lorick, Davis Webb

6. **STEWARDSHIP/ELECTED OFFICERS (Bldg 9 room B)**
   Chair: Rev. Edward Montoya **Co-Chair:** Rev. Cassandra Thomas
   Ministers: Glen Brister, Juan Castano, Fredy Diaz, TJ Malinoski, Fred Polacek
   Elders: Jennifer Curtis, John Koelz, Sheri Kuykendall, Adam McReynolds, Baker Thompson, Julio Cesar Urrutia
   Youth Advisory Delegates: Miles Bray, Arianna Whaley

7. **THEOLOGY/SOCIAL CONCERNS (Bldg 9 room A)**
   Chair: Rev. Lisa Anderson **Co-Chair:** Rev. Kip Rush
   Ministers: Fabio Ariza, Keith Lorick, Keith Mariott, Duawn Mearns, Rich Shugert, Jesse Thornton
   Elders: Andrew Castleman, Dean Dancer, Randy Miller, Gloria Ortiz, Leigh Prosser, Naomi Smith
   Youth Advisory Delegates: Kelsey Hayes, Tanner Lindsey, William Moss

8. **CREDENTIALS:**
   Chair: Reverend Stephanie Brown
   Members: Reverend Brent Wills, Elder Sylvia Hall
   Youth Advisory Delegate: Benjamin Diaz

ASSEMBLY MEETINGS AND OFFICERS

Historical Review of the Stated Meetings and Officers of:

THE CUMBERLAND PRESBYTERY, 1810-1813

Date	Place	Moderator	Clerk	Members
1810, February	Sam McAdow's House, Dickson Co., TN	Samuel McAdow	Young Ewing	3
1810, March 20	Ridge Meeting-House, Sumner Co., TN.	Samuel McAdow	Young Ewing	14
1810, October 23	Lebanon Meeting-House	Finis Ewing	Young Ewing	16
1811, March 19	Big Spring, Wilson Co., TN	Robert Bell	Young Ewing	19
1811, October 9	Ridge Meeting-House	Thomas Calhoun	David Foster	23
1812, April 7	Suggs Creek Meeting-House	Hugh Kirkpatrick	James B. Porter	28
1812, November 3	Lebanon, KY	Finis Ewing	Hugh Kirkpatrick	22
1813, April 6	Beech Meeting-House, Sumner Co. TN	Robert Bell	James B. Porter	34

THE CUMBERLAND SYNOD, 1813-1828

Date	Place	Moderator	Clerk	Members
1813, October 5	Beech Meeting-House	William McGee	Finis Ewing	13
1814, April 5	Suggs Creek	David Foster	James B. Porter	27
1815, October 17	Beech Meeting-House	William Barnett	David Foster	15
1816, October 15	Free Meeting-House, TN	Thomas Calhoun	David Foster	22
1817, October 21	Mt. Moriah, KY	Robert Donnell	Hugh Kirkpatrick	27
1818, October 20	Big Spring, TN	Finis Ewing	Robert Bell	27
1819, October 19	Suggs Creek, TN	Samuel King	William Barnett	24
1820, October 17	Russellville, KY	Thomas Calhoun	William Moore	30
1821, Third Tues. in Oct.	Russellville, KY	Minutes not recorded		
1822, October 15	Beech Meeting-House	James B. Porter	David Foster	47
1823, October 21	Russellville, KY	John Barnett	Aaron Alexander	48
1824, October 19	Cane Creek, TN	Samuel King	William Moore	68
1825, October 18	Princeton, KY	William Barnett	Hiram McDaniel	76
1826, Third Tues. in Oct.	Russellville, KY	Minutes not recorded		
1827, November 20	Russellville, KY	James S. Guthrie	Laban Jones	63
1828, October 21	Franklin, TN	Hiram A. Hunter	Richard Beard	94

THE GENERAL ASSEMBLY, 1829-

Date	Place	Moderator	Clerk	Members
1829, May 19	Princeton, KY	Thomas Calhoun	F. R. Cossitt	26
1830, May 18	Princeton, KY	James B. Porter	F. R. Cossitt	36
1831, May 17	Princeton, KY	Alex Chapman	F. R. Cossitt	34
1832, May 15	Nashville, TN	F. R. Cossitt	F. R. Cossitt	36
1833, May 21	Nashville, TN	Samuel King	F. R. Cossitt	35
1834, May 20	Nashville, TN	Thomas Calhoun	James Smith	48
1835, May 19	Princeton, KY	Sam King	James Smith	42
1836, May 17	Nashville, TN	Reuben Burrow	James Smith	43
1837, May 16	Lebanon, TN	Robert Donnell	James Smith	49
1838, May 15	Princeton, KY	Hiram A. Hunter	James Smith	47
1840, May 19	Elkton, KY	Reuben Burrow	James Smith	55
1841, May 18	Owensboro, KY	William Ralston	C. G. McPherson	56
1842, May 17	Owensboro, KY	Milton Bird	C. G. McPherson	57
1843, May 16	Owensboro, KY	A. M. Bryan	C. G. McPherson	68
1845, May 20	Lebanon, TN	Richard Beard	C. G. McPherson	95
1846, May 19	Owensboro, KY	M. H. Bone	C. G. McPherson	86
1847, May 18	Lebanon, Ohio	Hiram A. Hunter	C. G. McPherson	71
1848, May 16	Memphis, TN	Milton Bird	C. G. McPherson	100
1849, May 16	Princeton, KY	John L. Smith	C. G. McPherson	75
1850, May 21	Clarksville, TN	Reuben Burrow	Milton Bird	102
1851, May 20	Pittsburgh, PA	Milton Bird	Milton Bird	71
1852, May 18	Nashville, TN	David Lowry	Milton Bird	107
1853, May 17	Princeton, KY	H. S. Porter	Milton Bird	108
1854, May 16	Memphis, TN	Isaac Shook	Milton Bird	112
1855, May 15	Lebanon, TN	M. H. Bone	Milton Bird	101
1856, May 15	Louisville, KY	Milton Bird	Milton Bird	99
1857, May 21	Lexington, MO	Carson P. Reed	Milton Bird	106
1858, May 20	Huntsville, AL	Felix Johnson	Milton Bird	124
1859, May 19	Evansville, IN	T. B. Wilson	Milton Bird	131
1860, May 17	Nashville, TN	S. G. Burney	Milton Bird	168
1861, May 16	St. Louis, MO	A. E. Cooper	Milton Bird	51
1862, May 15	Owensboro, KY	P. G. Rea	Milton Bird	58
1863, May 21	Alton, IL	Milton Bird	Milton Bird	73
1864, May 19	Lebanon, OH	Jesse Anderson	Milton Bird	65
1865, May 18	Evansville, IN	Hiram Douglas	Milton Bird	78
1866, May 17	Owensboro, KY	Richard Beard	Milton Bird	155
1867, May 16	Memphis, TN	J. B. Mitchell	Milton Bird	176
1868, May 21	Lincoln, IL	G. W. Mitchell	Milton Bird	184
1869, May 20	Murfreesboro, TN	S. T. Anderson	Milton Bird	173
1870, May 19	Warrensburg, MO	J. C. Provine	Milton Bird	167

Date	Place	Moderator	Clerk	Members
1871, May 18	Nashville, TN	J. B. Logan	Milton Bird	173
1872, May 16	Evansville, IN	C. H. Bell	Milton Bird	182
1873, May 15	Huntsville, AL	J. W. Poindexter	John Frizzell	165
1874, May 21	Springfield, MO	T. C. Blake	John Frizzell	185
1875, May 20	Jefferson, TX	W. S. Campbell	John Frizzell	169
1876, May 18	Bowling Green, KY	J. M. Gill	John Frizzell	184
1877, May 17	Lincoln, IL	A. B. Miller	John Frizzell	171
1878, May 16	Lebanon, TN	D. E. Bushnell	John Frizzell	205
1879, May 15	Memphis, TN	J. S. Grider	John Frizzell	143
1880, May 20	Evansville, IN	A. Templeton	John Frizzell	194
1881, May 19	Austin, TX	W. J. Darby	John Frizzell	187
1882, May 18	Huntsville, AL	S. H. Buchanan	John Frizzell	188
1883, May 17	Nashville, TN	A. J. McGlumphey	T. C. Blake	204
1884, May 15	McKeesport, PA	John Frizzell	T. C. Blake	148
1885, May 21	Bentonville, AR	G. T. Stainback	T. C. Blake	185
1886, May 20	Sedalia, MO	E. B. Crisman	T. C. Blake	193
1887, May 19	Covington, OH	Nathan Green	T. C. Blake	187
1888, May 17	Waco, TX	W. H. Black	T. C. Blake	217
1889, May 16	Kansas City, MO	J. M. Hubbert	T. C. Blake	217
1890, May 15	Union City, TN	E. G. McLean	T. C. Blake	220
1891, May 21	Owensboro, KY	E. F. Beard	T. C. Blake	213
1892, May 19	Memphis, TN	W. T. Danley	T. C. Blake	229
1893, May 18	Little Rock, AR	W. S. Ferguson	T. C. Blake	226
1894, May 17	Eugene, OR	F. R. Earle	T. C. Blake	167
1895, May 16	Meridian, MS	M. B. DeWitt	T. C. Blake	208
1896, May 21	Birmingham, AL	A. W. Hawkins	J. M. Hubbert	200
1897, May 20	Chicago, IL	H. S. Williams	J. M. Hubbert	224
1898, May 19	Marshall, MO	H. H. Norman	J. M. Hubbert	221
1899, May 18	Denver, CO	J. M. Halsell	J. M. Hubbert	181
1900, May 17	Chattanooga, TN	H. C. Bird	J. M. Hubbert	230
1901, May 16	West Point, MS	E. E. Morris	J. M. Hubbert	226
1902, May 15	Springfield, MO	S. M. Templeton	J. M. Hubbert	255
1903, May 21	Nashville, TN	R. M. Tinnon	J. M. Hubbert	247
1904, May 19	Dallas, TX	W. E. Settle	J. M. Hubbert	251
1905, May 18	Fresno, CA	J. B. Hail	J. M. Hubbert	249
1906, May 17	Decatur, IL	Ira Landrith	J. M. Hubbert	279
1906, May 24	Decatur, IL	J. L. Hudgins	T. H. Padgett	106
1907, May 17	Dickson, TN	A. N. Eshman	J. L. Goodknight	140
1908, May 21	Corsicana, TX	F. H. Prendergast	J. L. Goodknight	136
1909, May 20	Bentonville, AR	J. T. Barbee	J. L. Goodknight	142
1910, May 19	Dickson, TN	J. H. Fussell	J. L. Goodknight	144
1911, May 18	Evansville, IN	J. W. Duvall	J. L. Goodknight	109
1912, May 16	Warrensburg, MO	J. D. Lewis	J. L. Goodknight	119
1913, May 15	Bowling Green, KY	J. H. Milholland	J. L. Goodknight	112
1914, May 21	Wagoner, OK	F. A. Brown	J. L. Goodknight	105
1915, May 20	Memphis, TN	William Clark	D. W. Fooks	116
1916, May 18	Birmingham, AL	J. L. Price	D. W. Fooks	125
1917, May 17	Lincoln, IL	F. A. Seagle	D. W. Fooks	102
1918, May 16	Dallas, TX	C. H. Walton	D. W. Fooks	117
1919, May 15	Fayetteville, AR	J. H. Zwingle	D. W. Fooks	101
1920, May 15	McKenzie, TN	J. E. Cortner	D. W. Fooks	123
1921, May 19	Greenfield, MO	Judge John B. Tally	D. W. Fooks	108
1922, May 18	Greeneville, TN	Hugh S. McCord	D. W. Fooks	102
1923, May 17	Fairfield, IL	P. F. Johnson, D. D.	D. W. Fooks	105
1924, May 15	Austin, TX	D. M. McAnulty	D. W. Fooks	93
1925, May 21	Nashville, TN	W. E. Morrow	D. W. Fooks	114
1926, May 20	Columbus, MS	I. K. Floyd	D. W. Fooks	111
1927, May 19	Lakeland, FL	T. A. DeVore	D. W. Fooks	97
1928, May 21	Jackson, TN	J. L. Hudgins	D. W. Fooks	97
1929, May 16	Princeton, KY	H. C. Walton	D. W. Fooks	98
1930, May 15	Olney, TX	O. A. Barbee	D. W. Fooks	92
1931, May 21	Evansville, IN	J. L. Elliot	D. W. Fooks	98
1932, May 19	Chattanooga, TN	G. G. Halliburton	D. W. Fooks	104
1933, June 14	Memphis, TN	W. B. Cunningham	D. W. Fooks	94
1934, June 14	Springfield, MO	A. C. DeForest	D. W. Fooks	103
1935, June 13	McKenzie, TN	C. A. Davis	D. W. Fooks	104
1936, June 18	San Antonio, TX	E. K. Reagin	D. W. Fooks	100
1937, June 16	Knoxville, TN	George E. Coleman	D. W. Fooks	109
1938, June 16	Russellville, AR	D. D. Dowell	D. W. Fooks	117
1939, June 15	Marshall, MO	E. R. Ramer	D. W. Fooks	126
1940, June 13	Cookeville, TN	Keith T. Postlethwaite	D. W. Fooks	116
1941, June 19	Denton, TX	L. L. Thomas	D. W. Fooks	120
1942, June 18	McKenzie, TN	George W. Burroughs	D. W. Fooks	108
1943, June 17	Paducah, KY	A. A. Collins	D. W. Fooks	94
1944, June 15	Bowling Green, KY	I. M. Vaughn	D. W. Fooks	94
1945, May 31	Lewisburg, TN	S. T. Byars	Wayne Wiman	103
1946, June 13	Birmingham, AL	C. R. Matlock	Wayne Wiman	105
1947, June 12	Knoxville, TN	Morris Pepper	Wayne Wiman	108

Date	Place	Moderator	Clerk	Members
1948, June 17	Nashville, TN	Paul F. Brown	Wayne Wiman	105
1949, June 16	Muskogee, OK	Blake Warren	Wayne Wiman	109
1950, June 15	Los Angeles, CA	L. P. Turnbow	Wayne Wiman	98
1951, June 14	Longview, TX	John E. Gardner	Wayne Wiman	105
1952, June 12	Memphis, TN	Emery A. Newman	Wayne Wiman	120
1953, June 18	Gadsden, AL	Charles L. Lehning, Jr.	Wayne Wiman	107
1954, June 17	Dyersburg, TN	John S. Smith	Wayne Wiman	124
1955, June 16	Lubbock, TX	Ernest C. Cross	Shaw Scates	118
1956, June 21	Cookeville, TN	Hubert Morrow	Shaw Scates	118
1957, June 21	Evansville, IN	William T. Ingram, Jr.	Shaw Scates	119
1958, June 18	Birmingham, AL	Wayne Wiman	Shaw Scates	116
1959, June 17	Springfield, MO	Virgil T. Weeks	Shaw Scates	120
1960, June 15	Nashville, TN	Arleigh G. Matlock	Shaw Scates	130
1961, June 21	Florence, AL	Ollie W. McClung	Shaw Scates	126
1962, June 20	Little Rock, AR	Eugene L. Warren	Shaw Scates	126
1963, June 19	Austin, TX	Franklin Chesnut	Shaw Scates	117
1964, June 17	Chattanooga, TN	Vaughn Fults	Shaw Scates	123
1965, June 16	San Francisco, CA	Thomas Forester	Shaw Scates	114
1966, June 15	Memphis, TN	John W. Sparks	Shaw Scates	124
1967, June 21	Paducah, KY	Raymon Burroughs	Shaw Scates	123
1968, June 19	Oklahoma City, OK	Loyce S. Estes	Shaw Scates	115
1969, June 18	San Antonio, TX	J. David Hester	Shaw Scates	116
1970, June 17	Knoxville, TN	L. C. Waddle	Shaw Scates	116
1971, June 16	Jackson, TN	E. Thach Shauf	Shaw Scates	116
1972, June 19	Kansas City, MO	Claude D. Gilbert	Shaw Scates	110
1973, June 18	Ft. Worth, TX	Thomas H. Campbell	Shaw Scates	101
1974, June 17	Bowling Green, KY	David A. Brown	Shaw Scates	116
1975, June 16	McKenzie, TN	Roy E. Blakeburn	Shaw Scates	120
1976, June 21	Tulsa, OK	Hubert W. Covington	T. V. Warnick	115
1977, June 30	Tampa, FL	Fred W. Bryson	T. V. Warnick	122
1978, June 19	McKenzie, TN	Jose Fajardo	T. V. Warnick	120
1979, June 18	Albuquerque, NM	James C. Gilbert	T. V. Warnick	126
1980, June 16	Evansville, IN	Robert L. Hull	T. V. Warnick	126
1981, June 15	Denton, TX	W. Jean Richardson	T. V. Warnick	126
1982, June 21	Owensboro, KY	W. A. Rawlins	T. V. Warnick	124
1983, June 20	Birmingham, AL	Robert G. Forester	T. V. Warnick	127
1984, June 11	Chattanooga, TN	C. Ray Dobbins	T. V. Warnick	125
1985, June 17	Lexington, KY	Virgil H. Todd	Roy E. Blakeburn	125
1986, June 23	Odessa, TX	James W. Knight	Roy E. Blakeburn	125
1987, June 15	Louisville, KY	Wilbur S. Wood	Roy E. Blakeburn	125
1988, June 6	Tulsa, OK	Beverly St. John	Robert Prosser	119
1989, June 12	Knoxville, TN	William Rustenhaven, Jr.	Robert Prosser	96
1990, June 25	Ft. Worth, TX	Thomas D. Campbell	Robert Prosser	88
1991, June 24	Paducah, KY	Floyd T. Hensley, Jr.	Robert Prosser	106
1992, June 22	Jackson, TN	John David Hall	Robert Prosser	102
1993, June 21	Little Rock, AR	Robert M. Shelton	Robert Prosser	100
1994, June 20	Albuquerque, NM	Donald C. Alexander	Robert Prosser	100
1995, June 19	Nashville, TN	Clinton O. Buck	Robert Prosser	102
1996, June 17	Huntsville, AL	Merlyn A. Alexander	Robert Prosser	95
1997, April 11	Nashville, TN	Merlyn A. Alexander	Robert Prosser	80
1997, June 16	Louisville, KY	W. Lewis Wynn	Robert Prosser	95
1998, June 15	Chattanooga, TN	Masaharu Asayama	Robert Prosser	97
1999, June 21	Memphis, TN	Gwendolyn Roddye	Marjorie Shannon	96
2000, June 19	Bowling Green, KY	Bob G. Roberts	Robert D. Rush	96
2001, June 18	Odessa, TX	Randolph Jacob	Robert D. Rush	88
2002, June 17	Paducah, KY	Bert L. Owen	Robert D. Rush	95
2003, June 23	Knoxville, TN	Charles McCaskey	Robert D. Rush	96
2004, June 21	Irving, TX	Edward G. Sims	Robert D. Rush	87
2005, June 27	Franklin, TN	Linda H. Glenn	Robert D. Rush	91
2006, June 18	Birmingham, AL	Donald Hubbard	Robert D. Rush	87
2007, June 18	Hot Springs, AR	Frank Ward	Robert D. Rush	84
2007, December 7	Nashville, TN	Frank Ward	Robert D. Rush	62
2008, June 7	Japan	Jonathan Clark	Robert D. Rush	82
2009, June 15	Memphis, TN	Sam Suddarth	Robert D. Rush	86
2010, June 13	Dickson, TN	Boyce Wallace	Robert D. Rush	88
2011, June 20	Springfield, MO	Don M. Tabor	Michael Sharpe	82
2012, June 18	Florence, AL	Robert D. Rush	Michael Sharpe	90
2013, June 17	Murfreesboro, TN	Forest Prosser	Michael Sharpe	93
2014, June 16	Chattanooga, TN	Lisa Anderson	Michael Sharpe	86
2015, June 22	Cali, Colombia	Michele Gentry	Michael Sharpe	91

BYLAWS

Bylaws of the Cumberland Presbyterian Church General Assembly Corporation
A Non-profit Religious Corporation Organized and Existing
Under the Laws of the State of Tennessee

ARTICLE 1-RELIGIOUS CORPORATION

1.01 Purpose. The Cumberland Presbyterian Church is a spiritual body comprised of a portion of the universal body of believers confessing Jesus Christ as Lord and Savior. As an ecclesiastical body, the Cumberland Presbyterian Church is a connectional Church which includes all of the judicatories of the Church. The highest judicatory of this ecclesiastical body is the General Assembly of the Cumberland Presbyterian Church (referred to in these Bylaws as "the Church"). This corporation has been formed to serve and support the Church by holding real and personal property of the Church, employing staff to serve the Church, and performing other secular and legal functions.

1.02 Ecclesiastical Authority Not Limited by Corporate Powers. The enumeration in state statutes or these Bylaws of specific powers which may be exercised by the Commissioners, Board of Directors, or the officers of the corporation when acting in their corporate capacity shall not limit their authority when acting in their ecclesiastical capacity for the Church.

1.03 Church Authorities. The doctrine of the Cumberland Presbyterian Church, expressed in the Confession of Faith, Constitution, Rules of Discipline, and Rules of Order of the Cumberland Presbyterian Church, shall have precedence over any inconsistent provision of these Bylaws.

ARTICLE 2-TERMINOLOGY

2.01 Delegates. The corporation's delegates shall be called "Commissioners."
2.02 General Assembly. A meeting of the Commissioners shall be called a "General Assembly."
2.03 President. The corporation's president shall be called the "Stated Clerk."
2.04 Ecumenical Representative. A person who is not a member of a Cumberland Presbyterian Chuch or presbytery but who supports the mission of a denominational entity and is elected to a term of service on that entity shall be called an "Ecumenical Representative."

ARTICLE 3-OFFICES

3.01 Location. The principal office of the corporation in the State of Tennessee shall be located in Shelby County, Tennessee. The corporation may have such other offices, either within or outside the State of Tennessee, as the General Assembly or the Board of Directors may direct from time to time.

ARTICLE 4–COMMISSIONERS

4.01 Commissioners. The Commissioners shall have the powers and authority described in the corporation's charter and these Bylaws. Included among them are the power to:

   a. Elect the elected members of the Board of Directors.
   b. Approve any amendment to the corporation's charter except an amendment to delete the names of the original directors; to change the name of the registered agent, or to change the address of the registered office;
   c. Elect and remove the Moderator, Stated Clerk, and the Engrossing Clerk.
   d. Fill vacancies on the corporation's various boards, agencies and committees, and on the boards of any subsidiaries;
   e. Approve the merger or dissolution of the corporation, or the sale of substantially all of the corporation's assets; and
   f. Transact such other business of the corporation as may properly come before any meeting of the Commissioners.

4.02 Selection of Commissioners: Number and Qualifications. Commissioners shall be selected by the presbyteries. A presbytery shall be entitled to send one minister and one elder for each 1,000, or fraction thereof, active members (including ordained clergy) in the presbytery. Each elder selected as a

Commissioner must be serving as a member of a session at the time of the General Assembly at which he or she will serve. A Commissioner shall continue to serve until no longer qualified or until his or her successor is selected and qualified. The clerk of each presbytery shall certify the presbytery's duly elected commissioners, youth advisory delegates, and alternates to the Stated Clerk in a manner provided by the Stated Clerk.

4.03 Youth Advisory Delegates. Each presbytery may select not more than two youth advisory delegates who should be from 15 through 19 years of age. Advisory delegates may serve as members with full rights on General Assembly committees, but shall not vote as Commissioners.

4.04 Annual Meeting and Notice. The Commissioners shall meet annually at a date and time established by the General Assembly. The meeting shall be continued from day to day until adjournment. Written notice of the meeting shall be mailed to the stated clerks of all presbyteries and published in the Cumberland Presbyterian at least sixty (60) days prior to the proposed meeting.

4.05 Special Meetings and Notice. The Moderator, or in case of the Moderator's absence, death, or inability to act, the Stated Clerk, may with the written concurrence or at the written request of twenty Commissioners, ten of whom shall be ministers and ten elders, representing at least five presbyteries, call a special meeting of the Commissioners. If warranted by a change of circumstances, a called special meeting may be cancelled by the Moderator, or in case of the Moderator's absence, death, or inability to act, the Stated Clerk, with the written concurrence of at least ten of the Commissioners who requested or concurred in the call of the special meeting. Written notice of any special meeting shall be mailed to the stated clerks of all presbyteries, to all Commissioners, and to their alternates at least sixty (60) days prior to the meeting. The notice shall specify the particular business of the special meeting, and no other business shall be transacted.

4.06 Place of Meeting. The General Assembly may designate any place within or outside the state of Tennessee as the place for an annual meeting. If the Commissioners fail to designate a place for an annual meeting, or if an emergency requires the place to be changed, the Board of Directors may designate a place for the annual meeting. The Moderator or the Stated Clerk, as the case may be, when calling a special meeting shall designate the time and place of the meeting in the notice of the meeting.

4.07 Quorum. Any twenty or more Commissioners, of whom at least ten are ministers and ten elders, entitled to vote shall constitute a quorum at any General Assembly. When a quorum is once present to organize a meeting, business may continue to be conducted and votes taken despite the subsequent withdrawal of any Commissioner. A meeting may be adjourned despite the absence of a quorum.

4.08 Voting. Every Commissioner shall be entitled to one vote, which must be cast by the Commissioner in person; no proxies are permitted. All corporate actions shall be taken by majority vote except as otherwise provided by the corporation's parliamentary authority. Voting for members of the Board of Directors shall be non-cumulative.

ARTICLE 5-BOARD OF DIRECTORS

5.01 Authority. The Board of Directors shall manage the business and affairs of the corporation except for any power or authority which is reserved to the Commissioners or delegated to any other agency of the corporation. The Board of Directors is authorized to amend the corporation's charter only to delete the names of the original directors; to change the name of the registered agent; or to change the address of the registered office.

5.02 Composition of the Board of Directors. The Board of Directors shall consist of seven (7) members, who shall be the directors of the corporation. Six (6) members shall be elected by the Commissioners and the Stated Clerk shall serve by virtue of office. All members, whether elected or ex officio, shall have all of the privileges of office.

5.03 Qualification for Election. Each person elected to the Board of Directors shall be a natural person who is a person in good standing of a presbytery or local Cumberland Presbyterian Church. No two directors shall be from the same presbytery, provided, however, that a director who moves from one presbytery to another may continue to serve until the expiration of his or her term of office.

5.04 Election and Tenure. The elected members of the Board of Directors shall serve terms of three (3) years each. The terms shall be staggered so that two (2) directors shall be elected each year. Each person elected shall serve until his or her successor has been elected and qualified.

5.05 Action of Board in Emergency or By Default. If, for any reason, the General Assembly fails to fill a vacancy on the Board of Directors at the next General Assembly, then the Board of Directors may fill the vacancy by majority vote of the members then in office.

5.06 Meetings. The Board of Directors shall meet annually or more often at such time and place as it may set. Special meetings may be called by or at the request of the Stated Clerk or any three directors at any place, either within or outside the state of Tennessee.

5.07 Notice. Notice of any meeting shall be given at least five (5) days before the date of the meeting, except that notice by mail shall be given at least ten (10) days before the date of the meeting. Notice may be communicated in person; by telephone, fax, or electronic mail; or by first class mail or courier. Except as specifically provided by these Bylaws, neither the business to be transacted at nor the purpose of any special or regular meeting of the Board of Directors need be specified in the notice of the meeting.

5.08 Notice of Special Actions. Any meeting of the Board of Directors at which one or more of the following actions shall be considered must be preceded by seven (7) days written notice to each member that the matter will be voted upon, unless notice has been waived. Actions requiring such notice are: amendment or restatement of the corporate charter; approval of a plan of merger for the corporation; sale of all or substantially all of the corporation's assets; and dissolution of the corporation.

5.09 Officers of the Board of Directors. The Board of Directors may have such officers of the board as it may deem appropriate.

5.10 Quorum and Voting. A majority of the members shall constitute a quorum for the transaction of business at any meeting of the Board of Directors. When a quorum is once present to organize a meeting, it is not broken by the subsequent withdrawal of any of those present. A meeting may be adjourned despite the lack of a quorum. The vote of a majority of the members present at a meeting at which a quorum is present shall be the act of the Board of Directors unless a greater vote is specifically required by the Charter or the Bylaws.

5.11 Conference Meetings. Any or all the members of the Board of Directors or any committee designated by it may meet by means of conference telephone or similar communications equipment which permits all persons participating in the meeting to hear each other simultaneously. A member who participates in a meeting by such means is deemed to be present in person at the meeting.

5.12 Action by Written Consent. Whenever the members of the Board of Directors are required or permitted to take any action by vote, such action may be taken without a meeting on written consent, setting forth the action so taken and signed by all of the members entitled to vote,

5.13 Emergency Actions. If the Board of Directors determines by a vote of three-fourths of all its members that an emergency exists of such magnitude as to threaten the work of the whole Church, or of all boards and other agencies of the Church, and that the emergency requires action before the next meeting of the General Assembly, then the Board of Directors shall exercise the powers of the Commissioners in such emergency.

5.14 Compensation. Members of the Board of Directors shall receive no compensation in their capacity as members of the Board of Directors. Members may be paid their expenses, if any, of attendance at each meeting of the Board of Directors.

5.15 Removal of Directors. An elected member of the Board of Directors may be removed by the Commissioners for misfeasance or if he or she is no longer qualified to be elected to the Board of Directors.

ARTICLE 6-WAIVER OF NOTICE

6.01 Written Waiver. Any notice required to be given to any member of the Board of Directors or a Commissioner under these Bylaws, the Charter, or the laws of Tennessee may be waived. The waiver shall be in writing, signed (either before or after the event requiring notice) by the person entitled to the notice, and delivered to the corporation.

6.02 Waiver by Attendance. The attendance of a member of the Board of Directors or a Commissioner at any meeting shall constitute a waiver of notice of the meeting, unless the person attends a meeting for the express purpose of objecting to the transaction of any business because the meeting was not properly called or convened.

ARTICLE 7-MODERATOR AND VICE-MODERATOR

7.01 Nomination and Election. At the beginning of each annual meeting the General Assembly shall elect a Commissioner to serve as Moderator until the next annual meeting. Nominations for Moderator shall come from the floor. One nominating speech, not to exceed ten minutes, shall be permitted on behalf of each nominee. If there is more than one nominee, the election shall be conducted by written ballot. A committee appointed and supervised by the Stated Clerk shall receive the ballots, count them, and certify the election. If no nominee receives a majority of the votes cast, a run-off election shall be conducted. Only those leading nominees who together received a majority of the votes cast on the preceding ballot shall be included in the run-off election.

7.02 Nature of Office. The Moderator of the General Assembly is the ecclesiastical head of the Cumberland Presbyterian Church during the tenure of the office and a spiritual representative of the Cumberland Presbyterian Church wherever God leads. The Moderator receives a precious gift and great opportunity for service in the Church: the freedom to go anywhere and to listen to the mind, heart and spirit of the denomination and to speak with and to the Church. The office of Moderator has great honor and respect, and the person elected to the Office is a priest, prophet, and pastor of the Church at large. The Moderator prays with and for the work of the Spirit of God in the life of the denomination at every opportunity. The Moderator participates in the life and work of the Church as far as possible, and pays particular attention to ecumenical relations, especially with the Cumberland Presbyterian Church in America. Judicatories, congregations, and others are urged to invite the Moderator, and the Moderator is encouraged to attend meetings of Church entities and judicatories to observe the life and work of the Church at every level.

7.03 Duties and Privileges of Office.
   a. The Moderator shall preside at all meetings of the General Assembly.
   b. The Moderator shall appoint, with the consent of the General Assembly, such special committees as are needed;
   c. The Moderator shall serve as chairperson of the General Assembly Program Committee and as a member of the Place of Meeting Committee;
   d. The Moderator shall perform such other duties as may be assigned by the General Assembly.
   e. The Moderator shall serve as an advisory member of the Ministry Council during tenure in office and for the year following tenure.
   f. The Moderator shall observe the places and times God is calling the Church to service, assess the need for a Denominational response to God's call, and report items that concern the General Assembly.
   g. The Moderator shall wear the official cross and stoles of office during the term of office.

7.04 Expenses of Office. Any allowance budgeted by the General Assembly to offset the expenses of the Moderator shall be administered by the Stated Clerk. Persons issuing an invitation to the Moderator are encouraged to agree in advance on arrangements for the payment of travel expenses. Upon the Moderator's retirement from office, a gavel and a replica of the Moderator's cross shall be presented to the Moderator.

7.05 Vice-Moderator. The General Assembly shall elect a Vice-Moderator in like manner. The Vice-Moderator shall perform such duties as may be assigned by the Moderator of the General Assembly and perform the duties of the Moderator in the event of the Moderator's disability or absence from office for any reason.

7.06 Removal. The Moderator or Vice-Moderator may be removed by the General Assembly whenever in its judgment the removal would serve the best interests of the corporation.

ARTICLE 8-STATED CLERK

8.01 President. The Stated Clerk is the principal executive officer of the corporation and shall also have the titles of "president" and "treasurer".

8.02 Nomination and Election. The Nominating Committee may nominate the serving Stated Clerk for re-election. If the Nominating Committee declines to nominate the serving Stated Clerk for re-election, or if the Stated Clerk has vacated the office, resigned, or declined to be re-nominated, then the Corporate Board shall conduct a search for and nominate a candidate to the General Assembly. In either event, further nominations may be made by the Commissioners. The Commissioners shall elect the Stated Clerk by majority vote.

8.03 Term of Office. The Stated Clerk shall be elected to a term of four (4) years. The regular term of office begins on January 1 and ends on December 31. There is no limit on the number of terms which may be served by an individual Stated Clerk.

8.04 Duties. The Stated Clerk shall be concerned with the spiritual life of the Church and with maintaining and strengthening a united witness for the Church. The Stated Clerk shall also generally supervise and control the business affairs of the corporation and see that all orders and resolutions of the General Assembly are carried into effect. In fulfillment of these duties, the Stated Clerk shall:
   01. Have responsibility to provide for the orderly governance of the Church in accordance with the Constitution, Rules of Order and Rules of Discipline.

02. Maintain records of the corporation and respond to requests for official records of General Assembly actions and interpretations of its actions.
03. Represent the Church when an official of the General Assembly is needed.
04. Represent the Cumberland Presbyterian Church in establishing and maintaining relations with other Churches, particulary those of the Presbyterian and Reformed tradition, and in addressing common concerns.
05. Sign all documents on behalf of the corporation or the Cumberland Presbyterian Church.
06. Represent the corporation or the Church in litigation or other legal matters affecting the Cumberland Presbyterian Church, including the selection and employment of legal counsel.
07. Make suitable arrangements for General Assembly meetings, including researching possible meeting sites, contracting for facilities, and arranging space for committee meetings and sessions of the General Assembly;
08. Provide for printing and other communication needs of the General Assembly while in session.
09. Call meetings of the Place of Meeting Committee and the Program Committee.
10. Prepare and distribute an information form to be completed by Commissioners for the Moderator's use in making committee appointments.
11. Advise the Moderator in the appointment of committees.
12. In consultation with the Moderator, refer all matters to come before the next General Assembly; and provide copies of all such referrals to the Commissioners and advisory delegates before the General Assembly convenes.
13. Prepare and distribute preliminary minutes and an agenda for General Assembly meetings which shall provide time for the consideration of any appropriate business, including memorials from a judicatory or denominational entity delivered to the Stated Clerk in writing by April 30.
14. Supervise the recording and publication of minutes and a summary of actions taken by each General Assembly.
15. Make copies of General Assembly minutes available to ordained ministers, licentiates, candidates, commissioners, clerks of sessions, members of denominational entities, schools of the Church, synod, and presbytery clerks, to the Stated Clerk's exchanges and other interested persons in order to encourage lower judicatories and persons in the Church to implement the actions of the General Assembly.
16. File the minutes of each General Assembly with the Historical Foundation as a permanent record.
17. Maintain and update annually the Digest of the General Assembly actions.
18. Represent the Church at large on the Ministry Council.
19. Provide support services for the Moderator and all denominational entities.
20. Receive and make any appropriate response to communications to the Cumberland Presbyterian Church or General Assembly.
21. Maintain a name and address file on congregations, session clerks, pastors, and other leadership of congregations with statistical information about congregations, presbyteries, and synods.
22. Solicit, receive, publish, and disseminate annual reports from churches.
23. Review reports by denominational entities and assist them in complying with correct reporting and budgeting procedures and in avoiding duplication of work.
24. Hold, report annually, and distribute as authorized by the General Assembly or the Ministry Council the Contingency Fund and all other General Assembly Funds not entrusted to the care of a denominational entity.
25. Call the Judiciary Committee into session or by other means secure the advice of the committee on appropriate matters.
26. Communicate with presbyteries and synods on behalf of the General Assembly and attend their meetings from time to time.
27. Provide training for presbytery and synod clerks and orientations for General Assembly commissioners.
28. Generally perform duties as are prescribed in the Constitution or directed by the General Assembly.

8.05 Removal. The Stated Clerk may be removed by the General Assembly whenever in its judgment the removal would serve the best interests of the corporation.

ARTICLE 9-OTHER OFFICERS

9.01 Secretary. The chief executive officer of the Ministry Council shall, by virtue of office, be the secretary of the corporation, and shall in general perform all duties incident to the office of secretary.

9.02 Engrossing Clerk. The Engrossing Clerk shall be elected by the General Assembly to a term of four (4) years. The regular term of office begins on January 1 and ends on December 31. There is no limit on the number of terms which may be served by an individual Engrossing Clerk. The Engrossing Clerk shall serve as Stated Clerk pro tempore during the meeting of the General Assembly in the event the Stated Clerk is absent or unable to serve. The Engrossing Clerk shall perform such other duties as may from time to time be prescribed by the Board of Directors or the General Assembly.

9.03 Additional Officers. The corporation may have such additional officers as it may from time to time find necessary or appropriate.

ARTICLE 10-ORGANIZATION AND RELATIONSHIPS

10.01 Generally. The following are denominational entities related to the Cumberland Presbyterian Church:
   01. Subsidiary corporations: Board of Stewardship, Foundation and Benefits of the Cumberland Presbyterian Church; Memphis Theological Seminary of the Cumberland Presbyterian Church; Ministry Council of the Cumberland Presbyterian Church.
   02. Related corporations: Bethel University; Cumberland Presbyterian Children's Home; Historical Foundation of the Cumberland Presbyterian Church and the Cumberland Presbyterian Church in America.
   03. Commissions: Chaplains and Military Personnel.
   04. Committees: Committee on Nominations; Joint Committee on Amendments; Judiciary, Our United Outreach; Place of Meeting Committee; Program Committee; Unified Committee on Theology and Social Concerns.

10.02 Election and Tenure. The following qualifications and rules relate to service on any denominational entity.
   01. Unless elected as an Ecumenical Representative, no person shall be qualified to serve except a member in good standing in a presbytery or local congregation of the Cumberland Presbyterian Church.
   02. No person who is employed in an executive capacity including Chief Executive, Vice-President, Team Leader, Director, or equivalent in the Cumberland Presbyterian Church is eligible to serve on a denominational entity. No employee of a denominational entity is eligible for service on the same denominational entity.
   03. Each person shall be elected for a term of three years unless elected to fill the remainder of an unexpired term. However, if a person elected to serve on a denominational entity where residence in a particular synod is a qualification for election shall move to another synod while in office, the term to which he or she was elected shall terminate at the close of the next meeting of the General Assembly.
   04. Members of the Committee on Nominations may not be elected to a consecutive term. All other persons may serve up to three consecutive terms for a total not to exceed nine years in office.
   05. A Cumberland Presbyterian who has served on any entity is not eligible to serve on the same entity (except for an authorized consecutive term) until at least two (2) years have elapsed since the conclusion of the previous service.
   06. A Cumberland Presbyterian who is serving on any entity is not eligible to serve on another entity until at least one (1) year has elapsed since the conclusion of the previous service.
   07. An Ecumenical Representative who is serving or has served on any entity is not eligible to serve on any other entity (except for an authorized consecutive term on the same entity) until at least one (1) year has elapsed since the conclusion of the previous service.

10.03 Resignation or Removal.
- 01. Any person serving on a denominational entity who is no longer qualified or eligible to serve shall be deemed to have resigned.
- 02. Any person serving on an incorporated denominational entity may resign by delivering written notice of resignation to the secretary or an executive officer of the denominational entity, who shall promptly report the resignation to the Stated Clerk. Any person serving on an unincorporated denominational entity may resign by delivering written notice of resignation to the Stated Clerk. A resignation is effective when delivered unless some other effective date is specified in the written resignation.
- 03. No member who continues to meet the standard requirements for election or appointment to any denominational entity shall be removed from office except for misfeasance. Removal of a person elected by the General Assembly shall be by vote of the General Assembly.

10.04 Board of Stewardship, Foundation and Benefits. The corporation shall elect the eleven (11) directors of the Board of Stewardship as provided in its charter.

10.05 Cumberland Presbyterian Children's Home. The corporation shall elect the fifteen (15) directors of Children's Home as provided in its corporate articles. The corporation shall elect the directors in such a manner that, immediately following any election, there shall be at least six (6) directors who are members of ecumenical partners of the Children's Home.

10.06 Historical Foundation. The corporation shall elect six (6) of the twelve (12) directors of the Historical Foundation as provided in its charter. The corporation shall elect the directors of the Historical Foundation in such a manner that, immediately following any election, there shall be at least one (1) member from each synod and no person shall be elected if the election would cause two directors from the same presbytery to be serving simultaneously. The remaining six (6) directors shall be elected by the Cumberland Presbyterian Church in America.

10.07 Memphis Theological Seminary. The corporation shall elect the twenty-four (24) directors of Memphis Theological Seminary as provided in its charter. The corporation shall elect the directors in such a manner that, immediately following any election, there shall be at least eleven (11) directors who are members of ecumenical partners of the Seminary.

10.08 Ministry Council.
- 01. The corporation shall elect the fifteen (15) directors of the Ministry Council as provided in its charter.
- 02. The corporation shall elect the directors of the Ministry Council in such a manner that immediately following any election, there shall be three (3) directors from each synod; at least six (6) but no more than nine (9) directors who are ordained clergy; and no more than nine (9) directors of the same gender.
- 03. The Stated Clerk and Moderator shall be designated as Advisory Members to the board of directors of the Ministry Council. In addition, the corporation shall elect three (3) Youth Advisory Members who shall be between the ages of 15 - 17 for 1-year terms, with eligibility for re-election for one additional term.

10.09 Commission on Chaplains and Military Personnel. The commission shall consist of three (3) members elected by the corporation.

ARTICLE 11-COMMITTEES

11.01 General. The corporation shall have the committees provided for in these Bylaws and such other standing or special committees as the General Assembly may create from time to time. Except as otherwise provided in these Bylaws, the Moderator, in consultation with the Stated Clerk, shall appoint all committees.

11.02 Committees of Commissioners and Youth Advisory Delegates. Prior to each General Assembly, the Moderator, in consultation with the Stated Clerk, shall organize the Commissioners and Youth Advisory Delegates into the following committees: Chaplains/Missions/Pastoral Development, Children's Home/Historical Foundation, Higher Education, Judiciary, Ministry Council/Communications/Discipleship, Stewardship/Elected Officers, and Theology and Social Concerns. Each committee shall consider such matters expected to come before the General Assembly as are referred to it by the Stated Clerk. Any denominational organization, the work of which is affected by a matter before a committee, shall be entitled to address the committee.

11.03 Committee on Nominations.
- 01. The committee shall consist of ten (10) persons elected by the corporation in such a manner that, immediately following any election, the committee shall have at least one minister and one lay person from each synod. It is preferred but not required that no two members shall be from the same presbytery.
- 02. Approximately one third of the members of the committee shall be elected each year by the General Assembly and shall serve one term not to exceed three years.
- 03. The committee shall meet not earlier than February 15 each year and shall nominate to the General Assembly qualified persons to fill all vacancies to be filled by vote of the General Assembly, including vacancies on the Committee on Nominations, unless another method of nomination is provided in these Bylaws. The report of the committee shall list the names of nominees, the presbytery if a minister, and the presbytery and the local congregation if a lay person. The Committee on Nominations shall be intentional in nominating persons who represent the global nature of the Church.
- 04. Presbyteries and synods and their moderators and stated clerks are requested to assist the Committee on Nominations by recommending persons for any position by providing the name and qualifications of the potential nominees to the Stated Clerk no later than February 1 on a form to be provided by the Stated Clerk. Nominations from the floor shall also be in order.
- 05. No person shall be nominated for election by the General Assembly unless the nominee has within the past year given his or her consent to the nomination and has been endorsed by his or her presbytery/session clerk.

11.04 Joint Committee on Amendments. The Judiciary Committee shall appoint as many as five of its members to act in committee with an equal number of members of the Judiciary Committee of the Cumberland Presbyterian Church in America. Upon the request of the General Assembly of the Cumberland Presbyterian Church or the General Assembly of the Cumberland Presbyterian Church in America, this Joint Committee shall prepare for the consideration of both general assemblies proposed amendments to the Confession of Faith, Catechism, Constitution, Rules of Discipline, Directory for Worship, and Rules of Order.

11.05 Judiciary Committee.
- 01. The committee shall consist of nine (9) persons elected by the corporation in such a manner that, immediately following any election, the committee shall have at least four members (4) who are ordained ministers and at least three (3) members who are licensed attorneys-at-law. The Stated Clerk shall be staff liaison to the committee, attending its meetings and providing resources and counsel.
- 02. The committee shall meet at least annually upon the call of its chairperson or the Stated Clerk.
- 03. The committee shall provide advice and counsel to the Stated Clerk. Upon the written request of any judicatory or denominational entity made to the chairperson or Stated Clerk, the committee shall render an advisory opinion on matters of church law or procedure. The chairperson shall secure the views of all members of the committee and write the advisory opinion based on the majority view of the members. The committee shall not render legal opinions on matters of civil law nor otherwise engage in the practice of law.
- 04. At least one member of the committee shall attend each meeting of the General Assembly to advise with its officers and Commissioners on matters of church law or procedure. At the Moderator's request a member of the committee shall be available to advise the Moderator during the business sessions of the General Assembly.
- 05. The committee shall be a commission within the meaning of section 2.5 of the Rules of Discipline to hear and determine appeals from synods.

11.06 Our United Outreach Committee.
- 01. The committee shall consist of five (5) persons elected by the corporation in such a manner that, immediately following any election, the committee shall have one person from each synod. Seven (7) additional members will include a member of the Ministry Council, a member of the Corporate Board, a member of the Board of Stewardship, Foundation and Benefits, a member of the Board of Trustees of the Historical

Foundation, and a Cumberland Presbyterian member of the Boards of Trustees of Bethel University, the Cumberland Presbyterian Children's Home, and Memphis Theological Seminary. The executives of the above named denominational entities shall serve as non-voting, Resource/Advocacy members.

    02. The Office of the General Assembly will be responsible for the expenses of the representative of each synod. The represented denominational entities will be responsible for the expenses of their representatives and executives.

11.07 Place of Meeting. The committee shall consist of the Moderator, the Stated Clerk and a representative of the Cumberland Presbyterian Women's Ministries.

11.08 Program Committee. The committee shall consist of the Moderator, Stated Clerk, Director of Ministries, Assistant to the Stated Clerk who serves as secretary, the pastor of the host church, four elected representatives designated by the Ministry Council from among its ministry teams, and one representative designated by each of the following: Bethel University, Board of Stewardship, Foundation, and Benefits, Cumberland Presbyterian Children's Home, Historical Foundation, Memphis Theological Seminary, and the Cumberland Presbyterian Women's Ministry. The committee will begin planning for two years prior to the meeting of a particular General Assembly.

11.09 Unified Committee on Theology and Social Concerns. The committee shall consist of eight (8) members elected by the corporation, the Stated Clerk, and the President of Memphis Theological Seminary. At least one member of the committee other than the Seminary's president shall be a Cumberland Presbyterian member of the faculty of Memphis Theological Seminary.

ARTICLE 12-INDEMNIFICATION

12.01 Indemnification. The corporation shall indemnify any director, officer or employee who is, or is threatened to be, made a party to a completed, pending, or threatened action or proceeding from any liability arising from the director's, officer's or employee's official capacity with the corporation. This indemnification shall extend to the personal representation of a deceased person if the person would be entitled to indemnification under these Bylaws if living.

12.02 Costs and Expenses Covered by Indemnification. Indemnification provided under these Bylaws shall extend to the payment of a judgment, settlement, penalty, or fine, as well as attorney's fees, court costs, and other reasonable and necessary expenses incurred by the director or officer with respect to the action or proceeding.

12.03 Limitation on Indemnification. No indemnification shall be made to or on behalf of any person if a judgment or other final adjudication adverse to that person establishes his or her liability:

    01. for any breach of the duty of loyalty to the corporation;
    02. for acts or omissions not in good faith or which involve intentional misconduct or a knowing violation of law; or
    03. for any distribution of the assets of the corporation which is unlawful under Tennessee law.

ARTICLE 13-TRUSTEE FOR THE CORPORATION

13.01 Trustee. The Board of Stewardship, Foundation and Benefits of the Cumberland Presbyterian Church, a nonprofit corporation existing under the laws of the state of Tennessee, holds certain real property and other assets of the Church as trustee for the use and benefit of the Church. The Board of Stewardship may continue to hold such real property and other assets, but after the adoption of these Bylaws, it shall hold those assets as trustee for the use and benefit of the Cumberland Presbyterian Church General Assembly Corporation.

13.02 Other Assets. Other, additional property may from time to time be conveyed to the Board of Stewardship to be held by it as trustee for the corporation. All assets held by the Board of Stewardship as trustee for the corporation shall be held at the pleasure and direction of the General Assembly.

ARTICLE 14-PARLIAMENTARY AUTHORITY

14.01 Designation. The parliamentary authority of the corporation in all meetings shall be the latest revised edition of the Rules of Order as set out in the Confession of Faith and Government of the Cumberland Presbyterian Church. In matters not provided for in the Rules of Order, the parliamentary authority shall be Robert's Rules of Order, latest revised edition.

14.02 Standing Rules. The following shall be Standing Rules for meetings of the General Assembly and may be suspended as provided in the parliamentary authority. (see Rules of Order 8.34c)

Standing Rules

1. Unless otherwise determined by the General Assembly or by the Stated Clerk in the event of an emergency, the annual General Assembly shall meet on the third or fourth Monday of June at two o'clock in the afternoon to organize, elect a moderator and transact business, and shall close on Thursday or Friday of the same week.

2. Reports of all standing and special committees shall be considered in the order established by the Moderator in consultation with the Stated Clerk. Committee reports may be presented orally or in writing provided to all Commissioners and youth advisory delegates. Those presenting committee reports shall have the opportunity to make remarks and give explanation, such presentations not to exceed ten minutes unless time is extended by two-thirds vote taken without debate. All committee recommendations shall be submitted in writing.

3. All materials from denominational entities for consideration or action by a General Assembly shall be submitted to the Stated Clerk at least thirty (30) days before the meeting of General Assembly.

4. Resolutions and memorials proposed for adoption by individual commissioners rather than denominational entities or judicatories of the Cumberland Presbyterian Church shall be introduced no later than the close of business on the second day of a meeting of General Assembly, and, when introduced, shall be referred by the Moderator, in counsel with the Stated Clerk, to the appropriate committee or committees for report and recommendations to the Assembly.

ARTICLE 15-REPORTS AND AUDITS

15.01 Congregational Reports. Annually by December 1, the Stated Clerk shall send to session clerks statistical forms for reporting congregational data. Session clerks shall mail the completed forms to presbytery clerks by February 1. The presbytery clerk shall mail the composite statistical report for all congregations of a presbytery to the Stated Clerk by February 10.

15.02 Institutional Reports. In order to be considered for inclusion in the General Assembly budget, all denominational entities shall deliver to the Stated Clerk an annual report including a concise description of the organization's work during the previous year and a line item budget for the forthcoming year. Financial reports should be condensed as much as possible while conveying all essential information on the organization's operations. All denominational entities except academic institutions on a fiscal year are requested to maintain their books on a calendar year.

15.03 Reporting Schedule. An electronic copy and two written copies of the annual report signed by two officers of the organization shall be delivered to the Stated Clerk by March 15 each year. Organizations requesting funds from Our United Outreach shall submit multi-year program budgets to the Our United Outreach Committee.

15.04 Audits. Organizations and operations included in the General Assembly budget shall be audited annually by a certified public accountant. Copies of the auditor's report, including any recommendations for changes in the procedures relating to internal financial controls, shall be delivered to the Stated Clerk. Organizations with total receipts of $100,000 or less are not required to have an audit but shall submit their books and financial statements to the Stated Clerk annually.

15.05 Bonds. Each organization or person whose financial records are required to be audited shall have a fidelity bond in an amount adequate to protect all funds held by the organization or person.

ARTICLE 16-AMENDMENTS

16.01 Manner of Amendment. Except as provided below, these Bylaws may be amended or repealed only by the affirmative vote of two-thirds of the votes cast in a duly constituted meeting of the General Assembly. No portion of the Bylaws may be amended or repealed by the Board of Directors. Fair and reasonable notice of any proposed amendment shall be provided as required by state law.

16.02 Extraordinary Actions. In order to be effective the following actions must be approved by (1) the affirmative vote of two consecutive General Assemblies, or (2) a ninety percent (90%) vote of a single General Assembly.
- 01. Terminating the existence of a denominational entity named in Bylaw 10.01
- 02. Creating a new denominational entity other than a temporary committee or task force.
- 03. Decreasing the Our United Outreach budget allocation to a denominational entity by more than 40% of the amount distributed to it during the previous calendar year; or
- 04. Taking any other actions which would cause a drastic change in the mission or structure of the Cumberland Presbyterian Church.

MEMORIAL ROLL OF MINISTERS

IN MEMORY OF
MINISTERS LOST BY DEATH

NAME	PRESBYTERY	AGE	DATE
Brodeur, Evelyn M.	Robert Donnell	91	12/02/14
Chang, John	del Cristo		03/08/14
Chesnut, Walter	Cumberland	98	12/26/14
Cravens, Marvin	Missouri	86	08/02/14
Denton, Clyde M.	Columbia	72	06/27/14
Drylie, James T	West Tennessee	75	02/14/15
Fajardo, Jose	Red River	101	02/21/15
Gerard, Eugene "Stan"	Covenant	82	04/26/15
Hester, J. David	East Tennessee	83	07/31/14
Leslie, Eugene	West Tennessee	83	03/10/15
Matlock, Joe	del Cristo		02/26/15
McGregor, David	Columbia	86	01/23/14
McKee, Margaret	West Tennessee	87	11/06/14
Morgan, Jerry	Red River		09/19/14
Palmer, Walter (Pete)	Red River	87	07/26/14
Powell, Omer Thomas	Cumberland	90	01/30/15
Rapson, Tim <Candidate>	Tennessee-Georgia		03/30/14
Rodriguez, Paul	Cauca Valley		03/10/14
Todd, Virgil	Nashville	93	10/20/14
White, Bobby Earl <Lay Speaker>	Cumberland	71	09/03/14
Wilkins, Marvin E	Columbia	65	04/01/14

LIVING GENERAL ASSEMBLY MODERATORS

2014—REV. LISA ANDERSON, 1790 Faxon Avenue, Memphis, TN 38112
2013—REV. FOREST PROSSER, 1157 Mountain Creek Road, Chattanooga, TN 37405
2012—REV. ROBERT D. RUSH, 17822 Deep Brook Drive, Spring, TX 77379
2011—REV. DON M. TABOR, 9611 Mitchell Place, Brentwood, TN 37027
2010—REV. BOYCE WALLACE, Cra 101 No 15-93, Cali, Colombia, South America
2009—ELDER SAM SUDDARTH, 206 Ha Le Koa Court, Smyrna, TN 37167
2008—REV. JONATHAN CLARK, 88 Woodcrest Drive, Winchester, TN 37398
2007—REV. FRANK WARD, 8207 Traditional Place, Cordova, TN 38016
2006—REV. DONALD HUBBARD, 2128 Campbell Station Road, Knoxville, TN 37932
2005—REV. LINDA H. GLENN, 49 Mason Road, Threeway, TN 38343
2004—REV. EDWARD G. SIMS, 2161 N. Meadows Drive, Clarksville, TN 37043
2003—REV. CHARLES MCCASKEY, 679 Canter Lane, Cookeville, TN 38501
2001—REV. RANDOLPH JACOB, 610 W. Adams Street, Broken Bow, OK 74728
1999—ELDER GWENDOLYN G. RODDYE, 3728 Wittenham Drive, Knoxville, TN 37921
1998—REV. MASAHARU ASAYAMA, 3-15-9 Higashi, Kunitachi-shi, Tokyo, JAPAN
1996—REV. MERLYN A. ALEXANDER, 80 N. Hampton Lane, Jackson, TN 38305
1995—REV. CLINTON O. BUCK, 4986 Warwick, Memphis, TN 38117
1993—REV. ROBERT M. SHELTON, 7128 Lakehurst Avenue, Dallas, TX 75230
1992—REV. JOHN DAVID HALL, 109 Oddo Lane SE, Huntsville, AL 35802
1990—REV. THOMAS D. CAMPBELL, PO Box 315, Calico Rock, AR 72519
1989—REV. WILLIAM RUSTENHAVEN, Jr., 703 W. Burleson, Marshall, TX 75670
1988—ELDER BEVERLY ST. JOHN, 806 Evansdale Drive, Nashville, TN 37220
1982—REV. WILLIAM A. RAWLINS, 3100 Cook Lane, Longview, TX 75604
1981—REV. W. JEAN RICHARDSON, 7533 Lancashire, Powell, TN 37849
1975—REV. ROY E. BLAKEBURN, 111 Park Place, Greeneville, TN 37743

IN MEMORY OF:

Moderator of the 157th General Assembly

ELDER WILBUR S. WOOD

Died October 26, 2014

GENERAL ASSEMBLY OFFICERS

MODERATOR
THE REVEREND MICHELE GENTRY
Urb San Jorge casa 28
Km 8 via a La Tebaida
Armenia, Quindio, COLOMBIA, SA
gentry.andes@yahoo.com
(318)285-1161

VICE MODERATOR
THE REVEREND KIP RUSH
513 Meadowlark Lane
Brentwood, TN 37027
pastor@brenthaven.org
(615)376-4563

STATED CLERK AND TREASURER
THE REVEREND MICHAEL SHARPE
8207 Traditional Place
Cordova, TN 38016
(901)276-4572
FAX (901)272-3913
msharpe@cumberland.org

ENGROSSING CLERK
THE REVEREND VERNON SANSOM
7810 Shiloh Road
Midlothian, TX 76065
(972)825-6887
vernon@sansom.us

THE BOARD OF DIRECTORS OF THE GENERAL ASSEMBLY CORPORATION

(Members whose terms expire in 2016)
(1)MR. TIM GARRETT, 150 Third Avenue South, Suite 2800, Nashville, TN 37201
tgarrett@bassberry.com
(1)REV. BOBBY COLEMAN, 704 E Webb Street, Mountain View, AR 72560
bobby.coleman@gmail.com

(Members whose terms expire in 2017)
(1)REV. JOHN BUTLER, PO Box 257, Sacramento, KY 42372
jbutler@iccable.com
(1)MS. BETTY JACOB, PO Box 158, Broken Bow, OK 74728
chocpres@pine-net.com

(Members whose terms expire in 2018)
(1)MS. CALOTTA EDSEL, 7044 Woodsong Cove, Germantown, TN 38138
cedsell@hotmail.com
(1)REV. NORLAN SCRUDDER, 29688 S 534 Road, Park Hill, OK 74451
ndscrudder@gmail.com

*Ecumenical Partners   +Cumberland Presbyterian Church in America

MINISTRY COUNCIL

(Members whose terms expire in 2016)
(3)REV. JILL CARR, PO Box 1547, Lebanon, MO 65536
(2)REV. TROY GREEN, 105 Cobb Hollow Lane, Petersburg, TN 37144
(3)MS. ELIZABETH HORSLEY, 1200 Imperial Drive, Denton, TX 76201
(3)MS. GWEN RODDYE, 3728 Wittenham Drive, Knoxville, TN 37921
(3)REV. SAM ROMINES, PO Box 127, Lewisburg, KY 42256
(Members whose terms expire in 2017)
(2)REV. DONNY ACTON, 1413 Oakridge Drive, Birmingham, AL 35242
(3)REV. MICHELE GENTRY DE CORREAL, Urb San Jorge casa 28, Km 8 via a La Tebaida Armenia, Quinido, COLOMBIA, SOUTH AMERICA
(2)REV. LANNY JOHNSON, 120 S Mill Street, Morrison, TN 37357
(1)MR. ADAM MCREYNOLDS, PO Box 162, Bethany, IL 61914
(2)REV. TOM SANDERS, 4201 W Kent Street, Broken Arrow, OK 74012
(Members whose terms expire in 2018)
(2)MR. KENNETH BEAN, 1035 Stonewall Street N, McKenzie, TN 38201
(1)REV. PHILLIP LAYNE, 10699 Griffith Highway, Whitwell, TN 37397
(1)REV. PAULA LOUDER, 98 Gallant Court, Clarksville, TN 37043
(2)REV. RON MCMILLAN, 675 Kimberly Drive, Atoka, TN 38004
(1)MS. PATRICIA SMITH, PO Box 86, Smiths Grove, KY 42171

YOUTH ADVISORY MEMBERS
(1)MR. CALEB DAVIS, 502 S Alley Street, Jefferson, TX 75657
(1)MS. CAROLINA GILLIS, 6243 Sioux Lane, Birmingham, AL 35242
(2)MS. EMILY MAHONEY, 31 Barbara Circle, McMinnville, TN 37110

ADVISORY MEMBERS
REV. MICHELE GENTRY, Urb San Jorge casa 28, Km 8 via a La Tebaida, Armenia, Quindio, Colombia, South America
REV. MICHAEL SHARPE, 8207 Traditional Place, Cordova, TN 38016

COMMUNICATIONS MINISTRY TEAM

(Members whose terms expire in 2016)
(1)REV. NICHOLAS CHAMBERS, 11300 Road 101, Union, MS 39365
(1)REV. STEVEN SHELTON, 7886 Farmhill Cove, Bartlett, TN 38135
(Members whose terms expire in 2017)
(3)MS. B. DENISE ADAMS, 126 Ray, Monticello, AR 71655
(2)MS. DUSTY LUTHY, 400 S Friendship Road Apt G, Paducah, KY 42003
(Members whose terms expire in 2018)
(3)REV. MICHAEL CLARK, 80 Bryan Drive, Winchester, TN 37398
(3)REV. JAMES D. MCGUIRE, 220-2 Southwind Circle, Greeneville, TN 37743

DISCIPLESHIP MINISTRY TEAM

(Members whose terms expire in 2016)
(3)REV. MINDY ACTON, 1413 Oak Ridge Drive, Birmingham, AL 35242
(1)REV. NANCY MCSPADDEN, 120 Roberta Drive, Memphis, TN 38112
(1)REV. JOSEFINA SANCHEZ, 7 Hancock Street, Melrose, MA 02176
(Members whose terms expire in 2017)
(2)MS. LE ILA DIXON, 4406 John Reagan Street, Marshall, TX 75672
(2)REV. AARON FERRY, 122 Crimson Drive, Winchester, TN 37398 (resigned)
(3)MS. SAMANTHA HASSELL, 510 N Main Street, Sturgis, KY 42459
(Members whose terms expire in 2018)
(3)MS. JOANNA WILKINSON, 1174 Tanglewood Street, Memphis, TN 38114
(2)MS. RACHEL COOK, 210 Bynum Street, Scottsboro, AL 35768
(2)REV. CHRISTIAN SMITH, 475 State Street, Cookeville, TN 38501

MISSIONS MINISTRY TEAM

(Members whose terms expire in 2016)
(2)REV. MAKIHIKO ARASE, 3-355-4 Kamikitadai Higashiyamato-Shi, Tokyo, 207-0023 JAPAN
(1)REV. VICTOR HASSELL, 510 N Main Street, Sturgis, KY 42459
(1)MR. DOMINIC LAU, 3820 Anza Street, San Francisco, CA
(1)MS. BRITTANY MEEKS, 2664 Morning Sun Road, Cordova, TN 38016
(1)REV. CHRIS WARREN, 906 Prince Lane, Murfreesboro, TN 37129
(Members whose terms expire in 2017)
(2)REV. JAMES BUTTRAM, 103 Golfcrest Lane, Oak Ridge, TN 37830 (resigned)
(3)REV. JIMMY BYRD, 176 E Valley Road, Whitwell, TN 37397
(1)MS. DONNA CHRISTIE, 3221 Whitehall Road, Birmingham, AL 35209
(3)REV. RICARDO FRANCO, 7 Hancock Street, Melrose, MA 02176
(1)MRS. MS. KAREN TOLEN, 6859 A East County Road 000N, Trilla, IL 62469
(Members whose terms expire in 2018)
(3)REV. JIM BARRY, 1405 Anna Street, Hixson, TN 37343
(2)MR. TIM CRAIG, 8958 Carriage Creek Road, Arlington, TN 38002
(2)REV. CARDELIA HOWELL-DIAMOND, 1580 Jeff Road NW, Huntsville, AL 35806
(3)MS. SHERRY POTEET, P.O. Box 313, Gilmer, TX 75644
(2)MS. MELINDA REAMS, 10 W Azalea Lane, Russellville, AR 72802

PASTORAL DEVELOPMENT MINISTRY TEAM

(Members whose terms expire in 2016)
(1)REV. SANDRA SHEPHERD, 525 Summit Oaks Court, Nashville, TN 37221
(1)REV. PATRICK WILKERSON, 7719 S Whispering Oak Circle, Powell, TN 37849
(Members whose terms expire in 2017)
(2)REV. AMBER CLARK, 80 Bryan Drive, Winchester, TN 37398
(2)REV. DREW HAYES, 6322 Labor Lane, Louisville, KY 40291
(Members whose terms expire in 2018)
(2)REV.DUAWN MEARNS, 107 Westoak Place, Hot Springs, AR 71913
(3)REV. LINDA SNELLING, 15791 State Highway W, Ada, OK 74820

*Ecumenical Partners   +Cumberland Presbyterian Church in America

GENERAL ASSEMBLY BOARD OF:

I. TRUSTEES OF BETHEL UNIVERSITY

(Members whose terms expire in 2015)
(3)*MR. MICHAEL (MIKE) CARY, 181 Angel Cove, Huntingdon, TN 38344
(2)MR. CHARLIE GARRETT, 107 Willow Green Drive, Jackson, TN 38305
(1)+REV. ELTON C. HALL, SR., 305 Tiffton Circle, Hewitt, TX 76643
(1)REV. MARK S. HESTER, 763 Finn Long Road, Friendsville, TN 37737
(3)*MS. CHARLENE P. JONES, 137 Moore Avenue W, McKenzie, TN 38201
(1)MS. DEWANNA LATIMER, 1077 Jr. Jones Road, Humboldt, TN 38343

(Members whose terms expire in 2016)
(1)MR. JEFF AMREIN, 11711 Paramont Way, Prospect, KY 40059
(3)DR. LARRY A. BLAKEBURN, 790 Emory Valley Road Apt 714, Oak Ridge, TN 37830
(2)*JUDGE BEN CANTRELL, 415 Church Street #2513, Nashville, TN 37219
(2)+DR. ARMY DANIEL, 3125 Searcy Drive, Huntsville, AL 35810
(3)MR. LAWRENCE (LADD) DANIEL, 13023 Taylorcrest, Houston, TX 77079
(1)MR. BILL DOBBINS 5716 Quest Ridge Road, Franklin, TN 37064
(2)DR. ROBERT LOW, c/o New Prime, Inc., 2740 W Mayfair Avenue, Springfield, MO 65803
(3)MR. BEN T. SURBER, 1145 Hico Road, McKenzie, TN 38201

(Members whose terms expire in 2017)
(2)*MS. LISA COLE, PO Box 198615, Nashville, TN 37219
(2)MR. CHESTER (CHET) DICKSON, 24 W Rivercrest Drive, Houston, TX 77042
(2)*MR. ARTHUR (ART) LAFFER, JR., 410 Wilsonia Avenue, Nashville, TN 37205
(1)REV. NANCY MCSPADDEN, 120 Roberta Drive, Memphis, TN 38112
(3)MR. BOBBY OWEN, 1625 Cabot Drive, Franklin, TN 37064
(2)DR. ED PERKINS, 721 Paris Street, McKenzie, TN 38201
(1)MR. KENNETH (KEN) D. QUINTON, 2912 Waller Omer Road, Sturgis, KY 42459
(3)REV. ROBERT (ROB) TRUITT, 1238 Old East Side Road, Burns, TN 37029
(1)REV. ROBERT (BOB) WATKINS, 10950 West Union Hills Drive #1356, Sun City, AZ 85373

Trustee Emeritus – Dr. Vera Low, 3653 Prestwick Court, Springfield, MO 65809 (deceased)

II. TRUSTEES OF CUMBERLAND PRESBYTERIAN CHILDREN'S HOME

(Members whose terms expire in 2015)
(2)*MS. KAY GOODMAN, 1042 Bobcat Road, Sanger, TX 76266
(3)MS. PAT HUFF, 249 Rancho Drive, Saginaw, TX 76179
(2)REV. MELISSA KNIGHT, 5730 Haley Road, Meridian, MS 39305
(3)MS. RUBY LETSON, 2921 Alexander, Florence, AL 35633
(2)*MR. BARON H. SMITH, 3401 Hasland Drive, Flower Mound, TX 75022

(Members whose terms expire in 2016)
(2)*MR. RICHARD DEAN, 2140 Cove Circle North, Gadsden, AL 35903
(2)MS. PATRICIA LONG, 525 E Oak Street, Aledo, TX 76008
(3)REV. ALFONSO MARQUEZ, 389 Bethel Drive, Lenoir City, TN 37772
(3)MR. MICKEY SHELL, 2143 Griderfield-Ladd Road, Pine Bluff, AR 71601

(Members whose terms expire in 2017)
(1)REV. LISA ANDERSON, 1790 Faxon Street, Memphis, TN 38112
(1)MS. CAROLINE BOOTH, 2200 Westview Trail, Denton, TX 76207
(3)+MS. MAMIE HALL, 305 Tiffton Circle, Hewitt, TX 76643
(1)MR. CHARLES HARRIS, 3293 Birch Avenue, Grapevine, TX 76051
(1)MR. KNIGHT MILLER, 1035 Garden Creek Circle, Louisville, KY 40223
(1)MR. JOHN O'CARROLL, 1701 Live Oak Lane, Southlake, TX 76092
(2)*MS. TIFFANY SMITH, 2901 Corporate Circle, Flower Mound, TX 75028
(3)REV. DON TABOR, 9611 Mitchell Place, Brentwood, TN 37027

*Ecumenical Partners   +Cumberland Presbyterian Church in America

III. TRUSTEES OF HISTORICAL FOUNDATION

(Members whose terms expire in 2016)
(3)+MS. VANESSA BARNHILL, 819 King Street, Sturgis, KY 42459
(3)MS. PAMELA DAVIS, 5111 County Road 7545, Lubbock, TX 79424
(2)REV. MARY KATHRYN KIRKPATRICK, 401 1/2 Henley-Perry Drive, Marshall, TX 75670
(3)MS. SIDNEY MILTON, 27 Kalee Lane, Calvert City, KY 42029

(Members whose terms expire in 2017)
(3)+MS. EDNA BARNETT, 7 Breezewood Cove, Jackson, TN 38305
(2)MR. MICHAEL FARE, 401 E Deanna Lane, Nixa, MO 65714
(2)*MS. DOROTHY HAYDEN, 3103 Carolina Avenue, Bessemer, AL 35020
(1)+MS. PAT WARD, 2620 Rabbit Lane, Madison, AL 35756
(3)+REV. RICK WHITE, 124 Towne West, Lorena, TX 76655

(Members whose terms expire in 2018)
(1)REV. LISA OLIVER, 110 Allen Drive, Hendersonville, TN 37075
(3)DR. SIDNEY L. SWINDLE, 4407 Swann Avenue, Tampa, FL 33609

IV. TRUSTEES OF MEMPHIS THEOLOGICAL SEMINARY OF THE CUMBERLAND PRESBYTERIAN CHURCH

(Members whose terms expire in 2016)
(2)MR. MICHAEL R. ALLEN, 149 Windwood Circle, Alabaster, AL 35007
(1)*MR. JOHNNIE COOMBS, PO Box 127, Blue Mountain, MS 38610
(2)MS. DIANE DICKSON, 24 West Rivercrest, Houston, TX 77042
(3)*MR. DAN HATZENBUEHLER, 1544 Carr Avenue, Memphis, TN 38104
(1)*DR. RICK KIRCHOFF, 2044 Thorncroft Drive, Germantown, TN 38138
(3)MR. TIM ORR, 1591 Laura Lane, Dyersburg, TN 38024
(2)*DR. INETTA RODGERS, 1824 S Parkway E, Memphis, TN 38114
(3)*MRS. K.C. WARREN, 215 Buena Vista Place, Memphis, TN 38112

(Members whose terms expire in 2017)
(1)*REV. NANCY COLE, 3346 Arcadia Drive, Tuscaloosa, AL 35404
(2)*REV. ROBERT MARBLE, 515 Shamrock Drive, Little Rock, AR 72205
(3)MS. PAT MEEKS, 8540 Edney Ridge Drive, Cordova, TN 38016 (resigned)
(2)REV. JENNIFER NEWELL, 2322 Marco Circle, Chattanooga, TN 37421
(1)REV. SUSAN PARKER, 655 York Drive, Rogersville, AR 35652
(3)REV. ROBERT M. SHELTON, 7128 Lakehurst Avenue, Dallas, TX 75230 (resigned)
(3)+DR. JOE WARD, 2620 Rabbit Lane, Madison, AL 35758
(3)*MS. RUBY WHARTON, 1183 E Parkway South, Memphis, TN 38114

(Members whose terms expire in 2018)
(3)REV. KEVIN BRANTLEY, 729 Old Hodgenville Road, Greensburg, KY 42743
(1)REV. KEVIN HENSON, 8220 Westwind Lane, N Richland Hills, TX 76182
(1)REV. LINDA HOWELL, PO Box 80050, Keller, TX 76244
(3)MR. MARK MADDOX, 225 Oak Drive, Dresden, TN 38225
(2)MS. SONDRA RODDY, 2583 Hedgerow Lane, Clarksville, TN 37043
(3)MR. TAKAYOSHI SHIRAI, 25 Minami Kibogaoka Asahi-ku, Yokohama, Kanagawa-ken 241-0824 JAPAN
(2)*REV. MELVIN CHARLES SMITH, 1263 Haynes Street, Memphis, TN 38114
(2)*MS. LATISHA TOWNS, The Med, 877 Jefferson Avenue, Memphis, TN 38103

V. STEWARDSHIP, FOUNDATION AND BENEFITS

(Members whose terms expire in 2016)
(3)MR. CHARLES G. FLOYD, 1617 Championship Drive, Franklin, TN 37064
(1)REV. CHARLES (BUDDY) POPE, 2391 Fairfield Pike, Shelbyville, TN 37160
(2)MS. SUE RICE, 1301 Brooker Road, Brandon, FL 33511
(2)MS. DEBBIE SHELTON, 1255 MG England Road, Manchester, TN 37355

---

*Ecumenical Partners   +Cumberland Presbyterian Church in America

(Members whose terms expire in 2017)
(1)REV. RANDY DAVIDSON, PO Box 880, Ada, OK 74821
(3)MR. CHARLES DAY, 9312 Owensboro Road, Falls of Rough, KY 40119
(3)MS. SYLVIA HALL, 930 Sherry Circle, Hixson, TN 37343
(3)MR. JACKIE SATTERFIELD, 2303 County Road 730, Cullman, AL 35055
(Members whose terms expire in 2018)
(3)MR. ANDREW B. FRAZIER, JR., 107 Doris Street, Camden, TN 38320
(1)MR. JAMES SHANNON, 2307 Littlemore Drive, Cordova, TN 38016
(2)MR. MICHAEL ST. JOHN, 324 Carriage Place, Lebanon, MO 65536

GENERAL ASSEMBLY COMMISSIONS:

I. MILITARY CHAPLAINS AND PERSONNEL

(1) Term Expires in 2016–REV. CASSANDRA THOMAS, 1920 Dancy Street, Fayetteville, NC 28301
(2) Term Expires in 2017–REV. MARY MCCASKEY BENEDICT, 892 Pen Oak Drive, Cookeville, TN 38501
(1) Term Expires in 2018–REV. TONY JANNER, 104 Northwood Drive, McKenzie TN 38201

These three persons and the Stated Clerk represent the denomination as members of the Presbyterian Council for Chaplains and Military Personnel, 4125 Nebraska Avenue NW, Washington, DC 20016

GENERAL ASSEMBLY COMMITTEES

I. JUDICIARY

(Members whose terms expire in 2016)
(3)REV. SHERRY LADD, 4521 Turkey Creek Road, Williamsport, TN 38487
    revsherryladd@gmail.com
(2)REV. ANDY MCCLUNG, 919 Dickinson Street, Memphis, TN 38107
    scubarev@att.net
(3)MS. FELICIA WALKUP, 179 Mary Anne Lane, Manchester, TN 37355
    fbwalkup@gmail.com
(Members whose terms expire in 2017)
(1)REV. HARRY CHAPMAN, 4908 El Picador Court SE, Rio Rancho, NM 87124
    wrightrev2gmail.com
(2)REV. ROBERT D. RUSH, 17822 Deep Brook Drive, Spring, TX 77379
    rushrd74@comcast.net
(3)MR. WENDELL THOMAS, JR., 1200 Paradise Drive, Powell, TN 37849
    volbaby@comcast.net
(Members whose terms expire in 2018)
(2)REV. ANNETTA CAMP, 2263 Mill Creek Road, Halls, TN 38040
    anetta@cumberlandchurch.com
(3)MS. KIMBERLY SILVUS, 1128 Madison Street, Clarksville, TN 37040
    kgsilvus@gmail.com
(1)MR. BILL TALLY, 907 Tipperary Drive, Scottsboro, AL 35768
    wtally@scottsboro.org

*Ecumenical Partners   +Cumberland Presbyterian Church in America

II. JOINT COMMITTEE ON AMENDMENTS

The committee consists of five members of the Judiciary Committee of the Cumberland Presbyterian Church in America and the Cumberland Presbyterian Church.

III. NOMINATING

(Members whose terms expire in 2016)
(1)MS. NANCY BEAN, 1035 Stonewall Street N, McKenzie, TN 38201
   beann@bethelu.edu
(1)REV. CHARLES MCCASKEY, 679 Canter Lane, Cookeville, TN 38501
   charles@cookevillecpchurch.org
(1)REV. JIMMY PEYTON, 1455 County Road 643, Cullman, AL 35055
   jakjpeyton@att.net
(1)MS. MARJORIE SHANNON, 2307 Littlemore Drive, Cordova, TN 38016
   margieshannon@att.net

(Members whose terms expire in 2017)
(1)REV. TOBY DAVIS, 502 S Alley Street, Jefferson, TX 75657
   pastortobydavis@gmail.com
(1)MS. CAROLYN HARMON, 4435 Newport Highway, Greeneville, TN 37743
   richardharmon09@comcast.net
(1)MS. ELLIE SCRUDDER, 29688 S 535 Road, Park Hill, OK 74451
   escrudder@gmail.com
(1)REV. KEVIN SMALL, 6492 E 400th Road, Martinsville, IL 62442
   revkev61@gmail.com

(Members whose terms expire in 2018)
(1)REV. THOMAS CAMPBELL, PO Box 343, Calico Rock, AR 72519
   tdcampbellar@gmail.com
(1)MS. HEATHER MORGAN, 1468 Williams Cove Road, Winchester, TN 37398
   htmorgan87@gmail.com

IV. OUR UNITED OUTREACH COMMITTEE

(Members whose terms expire in 2016)
(3)MR. RON D. GARDNER, 8668 Wood Mills Drive W, Cordova, TN 38016

(Members whose terms expire in 2017)
(3)MS. SHARON RESCH, PO Box 383, Dongola, IL 62926
(3)REV. WILLIAM RUSTENHAVEN III, PO Box 1303, Marshall, TX 75671

(Members whose terms expire in 2018)
(2)MR. RANDY WEATHERSBY, 1502 Pinecrest Street NW, Cullman, AL 35055
(2)MS. ROBIN WILLS, 4607 E Richmond Shop Road, Lebanon, TN 37090

V. PLACE OF MEETING

THE STATED CLERK OF THE GENERAL ASSEMBLY
THE MODERATOR OF THE GENERAL ASSEMBLY
A REPRESENTATIVE OF WOMEN'S MINISTRIES OF THE MISSIONS MINISTRY TEAM

---

*Ecumenical Partners   +Cumberland Presbyterian Church in America

VI. UNIFIED COMMITTEE ON THEOLOGY AND SOCIAL CONCERNS

(Members whose terms expire in 2016)
(3)MS. LEZLIE P. DANIEL, 13023 Taylorcrest Road, Houston, TX 77079
 lululoop@me.com
(2)+MRS. JIMMIE DODD, c/o Hopewell CPCA, 4100 Millsfield Highway, Dyersburg, TN 38024
 dodd125@gmail.com
(2)REV. BYRON FORESTER, 2376 Eastwood Place, Memphis, TN 38112
 bforester@bellsouth.net; (901)246-1242
(1)REV. JOHN A. SMITH, 916 Allen Road, Nashville, TN 37214
 john.a.smith.81@gmail.com; (573)453-8455
(2)+ELDER JOY WALLACE, 6940 Marvin D Love Freeway, Dallas, TX 75237
 jwallace@wlgllc.net

(Members whose terms expire in 2017)
(1)+MS. SHARON COMBS, PO Box 122, Sturgis, KY 42459
 (270)860-4175
(1)+REV. EDMOND COX, 249 Mimosa Circle, Maryville, TN 37801
 (865)789-6161
(2)+DR. NANCY FUQUA, 1963 County Road 406, Towncreek, AL 35672
 fuq23@bellsouth.net; (256)566-1226
(2)REV. RANDY JACOB, PO Box 158, Broken Bow, OK 74728
 chocpres@pine-net.com; (580)584-3770; (580)236-2469 cell
(1)+REV. LARUTH JEFFERSON, 25757 Primose Lane, Southfield, MI 48033
 (248)945-0349
(1)+DR. PHILLIP REDRICK, 228 Church Street NW, Huntsville, AL 35801
 (256)882-6333
(1)+REV. ROBERT E THOMAS, 1017 N Englewood, Tyler, TX 75702
 (903)592-0238

(Members whose terms expire in 2018)
(2)MR. DAVID PHILLIPS-BURK, 3325 Bailey Creek Cove N, Collierville, TN 38017
 dlphillipsburk@aol.com; (256)520-1380
(2)REV. GEORGE ESTES, 7910 Cloverbrook Lane, Germantown, TN 38138
 geoestes@gmail.com; (901)755-6673
(2)REV. SHELIA O'MARA, 533 Loughton Lane, Arnold, MD 21012
 chaplainshelia@aol.com; (410)757-5713; (443)370-7218 cell

President of Memphis Theological Seminary - Ex-officio Member
 REV. JAY EARHEART-BROWN, 866 N McLean Boulevard, Memphis, TN 38107
 jebrown@memphisseminary.edu; (901)278-0367

OTHER DENOMINATIONAL PERSONNEL

REPRESENTATIVES TO:
American Bible Society: REV. MICHAEL SHARPE, 8207 Traditional Place, Cordova, TN 38016

Caribbean and North American Area Council, World Communion of Reformed Churches:
STATED CLERK MICHAEL SHARPE, 8207 Traditional Place, Cordova, TN 38016

(Member whose terms expire in 2017)
(2)MS. LAURIE SHARPE, 3423 Summerdale Drive, Bartlett, TN 38133

THE REPORT OF THE MODERATOR

This year has been a gift to me as I have served The Cumberland Presbyterian Church as Moderator of the 184th General Assembly. Thank you for this privilege and for your support and confidence as I have done my best to represent the church well.

I have used the year to visit as many areas of the church as possible and would like to thank the many churches, presbyteries and institutions for your invitations and wonderful hospitality. These visits have given me a look at the denomination that has been a blessing. We have a historical tradition and theological grounding that ties us together with denominational encouragement to dream new dreams and live into a vision of being builders of the Kingdom of God where we live. I have seen that in the many places where Cumberland Presbyterians worship and serve.

One of the highlights of the year was the opportunity to visit Japan Presbytery and to experience the faithfulness of the church there. I am grateful for this time which offered me the chance to encourage the churches there but also to receive the blessing of encouragement from the gracious and faithful members of The Cumberland Presbyterian Church in Japan. I have a new appreciation for this global denomination and pray for the day when we all will truly see the global nature of our work for Christ.

Another blessing was to attend The Unification Task Force meeting and to see the dedication of this group of people. They have given their time and passion to guiding our two denominations into a conversation about unification that has been healthy and allowed for input from everyone who would take time to give opinions and ask questions. Although there are many reasons this is a difficult process I believe it is worth our efforts and willingness to embrace change. There are many issues still to be worked on the next two years and beyond so I ask for you to join me in praying daily with the Task Force for this work. We are one church in our history and theology, it is time we are one church in our mission and ministry.

This has also been a year when I have received many communications. So many that it has been difficult to respond to all of them. People in the church are concerned about a variety of issues that are dividing other denominations and we are right to be prayerful about the way that our denomination weathers this period. What I have learned from you, the church, is that we are a beautifully diverse. Some think that is a detriment but I believe it is our greatest strength. It requires being willing to live together and lean on the Gospel mandate to be loving and kind even in our disagreements. This period of time is our denominations opportunity to be an example of how to faithfully live in the world engaging in issues of justice and peace without becoming people of the world who become intolerant and divisive.

I cannot finish my time as Moderator without offering my appreciation to those who serve our denomination as staff. Mike Sharpe, stated clerk serves our church with a generous listening heart and does it in a very thankless position. I am thankful for all of the ways he has been supportive of me this year. Elizabeth Vaughn does so many jobs in the General Assembly office it is impossible to name them, she serves us well. The Ministry Council and Ministry Teams of the church work tirelessly, sometimes under great pressure and stress to make sure the church continues to serve God in active and evangelistic ways. The amount of time they spend away from family is overwhelming and never appreciated enough by those of us who benefit from their travels and gifts of ministry. They take criticism and praise in stride while staying focused on the mission of the church. I offer my gratitude to them as individuals and as a team.

Moderators often make suggestions and recommendations to the General Assembly. I would like to make the following based on my time this year listening to the church and observing the work of the church.

SUGGESTION 1: That the Cumberland Presbyterian Church renew commitment to study The Confession of Faith in churches, Sunday Schools, Bible Studies and small groups. Throughout the year many of the concerns of people in communication have been based on an inadequate and sometimes absent knowledge of the doctrine of the church. The health of our church depends on our study of scripture and our expression of Christianity spelled out in The Confession of Faith.

Sincerely and Thankfully,
Reverend Lisa Hall Anderson
Moderator of the 184th General Assembly

THE REPORT OF THE STATED CLERK

I. THE OFFICE OF THE STATED CLERK

The Constitution, the Rules of Discipline, the Rules of Order, and the General Assembly Bylaws (found in the front of the General Assembly Minutes) list the many responsibilities for the person who holds the position of Stated Clerk, the primary task is to maintain and strengthen a united witness for the Church. The Stated Clerk shall also generally supervise and control the business affairs of the Corporation, and see that all directives of the General Assembly are implemented.

The Office of the General Assembly also provides budgeting, accounting, and support services for commissions, committees, agencies and task forces without executive assistance.

Additional services and activities provided through the office of the Stated Clerk this past year include:
- Providing assistance to the Unification Task Force
- Developing and maintaining a web presence for the following General Assembly Committees/Commissions without staff: Nominating Committee, Unified Committee on Theology and Social Concerns, Commission on Military Chaplains and Personnel, Our United Outreach Committee and the Unification Task Force.
- Creation of spring and fall Denominational Updates, a compilation of talking points obtained from each board and agency that may be shared by visiting denominational staff and the moderator when making visits to presbyteries and in other settings. The updates are also shared with presbytery clerks.
- Development of a Travel Chart, to assist with the coordination of travel plans by denominational staff to meetings of presbyteries. The travel chart is also shared with presbytery clerks.
- Provided orientation/training to several of the General Assembly boards, agencies and presbyteries on the use of video conferencing technology for their meetings.
- Hosted the annual conference for Presbytery and Synod Clerks.

A significant portion of the Stated Clerk's time has been spent responding to various judicial and legal questions affecting local churches and presbyteries. The Clerk is appreciative for advice provided to this office from both the Permanent Judiciary Committee and from Mr. Jamie Jordan who serves as legal counsel for the Office of the General Assembly.

The Stated Clerk is grateful to the Church for calling him to serve in this position and appreciates the support of the Church for the Office and for the person who holds this position.

II. STAFF

Ms. Elizabeth Vaughn continues to serve as the Assistant to the Stated Clerk, a position that requires her to maintain accurate records of ministers, probationers, congregations, record income and expenses and to authorize payment of all items in the Office of the General Assembly budget. The Church is fortunate to have a person with such knowledge, efficiency and dedication to work. The Stated Clerk and the Assistant to the Stated Clerk are currently the only employees of the Office of the General Assembly.

Reverend Vernon Sansom was elected by the 182nd General Assembly to fill the position of Engrossing Clerk, and began his term of service January 1, 2013. Reverend Sansom is to be commended for the accuracy in recording the minutes of the General Assembly. Vernon also leads the orientation session for those who serve as the chairperson and co-chairperson for each General Assembly appointed Committee and provides valuable assistance in the preparation of committee reports at each meeting of the General Assembly.

III. ECUMENICAL RELATIONSHIPS

The Cumberland Presbyterian Church has always been involved in ecumenical relationships. Through co-operative ministries, chaplains for the military and veteran's hospitals are endorsed, migrant workers and persons in Appalachia are served, and missionaries are sent into a variety of countries. Through ecumenical partnerships disaster relief funds are distributed. Through working co-operatively church school and camping materials are developed. Habitat for Humanity enables many persons throughout the world to secure better housing. The Cumberland Presbyterian witness is more effective through participation with other Christians in these and various other ministries.

A. CUMBERLAND PRESBYTERIAN CHURCH IN AMERICA

The Cumberland Presbyterian Church in America and the Cumberland Presbyterian Church have one heritage, one Confession of Faith and share in several co-operative relationships and ministries such as the Historical Foundation, the United Board of Christian Discipleship, youth ministry, and the Unified Committee on Theology and Social Concerns. The Cumberland Presbyterian Church in America and the Cumberland Presbyterian Church also participate with other Reformed bodies in ministry. Although working through partnerships, the witness of the Cumberland Presbyterian Church in America and the Cumberland Presbyterian Church would be greatly enhanced through a union of the two denominations.

B. WORLD COMMUNION OF REFORMED CHURCHES

Both The Cumberland Presbyterian Church and the Cumberland Presbyterian Church in a America are members of World Communion of Reformed Churches (WCRC). The WCRC was formed in 2010 by a merger of the World Alliance of Reformed Churches and the Reformed Ecumenical Council. The WCRC represents approximately eighty million members of two hundred thirty denominations from one hundred seven countries, including Reformed, Congregationalists, Presbyterian and United Churches. Resources and updates from the World Communion of Reformed Churches are available on their website: (www.wcrc.ch).

Reverend Christopher Ferguson has been installed as the new general secretary of the WCRC and will office in Hanover, Germany where the headquarters for WCRC is now located. Setri Nyomi, former general secretary, concluded his second and final term (14 years) last summer, was not eligible to serve anther term.

The WCRC meets every seven years. The next meeting of the general Council will be held in Erfurt, Germany, June 2017 and will coincide with the 500th Anniversary of the Reformation. The theme for the 26th general Council is *Living God, Renew and Transform Us* (based on Romans 12:2 and Luke 4:16-19).

IV. THE CORPORATE BOARD

In the called meeting in December 2007, the General Assembly elected a new board of directors for the General Assembly Incorporation. With the merging of program boards into the Ministry Council, trust funds would become more vulnerable in the event the corporation was sued. The General Assembly Bylaws, Article 5 outlines the responsibilities for the Corporate Board.

The corporate board met once this past year, and is pleased to announce that as of April 1, 2015 all outstanding loans of the denomination have been retired. Plans for a note-burning celebration during the 186th meeting of the General Assembly in Nashville, Tennessee were approved.

Other actions taken: Re-allocated the remaining balance of the guaranteed debt retirement line item funds, to the various boards according using the allocation formula for 2015; approved the 2015 housing allowance for the stated clerk; received and approved a performance review report of the Stated Clerk

The Center Interagency Team (CIT) comprised of the Center's Principle Executive Officers, is responsible for oversight of the day-to-day maintenance and property needs at the Denominational Center. Current CIT members include: Mike Sharpe (Office of the General Assembly), Robert Heflin (Board of Stewardship, Foundation and Benefits), Susan Gore (Historical Foundation), and Edith Old (Ministry Council). The Shared Services budget covers the cost for maintaining the Center offices and property (see page 150).

V. MINUTES OF THE GENERAL ASSEMBLY

The Office of the General Assembly continues to make the minutes of the General Assembly available on a CD, and mailing them to persons requesting them. The resource center also prints and sells a few printed copies of the General Assembly Minutes each year. For information contact Matthew Gore, mhg@ cumberland.org. It is permissible to download and print a copy of the minutes from the website (www.cumberland.org/gao).

VI. ENDORSEMENT FOR MODERATOR

The Reverend Michele Gentry, Andes Presbytery, has been endorsed by her presbytery as Moderator of the 185th General Assembly.

VII. STATISTICAL INFORMATION

The annual congregational report forms are sent to the session clerk on December 1, and due in the office of the Stated Clerk of the Presbytery on February 1, and all reports are to be in the Office of the General Assembly by February 10.

In 2015, over a hundred congregations failed to report, thus statistics are not accurate. The statistics for a non-reporting congregation may be several years old, but it is the latest information available. The General Assembly Office continues to shorten and simplify the reporting process. Efforts also continue to further simplify online reporting for those able to utilize the technology. Hard copies of the report forms will still be made available for those congregations who do not have access to the internet.

The 178th and 179th General Assembly directed *"that each presbytery request that its Board of Missions or similar agency, as they minister to the needs of the churches within their presbyteries, remind the churches that it is important that they submit annual reports which are part of our history and offer assistance when needed in preparation of these reports."* If a congregation fails to receive a report, a duplicate form can be requested from the Office of the General Assembly or one may be printed from the web site (www.cumberland.org/gao), and going to the section on congregational reports.

Compiled statistical information is available in the annual Yearbook available online (www.cumberland.org/gao) or in print format, available through Cumberland Resource Distribution – resources@cumberland.org (901-276-4581)

VIII. CHURCH CALENDAR 2015-2016

The 182nd General Assembly, directed the Office of the General Assembly to be responsible for reporting the "Church Calendar" to the General Assembly for adoption in 2013 and all future years. Listed below are the dates received from the Boards and Agencies of the denomination.

RECOMMENDATION 1: That the 184th General Assembly approve the following dates for the 2015-2016 Church Calendar:

CHURCH CALENDAR 2015-2016

July-2015
5-10	Cumberland Presbyterian Youth Conference, Bethel, McKenzie, TN
11	Program of Alternate Studies Graduation
11-25	PAS Summer Extension School, Bethel, McKenzie, TN
18	Children's Fest, Bethel, McKenzie, TN
22-26	Ministers Retreat, Bethel, McKenzie, TN
25-28	Children's Fest On the Go, Casa de Fe, Malden, MA

August-2015
22	MTS Fall Semester Begins
30-Sept 27	Christian Education Season

September-2015
2	MTS Opening Convocation
13	Senior Adult Sunday
20	Christian Service Recognition Sunday
20	International Day of Prayer and Action for Human Habitat

October-2015
	Clergy Appreciation Month
4	Worldwide Communion Sunday
11	Pastor Appreciation Sunday
25	Native American Sunday

November-2015

	Any Sunday Loaves and Fishes Program
1	All Saints Day
1	Stewardship Sunday
6	World Community Day (Church Women United)
8	Day of Prayer for People with Aids and Other Life-Threatening Illnesses
8-11	The Forum, Brenthaven Chuch, Brentwood, TN
15	Bible Sunday
22	Christ the King Sunday
29-Dec 25	Advent in Church and Home

December-2015

	Any Sunday Gift to the King Offering
24	Christmas Eve
25	Christmas Day
27-30	Youth Evangelism Conference, Louisville, KY

January-2016

6	Epiphany
11	Human Trafficking Awareness Day
11	BU Spring Semester Begins
11-12	Stated Clerks' Conference
12-14	Ministers Conference, Brenthaven Church, Brentwood, TN
15	Deadline for receipt of 2015 Our United Outreach Contributions

February-2016

	Black History Month
1	Annual congregational reports due in GA office
7	Denomination Day
7	Historical Foundation Offering
7	Souper Bowl Sunday
10	Ash Wednesday, the beginning of Lent
10–Mar 27	Lent to Easter
14	Our United Outreach Sunday
21	Youth Sunday

March-2016

	Women's History Month (USA)
20	Palm/Passion Sunday
20	One Great Hour of Sharing
24	Maundy Thursday
25	Good Friday
27	Easter
27-April 1	National Farm Workers Awareness Week

April-2016

3-9	Family Week
10	CPCH Sunday
25-26	30-Hour Famine

May-2016

6	Friendship Day (Church Women United)
7	BU Commencement
14	MTS Closing Convocation & Graduation
15	Pentecost
15	Stott-Wallace Missionary Fund Offering
15	World Mission Sunday
30	Memorial Day Offering for Military Chaplains & Personnel for USA churches

June-2016
20-24	General Assembly, Nashville, TN
20-24	CPWM Convention, Nashville, TN
26-July 1	Cumberland Presbyterian Youth Conference, Bethel, McKenzie, TN

July-2016
9	Program of Alternate Studies Graduation
9-23	PAS Summer Extension School, Bethel, McKenzie, TN
19-23	Presbyterian Youth Triennium, Purdue University, Lafayette, IN

August-2016
6	BU Commencement
20	MTS Fall Semester Begins
22	BU Fall Semester Begins
28-Sept 25	Christian Education Season
30	BU Spring Convocation

September-2016
3	MTS Opening convocation
11	Senior Adult Sunday
18	Christian Service Recognition Sunday
18	International Day of Prayer and Action for Human Habitat

October-2016
	Clergy Appreciation Month
2	Worldwide Communion Sunday
9	Pastor Appreciation Sunday
23	Native American Sunday

November-2016
	Any Sunday Loaves and Fishes Program
1	All Saints Day
4	World Community Day (Church Women United)
6	Stewardship Sunday
6-9	The Forum
13	Day of Prayer for People with Aids and Other Life-Threatening Illnesses
13	Bible Sunday
20	Christ the King Sunday
27-Dec 25	Advent in Church and Home

December-2016
	Any Sunday Gift to the King Offering
10	BU Commencement
24	Christmas Eve
25	Christmas Day

IX. CONTINGENCY FUND

The Stated Clerk is to hold, distribute and report annually the General Assembly Contingency Fund (see Bylaws 8.04, #24). Below is a summary of 2013 Contingency Fund Activity.

Summary of 2014 Activity

Balance Forward 1/1/2014 $ 11413.06

Income in 2014:
    Our United Outreach $2,199.11
    Interest   425.43
    Reimbursement from CPCA for
        Unification expenses in 2013   2,533.35
    Total Income: **$5,157.89**

There were no expenditures in 2014:

Total Fund Balance as of 12/31/14   *$16,570.95

*Restricted Funds:

    $ 4,100.00   The current balance designated by the 178th General Assembly to print the Catechism in the various languages represented in the church.

    1,011.51   Pastoral Development Ministry Team/General Assembly Ordination Task Force

Total Amount of *Restricted Funds: $ 5,111.51 (12/31/14)

Total Amount of Unrestricted Amount: $11,459.44 (12/31/14)

Total Fund Balance: $16,570.95 (12/31/13)

Respectfully submitted,
Michael Sharpe, Stated Clerk

THE REPORT OF THE MINISTRY COUNCIL

To the 185th General Assembly of the Cumberland Presbyterian Church in session in Cali, Colombia, June 19-26, 2015.

I. MINISTRY COUNCIL

A. INTRODUCTION

Ephesians 4:12 states, "[11] And He [God] gave some *as* apostles, and some *as* prophets, and some *as* evangelists, and some *as* pastors and teachers, [12] for the equipping of the saints for the work of service, to the building up of the body of Christ;" (NASB). This text very plainly teaches something essential about church organization. Namely, that leaders are provided by the Lord to equip the saints (membership) for service.

Traditional Boards sit on top of the organizational structure to choose and decide what will or won't be done. The body is likewise expected to follow along (or resist!). In most churches it is the minister who is expected to do the ministry, but what would take place if the membership ("the saints") were the ones providing the ministry?

Over the last several months the Ministry Council has been wrestling with these important concepts and looking for ways we can become a more servant empowered organization. We have had Bible studies, held training workshops, read books and had many formal and informal discussions. We have prayed about it and for it, and we've experienced the Spirit's leading. It has become more and more evident to us that Jesus did not set up a traditional organizational structure when He formed the Church. Frankly, it was outrageous how much power Jesus entrusted to the most ordinary disciples. In a traditional organization the power is held by the few at the top, and the membership has very little power or responsibility. In the Church this has usually meant ministers provide the ministry and members consume ministry. Given that God supplies the Holy Spirit to every believer and calls each to service, we do not think it is supposed to be that way.

In a servant empowered organization the service of leadership is to equip, empower and engage members in the "work of service" also known as ministry. Therefore, we have worked to change the way the Ministry Council relates to the individual Ministry Teams and Ministry Team Leaders. The atmosphere has become more supportive and cooperative when Team Leaders meet with the Ministry Council proper. Every meeting the Ministry Council considers how we as leaders can best serve our Ministry Teams. It seems the Ministry Teams have very fully engaged in a servant empowered model where each team member has real responsibility and power to serve. That is a product of the caliber and humility of our Team Leaders and Executive Director. Those are real significant changes, but there is still work to do. In particular how can we foster this organizational restructuring throughout the denomination? How can the Ministry Council fulfill our leadership role and become more effective at engaging the membership of our denomination in active ministry? How can our Ministry Teams not just "do the work" but actually be leaders throughout the Church empowering and equipping them in Spirit led ministries?

Even though our culture expects "Church" to be a certain way, the vision of the Cumberland Presbyterian Church becoming a true servant empowered organization has taken hold. The empowerment and engagement of every member in the work of ministry is just too Christ honoring and world changing to leave undone.

1. Ministry Council (MC) Elected Membership and Terms

Ministry Council elected members are subject to General Assembly requirements of endorsement by presbytery (clergy) or church (laity), as well as geographical (synodic) and gender representation. *The Ministry Council urges all Commissioners to proactively encourage leaders in their respective presbyteries to seek opportunities to serve as elected board members at the denominational level.*

At present both the current Moderator and the Immediate Past Moderator serve as Advisory Members of the Ministry Council. The Moderator serves as a liaison between the General Assembly and the Ministry Council and as a conduit of information between the Church and the MC. That role is primarily associated with the Moderator's travels, and is greatly reduced once the person leaves office. Keeping stewardship of both human and financial resources in mind, the Ministry Council brings the following recommendation:

RECOMMENDATION 1: That the General Assembly amend the Bylaws of The Ministry

Council, **ARTICLE III, BOARD OF DIRECTORS, AUTHORITY, AND MEETINGS, Section C. Advisory Members "There shall be six Advisory Members to the board of directors, who shall be the Stated Clerk, the Moderator of General Assembly, the Immediate Past Moderator of the General Assembly, and three youth Advisory Members appointed by the member" to remove the Immediate Past Moderator as an Advisory Member, reducing the number of Advisory Members to five (Stated Clerk, Moderator, and three Youth Advisory Members.)**

The term of Carlton Harper expires in 2015. He has completed three terms and is not eligible to serve another term. Mary Ann Cole and Sally Allen have requested they not be considered for another term. The terms of Ron McMillan and Ken Bean expire in 2015; both are eligible for re-election. The Youth Advisory Member term of Eddie Montoya, Jr. expires in 2015, and he is not eligible for re-election. The Youth Advisory Member term of Emily Mahoney expires in 2015, and she is eligible for re-election. The Council expresses appreciation to Carlton Harper, Mary Ann Cole, Sally Allen, and Eddie Montoya, Jr. for their contributions to the work of the Ministry Council. The Council also wishes to express appreciation to Forest Prosser for his leadership and participation as a Ministry Council Advisory Member during his two years as Moderator and Immediate Past-Moderator of the General Assembly.

2. The Ministry Council's **Ministry Teams** plan and implement the program ministries of the Church and are made up of both Staff and Elected Team Members. The Ministry Teams report to the Ministry Council. **Staff Team Members** are employees of the Ministry Council; **Elected Team Members** are elected by the Ministry Council and reflect the General Assembly model to ensure representation among gender, laity and clergy.

Pastoral Development Ministry Team elected member, Micaiah Thomas, has resigned. The PDMT and the Ministry Council are grateful for her diligent and faithful service.

Ministry Team members recently reelected by the Council include: Jim McGuire, Michael Clark, Joanna Wilkinson, Rachel Cook, Christian Smith, Sherry Poteet, James Barry, Melinda Reams, Cardelia Howell-Diamond, Tim Craig, Linda Snelling, and Duawn Mearns.

New Ministry Team member elected by the Council is Sandra Shepherd, to replace Micaiah Thomas on PDMT.

Ministry Team Staff
 a. Communications Ministry Team (CMT): Senior Art Director Sowgand Sheikholeslami, and CMT Leader Mark J. Davis.
 b. Discipleship Ministry Team (DMT): Coordinator of Resource Development and Distribution Matt Gore; Coordinator of Youth and Young Adult Ministry Reverend Nathan Wheeler; Coordinator of Adult and Third-Age Ministry Cindy Martin; Coordinator of Children and Family Ministry Jodi Hearn Rush (Nashville, Tennessee office) Shipping Clerk Greg Miller; and DMT Leader Reverend Elinor S. Brown.
 c. Missions Ministry Team (MMT): Coordinator for Women's Ministry and Congregational Ministry Reverend Dr. Pam Phillips-Burk; Director Global Missions Reverend Lynn Thomas (Birmingham, AL office); Manager, Finance and Administration Jinger Ellis; Evangelism and New Church Development Reverend T. J. Malinoski; Cross-Culture Immigrant USA Ministry Reverend Johan Daza; and MMT Leader Reverend Dr. Milton Ortiz
 d. Pastoral Development Ministry Team (PDMT): PDMT Leader Reverend Chuck Brown.

3. **The Global Ministries Leadership Team (GMLT)** is made up of the four Ministry Team Leaders and the Director of Ministries. This body works together to apply the vision/mission of the Ministry Council to the many varied programs and resource materials planned and produced by the Ministry Teams, coordinating ministries in a unified, collaborative manner. The GMLT meets monthly and minutes are disseminated to all members of the Ministry Council and the four Ministry Teams.

4. **Administration:** Director of Ministries, Edith B. Old, and Executive Assistant to Director of Ministries, Megan Warren, provide administrative, financial and human resources to the Ministry Teams. The Director of Ministries is under direct employment of and is responsible to the Ministry Council. The Director gives executive leadership to the Ministry Council in accomplishing duties defined in its Bylaws and supervises the Global Ministries Leadership Team.

B. GENERAL INFORMATION

1. Meetings: The Council has met three times in regular session since the 184th General Assembly. To review the Summary of Actions for all Ministry Council meetings, please see (http://ministrycouncil.cumberland.org/summariesofaction).

2. Future Meeting Dates:
2015 Meeting Dates:
August 21 (Fri) – Orientation for **New Council and Elected Team Members** at the Denominational Center.
August 22 (Sat) – Council and Teams will meet concurrently at Faith Cumberland Presbyterian Church, Bartlett, Tennessee (10 minutes drive from the Denominational Center.)
August 23 (Sun) – Council and Teams will meet jointly in the Denominational Center Building One Conference Room then Worship together at a local CP Church.

2016 Meeting Dates:
January 29 – 30 (Fri/Sat)
April 15 – 16 (Fri/Sat)

3. Elected Member Accountability and Training: Elected Ministry Council members and elected Ministry Team members attend a day of orientation prior to their first MC/MT meeting to help them become acquainted with the many and varied programs and responsibilities of the Council and four Ministry Teams. Each year, all elected members sign a Covenant reinforcing their commitment to answering the call to serve God through service to the Church. Elected members set individual annual goals and complete annual self-evaluations reflecting on their service. These tools serve as metrics to help guide the Council and Ministry Teams. The Ministry Council Covenant may be seen at (http://ministrycouncil.cumberland.org/ministrycouncilcovenant).

4. Human Resources: The Council invests time in thorough revision of each MC/MT job description when the position becomes vacant. Input is gathered from elected Team and Council members, GMLT and relevant staff. In addition to ongoing coaching throughout the year, every MC staff member has an annual performance review completed by his or her supervisor; the Ministry Council appoints a committee to complete the annual review of the Director of Ministries. MC budgeted funds in 2014 for "on the spot" performance incentives (gift cards) to be distributed at the discretion of the Team Leaders/Director of Ministries to staff exceeding performance expectations. These performance incentives were in addition to the 2.4% cost of living raise recommended by the 183rd General Assembly that was implemented in 2014 and 2015.

5. Denominational Pool: The Ministry Council wishes to express our deep appreciation to the Nominating Committee of the General Assembly. That committee has the monumental task of matching individuals to boards in keeping with General Assembly required quotas (gender, synodic representation and clergy/laity) as well as the equally vital challenge of trying to match spiritual gifts of persons to those areas of need identified by the boards. This year, three elected members of the Ministry Council rotated off and the pool of eligible candidates was quite limited in number. It is our belief that God calls people all across the denomination to serve in leadership roles; the limited number of Personal Data Forms and related endorsements on file do not reflect the abundance of qualified leaders within the church. *The Ministry Council challenges all Commissioners to be proactive and intentional in efforts to encourage leaders in their respective spheres of influence to complete the necessary documents to be placed in the pool for future placement on a denominational board.*

6. Unification: The Ministry Council seeks out tangible ways to support Unification by forging strong relationships necessary to successful unification of the two denominations. Some tangible steps this year include the Council's decision that all elected members would subscribe to the CPCA magazine, *The Flag*; if members lacked the ability to pay for the subscription, the Council is underwriting the cost. MC has invited (and paid travel expenses for) CPCA leaders to attend four MC/MT meetings and there have been CPCA guests at all of these events. MC/MT staff have attended CPCA General Assembly meetings, focus groups and other CPCA events as a means of forging relationships.

Ministers Conference: At the annual Ministers Conference in January, one of the invited preachers for the Conference was Reverend Rhonda Westfield, minister from St. James CPCA in Hiwassee

Presbytery. Four CPCA ministers were in attendance at the conference, and a Pre-Conference Workshop provided opportunity for ministers from the two denominations to discuss ways that each denomination funds denominational ministries-- a fruitful discussion in light of the unification process. Making more opportunities for ministers of the two denominations to build relationships and share honest dialogue will be crucial as we continue this process. MC/MTs have underwritten scholarships specifically for CPCA members to attend MC/MT events including but not limited to the Ministers Conference.

United Board of Christian Discipleship (UBCD): DMT events are conducted jointly with the CPCA and thus open to both denominations. DMT has continued the decades of cooperative work begun by the former CP Board of Christian Education and the CPCA via the UBCD in planning and conducting discipleship/Christian education events.

Cumberland Presbyterians outside the bounds of the U. S. have asked MC and MT staff questions regarding Unification and have been encouraged by Ministry Council and Ministry Team staff to share their ideas, questions and concerns directly with the Unification Task Force. **Latino CP pastors from Tennessee, Georgia, and Alabama** gather quarterly to study themes of interest and to work on the Unification Task Force survey to provide Latino input about the expectations regarding unification with the CPCA.

C. REFERRALS FROM GENERAL ASSEMBLY

1. Presbyterian Church USA Evaluation

The 184th General Assembly directed Ministry Council to "evaluate our association with the Presbyterian Church USA to re-determine the boundaries of that association, pending the actions of the meeting of the Presbyterian Church USA 2014 General Assembly." The Ministry Council and Discipleship Ministry Team in particular have been and will continue to be vigilant to ensure any content or program in association with the PCUSA does not run counter to CP beliefs as articulated in the *Confession of Faith*. (Appendix A)

2. Mission Work/Mission Fields Relationship with Presbytery

The 184th General Assembly affirmed for a second consecutive year that the Missions Ministry Team is the agency responsible for oversight, guidance and authority for mission work and mission fields that cannot have a meaningful relationship with a presbytery due to distance and/or language. MMT is the official host of our mission work until such time as a presbytery can be formed. MMT continues to act as a judicatory of GA with respect to mission work outside the United States, and mission work not affiliated with a presbytery. In accordance with the 183rd GA ruling, the MMT elects a Judicatory Committee of elders and pastors from MMT members to deal with any issues on the mission field that require a judicatory action. As requested by the 184th GA, the MMT is working with the Permanent Judiciary Committee to develop a constitutional change to clear up any ambiguities with respect to the GA mission agency hosting mission work in areas where there are no presbyteries.

II. MINISTRIES

A. CROSS-CULTURE IMMIGRANT

1. Cross-Culture Immigrant Ministries Presence in the US: 14 out of 19 presbyteries in the US have at least one cross-culture ministry. Columbia Presbytery is starting a NCD within the presbytery regional boundaries with a multicultural ministerial goal.

2. Cross-Culture New Exploration Initiatives: The MMT is starting three New Exploration Initiatives in three different regions of the US within different cross-culture groups. The plan is to explore the possibility of establishing new cross-culture churches in three large cities within Tennessee, Georgia, and New Jersey.

3. Cross-Culture Probes and New Church Developments (NCDs): The progress of our cross-culture NCD is positive. Presbyteries are encouraged to remember the goal of planting new churches, and to find ways to celebrate these new church plants. Columbia Presbytery is intentionally working on the development of a probe plan with the goal of starting an intercultural church within their regional boundaries. It is a blessing to see how the cross-culture churches are growing spiritually and numerically. The list of CC-NCDs and churches is under New Church Development on the MC webpages.

RECOMMENDATION 2: That the General Assembly encourage all USA presbyteries to explore opportunities for Cross–Culture church starts within their boundaries.

4. Cumberland East Coast Korean Presbytery: We celebrate that the youngest presbytery in our denomination is working intentionally toward new leadership and NCD opportunities on the East Coast and other regions including Montreal, Canada. During 2014, six probationers were authorized by the Presbytery for ordination. The MMT has been involved in the process of leadership development by sponsoring the probationers who take the Program of Alternate Studies (PAS) CP courses established by General Assembly and approved by Presbytery.

5. Role of the Church and Immigration Education: The Cross-Culture Immigrant Ministries USA Program was created to assist presbyteries in the USA in starting new cross-culture churches. The CP Church is making a concerted effort to plant churches and develop ministries to meet the unique language and cultural needs of new arrivals to the USA. People from different countries are continuing to migrate to live in the USA as well as in other countries. This reality represents a great opportunity for the CP Church to welcome them as brothers and sisters by sharing the good news of Jesus Christ with them in their own languages and culture through immigrant pastors familiar with their cultures and languages.

Unfortunately, there is no single unifying way to embrace the issue of human migration, often called immigration. The people of Israel migrated through the Middle East and scriptural accounts help us better understand our role when dealing with people migrating. There are different perceptions and understandings of the dynamics of immigration around the world. In some cases different perceptions can affect the effectiveness and intentionality of ministering to brothers and sisters who have recently migrated. The Bible is full of stories of migration, refugees, and displaced people. Abraham, Israel, our Lord Jesus, and many first century Christians were migrants at some point in their journeys.

The Confession of Faith declares that "The covenant community, governed by the Lord Christ opposes, resists, and seeks to change all circumstances of oppression—political, economic, cultural, racial—by which persons are denied the essential dignity God intends for them in the work of creation" (Confession of Faith 6.30). This declaration highlights the expression "change all circumstances of…" and it means that as CPs we are agents of change and transformation. The CP Church is called to care for and minister to all human beings, especially those who suffer based on their culture, race, social economics, migration status, and/or political preference.

The United Nations Special Rapporteur of the Commission on Human Rights proposed in its report to the United Nations Educational, Scientific and Cultural Organization (UNESCO) that there is not an objective definition of migrant and migration. However, "The Special Rapporteur of the Commission on Human Rights has proposed that the following persons should be considered as **migrants**:

a. Persons who are outside the territory of the State of which they are nationals or citizens, are not subject to its legal protection and are in the territory of another State;

b. Persons who do not enjoy the general legal recognition of rights which is inherent in the granting by the host State of the status of refugee, naturalized person or of similar status;

c. Persons who do not enjoy either general legal protection of their fundamental rights by virtue of diplomatic agreements, visas or other agreements.

The dominant forms of migration can be distinguished according to the motives (economic, family reunion, refugees) or legal status (irregular migration, controlled emigration/immigration, free emigration/immigration) of those concerned. Most countries distinguish between a number of categories in their migration policies and statistics. The variations existing between countries indicate that there are no objective definitions of migration." (http://www.unesco.org/new/en/social-and-human-sciences/themes/international-migration/glossary/migrant/)

Following the example of Christ and examples of migration in scripture, we are called to love our brothers and sisters who have migrated to live in the countries where the CP Church is present. Therefore, observing the reality of migration in the world, the need to educate our church, and effectively express the love of God to all human beings; we make the following recommendations,

RECOMMENDATION 3: That according to the Confession of Faith for Cumberland Presbyterians, and the example of Christ, the General Assembly affirms that the Cumberland Presbyterian Church and all its judicatories and agencies are called to minister to all immigrants regardless of their nationality, culture, race, social economics, migration status, and/or political preference, who are coming to live in countries where the Cumberland Presbyterian Church is present.

RECOMMENDATION 4: That the Missions Ministry Team through the Cross-Culture Ministries USA program assists the judicatories of the Cumberland Presbyterian Church regarding immigration education and/or resources to embrace ministerial opportunities among communities made up of immigrants within all presbyteries and synods.

RECOMMENDATION 5: That the Missions Ministry Team engage new immigrants associated with the CP Church in the study of scriptures that ask followers of Christ to obey the laws imposed on society, providing theological guidance to Christian immigrants who may not be in compliant legal status.

B. EVENTS

Past Events

1. 125th Anniversary Celebration: 2014 marked the 125th anniversary of the ordination of Louisa Woosley, the first woman to be ordained in the CP Church. Various events were held during the year including celebration worship services at the Ministers Conference and General Assembly. The "standing room only" worship and celebration during General Assembly was sponsored by Missions Ministry Team, Discipleship Ministry Team, Pastoral Development Ministry Team, Ministry Council, MTS, and the Historical Foundation. A new endowment started by the Pastoral Development Ministry Team (PDMT), *Louisa M. Woosley Endowment for Sustaining Women's Ministry*, was introduced. Nearly fifty clergywomen were honored through a $10,300 contribution to the endowment during this inaugural year. In addition, a book of sermons by clergywomen, *Women Shall Preach*, was commissioned by the Historical Foundation. The book includes 69 sermons in 4 languages from 3 continents and can be purchased through CP Resource ($20).

2. 2014 Forum: November 2-5, 2014, at Camp Copass in Denton, Texas. Reverend Dr. Rodger Nishioka was keynote speaker. Evaluations reflected that all 35 participants considered the event "excellent" in every aspect. Mary Kathryn Kirkpatrick and Reverend Elton Hall (CPCA) served as worship leaders. Chuck Brown and Johan Daza led music.

3. Advanced CP Studies: The MMT has been a guiding force and strong participant with Memphis Theological Seminary in the development and implementation of the Advanced CP Studies Program. The MMT provided travel and scholarship grants to CP leaders outside the USA to travel to the USA to participate in this new program.

4. Children's Activities at General Assembly 2015: Saturday, June 20, 9 am-2 pm on the campus of the Colegio Americano. Beth Wallace and a local team of volunteers led the effort with Jodi Rush helping recruit volunteers from the USA who would be attending GA.

5. Children's Fest: Two Children's Fest events took place in the summer of 2014. These events brought together CP children, kindergarten – 6th grade, for a day of fellowship, Bible study, games, and worship. Forty children and 56 adults attended the Texas event; 166 children and 142 adults attended the Tennessee event. One of three Children's Fest events for 2015 will take place June 13, 2015, at the CP Children's Home in Denton, Texas.

6. Children's Fest On-the-Go took place at Casa de Fe CPC in Malden, Massachusetts, October 3 – 6, 2014. Renee Brown, Joanna Wilkinson, and Chris Warren accompanied Jodi Rush and provided leadership for Children's Fest as well as Sunday morning classes for all ages. Josefina Sanchez was the contact person for the local church and coordinated the events and meals for the team. This event hosted close to 50 children from the church and surrounding community.

7. 2014 Connect at General Assembly took place at GA in Chattanooga with more than 20 children participating. The group's activities included providing leadership for the morning devotion on Thursday for GA. These activities provided a time of relationship building, a creative and purposeful outlet for children and an opportunity to highlight the gifts and talents the children have to give to the larger Church.

8. 2014 Family Worship Space (FWS) was a designated space set up in three worship services at

GA. The space provided families of young children a place to worship that would engage and assist them in being involved in age appropriate ways. Jodi Rush and Sandra Shepherd provided leadership. The FWS was full to capacity each service and very well received by families and many others who inquired about it during the week.

9. Hong Kong Youth Team Summer 2014: MMT and DMT staff led a youth team to work in the Yao Dao High School, a school owned and administered by Hong Kong Presbytery. The team conducted interactive English classes for students and visited the CP Church in Macau (special district of China). Missionary Glenn Watts reported that after the team left there was a large group of teens from the high school that were now becoming involved in the Xi Lin CP church, located in the high school's facilities.

10. Women's Ministry Convention 2014: More than 250 attendees participated in worship, workshops, small groups, and a march at a Publix supermarket led by the Coalition of Immokalee Workers. More than 30 people urged the store manager to call upon the Publix CEO to join the Fair Food Campaign in support of farm workers across the nation. Attendees collected a trailer full of new and gently used shoes that were donated to *Soles for Souls* (http://soles4souls.org/). An afternoon joint meeting with 1CPCA women provided meaningful fellowship and prayer. The Convention Offering ($15,300) was divided among three ministry partners: Beth-El Farm Worker Ministry; National Farm Worker Ministry; and Project Vida. The 2015-2016 projects are Montgomery Bell Birthplace Shrine Chaplain and DMT Roadshow. A new 3-year focus on domestic abuse was announced as the Convention theme for 2016-2018: *Building a Promising Future in Guatemala.*

Future Events

1. 2015 Forum: November 8-11, 2015 at Brenthaven CPC, Brentwood, Tennessee (in the Nashville metro area). Mitzi Minor will teach "Unlocking the Scriptures." Kathy Wood-Dobbins will share spiritual practices both in worship and workshops. Brochures available; register online (http://ministrycouncil.cumberland.org/theforumregistration).

2. 2016 Ministers Conference: January 12-14, 2016 at Brenthaven Church, Brentwood, TN. The conference theme is "Ears to Hear - Preaching to Disciple Millennials." The keynote speaker is Rev. Dr. Rodger Nishioka, Columbia Theological Seminary, Benton Family Associate Professor of Christian Education.

3. Children's Fest: July 18, 2015 at Bethel University in McKenzie, Tennessee. Online registration information is at (http://ministrycouncil.cumberland.org/childrensfest2015).

4. Children's Fest On-the-Go: September 25-28, 2015 at Casa de Fe, Malden, Massachusetts, will be a part of a larger *quinceanera* (15th anniversary) celebration for Casa de Fe.

5. Cumberland Presbyterian Youth Conference (CPYC): July 5-10, 2015 at Bethel University, McKenzie, Tennessee. The theme, "Good as New" is from Ezekiel 36:24-29.

6. Colombian Youth Mission Trip: June 9-27, 2015, the mission team will attend a camp with youth from both the USA and Colombia, teach English as a Second Language classes, and then attend GA. Trip leaders are Erin and Johan Daza (MMT), Francia and Milton Ortiz (MMT) and Nathan Wheeler (DMT).

7. Presbyterian Youth Triennium (PYT): July 19-23, 2016 at Purdue University, Lafayette, IN. The theme is "Go." Nathan Wheeler (DMT) represents the CP Church and is on the PYT Administration Team. Samantha Hassell serves as manual writer. Aaron Ferry serves as Recreation Team Co-Leader and Mark Brown as Community Life Team Leader.

8. Youth Evangelism Conference (YEC): DMT and MMT are working together for the YEC December 27-30, 2015 in Louisville, Kentucky. The conference theme is *Ignite* based upon Matthew 3:11-12. YEC was created to engage youth (7th grade – college freshmen) and adult leaders in servant evangelism. (http://ministrycouncil.cumberland.org/2015-youth-evangelism-conference).

C. GLOBAL INITIATIVES

1. **Asia Mission Forum (AMF):** The AMF provides a platform for CP leaders in Asia to meet, learn about CP mission work in Asia, share information, plan shared events and activities for CPs in Asia and develop relational networks. The first AMF meeting was in 2014 in Japan with six Asian countries represented. The second AMF meeting was in Hong Kong, in March 2015. The third AMF meeting will be in Iloilo, Philippines in April 2016.

2. **Global Ministerial Aid Program:** MMT presented a plan to the Board of Stewardship for aid to ministers who are at retirement age outside the continental United States as part of the CP Ministerial Aid Program. The program will initially benefit retired Colombian ministers at or below the poverty line and may be used in other countries when needed.

3. **Cambodia Leadership Development and CP Expansion:** The MMT provided leadership training in Cambodia for CP leaders in Southeast Asia. In September 2014, Jim Barry and Lynn Thomas conducted leadership training in Cambodia with more than 30 in attendance. MMT helped facilitate continued video conference training with leaders in Southeast Asia via Bethel University's Certificate of Christian Studies. MMT also facilitated legal formation of the CP Church of Cambodia as a Non-Government Organization in Cambodia. MMT has allocated $100,000 of Gift of the King offerings to build a worship center in Cambodia. There are plans to start a second CP Church in Phnom Penh, Cambodia.

4. **Multi-Team Staff Visits to Guatemala 2014:** The MMT facilitated visits by three groups of Ministry Council/Ministry Team staff. These groups conducted workshops, a camp, and other events. They also visited the three new CP Churches/missions there and gained valuable insights as to the challenges and needs we face on the mission field. These MC/MT staff visits were in support of the GA decision to make Central America the denomination's mission priority for the next 10 years. This collaborative work of MC/MT staff is the first such outreach ministry by all four Ministry Teams and has done much to build good relationships with future Cumberlands in Central America.

5. **Deputation and Deployment of New Missionaries Fhanor and Socorro Pejendino to Guatemala:** In March 2014, MMT deployed Fhanor and Socorro Pejendino to Guatemala as new missionaries. They are from the Cauca Valley Presbytery and were recruited because of their experience as church planters. They currently provide pastor leadership to the Comunidad de Fe CP Church (Guatemala City), work with the CP council of churches, visit and encourage the other 2 CP churches in Guatemala, and are looking at places to initiate a NCD.

6. **New Clinic in Guatemala opened 2014:** A new medical clinic was placed in the Comunidad de Fe CP Church in Guatemala City. The first clinic founded by the CP Church was located approximately 45 minutes outside of Guatemala City on the Casa Shalom orphanage property owned by the Church of God. In late 2014, this clinic was transferred over to the board of directors of the orphanage. The new clinic is housed in a rented facility, which also serves as the Comunidad de Fe Church worship center. The clinic received start-up funds from the 2013 *Loaves and Fishes* program. The new clinic is under the direct administration of the Comunidad de Fe Church session, as established by action of the Guatemala Council of CP Churches. After months of red tape the permits and licenses needed to operate were granted by the Guatemalan government in late 2014. The new clinic has two doctors and a dental office.

7. **New Mission Policies:** MMT and MC approved a new policy manual in August 2014. The new policies involve various minor changes and two major changes: the CP Church now defines *partners in missions* as missionaries that work for a non-denominational mission organization and have a shared program with the CP Church; and CPs that work for other organizations and are not involved in a shared program are considered *colleagues in missions*, not CP missionaries. These policies better define what has in reality been taking place. It has also resulted in changes as to who the MMT considers CP missionaries.

8. **New Missionaries to the Philippines:** MMT endorsed Reverend John and Joy Park as new missionaries to the Philippines. Rev. Park is a CP minister in Tennessee-Georgia Presbytery, serving the Living Stone CP Church in the metro Atlanta area. The Parks are on deputation and hope to be in the Philippines by late 2015 or early 2016. They will work with Rev. Daniel and Kay Jang, CP missionaries serving in Iloilo.

9. **Possible New Mission Opportunities:** MMT is always in unofficial and fact-finding conversations

with different people about new fields of mission opportunity. CPs are often in contact with the MMT to explore ideas. There have been conversations about new mission efforts in: Australia, Brazil, Haiti, Liberia, and Central America. When opportunities are presented, whether promising or just remote possibilities, the MMT does give prayerful consideration.

RECOMMENDATION 6: That the General Assembly pray that God give us wisdom and leads us as a church into the places in the world where God can use the CP Church to show the love and compassion of Jesus Christ.

D. MISSIONARIES & MISSION FIELDS (Some names below are represented by initials only, for the protection of our missionaries in politically sensitive areas)

Endorsed CP Missionaries Expanding the CP Church
- **Anay Ortega** is a layperson from Andes Presbytery. She has been in Guatemala for almost five years and helps administer the Casa Shalom medical clinic. She is also working with the Council of CP Churches in Guatemala. Anay has a passion for evangelism and has been called on to lead workshops.
- **Boyce and Beth Wallace** are semi-retired CP missionaries in Cali, Colombia, who continue to provide leadership in Cauca Valley Presbytery. They remain very involved in the life of the CP Church in Colombia. They have been CP missionaries for more than 50 years.
- **Carlos and Luz Dary Rivera** are both pastors from the Andes Presbytery, working in Mexico City with the Mexico Council of Churches. Carlos provides leadership to the churches and pastors and Luz Dary has been developing women's ministry.
- **D and S** are missionaries who live in Laos, a closed country. They have a CP church in Laos. They also travel frequently to Cambodia and have started the Samaki CP Church in Phnom Penh.
- **Daniel and Kay Jang** are church planters in the Philippines. Daniel is the pastor of the Iloilo CP Church and also works with the Pavia and Oton CP missions.
- **Fhanor and Socorro Pejendino** arrived in Guatemala as new church planters in March 2014. They live in Guatemala City and work with the Council of CP Churches, in addition to their church planting responsibilities.
- **Glenn Watts** is a layperson serving in Hong Kong. He helps the Xi Lin CP Church with the development of an English worship service.
- **John and Joy Park** will be deployed to the Philippines as new missionaries when they finish with deputation.

Missionaries Working with Non-Denominational Mission Agencies
- **Kenneth and Delight Hopson** work with an interdenominational mission in Uganda, Africa. Kenneth is a layperson who uses his talents in printing to help mission organizations and Ugandan churches produce Christian materials. Delight works for the mission with which they are affiliated and also works in an international school.
- **N B** is a layperson and works with an interdenominational organization in the area of leadership development in China.
- **T and T G** work with an interdenominational mission in Central Asia. They use a business model as a means to improve the lives of Christians and to develop networks to share Christ.

There are currently 14 CP missionaries, 5 CP missionaries working with interdenominational mission organizations, and there are many other unlisted CPs who work for other agencies and organizations in mission fields around the world.

RECOMMENDATION 7: That CP churches everywhere light 19 candles or display 19 Bibles (or some other appropriate symbol) on Mission Sunday (Pentecost Sunday) to recognize the service of these 19 CP missionaries, and that they set aside special time for prayer for the work of these missionaries who are carrying the light of Christ into our world.

Young Adult Volunteer Program
Over the past several years, the Young Adult Ministry Council (YAMC) has explored ways for young adults to stay connected or reconnect with the Church, to discern callings, and to grow spiritually. For this reason, the YAMC has formed a committee to begin planning a program to give young adults an opportunity to serve as short-term missionaries within our global CP Church.

E. RESOURCES (http://ministrycouncil.cumberland.org/store)

New Resources

VBS Curriculum Projects: Last year, DMT worked with Chris Warren to edit and produce VBS curriculum. Plans are underway to produce a second VBS offering by Chris Warren for the summer of 2016 as well as a VBS curriculum (produced by DMT in collaboration with Bethel University)

Educational Resources

1. *50 Days of Prayer*: This new MMT resource is designed to support the Stott-Wallace Missionary Offering and can be found on the Missions section of the MC website.

2. *Advent Devotional:* The Jesse Tree, Gather 'Round the Circle, and Waiting and Wondering may all be purchased (http://ministrycouncil.cumberland.org/store). Designs on how to use each of the books and information about the three themes will be available online to download and use free of charge.

3. **CP Resources in Different Languages:** *About Being Cumberland Presbyterian* (Korean, Spanish), *Buenas Nuevas En La Frontera: Historia De La Iglesia Presbiteriana Cumberland* by Thomas H. Campbell, *El Pacto De Gracia: Un Hilo a Través De Las Escrituras* by Hubert Morrow, *La Confesion de Fe: Para Los Presbiterianos Cumberland, La Historia Y Las Doctrinas De La Iglelsia Presbiteriana Cumberland* compiled by Lynn Thomas, *Pacto de Confianza: Ética Ministerial para Presbiterianos Cumberland* by Milton L. Ortiz. The *Confession of Faith* in Korean is in development. The *Confession of Faith* in Japanese is a joint effort of Japan Presbytery and DMT that is now available. For online resources please visit (www.ministrycouncil.cumberland.org/crosscultureusaresources).

4. *Encounter*: Adult curriculum used by more than 6,500 CPs. Outlines are developed by a Committee on the Uniform Series, a group within the National Council of Churches of Christ. James McGuire represents the CP Church and serves as editor. Future writers are Victor Hassell, Sherry Ladd, Jerry Scott, George Estes, Jamie Lively, and Jimmy Byrd.

5. *Faith Out Loud*: CP youth curriculum with a solid scriptural and theological base, reflects the beliefs of the CP Church as stated in the Confession of Faith, invites young people into a deeper discussion of the Christian faith, and provides avenues through which young people can explore how their faith lives intersect. Faith Out Loud lessons include leader's tips, a comprehensive biblical background for teachers, reproducible pages, media connections that tie scripture with film, music, video, or website resources, and added options to take the lesson deeper.

6. *Intersections - Where Faith and Life Meet:* Adult curriculum released in 2014. Materials for Hope and Lent/Easter/Pentecost were shipped in February; materials on Faith, the next unit, will ship before General Assembly. Cardelia Howell-Diamond continues as the writer.

7. **Missions Gift Catalog:** Includes meaningful projects/programs and an educational component as a source for alternative gift-giving. (www.ministrycouncil.cumberland.org/giving).

8. **Clergy Crisis Fund:** Used to provide emergency financial support to clergy who are in crisis and in need of support and care. (http://ministrycouncil.cumberland.org/pastoraldevelopmentteam)

9. THE CUMBERLAND PRESBYTERIAN: The denominational magazine is published 11 times annually (November and December issues combined.) MC requested that a new mission statement be drafted for the magazine. Communications Ministry Team (CMT), with input from the Council, developed the following: "THE CUMBERLAND PRESBYTERIAN magazine exists to inspire, equip and engage readers in the work of Christian ministry." For subscription information, navigate to (http://tiny.cc/thecpmagazine). Some quick facts: 1,729 circulation of most recent issue, 416 individual subscribers, 20 Bulk orders (3 or more to the same address), 1,153 group subscribers, 10 seminaries have subscriptions, 24 states covered.

10. **New CP materials/books:** Ideas for new materials are developed as needed. The latest resources developed were *Women Shall Preach* (in cooperation with the Historical Foundation) and *It's All About Me* by Beverly St. John. A large print version of the updated *Confession of Faith* is available. A new printing of *The Covenant of Grace* by Hubert Morrow has also been made. Other CP publications include *Unity and Diversity*

in *Cumberland Presbyterian Education* by Clinton Buck, *38: The Chucky Mullins Effect* by Jody Hill, and *Family Stories* by Robert Truitt.

> **11. Missionary Messenger:** Quarterly publication delivered to more than 19,000 CP households at no charge to the recipient. Offers news of what the denomination is doing in missions, along with inspiring and thought-provoking stories of CPs engaged in missions in the USA and around the world. To subscribe (http://ministrycouncil.cumberland.org/themissionarymessenger)

12. Weekly eblasts: DMT sends eblasts to all CPs in the GA database. The monthly schedule for topics: General/Support Ministries (Week 1), Children/Family (Week 2), Youth/Young Adult (Week 3) and Adult/Third Age (Week 4).

F. PARTNERSHIPS

> **1. Beth-El Farm Worker Ministry:** Near Tampa, Florida, the ministry was begun by a small group of CPs in 1976 and has grown to encompass 27 acres and multi-faceted ministries. CPs who serve on the board include Eddie Jenkins, Penny Knight, Sue Rice, and Lita Swindle. Pam Phillips-Burk represents MMT on the board.

> **2. Coalition of Appalachian Ministries (CAM):** Strives to make a positive impact wherever Reformed tradition and Appalachian culture come together by networking with church and community to provide educational and service opportunities. CPs who serve on the board include Glen Brister, Gloria Gregory, Tommy Jobe, Nadara Jones and Mike Sharpe.

3. Curriculum Partnerships continue to exist with three curriculum publishers: *Faith Alive Resources*, *Feasting on the Word*, and *Shine*. Partners provide samples, brochures, and support to assist staff in making appropriate curriculum suggestions to CP congregations.

4. Ecumenical Stewardship Center (ESC): The DMT Leader serves on the Advisory Council of ESC and has done so since 1993. This group of some 25 communions enriches the stewardship ministry of the CP Church. Pastors and stewardship educators are invited to participate in the Leadership Seminar or the North American Conference on Christian Philanthropy, both sponsored by ESC.

> **5. National Farm Worker Ministry:** This faith-based organization supports farm workers as they organize for justice and empowerment. There are 33 member organizations. Joy Warren represents MMT on the board.

6. Presbyterian and Reformed Educational Partnership (PREP): Comprised of representatives from the PCUSA, Moravian Church, Presbyterian Church in Canada, Reformed Church in America, and CP Church, this group developed *Opening Doors to Discipleship*, an outline resource for leaders and seekers. This material is currently being translated into Korean and Spanish. It has been updated to include suggestions for people who have special needs. *Opening Doors to Discipleship* is available on mobile devices and free to CPs. Contact DMT for a special access code.

> **7. Project Vida:** Joint ministry of the CP Church and the PCUSA in El Paso, TX, in the center of the nation's most impoverished neighborhoods, serving more than 1,500 families. The multi-faceted ministry strives to change lives in a holistic way through health, education and economic development. CPs who serve on the board are Diane Sowell and Lee Bondurant.

G. PLANNING COUNCILS

1. Young Adult Ministry Council (YAMC): Young adult planning agency for United Board of Christian Discipleship (UBCD). **Term to Expire 2016:** Madison Rush (Nashville), Joshua Murray (Arkansas), Mary Ferry (Murfreesboro), Randy Barbour (CPCA/Huntsville); **Terms to Expire 2017:** Abby Prevost (Grace), Calvin Rogers (CPCA/Huntsville), Holton Sandiford (North Central), Emily Trapp (West Tennessee). YAMC is seeking four new members. Plans for the 2016 Young Adult Conference are on hold until these spots are filled and we can meet again.

RECOMMENDATION 8: That the General Assembly ask every presbytery to appoint a person to serve as a Youth and Young Adult Contact Person and send this person's name and pertinent information to the Discipleship Ministry Team Coordinator of Youth and Young Adult Ministry.

   2. **Youth Ministry Planning Council (YMPC)**: Youth ministry planning agency for the UBCD. **Terms to Expire 2015:** Nicole Franco (Red River), Cameron Lyons (CPCA/ Huntsville), Adriana Rodriguez (East Tennessee), Dailen Sutton (Red River), Dylan Weaver (Covenant); **Terms to Expire 2016:** Ivree Datcher (CPCA/Huntsville), Justin Dillard (Murfreesboro), Caleb Rhodes (Missouri), Joshua Tyler (West TN), Charli Uhlrich (North Central); **Terms to Expire 2017:** Ben Diaz (Trinity), Dezi Fletcher (CPCA/Huntsville), Eleanor Forester (West Tennessee), Levi Sweet (East Tennessee), Anna Yancy (Robert Donnell); **Adults:** Kip Rush (CPC) Term to Expire 2016

H. SPECIAL PROGRAMS

   1. **Birthplace Shrine Summer Chaplaincy:** MMT oversees this program. A worship service is held each Sunday, Memorial Day to Labor Day. Lisa Cook served as the chaplain for 2014. Attendance ranged from 8 to 47. Lisa Cook will serve as the 2015 chaplain.

   2. **Leadership Referral Services (LRS):** Provides assistance to churches searching for ministers/leaders and those ministers/leaders who want, need, or might be challenged to relocate. Pam Phillips-Burk coordinates and is aided by consultant George Estes. An online service was launched in 2015 providing enhanced efficiency in posting openings and searching for new calls. For churches *currently* in a search process, LRS will use both methods, but any NEW churches entering the search process will use only the online service. This service functions only as well as congregations and ministers utilize it. Therefore, we make the following recommendations:

   RECOMMENDATION 9: That each presbytery's Committee on the Ministry urge ministers/leaders who may be open to considering a call to create an online profile (http://ministrycouncil.cumberland.org/leadershipreferral).

   RECOMMENDATION 10: That each presbytery's Board of Missions urge churches who are searching for a pastor to create an online church profile to maximize the effectiveness of the Leadership Referral Services process (http://ministrycouncil.cumberland.org/leadershipreferral)

   3. **New Candidates and Licentiates**: As individuals come under the care of presbyteries and become candidates for the ministry, Pastoral Development Team (PDMT) gives them: *The Confession of Faith, Understanding God's Call to Ministry of Word and Sacrament in the Cumberland Presbyterian Church: Guide for Inquirers, Introduction to Christian Ministry* by Morris Pepper, and *What Cumberland Presbyterians Believe* by E. K. Reagin. New licentiates receive: *The Bible and the Calendar Year* by Thomas D. Campbell, and *Covenant of Grace* by Hubert Morrow.

   4. **Newly Ordained Ministers**: PDMT gives a travel communion set and a copy of *A Covenant of Trust* by Milton Ortiz to those who are newly ordained in the CP Church.

   5. **Work with Presbyterial Committees on Ministry and Clergy Care**: PDMT works with committees to prepare candidates for ministry and those who nurture ordained clergy. PDMT's *Understanding God's Call to Ministry of Word and Sacrament in the Cumberland Presbyterian Church: Guide for Inquirers* is a useful tool for persons inquiring about the process for ordination. PDMT developed *Understanding the Process for Ordination in the Cumberland Presbyterian Church: Handbook for Presbyterial Committees on the Ministry or Preparation for the Ministry*. PDMT is currently developing a manual for Committees on Clergy Care.

   6. **CP Learning Circles**: The first year of CP Learning Circles, done under the leadership of Design Group International, is complete. Participants expressed appreciation for the experience. PDMT is looking for ways to continue this initiative at a lower cost to participating clergy.

I. SPECIAL CP EMPHASIS

1. **Builder's Fellowship:** MMT approved a Builder's Fellowship call for the Amaga mission, an exciting mission point in need of their own worship facility outside of Medellin, Colombia (Andes Presbytery). Builder's Fellowship is a historic program of the CP Church. Members of the fellowship are asked to donate $50 to a particular NCD building project. Builders Fellowship last call of 2014 resulted in gifts totaling $9,501.

2. **Christian Service Recognition Sunday:** The third Sunday of September is a time to recognize and celebrate the skills and gifts of those who serve within, and outside, the Church. Worship resources are available online. (http://ministrycouncil.cumberland.org/liturgyforspecialsundays).

3. **Clergy Appreciation Month is October**: The second Sunday is Clergy Appreciation Sunday. Congregations have a month of opportunities to honor clergy and are encouraged to find ways to show their appreciation.

4. **Family Week:** Congregations are encouraged to plan activities that invite households of every size to find ways to share their faith with each other. The 2015 Family Week theme is *From God's House to Our House* and offers suggestions to families to worship together away from the church building. Free planning packs are available on request. In addition to Family Week materials, the Senior Adult Sunday brochure will be included as an added bonus.

5. **Gift to the King:** Celebrated on any Sunday in December or Epiphany Sunday. The 2013 offering was $56,549.25 and went toward purchasing a new building for the Samaki CP Church in Cambodia so they are not worshipping in a rented facility. 2014 offering up to April is $29,594 and will be toward a new church in Guatemala.

6. **Human Trafficking Awareness:** January 11 is set aside to raise awareness of sexual slavery and human trafficking worldwide. (http://ministrycouncil.cumberland.org/setthemfree)

7. **Loaves and Fishes:** Celebrated on any Sunday in November. The 2013 offering was $50,508.31 and went toward opening a second medical clinic in Guatemala. The 2014 offering up to April 2015 is $ 49,735 and will be directed toward the CP Children Development Program in the Philippines.

8. **National Farm Worker Awareness Week:** Celebrated the week closest to March 31, the birthday of Cesar Chavez, founder of National Farm Workers Association. Worship and educational resources are available on the MC website.

9. **Native American Sunday:** The CP Church designated the fourth Sunday of October to recognize and celebrate the first "foreign" mission work of the church. Worship resources at (https://ministrycouncil.cumberland.org/liturgyforspecialsundays). T. J. Malinoski of MMT serves as liaison for our brothers and sisters of Choctaw Presbytery. If your church would like to plan a short-term mission trip, provide financial assistance, participate in the camping program or offer other opportunities, please contact T. J. Malinoski or Betty Jacob, Choctaw Presbytery Coordinator, for more information.

10. **One Great Hour of Sharing (OGHS):** Annual offering received on Palm Sunday makes the love of Christ real for individuals and communities around the world who suffer the effects of disasters, conflict, or severe economic hardship. Projects are underway in more than 100 countries. OGHS is an ecumenical partnership among nine Christian denominations. The 2014 offering was $14,844.58. Seventy-five percent of this offering was sent to Church World Service, official sponsor of OGHS. The remaining 25% was used in support of ministries of compassion in CP fields of service.

11. **Safe Sanctuary:** The informational pieces for this emphasis are in the process of being revised. A checklist for things you need in your policy, release forms, and other information for criminal background checks. (http://ministrycouncil.cumberland.org/safesanctuary)

12. **Senior Adult Sunday:** "There's an App for That" written by Annetta Camp talks about ways older and younger generations can come together through the use of technology. A complete worship liturgy, written by Pat Pickett, is included. (http://ministrycouncil.cumberland.org/liturgyforspecialsundays)

13. Liturgies for Special CP Sundays: Liturgies are usually available a month prior to their celebration. (http://ministrycouncil.cumberland.org/liturgyforspecialsundays)

14. World Missions Day (Pentecost): *50 Days of Prayer and Action*, from Easter to Pentecost, is a time of prayer and action for missions. The focus culminates on Pentecost Sunday with a special offering for the Stott-Wallace Missionary Fund. (http://ministrycouncil.cumberland.org/liturgyforspecialsundays)

15. Stott-Wallace Missionary Offering: This special offering is the primary way CP missionaries are supported. Churches, groups, Sunday School classes, and individuals are encouraged to contribute. In this way, MMT can sustain salary and benefits packages for CP missionaries, giving them consistent income. The CP Church can raise a million dollars a year for missionaries if just 500 churches, groups or individuals give $2,000 a year. To date, $331,085 has been given.

RECOMMENDATION 11: That the General Assembly request that all pastors provide brochures and information about the Stott-Wallace Missionary Offering to their churches, explain the importance of the offering, and invite their church to participate in supporting CP missionaries through this offering.

J. STEP OUT

1. Evangelism

a. MMT held its first Missions Advocate Retreat in 2014 at the West Nashville CP Church to promote missions within the denomination. *Excited About New Church Development* provided participants with a focus on why start new churches and the various methods on how to start new groups.

b. MMT provided an evangelism themed pre-Assembly workshop in June 2014. The workshop, *I Was a Stranger*, provided training on church hospitality. The workshop was repeated at the August Ministry Council meeting.

c. In promotion of the Stott-Wallace Missionary Offering Sunday, MMT gave a presentation to the Manchester CP Church in Manchester, Tennessee.

d. T. J. Malinoski taught the Evangelism PM 106 course in the 2014 Program of Alternate Studies to develop leadership in the aspects of faith-sharing.

e. Congregations and presbyteries often seek assistance with evangelism, leadership development, demographic studies, church growth methods and church membership development. MMT provided training and consultation for the following congregations and presbyteries: Faith, Ebenezer, Glasgow, and High Point CP Churches and Arkansas and Choctaw Presbyteries along with training provided to the 3rd Age Retreat for CPs.

f. Presentations, training, and consultations are available for individuals, congregations and presbyteries. Columbia and Tennessee-Georgia Presbyteries are scheduled for faith-sharing training in early 2015.

g. The MMT, Office of General Assembly, and the CPCA are planning an evangelism conference at the beginning of the joint meeting of both denominations in June 2016.

h. The *Missionary Messenger* Summer 2015 issue is devoted to evangelism.

2. New Church Development (NCD)

MMT continued to support the following groups and congregations under NCD via means of administration, visits, regular contact, resources and/or guidance. This list is not exhaustive of all the NCDs within the denomination but those with which the MMT is involved at some level: 316 in Denver, Colorado; Ajusco (Mexico City, Mexico); Benton/Bryant Fellowship in Bryant, Arkansas; Bethesda Korean (El Paso, Texas); Calvary CP Church in Franklin, Tennessee; Casa de Fe (Malden, Massachusetts); Cristo Salva (Memphis, Tennessee); Eastlake CP Church in Oklahoma City, Oklahoma; Glory Korean (Atlanta, Georgia); High Point CP Church in Somerset, Kentucky; Hope Fellowship in Medina, Tennessee; Immanuel CP Church in Dade City, Florida; Japanese Christian Fellowship (Louisville, Kentucky); Luz de las Naciones (McMinnville, Tennessee); Maranatha East (El Paso, Texas); Nacion Santa International (Naples, Florida); Pikeville Mission, Pikeville, Tennessee; Stone Oak CP Church in San Antonio, Texas; Stonegate CP Church in Edmond, Oklahoma; The Connection CP Church in Nashville, Tennessee; Villavicencio (Villavicencio, Colombia); Ye Rang Korean (Round Rock, Texas). MMT met with the Murfreesboro Presbytery's Board of Missions to discuss the possibility of a NCD within its geographical bounds. Preliminary demographic studies have been conducted to explore possibilities and MMT continues to work with Murfreesboro

Presbytery to narrow down possibilities and determine God's call within these possibilities.

3. New Exploration Initiative: The purpose is to explore, study, secure leadership, and provide funding for geographical areas (USA) that do not have a CP presence. This process has a 12-month timeline to determine if a NCD may be established in a particular area. As the initiative grows, MMT will approach the respective presbytery with its findings to collaborate on a NCD. This frees the presbytery from initial financial burden and provides the expertise of the MMT to determine if a NCD is feasible before investing substantial resources that often discourage presbyterial board of missions from pursuing new endeavors. Currently, the MMT is setting up these pilot projects for feasibility.

K. TECHNOLOGY IN MINISTRY

1. Audio/Visual Services: CMT now offers Audio/Visual documentation services. The first use of this service was connected to the 2015 Ministers Conference. All three keynote lectures given by Reverend Dr. Cleophus J. LaRue were posted in March (http://tiny.cc/2015MinConfVideos). CMT developed a three-DVD set of the lectures, available for purchase at $24.95 per set ($20.00 plus $4.95 S/H). Purchasers of the DVD set will also receive a bonus DVD of the three sermons that were delivered during the conference. We anticipate extending this service to include meetings, seminars, conferences, and other CP gatherings, to benefit those who cannot physically attend. Contact cmt@cumberland.org for more information.

2. MC website, Facebook, Twitter: Visit (http://www.ministrycouncil.cumberland.org) for resources, news and information, event registration, blogs, announcements, and links of interest and use to CPs. Visit the Ministry Council, DMT and MMT on Facebook. Follow @MinistryCouncil on Twitter.

3, eVotions: Online devotions by youth and adults from a broad cross-section of CPs. (http://ministrycouncil.cumberland.org/evotions)

4. Telling Our Stories: We are collecting short video clips of CPs telling their faith stories. To see some of the videos already collected, navigate to (http://tiny.cc/cpfaithstories).

5. Stewardship Resources: Discussion starters and resources to help congregations: (http://ministrycouncil.cumberland.org/stewardshipdiscussionstarters).

6. The Well: Webpage for pastors and church leaders to help locate resources for planning and leading worship and other church programs. The Well will provide resources and will also be a place where CPs can post their own resources. (http://ministrycouncil.cumberland.org/thewell)

III. FUNDING

A. OUR UNITED OUTREACH

The Ministry Council assists with stewardship education efforts including but not limited to Our United Outreach. In 2014, Our United Outreach tithes fell short of the goal set by the General Assembly, resulting in a reduction of $158,795 to support ministries guided by the Council. Having consulted with the Stated Clerk to ensure compliance with GA policies, and recognizing that Our United Outreach tithes have not been a consistent/reliable source of dedicated income for many years, in 2014 the Ministry Council set up a subcommittee to consider long-term budgets and additional revenue sources. The subcommittee was charged to explore ways that the Ministry Council can help to promote Our United Outreach while thinking creatively/futuristically about new and additional methods of funding. The scope of the task exceeded the resources of the group. At the April 2015 meeting, the Ministry Council appointed a new ad hoc committee of members with interest and/or experience in fund development to bring ideas or proposals for ways to increase funding/revenue.

MC and MT staff demonstrate support of Our United Outreach by directing that portions of their paychecks go directly to OUO. MC and MT elected members have generously donated their reimbursed travel expense. As of April 2015, this resulted in donations totaling more than $6,600 from elected members Elizabeth Horsley, Adam McReynolds, Troy Green, Sam Romines, Lanny Johnson, Gwen Roddye, Ken Bean, Emily Mahoney, Denise Adams, Mary Ann Cole, Ron McMillan, Tom Sanders, Karen Tolen, Forest Prosser, James McGuire, Victor Hassell, Dominic Lau, and Linda Snelling. Included in that total are generous donations from Eleanor Scrudder of the Nominating Committee and Lewis Leon Cole of the CPCA.

B. ENDOWMENTS

All Endowments are listed within the Board of Stewardship section of the preliminary minutes. The MC hopes that highlighting some of the MT endowments that are not yet viable might prompt potential donors to help move these endowments to the point where interest income can be used to support programs. These include:

Need: $466.95	Christian Education Programs	Endowment No. 806330	Jeff and Angie Sledge	Level to reach: $3,000
Need: $758.72	Christian Education Programs	Endowment No. 806140	Jean Garrett	Level to reach: $5,000
Need: $2,564.44	Children's Ministry	Endowment No. 806370	Jake Tyler Children's Ministry	Level to reach: $5,000
Need: $449	General Support -Missions	Endowment No. 804150	Jose & Fanny Fajardo	Level to reach: $10,000
Need: $1,055	MM Magazine	Endowment No. 803400	Marguerite D. Richards	Level to reach: $10,000
Need: $1,565	General Support -Missions	Endowment No. 804200	Freda Mitchell Gilbert	Level to reach: $10,000
Need: $1,720	General Support -Missions	Endowment No. 804300	Rubye Johnson May	Level to reach: $10,000
Need: $5,190.52	Awards/Encouragement – CPC/CPCA Students at MTS	Endowment No. 810010	R & R Baugh	Level to reach: $10,000
Need: $8,466.01	Scholarships for Conference (Oklahoma, Red River Pres. & far away)	Endowment No. 810020	L Brown (Beth Brown)	Level to reach: $10,000

C. INVESTMENT LOAN PROGRAM (ILP)

ILPs serve as "savings accounts" for denominational entities to fund future programming. Currently, the Ministry Council/Teams have 54 ILPs.

D. CP RESOURCES AND SALES FIGURES

In 2014, 3,016 orders were shipped with $186,358.76 total billing for the year.

IV. MINISTRY COUNCIL CONCLUSION

In conclusion, growth and success of the varied ministries within the Ministry Council may be directly attributed to the concept of Servant Empowered Leadership. Even though our culture expects "Church" to be a certain way, the vision of the Cumberland Presbyterian Church becoming a true servant empowered organization has taken hold. The empowerment and engagement of every member in the work of ministry is just too Christ honoring and world changing to leave undone.

The Ministry Council elected members and staff remain committed to serving God through the Cumberland Presbyterian Church and ask that the Church remain in prayer for our work. We are thankful for the guidance of the Holy Spirit as we work to enhance and implement ministries that draw people to Christ.

Respectfully Submitted,
The Ministry Council of the Cumberland Presbyterian Church
Reverend Troy Green, President
Mary Ann Cole, First Vice President
Reverend Lanny Johnson, Second Vice President
Gwen Roddye, Secretary
Edith B. Old, Director of Ministries/Treasurer

MINISTRY COUNCIL APPENDICES

ECUMENICAL PARTNERSHIPS WITH MINISTRY TEAMS

(Appendix A)

In compliance with the General Assembly directive,
> "For the Ministry Council to evaluate our association with the Presbyterian Church USA to re-determine the boundaries of that association, pending the actions of the meeting of the Presbyterian Church USA 2014 General Assembly,"

Ministry Teams were asked to compile an inventory of direct relationships/associations/ partnerships of Ministry Teams with the Presbyterian Church USA and provide descriptions, purposes, and information about any agreements /memorandum of understanding, along with how often those agreements are reviewed/ when they were last reviewed.

COMMUNICATIONS MINISTRY TEAM
- no direct relationships/associations/partnerships with Presbyterian Church USA.

PASTORAL DEVELOPMENT MINISTRY TEAM
- no direct relationships/associations/partnerships with Presbyterian Church USA.

DISCIPLESHIP MINISTRY TEAM ECUMENICAL PARTNERSHIPS
(Representing the Cumberland Presbyterian Church)

PRESBYTERIAN AND REFORMED EDUCATIONAL PARTNERSHIP
    Partners: Cumberland Presbyterian Church, Moravians, Presbyterian Church USA, Presbyterian Church of Canada, Reformed Church in America
    Agreement/Memorandum of Understanding: Covenant formed after Presbyterian and Reformed Educational Ministry dissolved; renewed by attendance
    Description and Purpose: Members meet once a year to develop and work on joint projects such as Opening Doors to Discipleship; the Cumberland Presbyterian Church serves as treasurer and Partnership funds are invested in our Investment Loan Program (this money is not ours to spend but we are simply the stewards of it)
    Representative: Cindy Martin

COMMITTEE ON UNIFORM SERIES (creates outlines used for Encounter)
    Partners: African Methodist Episcopal, African Methodist Episcopal Zion, American Baptist Churches in the USA, Christian Methodist Episcopal, Church of the Brethren, Church of God (Anderson), Cumberland Presbyterian Church, Cumberland Presbyterian Church in America, Evangelical Lutheran Church in America, Mennonites (USA & Canada), National Baptists Convention of America, Inc., National Baptist Convention, USA, Inc., National Missionary Baptist Convention of America, Nigerian Baptist Convention, Presbyterian Church USA, Seventh Day Baptist, United Church of Christ, United Methodist Church.
    Agreement/Memorandum of Understand: Covenant renewed by attending the meeting, and the Discipleship Ministry Team gives a modest monetary gift that is used for administrative purposes.
    Description and Purpose: Meeting once a year together to develop and review scriptures to base Sunday school material on
    Representative: Jim McGuire

PRESBYTERIAN YOUTH TRIENNIUM
    Partners: Cumberland Presbyterian Church, Cumberland Presbyterian Church in America, Presbyterian Church USA
    Agreement/Memorandum of Understanding: Covenant; commitment renewed with evaluation of the previous year's speakers, programs, etc
    Description and Purpose: Youth event held every three years
    Representative: Nathan Wheeler plus various Cumberland Presbyterian Church members

CURRICULUM PARTNERSHIP
Partners: Faith Alive (Christian Reformed Church and Reformed Church in America)
Feasting on the Word (Presbyterian Church USA)
Shine (Church of the Brethren, Mennonites and Mennonites Canada)
Agreement/Memorandum of Understanding: Contract with each partner to receive discounts or money back for materials sold.
Description and Purpose: Meeting once a year or when representative in area; recommending curriculum and use of database of churches for approved mailings.
Representative: Jodi Rush

FAITH IN 3-D
Partners: Cooperative Baptist Fellowship, Cumberland Presbyterian Church, Presbyterian Church USA

ECUMENICAL STEWARDSHIP CENTER
Partners: African Methodist Episcopal, American Baptist Churches USA, Barnabas Foundation, Christian Church (Disciples of Christ), Church of the Brethren, Church of God, Community of Christ, Cumberland Presbyterian Church, Episcopal Church, Evangelical Covenant Church, Evangelical Lutheran Church in America, Evangelical Lutheran Church in Canada, Friends, Mennonites, Moravians, Presbyterian Church of Canada, Presbyterian Church USA, United Church of Canada, United Church of Christ, United Methodist Church
Agreement/Memorandum of Understanding: Meeting of Leadership Seminar once a year followed by Advisory Council meeting; Brown Bag Virtual meetings once a quarter; annual commitment of monetary gift from both Discipleship Ministry Team and Cumberland Presbyterian Church Board of Stewardship
Description and Purpose: Networking/relationship/sharing of resources through events and service on the Advisory Council; partnership of staff in a common area of stewardship ministry
Representative: Elinor Brown

GOD SO LOVES
Largest Purchaser: Presbyterian Church USA
Agreement/Memorandum of Understanding: none
Description and Purpose: video project about the Cumberland Presbyterian Church
Representative: Matthew Gore

CUMBERLAND PRESBYTERIAN HANDBOOK
Partners: Presbyterian Church USA, Evangelical Lutheran Church in America
Agreement/Memorandum of Understanding: Original one-time payment
Description and Purpose: book with major portions of it adapted from material they developed
Representative: Matt Gore

ECUMENICAL YOUTH MINISTRY STAFF TEAM
Partners: African Methodist Episcopal, Catholic Church, Christian Church (Disciples of Christ), Christian Methodist Episcopal, Church of the Brethren, Cooperative Baptist Fellowship, Cumberland Presbyterian Church, Episcopal Church, Evangelical Lutheran Church in America, Presbyterian Church USA, United Church of Christ, United Methodist Church,
Agreement/Memorandum of Understanding: Renewed annually with attendance
Description and Purpose: Meeting once a year; partnership of staff in a common area of youth ministry
Representative: Nathan Wheeler

CUMBERLAND PRESBYTERIAN YOUTH CONFERENCE, THE FORUM, THE EVENT
Partner: Cumberland Presbyterian Church in America
Agreement/Memorandum of Understanding: Covenant of attendance
Description and Purpose: United Board of Christian Discipleship events

THESE DAYS
Partners: Cumberland Presbyterian Church, Cumberland Presbyterian Church in America, Presbyterian Church of Canada, Presbyterian Church USA, United Church of Christ, United Church of Canada

Agreement/Memorandum of Understanding: recruit writers
Description and Purpose: meeting once a year to plan a devotional guide
Representative: Cindy Martin

ASSOCIATION OF PRESBYTERIAN CHURCH EDUCATORS
Partners: Cumberland Presbyterian Church, Moravians, Presbyterian Church of Canada, Presbyterian Church USA
Agreement/Memorandum of Understanding: individual membership; hope to be able to contribute as a denomination
Description and Purpose: Meeting once a year to train Christian educators through speakers, workshops, networking; they allow Cumberland Presbyterians to attend event even though we are not a denominational member at this time
Representatives: Discipleship Ministry Team staff

CUMBERLAND PRESBYTERIAN RESOURCE DEVELOPMENT
Partners: Beverly St. John, Chris Warren, etc.
Agreement/Memorandum of Understanding: case by case basis
Description and Purpose: Cumberland Presbyterian Church and other writers of resources, books, curriculum, etc. that we sell their product.
Representative: Matt Gore

MISSIONS MINISTRY TEAM ECUMENICAL PARTNERSHIPS
(Representing the Cumberland Presbyterian Church)

BETH-EL MISSION
Partners: Originally a tri-union project with the Cumberland Presbyterian Church, the Presbyterian Church in United States, and the United Presbyterian Church. These last two bodies eventually merged to become the Presbyterian Church USA.
Description and Purpose: Beth-El Mission helps farm workers achieve self-sufficiency through its open opportunities to worship, its extensive educational programs, and the many services it provides to meet basic needs. Started in 1976, as a mission out of Lewis Memorial Cumberland Presbyterian Church in Tampa, Florida. In June 1977, GA met in Tampa, and favorably supported the work among Hispanic population. A house was purchased in 1978, with funds from AL-FL-MS Synod. Rev. Jose Fajardo, preached at the first worship service in the new facility in August 1978. John Lovelace was appointed as Director of the Department of Hispanic Ministries in 1978. In 1979, he contacted representatives from United Presbyterian Church and the Presbyterian Church in United States about partnership.
Agreement/Memorandum of Understanding: there is a Covenant and Agreement signed in 2004 by all entities (Beth-El, Presbytery of Tampa Bay, Presbytery of Peace River, and Cumberland Presbyterian Church). "...shall be in effect indefinitely, with comprehensive review and evaluation every five years. Because of the sacred nature of covenant relationships, amendments shall require concurrence by the Board of Directors of Beth-El and each of the Presbyterian Churches."
Representatives: Cumberland Presbyterian Board Members: Eddie Jenkins, Joyce Kalemeris, Penny Knight and Don Schultz; Missions Ministry Team gives an annual contribution of $40,000

COALITION OF APPALACHIAN MINISTRIES (CAM)
Partners: Christian Reformed Church, Cumberland Presbyterian Church, Cumberland Presbyterian Church in America, Presbyterian Church USA, Reformed Church in America
Agreement/Memorandum of Understanding: The 1985 General Assembly voted to support recommendations from a task force comprised of four entities (Presbyterian Church USA, Reformed Church in America, Christian Reformed Church, and Cumberland Presbyterian Church) and the Coalition of Appalachian Ministries. Recommendations were B1) Y.that all entities Acommit themselves to a continuing partnership in missions in Appalachia; 2) that regional and area judicatories annually support the CAM budget to implement the mission strategies outlined in the task force's report; 3) name at least one staff person to serve with CAM as a resource person and liaison; 4) requested Synods of Kentucky, Tennessee, and AL-FL-MS to take initiative to become actively involved in CAM alongside Synod of East TN; and that, 5) current efforts of the (then) Board of Missions and (then) Board of Christian Education to be supportive of the work of CAM be affirmed.
Description and Purpose: The mission is to make a positive impact wherever Reformed tradition and Appalachian culture come together, by networking with church and community, to provide educational

and service opportunities.

Representatives: Cumberland Presbyterian Board Members: Nadara Jones, Tommy Jobe, Glen Brister with two new members yet to be named; the Missions Ministry Team gives an annual contribution of $11,500

PROJECT VIDA

Partners: Cumberland Presbyterian Church, Presbyterian Church USA

Agreement/Memorandum of Understanding:

Description and Purpose: Serves three neighborhoods of more than 1,500 families located within the nation's most impoverished neighborhoods. Based on the needs of these low-income neighborhoods, Project Vida has expanded over the years into a multi-faceted center striving to change lives in a holistic and profound way. Programs include low-cost health care (7 clinics); education (from newborn to 18 years); and economic development (micro-enterprise endeavors); housing (low-cost apartments, transitional housing for homeless single-parent families). Originally called AProject Verdad@ this was a holistic ministry to Hispanics in the El Paso/Juarez area under the auspices of the Tres Rio Presbytery (Presbyterian Church USA) and the National Presbyterian Church of Mexico. In 1982, the Cumberland Presbyterian denomination through the work of Western Presbytery became involved in this ministry as a result of the work of John Lovelace, Director of the Department of Hispanic Ministries. In 1990, the National Presbyterian Church of Mexico withdrew from the partnership, the name was changed to Project Vida and funding was provided through del Cristo Presbytery (Cumberland Presbyterian Church), Tres Rios (Presbyterian Church USA), and the national agencies of both denominations.

Representatives: Cumberland Presbyterian Board members: Diane Sowell, Rev. Lee Bondurant; Missions Ministry gives an annual contribution of $8,500.

NATIONAL FARM WORKER MINISTRY (NFWM)

Partners: 39 Member and Supporting Organizations (including Presbyterian Hunger Program of the Presbyterian Church USA).

Agreement/Memorandum of Understanding: General Assembly, during its 150th meeting (1980), voted to become a member of National Farm Worker Ministry. In March 1981, the National Farm Worker Ministry Executive Committee met and voted unanimously to receive the Cumberland Presbyterian Church as a new member group. The Cumberland Presbyterian connection with the National Farm Worker Ministry was first initiated through the work of John Lovelace, the Director of the Department of Hispanic Ministries. He served as the official representative for many years.

Description and Purpose: A faith-based organization committed to justice for and empowerment of farm workers. National Farm Worker Ministry educates, equips and mobilizes member organizations and other faith communities, groups and individuals to support farm worker led efforts to improve their living and working conditions.

Representative: Rev. Joy Warren representing the Missions Ministry Team; Missions Ministry Team gives an annual contribution of $2,200.

CHURCH WOMEN UNITED

Partners: 15 Partner organizations: Women of Faith for the 1,000 Days Movement, Ecumenical Women at the United Nations, Children's Defense Fund, UNICEF, Equal Justice Initiative, United Nations, United Nations Association of the United States, National Council of Churches of Christ USA, End Child Prostitution and Trafficking USA, Odyssey Networks, Church World Service, The Sister Fund, Religions for Peace, Faith Trust Institute, Campaign for Tobacco Free Kids; 30 participating denominations: African Methodist Episcopal Church (Women's Missionary Society), African Methodist Episcopal Zion Church (Women's Home and Overseas Missionary Society), American Baptist Churches in the USA (American Baptist Women's Ministries), Christian Church (Disciples of Christ) (International Christian Women's Fellowship), Christian Methodist Episcopal Church (Women's Missionary Council), Church of God (Women of the Church of God), Church of the Brethren (Program for Women), Church of the New Jerusalem (Swedenborgian) (Alliance of New Church Women), Community of Christ (Women's Ministries Commission), Council of Hispanic American Ministries (Ecumenical) (Women's Department of COHAM), Cumberland Presbyterian Church (Cumberland Presbyterian Women), The Episcopal Church (Women in Mission and Ministries), The Evangelical Lutheran Church in America (Women of the Evangelical Lutheran Church in America), International Council of Community Churches (Women's Christian Fellowship), Korean American Church Women United (Ecumenical Women's Fellowship), The Mar Thoma Church (Women's Evangelistic Service Association), The Mennonite Church (Women's Missionary & Service Commission),

The Moravian Church in America (North) (Provincial Women's Board, Northern Province), The Moravian Church in America (South) (Provincial Women's Board, Southern Province), National Baptist Convention of America (Women's Missionary Union), National Baptist Convention USA, Inc. (Women's Convention), National Council of Churches of Christ in America (Women's Ministries), Presbyterian Church (USA) (Presbyterian Women), Progressive National Baptist Convention, Inc. (Women's Department), Reformed Church in America (Reformed Church Women's Ministries), Religious Society of Friends (United Society of Friends Women International), United Church of Christ (Coordinating Center for Women in Church and Society), The Salvation Army, The United Methodist Church (United Methodist Women). The Young Women's Christian Association plus women from other Christian traditions (i.e. Roman Catholic, Orthodox, etc.) who support Church Women United individually.

Agreement/Memorandum of Understanding:

Description and Purpose: A racially, culturally, theologically inclusive Christian women's movement, celebrating unity in diversity and working for a world of peace and justice. Founded in 1941. Biblically based, shared Christian faith, a movement representing Protestant, Roman Catholic, Orthodox and other Christian women; organized into more than 1,200 local and state units working for peace and justice in the United States and Puerto Rico; supported by constituents in state and local units and denominational women's organizations; impassioned by the Holy Spirit to act on behalf of women and children throughout the world; and recognized as a non-governmental organization by the United Nations.

Representative: the Director of Cumberland Presbyterian Women's Ministry; Missions Ministry Team gives an annual contribution of $1,300.

ONE GREAT HOUR OF SHARING (OGHS)

Partners: From the beginning in 1946 this has been an ecumenical effort. As denominations changed and merged, One Great Hour of Sharing has varied from eight to twenty-nine participating communions. Currently, the One Great Hour of Sharing Committee officially comprises nine Christian denominations: American Baptist Churches USA, African Methodist Episcopal Zion Church, Church of the Brethren, Christian Church (Disciples of Christ), Cumberland Presbyterian Church, Presbyterian Church USA, Reformed Church in America, United Church of Christ, and Church World Service. In various ways, all work in cooperation with Church World Service, the relief, development, and refugee assistance arm of the National Council of the Churches of Christ in the USA

Agreement/Memorandum of Understanding: the Cumberland Presbyterian Church became partners in this offering in 1952 - "Board of Foreign Missions and the Board of Missions voted to recommend that denomination cooperate on a church-wide basis with the observance of One Great Hour of Sharing program to begin in March 1953."

Description and Purpose: An offering that makes the love of Christ real for individuals and communities around the world who suffer the effects of disaster, conflict, or severe economic hardship, and for those who serve them through gifts of money and time. Today, projects are underway in more than 100 countries, including the United States and Canada. In the 1990s, receipts exceeded $20 million annually. While specific allocations differ in each denomination, all use their One Great Hour of Sharing funds to make possible relief, refugee assistance, development aid and more. This was an outgrowth of Church World Service ministries following WWII - an effort to supply commodities such as corn, wheat, rice and beans to share around the world; and eventually became an "offering" of money.

Representative: Missions Ministry Team which collects the offering; 75% of the offering is sent to Church World Service for disaster relief; 25% is retained by Missions Ministry Team in support of ministries of compassion on Cumberland Presbyterian fields of service.

CHURCH WORLD SERVICE

Partners: Current membership - 37 organizations/denominations/communions: African Methodist Episcopal Church, African Methodist Episcopal Zion Church, Alliance of Baptists, American Baptist Churches USA, Armenian Church of America (including Diocese of California), Christian Church (Disciples of Christ), Christian Methodist Episcopal Church, Church of the Brethren, Community of Christ, The Coptic Orthodox Church in North America, Ecumenical Catholic Communion, The Episcopal Church, Evangelical Lutheran Church in America, Friends United Meeting, Greek Orthodox Archdiocese of America, Hungarian Reformed Church in America, International Council of Community Churches, Korean Presbyterian Church in America, Malankara Orthodox Syrian Church, Mar Thoma Church, Moravian Church in America, National Baptist Convention of America, National Baptist Convention, USA, Inc., National Missionary Baptist Convention of America, Orthodox Church in America, Patriarchal Parishes of the Russian Orthodox Church in the USA, Philadelphia Yearly Meeting of the Religious Society of

Friends, Polish National Catholic Church of America, Presbyterian Church USA, Progressive National Baptist Convention, Inc., Reformed Church in America, Serbian Orthodox Church in the USA and Canada, The Swedenborgian Church, Syrian Orthodox Church of Antioch, Ukrainian Orthodox Church in America, United Church of Christ, The United Methodist Church

Agreement/Memorandum of Understanding: "In compliance with the directive of the 1951 General Assembly, the Board of Foreign Missions and the Board of Missions and Evangelism have acted through an inter-board committee to work out a program for CP Church to participate in Church World Service."

Description and Purpose: Works with partners to eradicate hunger and poverty and to promote peace and justice around the world. Begun in 1946, in the aftermath of the WWII. Seventeen denominations came together to form an agency "to do in partnership what none of us could hope to do as well alone." The mission: Feed the hungry, clothe the naked, heal the sick, comfort the aged, shelter the homeless. The initial partnership work was sending food, clothing, and medical supplies to war-torn Europe and Asia. Now active in more than 30 countries globally and is a member of the ACT Alliance (a coalition of more than 140 churches and church-based humanitarian organizations working together in humanitarian assistance and development around the world), InterAction (comprised of more than 180 member organizations working in every developing country. Members are faith-base and secular, large and small, with a focus on the world's most poor and vulnerable populations), and International Council of Voluntary Agencies (the world's oldest non-governmental organization (NGO) network of humanitarian organizations, whose mission is to make humanitarian action more principled and effective by working collectively and independently to influence policy and practice.)

Representative: Missions Ministry Team which collects the offering; Use of Funds – 86.1% Programs, 9.8% Fundraising; 4.1% Administration.

THE REPORT OF THE BOARD OF STEWARDSHIP, FOUNDATION, AND BENEFITS

I. GENERAL INFORMATION

A. BOARD MEETINGS AND ORGANIZATION

The Board of Stewardship, Foundation and Benefits under the direction of its officers, President Charlie Floyd, Vice-president Rob Latimer, Secretary Debbie Shelton, and Treasurer Robert Heflin, met two times in regular session.

B. BOARD MEMBERS WHOSE TERMS EXPIRE

Members whose terms expire at the 2015 General Assembly, with their years of service, are as follows: Rob Latimer, nine years; Andy Frazier, six years and Mike St. John, three years. Rob Latimer is not eligible for another term. We want to thank him for him service and dedication to the Board of Stewardship, Foundation and Benefits. Andy Frazier and Mike St. John are eligible and have agreed to serve another three year term.

C. BOARD REPRESENTATIVE TO THE 185TH GENERAL ASSEMBLY

The board's representative to the 185th General Assembly is Sylvia Hall.

D. STAFF

Kathryn Gilbert Craig serves as Administrative Assistant, Mark Duck serves as Coordinator of Benefits and Robert Heflin serves as Executive Secretary. Carolyn Harmon serves as the Planned Giving Coordinator for the Presbytery of East Tennessee. The Board appreciates the work Carolyn Harmon does in educating congregations of the legacy ministry that can be accomplished as individuals make planned gifts to their local congregations.

E. 2016 BUDGET

The 2016 line-item budget has been filed with the Office of the General Assembly.

F. 2014 AUDIT

Certified copies of the 2014 audit reports from Fouts and Morgan will be filed with the Office of the General Assembly in compliance with General Regulations E.5. and E.6. The 2014 audit will be printed in the audit section of the 2015 minutes.

II. FINANCIAL FOUNDATION DEVELOPMENT AND MANAGEMENT

A. PURPOSE

One area of the work of the board is in financial foundation development and management. The purpose of this program is as follows:
To secure a firm financial undergirding for the ongoing ministry of congregations and the agencies of presbyteries, synods, and the General Assembly as they bear witness to the saving love of God, the grace of our Lord Jesus Christ, and the fellowship and communion of the Holy Spirit.
The Financial Foundation Program is reported in this section in general terms and more specifically under the headings III. Endowment Program, IV. Investment Loan Program, and V. Property and Casualty Insurance.

B. 2014 IN REVIEW

The year 2014 proved to be a difficult year to make money in investments. U. S. bonds continued to struggle as did domestic stocks. Foreign markets continued to be unstable. Commodity prices fell sharply in the last half of the year mainly due to the large drop in oil prices. For the past 12 months, ending September 30, 2014, only 17% of active managers outperformed the S&P500. The median price to earnings multiple for U. S. stocks is the highest is has been since 1950. The value of the 10 year Treasury bill fell throughout the year and is near its 50 year low. These conditions make it very difficult to make money with a traditional mix of 60/40 stocks and bonds for the next seven to ten years.

Throughout 2014 the markets were up and down, much like a roller coaster. This caused stress for many investors, making it more imperative that we focus on investing for the long term.

We need to continue to be cautious about looking too far down the road. Sentiment and emotion rule the short term. We are confident that our investment manager, Gerber/Taylor can continue to help us navigate the sometimes turbulent ups and downs of the market. Since October 1981, Gerber/Taylor has done a wonderful job for the Cumberland Presbyterian Church.

C. BOARD OF STEWARDSHIP

The Board of Stewardship ended 2012 with an unrestricted surplus of $52,113. We are ever mindful of expenses incurred and try to be good stewards of what has been entrusted to the Board. We are grateful for the faithful support from congregations and individuals through their contributions to Our United Outreach.

D. MANAGEMENT OF FUNDS

In January 2013, we combined the Growth/Income Endowment Fund and the Total Return Endowment Fund with a focus on not only interest and dividends but also growth in realized and unrealized gains/losses.

At the end of 2014 the Endowment Fund portfolio was under the co-management of Gerber/Taylor Management, Metropolitan West Asset Management, RREEF America II, Clarion, 1607 Capital and Eagle MLP. The funds of the Retirement Program were co-managed by Gerber/Taylor Management, Metropolitan West Asset Management and 1607 Capital.

The church loan portion of the endowment portion of the endowment portfolio and the investments of the Cumberland Presbyterian Church Investment Loan Program, Inc. were under the management of board staff with the help of Hilliard Lyons.

III. ENDOWMENT PROGRAM

Since 1836, the board and its corporate predecessors have sought to be faithful trustees of the funds given into their hands to provide a permanent financial foundation for the work of congregations, presbyteries, synods, and General Assembly agencies. The work of the Endowment Program is the oldest responsibility of the board and fulfills a portion of that task to which all Cumberland Presbyterians are called: "Christian stewardship acknowledges that all of life and creation is a trust from God, to be used for God's glory and service."—Confession of Faith for Cumberland Presbyterians 6:10.

A. COMMUNICATION

The Endowment Program report will be distributed to all endowment program participants, general assembly board members, churches, and individual contributors.

Agencies, other participants, and interested parties received quarterly detailed reports on the postings to all their endowments. With the addition of names supplied by the agencies during the year, the number of persons receiving these reports continues to expand. In addition, special reports were made as requested.

B. ASSETS, INVESTMENT MIX, AND PERFORMANCE

1. Assets and Investment Mix

The assets of the Endowment Fund totaled $55,082,008 for 2014 at market value. The following table provides a breakdown of the investment mix:

INVESTMENT MIX
Securities & Investments

15.8%	US Equity	$ 8,702,957
13.1%	Real Assets Investment Trusts	$ 7,215,743
14.6%	Fixed Income	$ 8,041,973
19.9%	Hedged Equity	$10,961,320
15.4%	Multi-Strategy	$ 8,482,629
2.1%	Opportunistic	$ 1,156,722
11.6%	International Stocks	$ 6,389,513
7.5%	Emerging Markets	$ 4,131,151
100.0%	Total	$55,082,008

2. Performance of the Endowment Fund

The Endowment Fund generated $3,019,891 in investment earnings during 2014. Net contributions and withdrawals were ($382,469). The change in market value was $2,637,422. Earnings paid and payable to congregations, presbyteries and agencies totaled $2,377,045 for 2014.

With the combining of the Growth/Income Fund and the Total Return Fund in January 2013, we also began paying out 5% (annualized) to the congregations, presbyteries and agencies. Previously agencies had difficulty in preparing budgets because of the unknown amount they would receive from endowment income. Now, they realize they will receive 5% in endowment income over a twelve month period. With this information, they have a better idea how much endowment income they can expect.

3. Rate of Income Paid Out by the Endowment Fund

The rate at which income was paid out to participants in the Endowment Fund for 2014 was 5%:

Percentage of Income Paid Out

2014	5.00%
2013	5.00%
2012	2.32%
2011	2.01%
2010	3.90%
2009	3.79%
2008	4.03%
2007	4.19%
2006	4.05%
2005	4.20%

4. Total Rate of Return for the Endowment Fund

The following table gives the annualized rates of return as contained in the report from Gerber/Taylor Associates for year end 2013:

	One Year Period 01/01/14-12/31/14	Five Year Period 01/01/10-12/31/14	Since Inception 09/30/81-12/31/14
Endowment Fund	5.9%	8.9%	10.3%

C. ESTABLISHING AN ENDOWMENT AS A LEGACY

The Board of Stewardship, Foundation and Benefits manages over 800 endowments established for the benefit of congregations, presbyteries, synods, agencies and other special ministries of the Cumberland Presbyterian denomination. Many of these endowments were established by individuals as a legacy to continue to benefit long after they are no longer with us. Some of the endowments were established by congregations, presbyteries and synods to help further their specific ministries. Some of the endowments were started with very little. Through the years these endowments have grown and the beneficiaries are reaping the gifts of the endowment income and using it in ministry in their local area or worldwide. Please consider establishing an endowment.

D. ENDOWMENT PROGRAM LOANS

Historical Review

Through investing up to 40% of the assets of the Endowment Program in the witness of the Church, the message of good news concerning Christ is strengthened both in the United States and overseas. A survey of old files in the Historical Foundation and in the vault of the Board of Stewardship reveals the important role played by this aspect of the investment policy. Over the past sixty-five years from 1944 to 2009, 841 loans were made to congregations, presbyteries, and synods. From 2010 through 2014 an additional 16 loans have been made. Through these loans, $42,474,405 has been provided in financing for expansion of facilities and extension of witness.

A look at the different periods during which loans have been made provides a picture of growing endowments (and of post World War II inflation!).

Period	Loans	Total Loaned	Average
1944-49	35	$ 145,755	$ 4,164
1950-59	171	$ 1,360,441	$ 7,955
1960-69	208	$ 3,056,891	$ 14,697
1970-79	166	$ 3,609,084	$ 21,741
1980-89	101	$ 4,349,120	$ 43,061
1990-99	102	$14,440,837	$141,577
2000-09	58	$10,571,723	$182,271
2010-14	16	$ 4,940,554	$308,785

While looking at the table above, it should be noted that the Cumberland Presbyterian Church Investment Loan Program began January 1, 2001. Since its creation most of the larger loans are made through the Investment Loan Program.

Down through the years, donors to endowments have found satisfaction in the knowledge that the prudent investment of their gifts strengthened not only the work of the particular churches, institutions, and causes which they designated to receive the income but also the broader witness of the Church.

E. OTHER CHURCH LOANS

In addition to loans from the Investment Loan Program and the Endowment Program there is another source available to the board for loans to churches.

1. Small Church Loan Fund

This fund, formerly none as the Revolving Church Loan Fund, was created through an endowment established by Lavenia Cole and gifts to the "Into the Nineties" Capital Gifts Campaign and all interest earned by the loans is added to the fund to increase the amount available for loans. There were seven loans from the Revolving Church Loan Program at the end of 2013 totaling $173,379.

The rate of interest for the Small Church Loans made during 2013 was based on the loan rate established by the Cumberland Presbyterian Church Investment Loan Program at the beginning of each quarter. These loans are generally small loans of $35,000 or less, amortized over five years.

F. REGIONAL PLANNED GIVING COORDINATORS

1. History

In 1993, the 163rd General Assembly commended the Board of Stewardship for "its vision in developing a program of planned giving in local congregations" and urged congregations "to be open to this new program and to take advantage of the assistance being offered" by the Board.

Further, it adopted recommendations to:

Approve a church-wide annual emphasis on planned gifts as a complementary part of the observation of the Family Week focus provided by the Board of Christian Education during May of each year; and

Urge each congregation to recognize the importance of promoting planned gifts as a part of its overall nurture of Christian stewardship among its members.

In response to the 1993 action, staff of the Board of Stewardship have made presentations to more than 150 congregations on the need to develop congregational endowments and encourage planned giving by church members.

At one time there were four Regional Planned Giving Coordinators. At the moment Carolyn Harmon is the only Regional Planned Giving Coordinators. She is an elder in the Cedar Hill Church, Greeneville, Tennessee, serving the Presbytery of East Tennessee. The other coordinators can no longer serve due to health conditions or other reasons. Though Carolyn is employed by the Presbytery of East Tennessee she has made presentations beyond her presbytery.

Through these regional coordinators education concerning the stewardship opportunities in planned giving has been made readily accessible to many churches. Often times the results of their work is not easily measured. It may be several years before their work bears fruit. The regional coordinators use their presentations to plant the seeds which may bear fruit immediately or years down the road. What is of utmost importance is that the seeds are being planted.

Regional coordinators are employed and their salaries paid by their respective presbyteries or by the Board of Stewardship. They are the living links of a partnership between the General Assembly and their presbyteries and they join in the semi-annual meetings of the Board of Stewardship and the biennial meetings of the North American Conference on Christian Philanthropy. In this partnership, the cost of their materials, travel, and continuing education opportunities are paid by the Board from Our United Outreach funds.

The Board of Stewardship would like to begin renewing efforts of educating local congregations about the opportunities available through planned giving. It is through planned giving that current Cumberland Presbyterians can provide for effective ministry long after they are gone.

It is our prayer that God will bless the work of encouraging Cumberland Presbyterians to give generously to enhance the future ministry of all our churches.

VII. CUMBERLAND PRESBYTERIAN CHURCH INVESTMENT LOAN PROGRAM, INC.

In 1976, the board began a program to provide an opportunity for flexible investment of current temporary cash assets of congregations and agencies of the church. The primary purpose of the program is to provide income to participants as a foundation for ministry. As of January 1, 2001, the assets of the original program, Cash Funds Management, were transferred to the new Cumberland Presbyterian Church Investment Loan Program, Inc.

For the year ending 2014, the assets for the Investment Loan Program were $16,435,223. There were 278 individual, congregation and agency accounts. At year end, deposits on account totaled $14,384,041. The total loans were $8,817,500 at year end.

For 2014, the corporation complied with the regulatory requirements in the states of Tennessee and Kentucky and was able to offer investment opportunities to individual Cumberland Presbyterians in the states of Tennessee, Kentucky, Texas, Missouri and New Mexico.

The board of directors is composed of the following: Rob Latimer, president; Charlie Floyd, vice-president and Debbie Shelton, secretary. Robert Heflin serves as Treasurer and Executive Secretary. During the past year, the board met twice in regular session.

In order to simplify administration and focus on the strengths of the Investment Loan Program, the board took action to limit the offering of notes and depository accounts to "ready access accounts." All note holders (individuals) and depository account holders (churches and church agencies) with funds invested in these "on demand" accounts participated in the $430,430 which the program paid in interest. For 2014 the interest rate paid to account holders was 3.0%. The interest rate paid to account holders can fluctuate from one quarter to the next. In recent years there has been renewed interest for congregations to open new accounts because the interest paid is higher than current CD rates.

The table below provides a breakdown of the investment mix.

INVESTMENT LOAN PROGRAM
Securities & Investments

15.78%	Cash Equivalents	$1,402,602
1.12%	Stocks	$ 99,640
82.69%	Taxable Fixed Income	$7,348,731
0.41%	Multi Asset	$ 36,185
100.00%		$8,887,158

At the end of 2014 there were 23 loans to congregations made through the Investment Loan Program. The loan balance was $8,817,500. Every accountholder is investing in the future ministry of the Cumberland Presbyterian Church as well as receiving interest on that investment.

VIII. EMPLOYEE BENEFITS ADMINISTRATION AND RESEARCH

A. PURPOSE

The second of two broad areas of the work of the board is in employee benefits administration and research. The purpose of this program is as follows:

To support the lay and ordained employees of the church as they venture to be faithful under the call of Christ and the Church to the daily demands of providing leadership to congregations and Church agencies whom are the incarnation of the Body of Christ, the family of God at work in the world.

Employee benefits are reported in detail under headings IX. Retirement Program, X. Ministerial Aid Program, and XI. Insurance Program.

B. VISION

The board has a vision of uniform benefits for all Cumberland Presbyterian clergy, including group health insurance, group long-term disability coverage, and participation in the General Assembly's retirement plan. Ministers would then know what to expect when they are called to another church. No longer would some ministers have to do without what is considered in the secular world to be basic employee benefits. No longer would ministers and their families have to settle for being relegated to second class status. The reality is, as several General Assemblies have recognized, that this is possible if we work together in much the same manner that we send out missionaries and do a lot of other ministry. Good employee benefit plans are in place and they would be healthier and stronger if used and supported by all employees of the Cumberland Presbyterian Church.

IX. RETIREMENT PROGRAM

Since 1952, the board has provided a retirement program open to all church employees of the Cumberland Presbyterian Church. The program gives opportunity for churches and their employees to provide a source of retirement income based on voluntary contributions. In 1987, a new Cumberland Presbyterian Retirement Plan No. 2 was established as a qualified 403(b) defined contribution plan and in 1990 the General Assembly amended the plan to include the churches and employees of the Second Cumberland Presbyterian Church, now known as the Cumberland Presbyterian Church in America.

A. PLAN AMENDMENTS

As new needs arise or deficiencies in the original plan document for Cumberland Presbyterian Retirement Plan No. 2 become apparent, the General Assembly has the authority under Article IX Section 9.01 of the Plan to amend the same. In 2012 a revised plan document was approved by the General Assembly.

B. YEAR END REPORT

On December 31, 2014, there were 321 active participants in the Retirement Plan. There were also 3 receiving direct monthly payments as a result of their elections under Plan 1. In addition to these participants, there were 12 persons who were receiving annuity payments purchased through the Plan and for whom the Plan issues 1099-R's.

During 2014, $1,091,879 was dispersed to or for participants, an increase of 31% over 2013's $834,080. Contributions totaled $713,181 and were up 17% over 2013's $610,467. Realized and unrealized gains on investments totaled $1,153,146 compared to a gain in 2013 of $2,456,153. The rate of return credited to the accounts for the year was 5.7% compared to 14% for 2013. (Comparative annual rates of return for: previous three years—+10.4%, previous five years—+9.2%, and from the beginning of professional management in March, 1982—+9.8%.)

Effective January 1, 2011, Gerber/Taylor Management was retained to manage our stock portfolio.

We have continued our relationship with Met West, a bond manager, and RREEF, a private real estate investment trust manager. Matt Robbins and Stacy Miller of Gerber/Taylor continue to be very helpful with keeping the board updated on market conditions and investment strategies.

X. MINISTERIAL AID PROGRAM

A. MINISTERIAL AID

1. Full Benefit Recipients

As of March 2015 there are 3 Cumberland Presbyterian Church recipients of the full benefit of $510 per month (increased from $300 on July 1, 2010). The monthly total of these payments are $1,530.00; annually, $18,360.00 is paid. The equivalent of benefits for four participants at $260, or $1040 per month, $12,480 annually, is sent to Cauca Valley Presbytery in Columbia. Those in need in Andes Presbytery also benefit from the payments made to Cauca Valley Presbytery. These payments are not designated for specific individuals but are distributed by the presbytery as it sees fit.

In October 2005, the board decided to distribute 75% of the previous year's surplus to the remaining recipients. This distribution was made in December 2014 with 3 state side recipients receiving $4,000.00 each for a total distribution of $12,000.00. The Board of Stewardship has approved a cap of a maximum of $4,000 in lieu of large distributions that can have a negative effect on other benefits received, such as SSI, or state assistance.

2. Basic Requirements.
The new basic requirements and amount for stateside recipients for the Ministerial Aid program were approved at the General Assembly of the Cumberland Presbyterian Church in June 2010. The poverty levels have been updated to the latest available figures. They are as follows:

Full Benefit of $510 a month for State Side Recipients

> 1. Minimum age is full retirement age set forth by the Social Security Administration.
> 2. Minimum years of service to the church - 15.
> 3. Can qualify for aid if a participant in the Cumberland Presbyterian Retirement Plan if income is below poverty level as established by the US Census Bureau.
> 4. Physical and/or mental disability (doctor's statement required) at any age, however, a minimum of ten years service is required if less than 60 years of age.
> 5. Individuals' income cannot exceed federal poverty guidelines set forth for the year by the US Census Bureau. Poverty level is $11,770 a year or $980.83 a month for 2015.
> 6. Couples income cannot exceed federal poverty guidelines set forth for the year by the US Census Bureau. Poverty level is $15,930 a year or $1,327.50 a month for 2015.
> (The GA Board of Stewardship is authorized to look at each case in light of unusual financial hardship; thus, application may be made even if income levels exceed the ceiling.)
> 7. Presbytery obtains information and approves (approval can be given by the committee or board charged by presbytery with this responsibility); certification of approval is sent to the General Assembly Board of Stewardship.
> 8. Surviving spouse is eligible if above items 2, 3 and 4 have been met.

> **Note: Recipient is responsible to verify if receiving Ministerial Aid would affect his or her SSI, Social Security or other benefits.

Cumberland Presbyterian Church applicants must submit to the board a listing of assets and liabilities so the net worth can be determined. The board urges presbyteries to maintain contact with persons under the Ministerial Aid Program who live within their bounds. Should there be serious unmet needs, the presbytery is urged to contact the board so that it may determine how the Ministerial Aid program can be of assistance in meeting those needs.

3. Cumberland Presbyterian Church in America.
The CPCA now has 3 participants who receive monthly payments at the originally agreed upon amount of $109 per month. Benefits for these recipients total $327.00 per month or $3,924.00 annually. The CPCA normally pays its share in June or July following their General Assembly.

4. Ministers in Overseas Presbyteries. Payments for ministers serving in overseas presbyteries (presently, a total of $12,480 annually) are being made to Cauca Valley Presbytery and administered through its budget.

B. SPECIAL FINANCIAL NEEDS

At the Spring 2014 Board of Stewardship meeting, the Board approved the use of funds from the Ministerial Aid Cash Fund ILP to be used in special situations where illness has caused a financial hardship for those that are not eligible for Ministerial Aid. At present there are two individuals who have received payments and the total of the payments were $16,200.

XI. INSURANCE PROGRAMS

The insurance programs of the board have been assigned by the General Assembly beginning in the middle of the previous century. Dental and Vision Insurance is the newest, begun in December 2008. Property and casualty insurance is the oldest, begun in 1951. While all of the insurance programs are important, group life and health insurance, begun in 1961, touches many lives in a personal way and often at times of deep anxiety. In all, about 245 men, women, and children depend on this program to meet their health care needs.

A. PROPERTY & CASUALTY INSURANCE

The Board of Stewardship, Foundation and Benefits secures property and casualty insurance coverage against accidental loss for the General Assembly Corporation, Board of Stewardship, Discipleship Ministry Team, Missions Ministry Team, Ministry Council, Communications Ministry Team, Pastoral Development Ministry Team, Memphis Theological Seminary, and Historical Foundation.

Our broker is Lipscomb & Pitts of Memphis, Tennessee. For 2015, Travelers Insurance carries our Property & Casualty policy and $2,500,000 in earth quake coverage, Mt. Hawley Insurance Company provides an additional $6,915,251 in earthquake coverage and Lloyds of London provides $10,000,000 in earthquake coverage. Philadelphia carries our Directors & Officers, Crime, Automobile, and Umbrella policies. Workers Compensation coverage as of October 23, 2014 is with Bridgefield Casualty.

B. GROUP LONG TERM DISABILITY INSURANCE

The presbyteries of Arkansas, Columbia, Covenant, Cumberland, del Cristo, East Tennessee, Missouri, Murfreesboro, Nashville, North Central, Red River, Robert Donnell, Trinity, West Tennessee and The Center have now established non-contributory long term disability programs insured currently through Cigna. This leaves only four stateside presbyteries (Choctaw, Hope, Grace and Tennessee Georgia) without a program. The quarterly rate applied to participant's salaries is .345 per $100 of salary.

There are three primary reasons for ministers to want the coverage and for presbyteries to want to provide the protection. The group rate is significantly lower than individual policy rates and does not require a large cash outlay to cover all full-time ministers in a presbytery; housing allowance and/or the fair rental value of a manse is included in the definition of salary for ministers; and, there is no medical qualification requirement in order to enroll. These advantages over individual policies make this coverage very attractive, especially to those who have previously purchased their own policies. In addition, a provision was negotiated with Cigna by the Board's consultant, whereby ministers, upon leaving a participating presbytery to serve in a non-participating presbytery, may continue the coverage if he or she so desires. The new employing church is then billed for the quarterly premium. There are now eight ministers and two employee who are receiving or have received benefits from this insurance program. There are approximately 196 participants.

C. GROUP TRAVEL ACCIDENT INSURANCE

This policy provides twenty-four hour coverage on "named employees" for accidental death, dismemberment, or loss of sight while on business travel. The maximum benefit is $50,000 and there is also a $1,000 medical benefit. The annual premium is $900. We renew this policy every 3 years. Thirty one named positions are covered under this policy.

D. GROUP HEALTH & LIFE INSURANCE

The board has used a fully-insured, managed care approach to provide group health insurance for Cumberland Presbyterian clergy and lay employees since March 1, 1999. Blue Cross / Blue Shield of Tennessee has been our insurance carrier since January 1, 2010. Blue Cross / Blue Shield of Tennessee (BCBST) is an independent, not-for-profit, locally governed health plan company that insures more than 5 million people nationwide. With an extensive network, BCBST is able to effectively service the employees of the Cumberland Presbyterian Church. In 2011 the deductible was increased for the two plans to $1,500 deductible and a $3,500 in-network deductible for the employee and has stayed the same for 2015. Spouse and Family deductibles are twice the amount of the employee only product. Lipscomb & Pitts, a Memphis based insurance company, is our insurance broker, and Craig Wright, our agent.

1. Loss Ratio.

A comparison of paid medical premiums and claims is made in order to calculate a loss ratio. The following table contains monthly and cumulative figures for the calendar year of 2014. For 2014, 111% of the medical premiums paid to Blue Cross were used to pay claims and stop-loss premiums. This compares to a loss ratio of 94% for 2013, 83% for 2012, 91% in 2011, 75% in 2010 (not a full year of claims due to moving to new carrier) 105% for the same period in 2009, 98% in 2008 and 112% in 2007 with our previous carrier, Unicare.

MEDICAL EXPERIENCE REPORT

MONTH	MONTHLY MEDICAL PREMIUM	MONTHLY PAID CLAIMS	MONTHLY LOSS RATIO	CUMULATIVE MEDICAL PREMIUM	CUMULATIVE PAID CLAIMS	CUMULATIVE LOSS RATIO
Jan. 14	176,825	125,856	71%	176,825	124,856	71%
Feb. 14	174,100	115,508	66%	350,925	241,364	69%
Mar. 14	167,974	124,866	74%	518,899	366,230	71%
Apr. 14	174,239	611,810	351%	693,138	978,040	141%
May 14	166,716	144,400	87%	859,854	1,122,440	131%
Jun. 14	164,548	99,304	60%	1,024,402	1,221,744	119%
Jul. 14	164,899	155,635	94%	1,189,301	1,377,379	116%
Aug. 14	164,899	141,613	86%	1,354,200	1,518,992	112%
Sept.14	159,915	137,825	86%	1,514,115	1,656,817	109%
Oct. 14	162,597	192,537	118%	1,676,712	1,849,354	110%
Nov. 14	163,469	201,698	123%	1,840,181	2,051,052	111%
Dec. 14	164,899	179,779	109%	2,005,080	2,230,8315	111%

2. Premiums.

Efforts to maintain affordable premiums and comprehensive coverage are the biggest challenges we face. Option 1 has a $1,500 employee only deductible and a $3,000 family deductible. Option 2 has a $3,500 employee only deductible and a $7,000 family deductible. Premiums for 2015 are shown in the table below.

Blue Cross / Blue Shield Health Insurance for 2015

	Option 1	Option 2
Deductible	$1,500 / $3,000	$3,500 / $7,000
Employee Only	$ 696	$ 601
Employee & Spouse	$1,476	$1,278
Employee & Child(ren)	$1,277	$1,105
Family	$2,166	$1,880

The Blue Cross Health Plan is now on a calendar year as far as deductible and pricing is concerned. It is our objective to have the renewal pricing by no later than September 1 so presbyteries and agencies can have the figures for their fall meetings and better plan their budgets for the coming year. Periodically we seek bids from other carriers in an effort to keep premiums competitive. When this is done, we may not have the new premium information by September 1.

Open enrollment period is the month of December. It is during this time that an employee can enroll or change their health insurance coverage unless there are special circumstances.

3. Participation.

As of February 1, 2015, 149 employees and 96 dependents for a total of 245 people depend on the Cumberland Presbyterian Church Health Insurance Program. A breakdown of family units by size at February 1, 2015 is listed below.

FAMILY UNITS BY SIZE

	Number of Units	Total
Emp. Only	97	97
Spouse Only	0	0
E & 1	4	8
E & 2	4	12
E & 3	0	0
E & S	24	48
Families of 3	4	12
Families of 4	13	52
Families of 5	2	10
Families of 6	1	6
Families of 7	0	0
Total	149	245

The following table shows the enrollment figures from January 2014 to December 2014. As one can see the numbers fluctuate from month to month.

MONTHLY GROUP INSURANCE ENROLLMENT

	EMPLOYEE COVERAGE	DEPENDENT COVERAGE	TOTAL
14-Jan	93	70	163
14-Feb	94	71	165
14-Mar	94	69	163
14-Apr	94	69	163
14-May	94	67	161
14-Jun	95	65	160
14-Jul	96	63	159
14-Aug	96	63	159
14-Sep	96	62	158
14-Oct	97	62	159
14-Nov	96	62	158
14-Dec	95	63	158

4. Premium Stabilization Reserve (Formerly Emergency Reserve)

The reserve is invested in the Endowment Program Total Return Fund account which had a balance of $2,060,032 on December 31, 2014. The Emergency Health Insurance Reserve was established in compliance with the 1992 General Assembly directive to be used in "emergency" situations to match presbyterial emergency fund disbursements. The 1998 General Assembly approved the Board's recommendation to allow the Board to use the Emergency Reserve to maintain the stability of the group health and life insurance plan. This allows these funds to be used for purposes outside of the original scope of the reserve. For 2014 the Board of Stewardship reduced the premiums charged by Blue Cross by $50 for Employee coverage and $80 for Dependent coverage. In 2014, the Board of Stewardship used $92,800 to help offset some of the cost of the health insurance premiums.

5. Dental and Vision Insurance

On December 1, 2008, we began offering Dental and Vision insurance, on a voluntary basis, for anyone working at least 30 hours or more for any Cumberland Presbyterian Church, its agencies, boards, and institutions. Peter Whitely is the agent of record. At present there are 73 participating employees.

6. Jessie W. Hipsher Health Insurance Endowment

The Jesse W. Hipsher Health Insurance Endowment was created as the first step in the board's goal to raise $10,000,000 in endowments for the support of the Cumberland Presbyterian Health and Life Insurance Program. The endowment was established on March 6, 2004. At its establishment $11,450 had been raised. The balance of the endowment as of December 31, 2014 was $41,138.34.

7. Health Education / E-Mail Newsletter

To further educate participants in matters concerning healthcare, participants receive a monthly e-newsletter entitled, TopHealth, published by Oakstone Publishing. The monthly e-newsletter is full of health related tips that can be easily implemented by readers. The two page newsletter can be read within a matter of minutes. Also initiated in 2008 is the E-Mail newsletter that is designed as an information tool to help the participants of the Health and Retirement programs stay on top of happenings within the Board of Stewardship.

8. Wellness Program

With their Well+Wise program, Blue Cross offers health coaching to help make positive lifestyle changes to improve health and wellness, provide support and answer any questions about medical conditions or surgical procedures and treatment decisions. A preventive health guide is also available and has been sent to all participants in the CP health program.

XII. RECOMMENDATION FROM THE 184TH GENERAL ASSEMBLY MEETING IN CHATTANOOGA, TENNESSEE

The 184the General Assembly meeting in Chattanooga, Tennessee passed the following recommendation:
"That the General Assembly ask the Board of Stewardship, Foundation, and Benefits to investigate what is being covered by the health insurance benefits offered and to clarify anything that might conflict with our Confession of Faith and previous General Assembly rulings regarding sanctity of life; if conflicts are found that they be referred to the Unified Committee on Theology and Social Concerns and that it be reported to the 185th General Assembly."

RECOMMENDATION 1: To properly answer the 184th General Assembly's inquiry pertaining to what is currently covered by the health insurance benefits and to clarify anything that might be in conflict with the Confession of Faith and previous General Assembly statements regarding the sanctity of life, the Board of Stewardship requests to refer the matter to Theology and Social Concerns.

Respectfully submitted,
Sylvia Hall, Board Member
Robert Heflin, Executive Secretary

Board of Stewardship Endowments

Endowment	Balance as of 12/31/2013	Balance as of 12/31/2014
Grace J. Beasley Memorial	$31,147.67	$31,439.61
Donald Bierhaus Trust	$73,319.29	$74,006.52
C. C. Brock Endowment Fund	$5,083.14	$5,130.80
Lavenia Campbell Cole Annunity Endowment	$69,185.53	$69,834.05
Lavenia Cole Testamentary Trust 25%	$564,997.51	$594,416.87
Lavenia Campbell Cole Trust 20%	$51,383.14	$51,869.50
Lavenia Campbell Cole Finance Endowment	$10,382.49	$10,479.77
Foundation & Finance Trust	$9,503.63	$9,608.94
Freeman Trust	$112,645.59	$113,701.44
Floyd Hensley Trust	$29,125.66	$29,398.67
P. F. Johnson Memorial Endowment	$9,846.25	$9,938.53
Robert H. Jordan Endowment Fund	$6,976.09	$7,041.47
Della Campbell Lowrie 20%	$467,662.13	$472,045.62
J. Richard Magrill, Jr. Endowment	$46,765.85	$47,415.70
Sam B. Miles Endowment	$86,542.45	$87,371.95
M. Dale Orr Endowment	$40,282.77	$40,660.34
William Dana Shriver Fund	$221,658.21	$223,735.85
Frontier Press 25%	$32,234.46	$32,536.59
Evelyn & Gene Walpole Endowment	$24,740.21	$26,151.35
Eugene Warren Endowment Fund	$26,032.83	$26,276.85
Dixie Campbell Zinn Memorial	$15,794.16	$15,947.42
Total	$1,935,309.06	$1,979,007.84

Ministerial Aid

Endowment	Balance as of 12/31/2013	Balance as of 12/31/2014
Ministerial Aid Endowment	$761,520.91	$804,956.90
Ministerial Aid Surplus Endowment	$29,573.59	$30,901.35
CPWM Endowment for Minister Care	$6,205.37	$6,559.26
Jesse W. Hipsher Endowment	$38,918.44	$41,138.34
Annie Lee Hogue Endowment	$37,437.20	$39,572.56
Herschel E. Jones Ministers' Trust	$10,976.15	$11,602.17
Kate H., Robert E. & Robert M. King	$148,151.75	$156,602.13
Della Campbell Lowrie Endowment 20%	$1,617,932.87	$1,710,217.26
Special Reserve Retirement Program	$1,223,535.52	$110,662.05
Sue Stiles Endowment Fund 50%	$91,037.41	$96,230.03
Premium Stabilization	$985,726.16	$2,076,130.16
Total	$4,951,015.37	$5,084,572.21

Missions Ministry Team

Endowment	Balance as of 12/31/2013	Balance as of 12/31/2014
Missions Ministry Team Budget Reserve Endowment	$0.00	$1,030,382.15
Church Loan Fund - General	$1,401,064.89	$1,414,199.88
McKenzie Endowment	$43,242.66	$43,648.07
Advance in Missions Trust Fund	$452,229.36	$456,469.03
Missions & Evangelism Endowment	$117,709.42	$118,817.77
Grace Johnson Beasley Memorial	$38,481.96	$38,842.73
Grace Beasley - Small Rural Church	$51,996.19	$52,483.66
Bennett & Mildred Brown Trust	$54,055.80	$55,848.80
David Brown Endowment	$11,033.16	$11,662.52
CPW Leadership Trust Fund	$93,818.10	$95,096.37
CPWM Bethel College Scholarship	$167,314.60	$174,665.46

Lavenia Campbell Cole Annuity Endowment	$63,945.97	$64,545.44
Lavenia Cole Testamentary Trust (25%)	$595,423.04	$625,144.14
Lavenia Campbell Cole Trust Endowment 20%	$22,693.07	$22,905.81
Rouine Vodra Coleman Endowment	$1,347.67	$1,424.53
Winnifred M. Dixon Endowment	$59,910.38	$60,472.03
Joseph B. Dungy Endowment	$93,604.15	$94,481.68
Louise & Sam R. Estes Endowment	$14,402.12	$14,548.27
Clifford Gittings Endowment	$5,890.28	$6,226.28
Lelia B. Goodman for Missions	$3,027.16	$3,199.83
P. F. Johnson Memorial End.	$19,704.72	$19,889.41
Finis Ewing & Bessie Keene Memorial	$153,704.19	$155,145.19
Chow King Leong Endowment	$52,868.63	$53,364.29
Mary Katherine Mize Longwell Endowment	$681.31	$720.16
Della Campbell Lowrie Trust 20%	$467,956.14	$472,343.23
Jamie Roy Chaffin Endowment	$2,086.69	$2,205.76
Mark G. Lynch Choctaw Presbytery	$10,159.98	$10,739.48
Clifford W. & Sarah C. McCall NCD	$6,850.14	$7,240.85
Joe E. Matlock Endowment	$53,190.63	$53,690.87
Robert E. Matlock Endowment	$168,762.84	$170,345.01
Robert T. & Dona Milam Endowment	$6,509.21	$6,880.51
Nancy J. Orr Bequest	$4,475.69	$4,730.93
New Church Development Endowment	$100,245.82	$101,185.63
S. Q. Proctor Home Mission Endowment	$11,923.32	$12,035.12
Marguerite D. Richards Rural Church	$25,389.25	$25,627.30
Maymie Stovall - Home Missions 25%	$12,516.74	$12,634.05
Paul & Geneva Richards Memorial	$12,651.71	$12,770.34
William A. & Beverly St. John Endowment	$13,088.52	$13,594.80
Madge Sprague Memorial Endowment	$5,773.80	$6,103.14
Lela Swanson Stricklen NCD	$66,964.75	$67,592.58
Cornelia Swain Endowment	$62,932.80	$63,842.66
Marguerite D. Richards MM Magazine	$8,463.04	$8,945.81
Walkerville CPC Memorial Endowment	$6,921.40	$7,316.17
Brown & Julia Welch Missions Endowment	$32,853.38	$33,161.36
Gina Marie Benzel Ableson Memorial	$10,384.45	$10,976.77
Ashburn-Graf Educational Endowment	$147,159.95	$155,790.92
Maree Blackwell Endowment	$2,533.20	$2,677.71
James A. Brintle II Scholarship	$6,217.62	$6,572.24
Mattie Ree Suddarth Brown Endowment - Missions	$21,546.08	$21,748.21
Gladys H. Bryson Scholarship Fund	$117,398.59	$124,284.09
Davis O. & Gladys H. Bryson Missionary	$88,021.92	$88,847.09
Mary Frances & William Carpenter	$12,365.10	$12,476.34
Mildred Chandler Scholarship Endowment	$145,286.43	$148,755.37
Colombian CPW Elementary Scholarships	$39,546.94	$41,802.63
Colombian University Scholarships	$71,980.95	$76,086.62
Helen Deal Endowment	$53,569.77	$54,072.03
John A. Deaver Mission	$10,475.51	$11,072.96
Chester E. Dickson Endowment	$46,600.77	$47,037.68
Jose & Fanny Fajardo Endowment	$9,076.94	$9,551.22
Foreign Missions Endowment	$354,714.88	$358,040.30
Mrs. G. W. Freeman Bible Woman Trust	$6,590.59	$6,966.51
McAdow and Mae Gam Endowment	$16,268.92	$16,420.97
Samuel King Gam	$22,041.27	$29,795.94
Freda Mitchell Gilbert Endowment (MMT)	$7,211.04	$8,435.36
Bernice Barnett Gonzalez Endowment	$1,438.56	$1,520.64
Gleniel Grounds Endowment	$2,210.77	$2,336.83
Holzer Trust	$86,779.62	$91,869.19
Hong Kong Mission	$41,945.56	$42,338.82
Marvin C. & Ruth M. Kinnard Trust	$16,783.19	$17,740.50
Warren and Carline Lowe Trust	$2,797.87	$2,957.44
Mamie McAdoo Endowment	$2,748.93	$2,905.75

McClung/Fowler Memorial Endowment	$91,366.55	$97,597.64
Holly Katelyn McClurkin	$692.12	$731.61
Rubye Johnson May Memorial 50%	$7,833.80	$8,280.63
Lucie C. Mayhew Fund for U-P Children	$17,193.74	$17,463.30
Elizabeth A. & James W. Morrow Trust	$25,184.71	$25,420.80
Richard Nicks Memorial Endowment	$57,687.83	$60,620.42
Hamilton & Merion S. Parks Family Trust #2	$11,255.88	$21,923.39
Patron Membership	$836,609.78	$848,212.53
Myra Patton Foreign Mission Endowment	$169,820.10	$171,412.17
Perpetual Membership Fund	$1,038,706.36	$1,052,365.00
Don & Gwen Peterson Endowment Fund	$108,046.32	$114,209.10
Rose Ella Porterfield Scholarship	$19,146.44	$20,238.50
Carl Ramsey Scholarship Fund	$37,315.23	$37,749.79
Marguerite D. Richards Japan	$16,953.61	$17,112.54
Elise Sanders Endowment	$313,288.13	$316,225.17
Scholarship-Universidad Evangelica	$11,167.75	$11,804.75
Buddy & Beverly Stott Endowment	$28,640.93	$28,910.15
Maymie Stovall - Foreign Mission 25%	$12,517.82	$12,635.20
Irvin & Annie Mary Draper Swain	$30,324.39	$30,827.95
Walter Swartz - Jose Fajardo Scholarship Fund	$45,596.29	$48,270.20
William B. & Emma Jo Denson Todd Endowment	$6,860.28	$7,251.61
Boyce & Beth Wallace Endowment	$52,104.87	$52,631.45
Robert J. & Marilee B. Watkins	$2,007.04	$2,121.51
Bill & Kathryn Wood	$66,022.23	$69,263.38
Forester World Missions Endowment	$3,693,017.36	$3,727,639.74
Bill & Iona Wyatt Endowment	$13,528.87	$13,655.70
Rev. & Mrs. Tadao Yoshizaki Memorial	$653.64	$690.95
Total	**$12,655,102.17**	**$13,915,514.41**

Communications Ministry Team

Endowment	Balance as of 12/31/2013	Balance as of 12/31/2014
Masaharu Asayama/CPWM Endowment	$10,446.99	$11,042.84
Ky Curry Publishing Endowment	$37,025.96	$39,137.84
C. Ray Dobbins Endowment	$34,736.98	$36,718.37
Dennis H. Kiefer Endowment	$940.08	$993.70
Marguerite D. Richards CP Magazine	$18,742.46	$19,811.52
Pat White Endowment	$7,395.97	$7,817.76
Total	**$109,288.44**	**$115,522.03**

Discipleship Ministry Team

Endowment	Balance as of 12/31/2013	Balance as of 12/31/2014
Paul Allen Endowment for C E	$11,663.23	$11,793.28
Grace Johnson Beasley Mem.	$11,281.33	$11,387.14
Bennett & Mildred Brown for C E	$26,245.47	$26,491.54
Christian Education Mid-Century	$257,628.17	$260,043.65
Christian Education Season Endowment	$186,452.78	$188,199.14
Carl Cook Outdoor Ministry Endowment	$5,001.70	$5,066.39
Lavenia Campbell Cole Annuity End.	$37,088.92	$37,436.68
Jill Davis Carr - Leadership Development	$11,845.98	$11,957.05
Consultant Training Fund	$59,780.33	$60,340.91
C. P. Youth Conference	$166,447.78	$170,504.34
H. Harold Davis Endowment Fund	$170,722.54	$172,329.51
Jack W. Ferguson, Jr. C E Endowment	$11,283.95	$11,389.71
Ira & Rae Galloway for C E	$14,695.88	$14,833.72
Jean Garret Endowment for C E	$4,012.45	$4,241.28
Louise Adams Heathcock Memorial	$11,335.92	$11,442.25
John Gilbert Horsley - Youth Leaders	$13,709.25	$13,904.00
Donald & Jane Hubbard Endowment for C E	$11,855.84	$11,967.01

Endowment	Balance as of 12/31/2013	Balance as of 12/31/2014
Into the Nineties for C E	$284,930.32	$287,601.99
Reverend Gayle J. Keown for C E	$3,692.86	$3,727.48
Earl King Memorial	$11,286.52	$11,392.35
Virginia Malcom Christian Education	$117,797.10	$118,901.58
Wesley & Jackie Mattonen Endowment	$35,574.68	$35,908.21
David & Mary McGregor C E Endowment	$57,196.61	$57,836.35
James D. McGuire Endowment for C E	$16,761.36	$16,918.85
Howell G. & Martha Jo Mims CPYC	$27,858.88	$29,690.96
Morris & Ruth Pepper for C E	$53,649.79	$54,153.16
Bill & Hazel Phalan Endowment	$14,882.36	$15,210.28
Claudette Hamby Pickle C E Endowment	$21,306.85	$21,506.62
Publishing House Endowment 33%	$148,045.81	$149,438.01
Dr. & Mrs. E. K. Reagin Endowment	$58,723.96	$59,274.55
Jodi Hearn Rush	$11,629.12	$11,740.27
Rev. Rusty Rustenhaven Youth Ministry	$14,076.76	$14,208.72
Jeff & Angie Sledge Endowment	$2,396.34	$2,533.05
John W. Speer Endowment for C E	$20,527.16	$20,719.62
Cornelia Swain Endowment for C E	$19,612.04	$20,116.03
Irvin & Annie Mary Swain Endowment	$23,786.88	$24,332.90
Jake Tyler Children's Ministry	$2,304.15	$2,435.56
Frank & Linda Ward Endowment (CE)	$36,641.04	$37,544.79
William Warren Endowment for C E	$12,079.43	$12,212.55
Clark Williamson Memorial	$42,655.60	$43,055.58
Helen Wiman Memorial	$4,418.39	$4,460.22
Young Adult Ministry Endowment	$24,308.17	$24,536.09
Terence R. McCain, Sr. Endowment	$5,968.50	$6,223.76
Total	**$2,083,162.20**	**$2,109,007.13**

Pastoral Development Team

Endowment	Balance as of 12/31/2013	Balance as of 12/31/2014
Awards for CP Ministers & Spouses	$25,701.70	$26,867.38
Roosevelt and Ruth Baugh	$4,549.92	$4,809.48
LaRoyce Brown Endowment	$1,451.22	$1,533.99
James & Helen Knight Endowment	$26,494.45	$27,696.04
Ministerial Endowment	$13,941.69	$14,574.46
Ministers Conference	$19,334.88	$20,211.82
Melvin & Naomi Orr Endowment	$21,709.29	$22,694.31
James Lee Ratliff Endowment	$6,752.48	$7,137.60
Norlan & Ellie Scrudder Endowment	$22,027.06	$23,026.06
James & Geneva Searcy Endowment	$33,552.58	$35,074.36
E. G. & Joy Sims Endowment	$23,369.60	$24,429.68
Leonard & Mary Jo Turner Endowment	$14,252.24	$14,898.64
Lyon Walkup Endowment	$14,560.19	$15,220.57
Arturo & Carmen Ortiz Endowment	$13,392.24	$14,156.10
Louisa M. Woosley Endowment for Sustaining Women in Ministry	$0.00	$9,932.72
Total	**$241,089.54**	**$262,263.21**

Office of The General Assembly

Endowment	Balance as of 12/31/2013	Balance as of 12/31/2014
D. W. Fooks Memorial Endowment	$19,238.06	$19,418.38
Publishing House Endowment (33%)	$49,339.14	$44,002.50
Robert & Olene Rush Endowment	$19,617.32	$19.76
Trustee Endowment	$378,370.25	$381,916.32
Total	**$466,564.77**	**$445,356.96**

Historical Foundation

Endowment	Balance as of 12/31/2013	Balance as of 12/31/2014

Anne Elizabeth Knight Adams Heritage Fund	$3,617.24	$3,923.79
Rosie Magrill Alexander Trust	$17,689.19	$17,860.92
Paul H. & Ann Middleton Allen Heritage Fund	$7,476.11	$7,546.24
Grace J. Beasley Birthplace Shrine	$59,428.30	$59,985.95
Birthplace Shrine Fund	$140,494.64	$156,260.08
James L. & Louise M. Bridges Heritage Fund	$18,883.98	$19,061.18
Mark and Elinor Swindle Brown Heritage Fund	$4,066.13	$4,604.39
Sydney & Elinor Brown Heritage Fund	$7,909.68	$8,302.24
Centennial Heritage Endowment	$90,221.60	$91,068.16
Walter Chesnut Endowment	$16,122.03	$16,827.18
Lavenia Campbell Cole Heritage Fund	$70,926.81	$71,592.30
C. P. Church in America Heritage Fund	$14,876.16	$15,015.77
CPW Archival Supplies Endowment	$31,560.55	$31,856.74
Bettye Jean Loggins McCaffrey Ellis Heritage Fund	$1,174.33	$1,241.36
Samuel Russell & Mary Grace Barefoot Estes	$24,526.29	$24,756.43
Family of Faith Endowment	$15,324.95	$15,468.73
Gettis & Delia Snyder Gilbert Heritage Fund	$7,012.08	$7,077.86
James C. & Freda M. Gilbert Heritage Fund	$23,705.18	$24,218.04
James C. & Freda M. Gilbert Trust (HF)	$65,513.54	$66,128.28
Mamie A. Gilbert Trust	$15,149.04	$15,291.23
Henry Evan Harper Endowment CP History	$1,954.21	$2,021.94
Ronald W. & Virginia T. Harper	$3,897.39	$4,119.68
Historical Foundation Trust	$97,609.29	$99,360.01
Donald & Jane Hubbard Heritage Fund	$12,186.94	$13,382.20
Cliff & Jill Hudson Heritage Fund	$6,161.51	$6,219.33
Robert & Kathy Hull Endowment	$16,878.85	$17,163.86
Into the Nineties Endowment	$40,686.36	$41,068.19
Joe Ben Irby Endowment	$5,640.32	$6,045.97
P. F. Johnson Memorial Endowment	$19,760.71	$19,946.13
Irene A. Kiefer Endowment	$1,543.50	$1,631.57
Mr. & Mrs. Chow King Leong Heritage Fund	$5,854.12	$5,909.03
Dennis L. & Elmira Castleberry Magrill 50%	$24,585.75	$24,816.43
J. Richard Magrill, Jr. Heritage Fund	$5,852.57	$6,186.42
Joe R. & Mary B. Magrill Trust	$175,856.71	$177,506.82
Jimmie Joe McKinley Heritage Fund	$8,671.70	$8,853.34
Edith Louise Mitchell Heritage Fund	$4,043.34	$4,273.99
Lloyd Freeman Mitchell Heritage Fund	$4,043.36	$4,274.00
Snowdy C. & Lillian Walkup Mitchell Heritage Fund	$7,012.16	$7,077.91
Rev. Charles & Paulette Morrow Endowment	$1,199.92	$1,268.35
Virginia Sue Williamson Morrow Heritage Fund	$13,386.79	$13,512.44
Anne E. Swain Odom Heritage Fund	$20,937.93	$22,501.39
Martha Sue Parr Heritage Fund	$35,030.34	$35,359.04
Florence Pennewill Heritage Fund	$4,872.43	$4,919.43
Morris & Ruth Pepper Endowment (HF)	$16,873.28	$17,138.41
Publishing House Endowment 33%	$81,732.96	$82,890.36
Mable Magrill Rundell Trust	$17,689.11	$17,855.08
Samuel Callaway Rundell Heritage Fund	$11,947.55	$12,059.66
Paul & Mary Jo Schnorbus Heritage Fund	$8,567.21	$8,647.62
Shiloh CPC Ellis County Texas Endowment	$7,820.59	$7,894.00
Hinkley & Vista Smartt Heritage Fund	$7,391.99	$7,678.07
John W. Sparks Heritage Fund	$101,613.15	$102,671.65
Irvin S. Annie Mary Draper Swain Heritage Fund	$27,707.44	$28,286.19
F. P. (Jake) Waits Heritage Fund	$12,407.97	$12,626.31
Roy & Mary Seawright Shelton Heritage Fund	$3,242.44	$3,527.65
Gwendolyn McCaffrey McReynolds Hertiage Fund	$10,417.84	$11,004.50
Total	$1,460,755.56	$1,497,783.84

Our United Outreach

Endowment	Balance as of 12/31/2013	Balance as of 12/31/2014

George F. Battenfield Memorial	$53,396.47	$53,920.21
Daisy Bray Freeman Trust	$58,065.14	$58,612.99
Bertha Feazel Hammons Memorial	$49,360.95	$49,823.67
Kenneth & Myrtle Holsopple Memorial	$243,885.98	$246,172.50
Cliff & Jill Hudson OUO Endowment Fund	$8,207.63	$9,995.86
Knights of Honor Association Trust	$3,440.81	$3,473.02
Lowrie Estate Oil Royalties	$1,601,475.13	$1,700,514.94
Robert L. McReynolds Endowment 50%	$43,314.19	$43,720.27
The Moderators' Endowment for Our United Outreach	$1,249.69	$6,070.41
Santa Anna Church Memorial Fund	$21,495.91	$21,697.42
Tithing and Budget Endowment	$384,595.19	$388,200.88

Children's Home

Endowment	Balance as of 12/31/2013	Balance as of 12/31/2014
Merlyn & Joann Kitterman Alexander	$1,453.23	$1,467.08
W. A. & Elizabeth Bearden Trust	$16,547.46	$16,703.79
Grace Johnson Beasley Mem	$38,528.05	$38,891.90
Bethlehem CPC, Maury County, TN	$6,297.55	$6,356.65
James L. & Louise Bridges Scholarship	$43,041.72	$43,445.36
J. T. & Dorothy Britt Trust	$11,651.68	$11,760.95
Children's Home Endowment	$336,117.45	$339,277.42
Lavenia Campbell Cole Annuity Endow	$86,076.90	$86,884.19
Lavenia Cole Testamentary Trust - 25%	$596,733.77	$626,468.87
Lavenia Campbell Cole Trust (20%)	$21,194.83	$21,393.59
Mrs. A. L. Colvin Memorial Fund	$999.04	$1,056.00
John H. & Eva Cox Trust Fund	$32,260.66	$32,563.21
Steve Currie Trust	$566,294.17	$571,605.20
Daniel Class, Morningside CPC	$33,316.73	$33,629.20
Donnie Curry Davis Memorial	$194,960.52	$196,788.98
Mary Elberta Davis Memorial	$20,803.07	$20,998.18
Fred & Mattie Mae Dwiggins Memorial	$83,529.74	$84,313.16
J. S. Eustis Memorial Trust Fund	$13,187.42	$13,311.07
Winnie & Clester H. Evans, Sr. Trust	$22,016.95	$22,223.39
John M. Friedel Trust	$22,774.25	$22,987.88
Joyce C. Frisby Memorial Endowment	$29,162.43	$29,527.58
Vaughn & Mary Elizabeth Fults Trust	$21,007.68	$21,204.67
Garner-Miller Memorial Trust	$12,960.43	$13,082.00
James C. & Freda M. Gilbert Endowment (CPCH)	$114,360.58	$115,704.01
Henry & Jayne Glaspy Memorial Fund	$8,597.52	$8,678.15
Rev. W. J. Gregory Memorial	$108,060.99	$109,074.46
Glenn Griffin Endowment 33%	$46,067.92	$46,499.94
Rev. & Mrs. Henry M. Guynn Memorial	$4,786.73	$4,831.65
Chad Evan Harper Memorial Endowment	$11,004.32	$11,631.98
Newsome & Imogene Harvey Endowment	$2,642.42	$2,667.18
Clarence & Lula Herring Endowment	$6,289.83	$6,348.83
Kenneth & Clara M. Holsopple Trust	$55,682.03	$56,204.23
George & Lottie M. Hutchins Trust	$1,184,216.43	$1,195,322.69
Norma K. Johnson Memorial Library	$11,884.36	$11,995.84
P. F. Johnson Memorial Endow	$19,728.40	$19,913.46
Robert H. & Genevie Johnson Endowment	$5,005.24	$5,052.17
Mr. & Mrs. Robert L. Johnson	$12,430.91	$12,547.49
Violet Louise Jolly Endowment	$1,255.14	$1,266.89
Eulava Joyce Memorial Trust	$10,372.86	$10,470.12
Ruth Cypert & Harlie Kugler Memorial	$20,888.50	$21,084.39
Blanche R. Lake Endowment	$15,053.88	$15,195.08
Wade P. Lane & Maude Dorough Memorial	$9,908.38	$10,001.31
Adolphus M. Latta Memorial Trust	$53,463.08	$53,964.51
Mr. & Mrs. Robert F. Little (CPCH)	$35,489.83	$36,554.36
Charles E. Addie Mae Lloyd Endowment	$23,549.03	$23,769.87

Tony & Ann Martin Endowment	$2,376.63	$2,512.17
Mrs. Lucille (Lucy) Mast Endowment	$2,415.89	$2,553.71
W. B. & Azalee McClurkan, Sr. Memorial	$20,133.50	$20,322.33
William J. McCall Memorial Trust	$10,372.82	$10,470.08
McEwen Church Trust	$7,968.87	$8,043.61
J. C. McKinley Endowment (CPCH)	$19,642.04	$19,826.27
Velma McKinley Trust Fund	$19,642.22	$19,826.40
McKinley & Barnett Families 33%	$830,194.65	$854,973.00
Mary McKnight Memorial Trust	$10,486.14	$11,134.44
Kenneth & Mae Moore Endowment Fund	$7,335.07	$7,403.87
Operational Trust Fund	$154,337.42	$155,784.92
Bert & Pat Owen Endowment for CPCH	$1,631.70	$1,646.98
Martha Sue Parr Endowment	$1,664.78	$1,680.51
Mary M. Poole Endwoment Fund	$997,789.82	$1,007,155.69
Jack & Mary Lou Proctor Memorial Trust	$66,528.88	$67,152.80
Mary Acenal Prewitt Trust Fund	$94,051.38	$94,933.48
S. Q. & K. Maurine Proctor Trust	$5,892.61	$5,947.86
Rev. & Mrs. Joe Reed Memorial	$2,715.62	$2,870.54
Marguerite D. Richards Endowment	$26,496.73	$26,745.36
Agnew Durbin Richardson Trust	$31,430.48	$31,725.24
Pat N. & Essie H. Roberts Memorial	$61,346.21	$61,922.08
Frances Benefield Roberts Trust	$2,429.95	$2,452.77
Rev. & Mrs. John A. Russell Memorial	$4,744.76	$4,789.00
John, Ann & Mary Elizabeth Shimer	$15,616.91	$15,763.51
Rev. W. B. & Lydia Snipes Memorial	$18,814.91	$19,888.09
Don M. Nancy E. Tabor Trust	$35,835.94	$36,172.35
Townsend Trust Fund	$40,038.07	$40,414.31
Hattie E. Wheelis Fund	$20,596.61	$20,790.00
Whitfield Family Endowment	$12,496.98	$12,643.06
Porter & Hattie S. Williamson Memorial	$178,651.83	$180,327.36
Helen and Lewis Wynn Endowment Fund	$10,431.04	$11,025.94
Maxie & Will Young Memorial Endowment	$21,624.69	$21,827.64
Dixie Campbell Zinn Memorial Trust	$6,501.02	$6,561.99
Joe Parr Trust Fund	$81,558.15	$82,322.97
Hamilton & Merion S. Parks Family Trust #3	$11,169.81	$11,697.04
Total	**$6,806,618.24**	**$6,916,026.30**

Memphis Theological Seminary

Endowment	Balance as of 12/31/2013	Balance as of 12/31/2014
African-American Studies Chair	$7,900.53	$8,351.16
Emerson A. Alburty Endowment	$6,248.03	$6,290.20
John W. Aldridge Memorial Scholarship	$8,431.82	$8,497.79
Merlyn A. & Joann K. Alexander	$9,059.31	$9,143.68
Alston Family Evangelistic Association	$48,990.49	$51,898.95
Polly Atterbury Aldridge Scholarship	$10,699.53	$10,788.02
Alternate Studies Endowment	$9,993.09	$10,079.86
Virgil R. Anderson Memorial Endowment	$9,684.92	$10,773.69
Baird-Buck Chair of CP Studies	$316,308.62	$325,516.85
Walter & Eula Baker Memorial Fund	$12,204.69	$12,268.16
O. A. Barbee Endowment	$1,793.71	$1,818.98
Richard M. & Martha Carol Barker Scholarship	$12,194.35	$12,377.09
Barnes Seminary Endowment	$63,846.86	$64,241.69
Isaac R. Barnes Scholarship Endowment	$16,775.76	$16,941.00
George B. Bates Trust	$3,643.65	$3,677.82
Grace Johnson Beasley Endowment	$85,363.88	$90,232.85
Joseph E. Bedinger Memorial Library	$5,055.44	$5,102.86
Tarlton M. Belles Fund	$24,162.37	$24,351.40
Marie Blackwell Endowment	$531.80	$546.00
Larry A. Blakeburn Endowment	$2,760.31	$2,786.24

Roy E. Blakeburn Scholarship	$5,863.70	$5,914.69
Bowen Chapel Church Trust	$30,068.99	$30,297.62
Bowen Lecture Fund	$21,087.60	$22,290.40
Kyle D. Brantley, M. D. Memorial	$18,351.35	$20,795.48
Wes & Susan Brantley Endowment	$0.00	$11,766.28
Brockwell Library Endowment	$11,303.45	$11,615.93
Evelyn Brodeur	$23,184.03	$23,824.68
Brooksville CPC Endowment	$21,892.69	$22,632.42
Beth-Helen-Peggy Brown Endowment	$29,190.02	$29,397.37
Paul B. Brown Endowment - MTS	$15,559.94	$17,104.30
Paul F. & Mattie Suddarth Brown - MTS	$37,764.38	$36.10
W. W. Brown Scholarship	$4,604.84	$4,654.46
Finis McAdoo Bruington Board-Designated Endowment	$43,312.97	$43,573.35
Davis & Gladys Bryson Education 50%	$25,709.68	$25,929.15
Henry & Alfreda Bunton Scholarship	$24,645.35	$25,395.98
Hal & Gladys Burks Memorial Fund	$7,685.63	$7,741.99
Thomas H. Campbell Library Endowment	$4,773.51	$4,824.70
Thomas H. & Margaret E. Campbell	$28,697.37	$31,539.52
Campbell-Todd Trust	$10,067.02	$10,698.25
Carlock Memorial Trust	$1,256.96	$1,267.93
Cawthon Memorial Fund	$4,173.74	$4,210.02
Mildred Chandler Endowment	$3,939.43	$3,985.59
Rev. Walter & Mrs. Sarah Chesnut Scholarship Endowment	$6,172.61	$8,780.54
Gladys Chumbler Endowment	$7,284.88	$7,347.32
Marian Lisenbee Clark Endowment	$5,381.26	$5,425.35
Sallie H. Clay & Alice J. Cooksey	$268,910.78	$270,694.54
Faye E. & Ford F. Claytor Endowment	$7,818.55	$7,889.21
Lavenia Campbell Cole Annuity Endow.	$55,693.22	$56,149.45
Lavenia Campbell Cole Testamentary Trust 25%	$451,808.32	$478,224.85
Lavenia Campbell Cole Trust	$20,116.63	$20,293.42
George E. & Rouine V. Coleman Endowment	$9,098.75	$9,167.24
George E. Coleman Scholarship	$59,017.26	$59,508.19
Willene Cooper Scholarship	$29,711.98	$31,246.31
Hubert & Dortha Covington Memorial	$3,872.66	$3,896.49
James Covington Scholarship	$8,270.99	$8,742.71
Thelma Craig Scholarship	$30,700.07	$30,932.44
Cora Hawkins Crutchfield Scholarship Endowment	$25,456.18	$27,105.03
Cumberland Hall Endowment	$5,225.61	$5,318.42
Cumberland Presbyterian Women	$29,350.76	$31,196.01
Sallie Stacy Davenport	$6,296.40	$6,712.53
Mary Elberta Davis Memorial	$5,940.31	$6,001.66
Paul & Nancy Dekar/Immersion Studies	$6,171.28	$6,629.35
James W. & Gladys Murray Diamond	$3,252.00	$3,280.26
Margaret M. Dirks*	$7,684.66	$8,180.02
Houston Dixon Memorial	$7,357.47	$7,410.96
Winifred M. Dixon Endowment	$28,701.29	$28,979.06
C. Ray Dobbins Endowment	$2,069.52	$2,087.47
Jesse R. & Virginia R. Durham Endowment	$905,612.02	$912,152.17
Rev. Dr. Loyce Estes Endowment Fund	$7,169.70	$7,669.14
Expansion & Development Fund	$3,240.58	$3,268.39
Faith CPC, Tulsa, OK - Scholarship	$47,184.07	$47,625.83
Alice Fay Finley	$5,560.02	$5,602.34
H. Glenn Finley Library Fund	$2,937.21	$2,964.73
E. H. & Millie Finley	$2,396.36	$2,418.82
Linda Hester Fooks Memorial	$16,364.15	$16,579.75
Jere B. Ford Family Endowment	$11,533.28	$11,600.72
Rev. J. C. & Willie Mae Forester Library	$4,844.66	$5,320.23
Vaughn Fults Endowment	$10,911.69	$10,996.32
Gadsden Area Churches Trust	$41,643.34	$43,619.95
McAdow Gam Endowment Fund	$28,293.29	$29,697.23

John E. & Anna B. Gardner Endowment	$16,557.52	$16,700.59
Jessie B. & Noella Garner	$1,336.96	$1,348.62
W. L. & Dot Lacey Gaston Endowment	$6,640.07	$7,230.80
Louis E. & Millie Coats Gholson	$157,976.86	$159,132.83
James C. & Freda M. Gilbert Endowment (MTS)	$13,414.35	$14,179.49
James & Martha Gill Sacred Theology	$12,417.67	$12,482.06
David E. Glasgow Endowment	$1,516.01	$1,529.20
James A. & Lenora Greer Endowment	$3,066.74	$3,241.70
Mary Guice Memorial	$14,589.95	$15,149.51
Margaret I. Gunn Memorial	$23,381.08	$24,714.66
Hamilton Chapel Fund	$565,836.47	$461,480.04
Mrs. George N. Harris Library Memorial	$3,540.03	$3,573.20
Newsome & Imogene Daniel Harvey	$6,803.90	$6,853.01
Bettye & Dick Hendrix Scholarship	$16,085.59	$17,003.12
Henshaw Family Endowment Fund	$5,814.05	$5,864.63
Frank & Margaret Henshaw Endowment 1	$12,462.10	$13,628.97
J. David & Barbara Hester Endowment	$33,800.54	$45,051.80
Rev. E. Samuel Hicks Endowment Fund	$4,668.01	$4,705.86
Dr. Alfred D. Hill Scholarship	$7,738.65	$8,392.11
Cortis E. Hill Library	$3,813.15	$3,848.92
David & Patsy Hilliard	$10,263.64	$10,472.63
Francis A. Hobgood Trust	$27,492.45	$27,659.55
William Clarence Hodge Memorial	$3,413.86	$3,445.88
B. L. & Jewel Looper Holder	$11,821.35	$12,552.65
Lee Hollowell Trust	$14,450.23	$14,587.89
Barbara A. Holmes Lectures	$13,536.13	$9,028.27
Mr. & Mrs. J. S. Holmes Trust	$5,200.12	$5,248.87
Kenneth & Myrtle Holsopple Endowment	$27,312.13	$27,595.44
Jack & Gwen Hood Scholarship	$40,775.55	$46,527.48
Rev. John William Howell Memorial	$2,374.33	$2,404.63
Cardelia Howell-Diamond Scholarship	$77,409.89	$77,753.20
Donald & Jane Hubbard Endowment for MTS	$8,355.93	$9,332.66
Bernice A. Humphreys Endowment	$17,444.54	$17,567.38
Charles E. & Helen Humphreys Endowment	$11,231.75	$11,238.15
Gerald S. & Louise Felts Hunter	$2,890.52	$2,915.69
George & Lottie M. Hutchins 33%	$223,897.81	$225,255.32
Mattie Hutchison Seminary Fund	$1,722.88	$1,739.03
Eugenia Turner Ingram Endowment	$3,242.32	$3,280.18
Lillian Johnston Ingram Library	$5,898.31	$5,959.29
Tom & Barbara Ingram Student Asst.	$38,592.98	$42,383.48
Virginia Howell Ingram Endowment Fund	$78,769.79	$83,262.71
Rev. W. T. Ingram, Sr. & Family Scholarship	$96,475.94	$100,507.95
William T. & Virginia H. Ingram Lectures	$111,061.98	$117,853.11
Joe Ben Irby Trust	$4,263.98	$4,303.94
Joe Ben & Julia Irby Endowment Fund	$88,642.85	$89,218.02
Virginia Irwin Memorial Endowment	$5,009.38	$5,056.16
Johns Lectures	$14,607.36	$15,440.52
P. F. Johnson Memorial	$50,952.37	$51,365.22
Robert A. & Jo S. Johnson (MTS)<	$58,279.70	$61,717.96
Roby M. Johnston Endowment	$85,772.47	$86,449.96
Joiner Ministerial Scholarship	$6,233.85	$6,286.35
(. A. Jones Library Memorial	$4,194.06	$4,230.55
Kiningham-Kuehn Endowment	$10,983.58	$11,088.62
Franklin W. Latta Memorial Scholarship	$15,164.95	$15,306.11
Ruth Fumbanks Latta Endowment	$15,289.51	$15,411.85
Randal (Randy) Leslie Endowment Fund	$16,009.98	$16,127.69
C. S. Lewis & His Friends Lecture	$27,355.42	$29,451.34
Library Reserve - Seminary Development	$2,550.82	$2,582.68
Mr. & Mrs. Robert F. Little (MTS)	$28,612.17	$29,592.67
James & Louella Lively Family Endowment	$8,582.19	$8,668.23

Inez Lovelace Endowment	$33,036.16	$33,265.67
Virgil L. & Della M. Lowrie Lectures	$105,182.44	$105,197.31
Della Campbell Lowrie Endowment 20%	$423,401.16	$426,661.87
Dennis L. & Elmira C. Magrill 50%	$29,704.38	$30,001.03
Rev. George Malone / Rev. Edmong Weir	$73,969.02	$78,302.19
W. A. Johnson Family Endowment	$2,984.51	$3,036.86
Dessa Jane Manuel Scholarship 50%	$43,004.09	$43,414.81
Marshall (Texas) CPW Endowment	$9,903.62	$10,498.63
Dr. & Mrs. Arleigh G. Matlock Scholarship	$34,350.32	$34,675.34
Charles R. Matlock Library Endowment	$5,257.75	$5,303.49
Walter L. Mayo Endowment Fund	$5,931.36	$5,986.94
Mr. & Mrs. David M. McAnulty Memorial	$14,111.86	$14,193.26
Doris McCall Memorial Endowment	$12,787.93	$12,886.52
James W. & Mary H. McCulloch Memorial	$12,709.62	$13,434.52
Margaret McCulloch Scholarship	$9,228.83	$9,812.27
F. Dwight & Bernice K. McDonald	$185,962.18	$187,391.87
McGuinness-Wood Endowment	$21,171.37	$21,358.08
Jack B. McKamey Endowment Fund	$5,727.85	$5,741.09
Velma McKinley Memorial Endowment	$4,683.31	$4,727.20
McKinley & Barnett Families 33%	$262,113.04	$280,547.17
Wesley McKinney Memorial Endowment	$11,119.75	$11,811.01
Maude McLin Memorial Endowment	$4,414.99	$4,456.23
Robert W. McReynolds Memorial	$5,559.32	$5,607.27
Mr. & Mrs. W. J. McReynolds Trust	$6,125.68	$6,168.89
Memphis Methodist Conference Fund	$30,701.99	$30,915.95
Ed Mikel Doctoral Scholarship Memorial	$9,494.79	$10,036.36
Sam B. & Naurine W. Miles Endowment	$4,972.34	$5,015.59
Sam B. Miles Board Designated Endowment	$72,557.07	$76,695.61
Mary Elliott Miller Endowment	$8,171.87	$8,638.01
Rev. & Mrs. W. E. Miller Scholarship	$5,788.81	$5,848.76
Robert Lynn & Elizabeth P. Mills	$8,675.53	$8,873.98
Ministerial Scholarship Endowment 40%	$19,113.98	$19,176.14
Missouri-Arkansas CO-OP PCUSA*	$4,524.13	$4,628.39
John L. Mize Scholarship	$8,882.49	$8,959.29
Clinton & Eva B. Moore Endowment	$31,004.46	$31,177.94
Frank C. Moore Endowment Fund	$10,933.77	$10,997.63
Mary E. Morefield Memorial 40%	$5,323.96	$5,360.21
Hubert W. Morrow Endowment PAS	$32,000.52	$33,939.84
Virginia Sue Williamson Morrow MT	$29,342.73	$31,130.50
Ruby Page Morton Endowment	$9,956.12	$11,083.18
William Taylor Morton Endowment	$11,150.73	$11,916.53
John & Gail Moss Endowment	$4,675.49	$4,716.13
Dr. Arthur Murrell Memorial Scholarship	$4,622.01	$4,661.85
Walter & Anna Murrie Endowment	$6,454.15	$6,510.29
Willard & Bettie Murrie Endowment	$10,027.75	$10,161.26
Gladys Teter Nichols	$100,220.04	$100,957.29
North Central Texas Presbytery Scholarship	$5,312.50	$5,362.29
William H. & Nola A. Oliver Scholarship	$5,691.21	$5,750.36
Bert & Pat Owen - Shepherd's Rest	$95,108.19	$100,533.01
Palestine CPC Endowment at MTS	$3,846.08	$3,879.51
Paskell & Bernice Parker Endowment	$4,507.38	$4,549.71
Parr Scholarship Endowment	$55,120.52	$55,538.91
Rev. G. F. Phelps Memorial Scholarship	$17,691.78	$17,806.71
John W. Piper Endowment Fund	$24,521.80	$24,683.37
Platte-Lexington Seminary	$21,514.90	$21,655.22
Pleasant Hill CP Endowment	$6,685.55	$6,737.65
Bernice A. Humphreys Scholarship Endowment	$134,428.32	$142,095.88
Bettie Press Library Fund	$4,791.42	$4,816.90
S. Q. Proctor Ministerial Scholarship	$8,366.86	$8,463.90
Klahr & Iris Raney Endowment Fund	$19,162.70	$19,308.17

Eugene & Agnes Richardson Endowment	$7,710.55	$7,781.73
Evelyn B. Crick Richmond Endowment	$52,792.94	$53,145.46
Roy Roberts Memorial Endowment	$1,668.75	$1,684.39
Mrs. W. H. Rochelle Endowment Fund	$10,058.73	$10,141.23
Hudson & Robbie C. Roseberry	$74,024.15	$78,246.33
W. L. & Mary K. Rolman Scholarship	$20,098.97	$20,287.45
William & Dolores Rustenhaven Endowment	$5,501.47	$5,553.02
Beverly St. John/Theology & Arts	$8,487.20	$8,716.43
Saint Timothy CPC	$3,486.12	$3,516.46
Herschel A. & Iris L. Schultz	$131,889.08	$132,881.57
Clara Scott Family Chair - Part I	$349,259.33	$351,341.85
Clara Scott Family Chair - Part II	$216,967.41	$220,956.78
George W. Scott Endowment Fund	$6,373.49	$6,433.30
W. H. Scott Family Endowment	$11,022.02	$11,117.33
Marie C. Scrudder Memorial	$4,416.00	$4,457.39
Seminary Commitment Campaign	$3,174.83	$3,215.73
Seminary Development Fund Endowment	$818.23	$825.32
Seminary Scholarship Fund	$9,149.94	$9,202.25
Ed Shannon Endowment	$7,659.15	$8,153.06
E. Thach & Jerry Shauf Endowment	$16,141.09	$16,269.14
Robert E. Shelton Scholarship	$3,542.80	$3,845.75
Robert M. Shelton Scholarship	$3,479.59	$3,512.67
Ruby Burris Shelton Endowment	$5,147.48	$5,195.77
Dick & Virginia Singellton Endowment	$13,965.75	$14,045.72
Esther Smith & Search Parish Endowment	$2,170.94	$2,191.29
Odus H. Smith Memorial Endowment	$4,887.32	$4,933.13
Katherine Hinds Smythe Endowment	$5,797.74	$5,842.11
W. B. Snipes Memorial Scholarship	$15,778.68	$15,875.67
Truman Barrett Snowden Memorial	$4,874.79	$4,929.70
Dorothea Snyder Endowment	$5,009.90	$5,047.35
L. D. & Dathel Jones Stacey Endowment	$657.14	$662.86
Henry L. Starks Scholarship	$172,711.14	$178,134.54
Anne Stavely Endowmet Fund	$2,356.23	$2,378.32
Eva Jane Stewart Trust 50%	$48,688.52	$49,060.25
J.W. Stiles Lectures	$38,531.31	$40,828.32
Rev. Elizabeth Stone Mem. Schol.	$2,104.49	$2,122.79
Lela Stricklen Endowment	$45,179.18	$45,161.83
Maymie Stovall Memorial Trust 25%	$11,944.45	$12,050.54
Roy Stucker Scholarship Fund 50%	$38,238.35	$38,697.54
Charles Studdard Memorial	$18,429.25	$18,600.73
Emma Elizabeth Suddarth Memorial	$6,922.16	$6,987.07
Robert H. & Lois Went Taylor Endowment	$11,892.29	$12,013.03
Thomas V. Taylor Seminary Student	$6,169.00	$6,236.21
Verdys E. Taylor Trust	$2,337.85	$2,359.75
A. J. Terry Scholarship	$2,225.50	$2,246.37
Theological Seminary General Endowment	$81,081.82	$79,881.20
Virgil H. & Irene R. Todd - OT EXCL	$69,562.37	$73,997.59
Tri-Mu Bible Class Scholarship	$63,401.44	$66,163.32
R L Truax, M L Truax, R L Truax, Jr Award for Academic Ach	$7,639.73	$8,075.44
Carl Walker Endowment	$8,285.25	$8,372.11
Mr. & Mrs. Carl Forbis Ward Memorial	$5,511.62	$5,543.46
Tom V. Warnick Memorial	$33,835.87	$37,134.34
Geneverette Warr Endowment	$5,798.91	$5,842.86
Warren, MI, First CPC Endowment	$7,705.67	$7,766.44
Rev. David & Leota Watson Scholarship Endowment	$0.00	$4,056.94
The Rev. Harlon & Mary Edith Watson Endowment	$38,088.61	$38,796.58
Virgil T. & Sue B. Weeks	$7,638.85	$7,705.15
Lynn Westbrook Memorial Endowment	$9,130.61	$9,219.67
Mae Westbrook Memorial Endowment Fund	$4,357.39	$4,395.25
The Weston Endowment	$14,797.67	$14,896.93

	Balance as of 12/31/2013	Balance as of 12/31/2014
J. W. Wilder Scholarship	$197,539.48	$198,637.99
Alline Williams Endowment	$8,922.23	$9,005.90
Wayne Wiman Scholarship	$27,712.89	$28,105.81
Davis/Winston Scholarship for National Baptist Students	$1,212.24	$1,281.39
Lamar & Ellen Wilson Memorial Scholarship	$21,220.10	$20,921.62
Women's Issues in Ministry Endowment	$5,273.76	$5,574.57
Louisa Woosley Endowment Fund	$67,521.11	$72,450.62
Rev. Charles W. Hall Endowment for Pastoral Excellence	$12,934.23	$14,899.45
Dr. Thomas D. Campbell Endowment	$9,128.57	$9,649.25
Rev. Matthew Miller Endowment	$1,742.38	$2,042.78
Total	**$9,677,002.97**	**$9,791,239.41**

Miscellaneous

Endowment	Balance as of 12/31/2013	Balance as of 12/31/2014
Lavenia Cole Test. Trust Temp.	$20,778.13	$29,552.00
CP Retirement & Health Maintenance (Sue Galey)	$13,419.37	$14,184.74
Lillie M. Dickerson Memorial Fund	$73,741.56	$75,062.09
Verna Fillius Green Charities Endowment	$5,836.72	$7,893.22
Hodgeville Cemetery Association	$13,249.80	$14,005.56
Laddie Lollar Scholarship	$48,688.76	$35,483.46
McKinley & Barnett Families Temp.	$6,518.42	$5.60
Matching Gift Endowment Fund	$47.22	$49.92
Terrell D. and Jacqueline C. Maynard Endowment	$17,180.84	$19,314.17
Anay Ortega Montroy Missionary Endowment Fund	$0.00	$4,371.11
Ethel Phillips Endowment	$47,953.39	$52,691.97
Thomas P. & Barbara J. Semmens Scholarship	$1,627.35	$1,720.22
Stobbe Mathematics Scholarship	$46,947.90	$49,625.71
Maymie Stovall Trust	$278,095.00	$285,243.49
Mary Ann Walton Trust	$2,380,680.34	$2,409,695.76
Parr Estate/Mission Synod Ministerial Aid	$132,560.29	$140,121.35
Total	**$3,087,325.09**	**$3,139,020.37**

Bethel University

Endowment	Balance as of 12/31/2013	Balance as of 12/31/2014
J. E. Ash Memorial	$8,007.57	$8,086.20
Daisy J. Barger & Lena J. Davis	$20,317.52	$20,508.09
Grace Johnson Beasley (Memorial)	$17,887.13	$18,054.90
Herman Osteen Beasley Memorial	$44,149.61	$44,563.66
Bethel CPC, Columbia Presbytery	$2,031.81	$2,050.88
Boyett Trust	$35,738.44	$36,073.63
Rev. & Mrs. C. L. Bruington Library	$11,939.61	$12,051.55
Davis O. & Gladys Bryson Educ. 50%	$44,539.57	$44,957.74
Lavenia Campbell Cole Annuity End	$80,239.49	$80,992.03
Lavenia Campbell Cole Trust - 20%	$19,535.60	$19,718.80
Cumberland Presbytery Scholarship	$13,108.08	$13,231.06
J. Claud & Mary L. Dickinson Fund	$8,060.20	$8,135.75
Mary L. Claud Dickinson Educ.	$458,150.75	$462,447.52
Rev. & Mrs. Walter E. Dillow Memorial	$25,362.00	$25,599.84
Winifred M. Dixson Endowment	$50,919.44	$51,397.00
Jack & Ewie Freeman Trust	$20,865.81	$21,061.46
Vaughn & Mary E. Fults Min. Scholarship	$40,339.33	$40,717.68
Samuel K. Gam & Mamie S. Gam Endowment	$17,933.66	$25,649.88
Greensburg CPC Memorial Scholarship	$8,164.10	$8,240.70
Glenn Griffin Endowment - 33%	$39,107.42	$39,474.17
Fenner Heathcock Memorial Fund	$83,704.53	$84,489.55
Roy Hickman & Ruth Hughes Hickman	$43,892.58	$44,304.19
Francis A. Hobgood Trust 25%	$34,368.73	$34,691.04
George & Lottie M. Hutchins (Trust)	$281,738.31	$284,380.59

Dr. P. F. Johnson Memorial Endowment	$62,296.59	$62,880.85
Joiner Ministerial Scholarship	$6,750.75	$6,814.03
Rev. E. R. & Forest Ladd Memorial	$2,650.91	$2,675.78
Robert F. & Jane L. Little (BC)	$29,105.10	$29,378.01
Della Campbell Lowerie 20%	$402,731.40	$406,508.52
Dessa Jane Manuel Scholarship 50%	$188,261.48	$190,027.09
Albert & Belle McDonald Trus	$505,615.59	$510,357.54
Cliff McElroy Memorial Trust	$19,535.23	$20,649.51
Nyta Miller Scholarship	$7,535.25	$7,605.88
Nell Miller Scholarship	$3,371.03	$3,402.64
Ministerial Scholarship Endowment 60%	$132,534.71	$133,777.70
Bert & Pat Owen Endowment for Bethel	$2,248.80	$2,269.87
Max & Ethel Mize Parker Scholarship	$21,860.68	$22,065.73
S. Q. Proctor Ministerial Scholarship	$12,988.01	$13,109.79
Agnes D. Richardson Endowment Fund	$10,283.24	$10,379.66
Pauline Rucker Memorial	$4,619.54	$4,662.92
Rev. & Mrs. J. Howard Scott Memorial	$11,277.95	$11,383.65
Esther M. Smith Trust	$7,644.17	$7,715.88
Martha S. & W. Horace Snipes Scholarship	$2,088.52	$2,586.74
Eva Jane Stewart Trust - 50%	$64,360.90	$64,964.53
Roy Stucker Scholarship 50%	$54,391.40	$54,901.46
Richard Swain Memorial Scholarship	$24,966.99	$25,201.16
Weigel Bible CLass	$10,763.60	$10,864.56
Total	**$2,997,983.13**	**$3,035,061.41**

Cumberland Presbyerian Church in America

Endowment	Balance as of 12/31/2013	Balance as of 12/31/2014
CP Church in America Min. Education	$4,184.14	$4,422.80
CP Church in America World Mission	$8,533.35	$9,020.09
Total	**$12,717.49**	**$13,442.89**

Congregations

Endowment	Balance as of 12/31/2013	Balance as of 12/31/2014
Kate Maxwell Allen Trust	$6,356.69	$6,418.32
Grace Bright Circle Missions	$9,504.55	$10,046.72
Brunswick Cumberland Presbyterian Church Trust	$13,886.65	$13,272.85
Jane and Ed Chapman Endowment	$5,036.75	$4,285.07
Chinese Mission of San Francisco	$28,642.58	$28,920.61
Christ (FL) Tom W. Kelley Ed Fund	$28,902.57	$30,551.13
Christ (FL) Mary Beth Swindle Scholarship	$87,839.85	$90,401.07
Calico Rock - Christian Service Center End	$5,867.73	$6,100.95
The Mary Cloud Fund	$44,560.10	$44,978.96
Lavenia Campbell Cole Endowment	$275,624.65	$276,809.65
Dyersburg - Charles F. Moore C/T	$49,854.60	$52,698.22
Dyersburg - Jenny Edwards Endowment	$29,837.09	$31,538.97
Elliottsville - Gillis Endowment	$10,033.93	$10,606.24
Elliottsville - Kent Endowment	$7,512.47	$7,940.97
Fairfield C P Church Trust	$91,456.52	$92,316.28
Frankie Floyd Fund for Education	$12,788.53	$13,517.99
Faith-Hopewell CPC Ministries Endowment	$0.00	$1,007.33
Germantown - Christian Education Ministry	$26,267.43	$27,765.67
Germantown - Outreach Ministry	$6,372.87	$6,736.39
Germantown - Worship Ministry	$1,986.35	$2,149.61
Germantown - Eugene/Rosa Mae Warren	$13,327.66	$13,895.95
Germantown - William Pickle Member Care	$5,025.63	$5,535.53
Basil & Gertrude Green Scholarship Fund	$60,913.71	$62,131.92
Glenn Griffin Endowment 33%	$46,383.51	$46,819.55
Francis A. Hobgood Trust 50%	$69,562.18	$70,216.18

Hohenwald CPC	$355,112.22	$358,436.96
Hopewell Cumberland Presbyterian Church Endowment	$0.00	$503.67
Albert M. & Delia Jackson Memorial	$4,328.88	$5,101.24
Albert S. Johnston Trust	$62,130.10	$62,714.15
Orn/Laughlin Trust	$6,860.58	$6,925.12
Lawrenceburg CPC - Jack & Marjorie Anderson Endowment	$144,406.86	$152,643.57
Lawrenceburg CPC - Springer	$34,843.67	$29,242.41
Lawrenceburg CPC - Every Member	$8,416.44	$145.79
Lawrenceburg CPC - Mason/Jennings	$99,595.35	$100,531.64
Della Campbell Lowrie Trust	$84,135.76	$84,926.74
Lucado Endowment	$630,914.76	$666,901.17
Manchester CPC - Christian Education Endowment	$9,003.50	$11,229.41
Marshall (MO) David Guthrie Youth	$5,962.22	$6,302.24
Marshall (MO) 50 Year Church Member Rec	$6,987.46	$7,386.08
Marshall (TX) CPC of, Endowment	$300,309.57	$226,424.88
Marshall (TX) Ewing Chapel Cemetery	$58,291.23	$62,540.93
McKenzie CPC - Beasley Endowment	$75,151.31	$75,857.80
McKenzie CPC - Julia Patterson Irby	$13,520.13	$13,647.23
Medina CPC Trust	$2,477.80	$2,619.11
Mesquite CPC - Every Member Endowment	$10,842.80	$11,461.26
Louise Moffitt Trust Fund	$306,833.74	$309,706.46
Mount Moriah Cemetery Fund (W. TN Presbytery)	$326,989.03	$334,211.63
Murfreesboro First CPC Trust	$1,654.94	$1,749.33
New Salem Cemetery Fund	$97,063.91	$101,459.74
Oliver's Chapel Cemetery Trust	$91,408.63	$96,622.43
Trimble CPC - Horace J. Coffer Memorial Trust	$5,706.66	$5,763.50
Trimble CPC - Howard Glasgow Memorial Trust	$5,706.65	$5,763.49
Trimble CPC - Bob & Chris Page Family Trust	$3,552.68	$3,595.27
Carolyn Smythe Parks Memorial Trust	$168,636.73	$170,230.43
E. E. Parks Memorial Trust	$4,372.15	$4,413.26
Hamilton & Merion S. Parks Family	$44,206.24	$44,628.58
Rev. Hamilton Parks Memorial Trust	$2,023.01	$12,081.67
W. H. Parks Memorial Trust	$6,937.83	$7,003.08
Franklin Pierce Memorial Trust	$9,996.15	$10,090.06
William W. & Lou W. Pierce Memorial	$1,997.76	$2,016.59
J. Dixie Johnson Primm Endowment	$1,633.30	$1,726.50
Red Bank CPC Endowment	$27,161.27	$29,467.25
Robinson Cemetery Endowment	$33,920.09	$35,854.89
Saint Timothy CPC Trust	$29,639.88	$29,922.86
Short Creek CPC Memorial Fund	$16,715.89	$19,149.05
Swan Cumberland Presbyterian Church	$13,629.78	$14,407.18
Inman & Mildred Swain Memorial	$67,202.07	$67,833.87
Thomas D. & Mary Jo (Adams) Vaughan	$564,371.59	$569,655.46
Thomas & Mary Jo Vaughan Outreach	$56,767.34	$57,298.83
West Union Cemetery - Old Committee	$59,112.12	$62,483.78
Rev. Jonathan Clark Endowment	$649.21	$686.24
Calico Rock - Mildred B. Curless Danielson	$1,672.93	$1,768.36
Calico Rock - Every Member Endowment	$7,635.90	$8,460.50
Calico Rock CPC -Dixie Jennings Gray Endowment	$7,749.21	$8,191.22
Calico Rock - Ernie Horton Gray Endowment	$6,825.43	$7,214.76
Calico Rock - Willis Newton Hankins End.	$690.79	$730.15
Calico Rock - Joann Smith Hudson Endowment	$1,933.39	$2,043.70
Calico Rock - Zelda Killian Endowment	$1,472.28	$1,556.25
Calico Rock - James & Ariel Utt-Landrus End	$6,887.57	$7,280.45
Calico Rock CPC - John & Ernette "Ernie" Parker	$1,541.94	$1,629.85
Calico Rock - Ray & Velma Perryman End	$7,599.10	$8,032.57
Calico Rock - Beatrice Virginia Pino End	$604.24	$638.68
Calico Rock - Pietro "Pete" Pino Endowment	$4,758.65	$5,030.12
Calico Rock - Muriel Thompson Ryan End	$1,481.14	$1,565.58
Calico Rock - Sean Vann Endowment	$4,004.03	$4,232.46

Calico Rock - Seay Endowment		$6,712.45	$11,176.03
Calico Rokc - Wayne & Gaye Wood End		$10,742.53	$11,355.27
Calico Rock - Trimble House Maintenance Endowment		$6,509.94	$6,881.26
Calico Rock - Pete & Betty Riggins		$1,823.09	$1,927.04
	Team	$4,879,368.50	$4,929,739.21

Presbyteries

Endowment	Balance as of 12/31/2013	Balance as of 12/31/2014
Arkansas Presbytery - Camp Peniel	$25,720.09	$27,186.56
Arkansas Presbytery - Higher Education	$65,511.08	$66,126.90
Rev. Leo E. Smith Min. Memorial Scholarship	$10,857.45	$11,863.59
Daisy Bell Belcher Estate	$29,483.29	$31,164.99
Cauca Valley Presbytery - Hogar Samaria	$73,418.00	$100,788.11
Columbia Presbytery Endowment	$74,596.79	$440,165.51
Crystal Springs Camp - Fred Ramsey	$27,363.19	$28,923.93
East Tennessee - Philip Norris Jones	$8,990.42	$9,503.24
William J. Eldredge Trust Fund	$12,019.32	$12,132.32
Ephraim McLean Sr. Memorial Fund	$51,402.24	$54,334.11
Missouri Presbytery - Education Fund	$16,545.55	$38,200.28
Missouri Presbytery - Church Development & Revitalization	$1,299.94	$22,138.48
Missouri Presbytery - Missions Growth	$22,674.06	$23,967.36
Oklahoma/Kansas/Nebraska Mission	$481,463.73	$508,925.69
Red River Presbytery - Camp	$42,380.28	$44,797.56
Red River Presbytery Christian Ed. General	$7,993.73	$8,449.71
Tennessee Georgia Presbytery Capital	$28,604.69	$25,716.70
Tennessee Georgia Presbytery Candidate Education	$10,341.40	$11,516.88
Trinity Presbytery - Saint Paul	$180,699.95	$133,197.37
Trinity Presbytery - Saint Paul Interest	$169,833.79	$118,006.53
W. Tennessee Presbytery - Grace Beasley Fund	$149,527.17	$158,055.96
W. Tennessee Presbytery - Camp Clark Williamson	$16,999.42	$17,969.08
Covenant Presbytery - Russ Milton Scholarship Endowment	$11,717.82	$12,888.22
Cumberland Presbtery - Missions - McInteer End	$65,417.91	$66,030.37
Cumberland Presbtery - Missions - Millwood	$5,564.39	$5,616.53
Cumberland Presbtery - Missions - Ray A. Morris	$2,044.31	$2,063.37
Cumberland Presbtery - Missions - NCD	$138,570.37	$140,924.38
Cumberland Presbtery - Missions - Reid's Chapel End	$47,018.99	$47,459.20
Cumberland Presbtery - Missions - Royal Oak End	$44,974.79	$45,395.84
Cumberland Presbtery - Scholarships - Freeman End	$136,968.59	$138,250.93
Cumberland Presbtery - Scholarships - E. L. Freeman Farms	$192,568.12	$194,371.02
Cumberland Presbtery - Scholarships - Howard End	$51,107.68	$51,586.16
Cumberland Presbtery - Min. Educ - Bremen CPC 25%	$53,067.74	$53,564.58
Cumberland Presbtery - Cont Edu - Hampton End	$122,658.59	$123,806.99
Cumberland Presbtery - Cont Edu - KY Synod	$5,097.73	$5,145.48
Cumberland Presbtery - Gen. Program - Bremen CPC 75%	$159,203.15	$160,693.64
Cumberland Presbtery - Gen. Program - KY Synod	$10,221.63	$10,317.33
Cumberland Presbtery - Gen. Program - Eugene A. Leslie	$2,975.21	$3,003.08
Cumberland Presbtery - Gen. Program - Wilcoxson End.	$4,088.58	$4,126.88
Cumberland Presbtery - Christian Ed - Camp Koinonia	$33,352.14	$33,664.37
Cumberland Presbtery - Christian Ed - Cecil Huff	$4,333.25	$4,373.80
Cumberland Presbtery - Christian Ed - Sam Macy	$1,293.46	$1,512.08
Cumberland Presbtery - Higher Ed - Joseph H. Butler	$1,902.14	$1,919.94
Cumberland Presbtery - Higher Ed - Sharon Church	$27,660.23	$27,919.20
Cumberland Presbytery -Robert L. McReynolds 50%	$43,523.74	$43,931.62
Total	$2,673,056.14	$3,071,695.87

THE REPORT OF THE HISTORICAL FOUNDATION

I. GENERAL INFORMATION

A. OFFICERS OF THE BOARD

The officers of the board are as follows: Reverend Rick White, president; Pam Davis, vice-president; and Sidney Milton, secretary. Susan Knight Gore is the director and treasurer of the Historical Library and Archives.

B. BOARD REPRESENTATIVE TO THE 184TH CPC GENERAL ASSEMBLY

The board's representative to the 184th General Assembly of the Cumberland Presbyterian Church (CPC) is Reverend Tommy Jobe. The alternate is Reverend Mary Kathryn Kirkpatrick.

C. MEMBERSHIP AND MEETINGS OF THE BOARD

The board is currently composed of the following members: from the Cumberland Presbyterian Church in America—Edna Barnett, Vanessa Barnhill, Dorothy Hayden, Pat Ward, and Rick White, from the Cumberland Presbyterian Church—Pam Davis, Michael Fare, Tommy Jobe, Mary Kathryn Kirkpatrick, Sidney Milton, and Sidney Swindle.
The Board of Trustees met, September 19-20, 2014.

D. MEMBERS WHOSE TERMS EXPIRE

The second term of Michael Fare expires with the 2015 meeting of the Cumberland Presbyterian General Assembly, and he is eligible for reelection. The third term of Tommy Jobe expires with the 2015 meeting of the Cumberland Presbyterian Church in America General Assembly, and he is not eligible for reelection.

E. STAFF

Susan Knight Gore serves as the Archivist of the Historical Foundation. Lauren Gam Gilliland is the archival assistant for the Foundation.

II. ASSEMBLY REPORTING

As a matter of official structure, relative to the CPC, there is a Board of Trustees composed of members from both the CPC and CPCA, and relative to the CPCA, there is a committee composed of members from the CPCA.

III. PROGRAMS AND ACTIVITIES

A. HISTORY INTERPRETATION AND PROMOTIONAL ACTIVITIES

1. The 1810 Circle
In order to enlist the financial support of interested members of our churches in the work of the Foundation, the 1810 Circle was created. Membership is based on a financial contribution of $25 or more per year. Income through such gifts enables the Foundation to meet expenditures and is vital to the continued work of the Foundation.
We appreciate the support given to the Foundation by all members of the 1810 Circle and encourage other members of the Cumberland Presbyterian Church and the Cumberland Presbyterian Church in America to join this donor group.

RECOMMENDATION 1: That the General Assembly make congregations and presbyteries aware of the 1810 Circle and encourage new members to support this endeavor annually.

2. Patrons

Persons who contribute $100 or more to one of the endowments of the Historical Foundation become patron members and receive a certificate. Patron memberships may also be given in honor or in memory of an individual.

3. Heritage Churches

Congregations contributing a minimum of $1,000 to an endowment of the Historical Foundation become Heritage Churches and receive a framed certificate. There are six categories of recognition and churches can move from one level to another.

Heritage Church	$1,000 - $4,999
Silver Heritage Church	$5,000 to $9,999
Golden Heritage Church	$10,000 to $24,999
Platinum Heritage Church	$25,000 to $49,999
Diamond Heritage Church	$50,000 to $99,000
Jubilee Heritage Church	$100,000 and up

4. Presbyterial Heritage Committees/Presbyterial Historians

To promote interest in the work of the Foundation and to nurture work in history on the presbyterial level, the Historical Foundation seeks to work cooperatively with the Presbyterial Heritage Committees/Presbyterial Historians of both general assemblies. The brochure, Suggestions for Heritage Committees and Presbyterial Historians, is available from the Foundation. The board expresses its appreciation to the presbyteries that have Heritage Committees/Presbyterial Historians.

5. Denomination Day Offering

The 2015 Denomination Day Offering was designated to help preserve the history of Choctaw Presbytery.

The Foundation expresses appreciation to congregations and others groups who received special offerings for the work of the Historical Foundation on Denomination Day. This special offering provides an opportunity for congregations to directly contribute to the support of the Historical Foundation as well as the Foundation supplying educational materials to each congregation.

RECOMMENDATION 2: That congregations be encouraged to have a special offering on the Sunday designated as Denomination Day to help support the special project designated for that year.

B. PUBLICATIONS

1. Promotional Materials

The Historical Foundation provides promotional materials describing its purpose and work, the various means of financially supporting this work, and listings of available publications and prints for sale through the Foundation. These materials are available on the Foundation's website.

2. Publication Series

The Foundation has a number of titles and prints available for purchase. Income from the sale of these items goes into the Historical Foundation Trust, a permanent endowment supporting the Foundation's work. Titles available are:

1883 Confession of Faith.
1895 Cumberland Cook Book.
Cumberland Presbyterianism and Arminianism Compared/Contrasted on Selected Doctrines by Joe Ben Irby.
Faith Once Delivered; Some Indispensable Doctrines of the Christian Faith by Joe Ben Irby.
Family of Faith: Cumberland Presbyterians in Harrison County [Texas], 1848-1998 by Rose Mary Magrill.
History of East Side Cumberland Presbyterian Church, Memphis, Tennessee, Memphis Tennessee: 1926-1986, by the Historical Committee.
History of the Cumberland Presbyterian Church by B. W. McDonnold.

Jerusalem Cumberland Presbyterian Church: A Documentary and Pictorial History by Anne Elizabeth Swain Odom.
Legacy of Grace: Louisiana and Texas Cumberland Presbyterian People & Places of Trinity Presbytery by Rose Mary Magrill.
Life and Thought of Finis Ewing by Joe Ben Irby.
Life and Thought of Milton Bird by Joe Ben Irby.
Life and Thought of Reuben Burrow by Joe Ben Irby.
Life and Thought of Robert Verrell Foster by Joe Ben Irby.
Life and Thought of Stanford Guthrie Burney by Joe Ben Irby.
Life and Times of Finis Ewing by F. R. Cossitt.
Soundings by Morris Pepper.
Theological Snippets by Joe Ben Irby.
This They Believed by Joe Ben Irby.
What Cumberland Presbyterians Believe by E. K. Reagin.
Women Shall Preach: Celebrating 125 Yeas of Ordained Women in Ministry in the Cumberland Presbyterian Church.
Prints of the *Samuel McAdow Home* and the *First Meeting of Cumberland Presbytery*.
These items are available for sale from Cumberland Presbyterian Resources.

RECOMMENDATION 3: That the General Assembly make presbyteries, congregations, and individuals aware that the Historical Foundation is interested and has funds to publish books on topics concerning the Cumberland Presbyterian Church and Cumberland Presbyterian Church in America.

3. Denomination Day Resources

All the Past is but the Beginning of Beginning (Denomination Day resource) is available on the Foundation's web site under the Resources section: http://www.cumberland.org/hfcpc/resource/. It includes eight dramas intended to present the birth of the Cumberland Presbyterian Church and the Cumberland Presbyterian Church in America. A hard copy may be requested from the Foundation office.

4. Online Promotion

Recognizing the increasing value of emerging social media, the Historical Foundation employs a Facebook group, "Historical Foundation of the CPC & CPCA," to engage an expanding audience of Cumberland Presbyterians in denominational history and heritage. By showcasing collection acquisitions, the Foundation expands the knowledge of those materials sought for preservation as well as the nature of archival development.

RECOMMENDATION 4: That the General Assembly encourage presbyteries, congregations, and individuals active on the Internet to join the Historical Foundation of the CPC & CPCA Facebook group.

C. HISTORICAL FOUNDATION AWARDS

1. Award in Cumberland Presbyterian History

The Foundation encourages the writing and publication of papers on all aspects of the history of the Cumberland Presbyterian Church in America and the Cumberland Presbyterian Church. One means of promoting such writing is the Historical Foundation Award in Cumberland Presbyterian History. A $300 prize is awarded to the author entering the best paper on any CP or CPCA history subject which meets in form and content the requirements set by the Board of Trustees and judged by the board appointed awards committee. All manuscripts submitted to the competition become property of the Foundation and are added to the Historical Library and Archives.

The contest follows the calendar year, and entries for the 2015 competition are encouraged. All entries will be accepted through December 2015 for this year's contest. Any entries received following the deadline of December 31st will be automatically entered in the 2016 competition.

Guidelines and entry forms for submitting manuscripts to the competition are available from the Foundation office as well as on the internet, http://www.cumberland.org/hfcpc/Awards.htm. The Historical Foundation appreciates the participation of past and future CPCA and CP historians in this program.

2. Awards of Recognition

Awards of recognition are certificates given to organizations or individuals in recognition of historic events or contributions to the preservation of our heritage as Cumberland Presbyterians. Appropriate applications for the award are: particular churches celebrating anniversaries of their organization; any judicatory or agency celebrating publication of a written history; celebrations of history or historic event in a creative or unusual manner; individuals who have provided continued service for 50 years or more as members of a local congregation or presbytery; individuals who have served for 40 years or more in a continuing leadership role (including pastors) within a local church. Individuals, churches, or presbyterial heritage committees may make application for the issuing of an award by contacting the Foundation office. Application forms are supplied by the Foundation office as well as the internet, http://www.cumberland.org/hfcpc/Awards.htm.

D. RELATIONSHIPS

The Presbyterian Historical Society of the Southwest is an agency of The Synod of the Sun, Presbyterian Church (USA) and Cumberland Presbyterian Churches in Arkansas, Louisiana, Oklahoma and Texas. Members of the Cumberland Presbyterian Church who serve on the board of this organization are Reverend Norlan Scrudder and Dr. Rose Mary Magrill.

IV. HISTORICAL LIBRARY AND ARCHIVES

A. RESEARCH SERVICE

The Foundation's main research commitment is to the agencies, local congregations, and members of the Cumberland Presbyterian Churches. Since the Historical Library and Archives of the Historical Foundation serves as the official repository for the Cumberland Presbyterian General Assemblies, this is our focus. Although the separation of research into two types designated by their mode of access has been rapid and dramatic, both the traditional and "cyber" mode contribute to and enhance the other.

1. Traditional/Physical Access

Hands on access to primary source material remains the vital heart of historic and theological research. Rather than being diminished by increased electronic resources, traditional research has broadened due to heightened awareness of primary sources in an expanding information age. The Foundation receives research requests by personal visitors, mail, e-mail, and telephone. As time permits, requests are researched. Responses are sent to the requestor, as well as pertinent information on ministers, congregations, presbyteries and synods being placed on our website for future researchers.

2. Electronic Access

The Foundation's website continues to expand in order to provide greater access to the materials in the Historical Library and Archives. As well as being a research tool, the internet provides an invaluable and inexpensive means of promotion for the physical collections of the Historical Library and Archives, the activities of the Historical Foundation, and for the greater community of faith called Cumberland Presbyterians. Information at the site includes: general information about the Foundation, entire texts of important historical documents, historical information on particular congregations, ministers, presbyteries, and synods. The gateway URL to the Foundation's website is http://www.cumberland.org/hfcpc/.

B. ACQUISITIONS

The Historical Library and Archives regularly receives items published by the two denominations, *Minutes of the General Assembly of the Cumberland Presbyterian Church, Preliminary Minutes of the General Assembly of the Cumberland Presbyterian Church, Yearbook of the General Assembly of the Cumberland Presbyterian Church, The Cumberland Presbyterian, Missionary Messenger, Minutes of the General Assembly of the Cumberland Presbyterian Church in America, Preliminary Minutes of the General Assembly of the Cumberland Presbyterian Church in America,* and *The Cumberland Flag.* Synods and presbyteries deposit four copies of their printed minutes in the Historical Library and Archives. In addition, books, pamphlets, theses, dissertations, records and publications of general assembly, boards, agencies, institutions, and task forces; records and publications of synods and presbyteries, session records and other materials of particular churches, biographical material of Cumberland Presbyterian and Cumberland Presbyterian Church in America ministers, photographs, audiovisual materials, and museum items were among the accessions received. The 2014 Accession List closed with 238 accession groups.

Some of the highlights added to the collection in 2014 include:

Audiovisual Items

Beech Cumberland Presbyterian Church. Hendersonville, Tennessee. *Historic Beech Cemetery Tour*. DVD. 2005-2014.

Camp Peniel. Arkansas Presbytery. Cumberland Presbyterian Church. *Camp Peniel: Where I Met God Face to Face*. DVD.

Books

Baugh, Milton L. *Social Views Reflected in Official Publications of the Cumberland Presbyterian Church, 1875-1900*. [Nashville]: Vanderbilt University, 1954.

Bird, Milton, and S. B. Howard. *The Social Harp: Comprising the Richest Variety of Spiritual Songs : Also Some of the Best Hymns for the Use of Christians in Their House of Pilgrimage, Adapted to All Occasions and Seasons*. Louisville: Cumberland Presbyterian Board of Publications, 1851.

Brown, Betty Bolin and Rose Mary Magrill. *History of the Ewing Chapel Cemetery*. Marshall, Texas: Ewing Chapel Cemetery Committee, 2013.

Buck, Clinton Owen. *Unity and Diversity in Theological Education: A Supplement 1964-1990 and a Sequel 1990-2008 of A History of Memphis Theological Seminary*. Printed by The King's Press Publications, Southaven, Mississippi. Memphis, Tennessee: Memphis Theological Seminary, 2014.

Constitution of the Cumberland Presbyterian Church, in the United States of America: Containing The Confession of Faith, The Catechism, and a Directory for the Worship of God: Together with the Form of Government and Discipline, as Revised and Adopted by the General Assembly at Princeton, Ky. May 1829. 3rd ed. Nashville: Printed by James Smith, 1834.

Gore, Susan Knight, comp. *Women Shall Preach: Celebrating 125 Years of Ordained Women in Ministry in the Cumberland Presbyterian Church*. Memphis, Tennessee: Historical Foundation of the Cumberland Presbyterian Church and the Cumberland Presbyterian Church in America, 2014.

Odom, Anne Elizabeth Swain. *Jerusalem Cumberland Presbyterian Church: A Documentary and Pictorial History*. Cordova, Tennessee: Historical Foundation of the Cumberland Presbyterian Church and the Cumberland Presbyterian Church in America, 2013.

Rush, Jodi Hearn, ed. *Advent Devotional: Gather 'Round the Circle*. Cordova, Tennessee: Discipleship Ministry Team, Ministry Council, Cumberland Presbyterian Church, September 2013.

St. John, Beverly, *It's All About Me: The Best Life Anyone Could Have. Being an Autobiography of Beverly Head Pickup St. John*. Cordova, Tennessee: Cumberland Presbyterian Church, 2014.

Periodicals

Cumberland Presbyterian Church in America. *The Cumberland Flag*. May 1996.

Missionary Record. *A Monthly Magazine Devoted to the Subject of Christian Missions*. September 1892, January 1894, April 1896, June 1901, and May 1903.

The Union Evangelist (Uniontown, Pennsylvania), 1841-1842, scattered issues.

General Assembly

Board of Missions. Cumberland Presbyterian Church. Miscellaneous files. 18 boxes.

General Assembly. Cumberland Presbyterian Church in America. *Minutes of the General Assembly of the Cumberland Presbyterian Church in America*. June 14-16, 1995. Nashville, Tennessee.

National Missionary Society. Cumberland Presbyterian Church in America. Annual Luncheon Program. June 7, 2011 in Dallas, Texas.

Institutions

Beverly College. Beverly, Ohio. Report of the Trustees of Beverly College to the Cumberland Presbyterian Synod of Ohio. Manuscript, 1872.

Cumberland University. Lebanon, Tennessee. *Catalogue of the Theological Seminary at Lebanon, Tennessee*. Theological Department of Cumberland University. 1902-1903.

Minister's Records

Holtsinger, John Patton (1813-1875). Notes on Infant Baptism.

McKee, Margaret Elizabeth Scott (1927-2014). Papers. 1 box.

McMillan Ronald L. Files. 8 boxes.

Museum Items

Austin, First Cumberland Presbyterian Church. Austin, Texas. Commemorative Plates.

Communion Set. Sanitary Communion Outfit Company, Rochester, New York. Found at Brenthaven Cumberland Presbyterian Church, Brentwood, Tennessee.

Crystal Springs Camp. Kelso, Tennessee. Tennessee Synod. Mug.

Garfield Cumberland Presbyterian Church. Garfield, Washington. Paperweight. Glass with photographs of church building and Rev. Solon McCroskey, pastor.

Hiwassee Presbytery. Cumberland Presbyterian Church in America. Commemorative Cup. Hiwassee Presbytery. CPCA 2014.

Jerusalem Cumberland Presbyterian Church. Murfreesboro, Tennessee. Tee Shirt and Tote bag.

Lewis Memorial Cumberland Presbyterian Church. Tampa, Florida. Commemorative Plate.

Osaka Jogakuin School. Osaka, Japan. Notepaper. Set of notepaper and envelopes. 2009. (Dr. Eilo Kato-Otani, President of Osaka Jogakuin School in Osaka, Japan).

Pacific Synod. Cumberland Presbyterian Church. Ribbon. Pacific Synod. Delegate. Selma Cal. Oct. 7 to 13. 1902 C. P. C.

Red River Meeting House. Logan County, Kentucky. Christmas Ornament. Red.

Sewanee Cumberland Presbyterian Church. Sewanee, Tennessee. Metal Tray. Picture of building.

Other Congregational Records

Beech Cumberland Presbyterian Church. Hendersonville, Tennessee. Newsletters. 2006-2010.

Clarksville Cumberland Presbyterian Church. Clarksville, Montgomery County, Tennessee. Bulletins. 1964-1978, 1982-1983, 1990-2012.

Cleveland Cumberland Presbyterian Church. Cleveland, Tennessee. Sunday School Records. 1907-1911, 1913, 1915-1916.

Cleveland Cumberland Presbyterian Church. Cleveland, Tennessee. Treasurer's Book. 1911-1922; 1930-1954.

High Hill Cumberland Presbyterian Church Cemetery Association. Sturgis, Kentucky. Trustees Record Book. 1932-1982.

Cleveland Cumberland Presbyterian Church. Cleveland, Tennessee. Church Directory. 1918, 1957, 1963, 1964.

Jerusalem Cumberland Presbyterian Church. Murfreesboro, Tennessee. Cookbook. *Faithful Favorites*. Kearney, Nebraska: Morris Press Cookbooks, 2009.

Moberly Cumberland Presbyterian Church. Moberly, Missouri. Miscellaneous Records. 1 box.

Westside Cumberland Presbyterian Church. Nashville, Tennessee. Guest Book. 1987-1994.

Woodlawn Cumberland Presbyterian Church. Paducah, Kentucky. *Woodlawn's Rich Heritage and Legacy: A Collection of Memories of Woodlawn Cumberland Presbyterian Church, Paducah, Ky*. Compiled by Sidney Milton.

Photographs

Crisman, Rev. Edwin Burnett (1831-1899). Photograph. 2 ½ x 4. Sepia.

Cumberland University. Lebanon, Tennessee. Senior Theological Class, 1903. Photograph. B & W, 12 ½ x 15 ½. J. S. Stapleton, Mo.; I. G. Boydston, Tenn.; A. F. Eddings, Tenn.; S. G. McCluney, Tex.; R. E. Sherman, Mo.; J. W. Haggard, Tenn.; G. S. Jenkins, Mo.; A. M. Williams, Cal.; L. B. Gray, Tex.; I. L. Myers, Ohio; Dr. J. Stephens, Tenn.; Dr. R. G. Pearson, N.C.; Dean J. R. Henry, Tenn.; Dr. C. H. Bell, Tenn.; Prof. F. K. Farr, Tenn.; Prof. W. P. Bone, Tenn.; Dr. R. V Foster, Tenn.; Prof. F. J. Stowe, Tenn.

Lewis Memorial Cumberland Presbyterian Church. Tampa, Florida. Photograph. 4 ½ x 6 ½. B&W. 1930s. Rev. Henry Graf and wife and group.

Mt. Sterling Cumberland Presbyterian Church in America. Sturgis, Kentucky. Photographs. Resurrection Day Program. 4 photographs.

Postcards

Bethel College. McKenzie, Tennessee. Postcard. Photograph of building. Divided back, real photo, c1910. Written by Julia McCaslin mailed in 1911.

Evansville Cumberland Presbyterian Church. Evansville, Indiana. Postcard. First Cumberland Presbyterian Church, Evansville, Ind. Divided back, color tinted, c1905.

Presbyterial Records

Knoxville Presbytery. Cumberland Presbyterian Church. Minutes. April 3-5, 1873 and October 9-11, 1873. Manuscript minutes.

Ocoee Presbytery. Cumberland Presbyterian Church. Presbytery Minutes. April 1867-October 1873. Original Volume.

Ohio Valley Presbyterial Musical Clinic. Second Cumberland Presbyterian Church. Minutes. Original Volume. 1963-1978.

Sermons

Forester, Jesse Clem (1915-1983). Sermons. 2 boxes.

McGregor, David Vincent, Jr. (1927-2014). Sermons. 8 boxes.

Session Records

Beech Cumberland Presbyterian Church. Hendersonville, Tennessee. Session Records. 1962-2005.

Thurman's Chapel Second Cumberland Presbyterian Church. Marion, Kentucky. Session Records. April 4, 1973-October 10, 1986.

Bethesda Cumberland Presbyterian Church. Fall Branch, Greene County, Tennessee. Session Records. September 14, 1847; October 7, 1847; October 14, 147, April 1, 1848; October 2, 1848.

Calico Rock Cumberland Presbyterian Church. Calico Rock, Izard County, Arkansas. Session Records. 1923-2013.

Cedar Hill Cumberland Presbyterian Church. Greeneville, Tennessee. Session Records. 2008-2011.

Chandler Cumberland Presbyterian Church. Chandler, Warrick County, Indiana. Session Records. 1892-1978.

Clarksville Cumberland Presbyterian Church. Clarksville, Montgomery County, Tennessee. Session Records. 1928-2004.

Cleveland Cumberland Presbyterian Church. Cleveland, Bradley County, Tennessee. Session Records. 1837-1986. 20 volumes. Microfilm. 1 reel.

Ethel Cumberland Presbyterian Church. Collinsville, Grayson county Texas. Session Records. 1914-1968.

Glenwood Cumberland Presbyterian Church. Maury County, Tennessee. Session Records. 1956-1993.

Holly Grove Cumberland Presbyterian Church. Princeton, Jackson County, Alabama. (Name changed from Paint Rock on October 1, 1860 by Jackson Presbytery.) Session Records. 1889-1962.

Medina Cumberland Presbyterian Church. Medina, Gibson County, Tennessee. Session Records. 1956-1964

Oak Grove Cumberland Presbyterian Church. Cottonwood, Gallatin County, Illinois. Session Records. 1874-2010.

Pleasant Hill Cumberland Presbyterian Church. Owensboro, Daviess County, Kentucky. Session Records. 1976-1986.

Union Grove Cumberland Presbyterian Church. Dyer county, Tennessee. Session Records. 1863-1901.

Watkins Park Cumberland Presbyterian Church. Nashville, Tennessee. Session Records. 1926-1936.

Watkins Park Cumberland Presbyterian Church. Nashville, Tennessee. Name changed in 1942 to Westside Cumberland Presbyterian Church. Nashville, Tennessee. Session Records. 1940-2012.

Synodical Records

Kentucky States Synod. Cumberland Presbyterian Church in America. Minutes. August 14-15, 1998.

RECOMMENDATION 5: That the General Assembly encourage all congregations to preserve their session records by depositing them in the Historical Foundation.

RECOMMENDATION 6: That the General Assembly instruct each synod and presbytery to deposit their minutes in a timely fashion with the Historical Foundation.

The Historical Foundation can provide on-site assistance to both presbyteries and individual congregations. On the presbyterial level, we can assist the appropriate agency to evaluate materials left when a church has ceased to be viable and has been closed. This can eliminate speculation on the presbytery's part as to what is, or is not, material to be preserved. For congregations we can provide a similar service helping them to determine what can and should be archived.

RECOMMENDATION 7: That the General Assembly instruct presbyteries to locate the session records when closing a church and then deposit them in the Historical Foundation.

V. BIRTHPLACE SHRINE

The Birthplace Shrine located at Montgomery Bell State Park near Dickson, Tennessee was dedicated June 18, 1960. This site consists of the Memorial Chapel and a replica of the Reverend Samuel

McAdow's log house. Since 1994, the Foundation has been responsible for the preservation of the Birthplace Shrine. Four endowments provide funds for maintenance and repairs: the Grace Johnson Beasley Birthplace Shrine Fund, the Birthplace Shrine Fund, the Henry Evan Harper Endowment for Cumberland Presbyterian History, and the P.F. Johnson Memorial Endowment. Gifts to these endowments provide for the continued preservation of the Birthplace Shrine. Interested donors are encouraged to contact the Foundation office. Another means of support are the fees collected from couples who use the chapel for their wedding ceremony. These funds are added to the Birthplace Shrine Fund and earnings are used for maintenance and special projects. The Board encourages individuals and groups to visit the Birthplace Shrine as an act of remembering our heritage and envisioning our future as Cumberland Presbyterians.

Groups and individuals are encouraged to contact the Foundation to set up work days and special projects. The Foundation thanks the Heritage Committee of Nashville Presbytery and the Charlotte Cumberland Presbyterian Church for their continuing volunteer upkeep of the property.

VII. FINANCIAL CONCERNS AND 2016 BUDGET

A. BUDGETS

The 2016 line-item budget of the Historical Foundation has been filed with the CPC General Assembly Office.

B. ENDOWMENTS

- Anne Elizabeth Knight Adams Heritage Fund
- Rosie Magrill Alexander Trust
- Paul H. and Ann M. Allen Heritage Fund
- Grace Johnson Beasley Birthplace Shrine Fund
- Birthplace Shrine Fund
- James L. and Louise M. Bridges Heritage Fund
- Mark and Elinor Swindle Brown Heritage Fund
- Sydney and Elinor Brown Heritage Fund
- Centennial Heritage Endowment
- Walter Chesnut Heritage Fund
- Lavenia Campbell Cole Heritage Fund
- Cumberland Presbyterian Church in America Heritage Fund
- Cumberland Presbyterian Women Archival Supplies Endowment
- Bettye Jean Loggins McCaffrey Ellis Heritage Fund
- Samuel Russell & Mary Grace (Barefoot) Estes Endowment
- Family of Faith Endowment
- Gettis and Delia Snyder Gilbert Heritage Fund
- James C. and Freda M. Gilbert Heritage Fund
- James C. and Freda M. Gilbert Trust
- Mamie A. Gilbert Trust
- Henry Evan Harper Endowment for Cumberland Presbyterian History
- Ronald Wilson and Virginia Tosh Harper Endowment
- Historical Foundation Trust
- Donald and Jane Hubbard Heritage Fund
- Cliff and Jill Hudson Heritage Fund
- Robert and Kathy Hull Endowment
- Into the Nineties Endowment
- Joe Ben Irby Heritage Fund
- P.F. Johnson Memorial Endowment
- Irene A. Kiefer Endowment
- Chow King Leong Endowment
- Dennis Lawrence & Elmira Castleberry Magrill Trust
- J. Richard Magrill Heritage Fund
- Joe Richard and Mary Belle Magrill Trust
- Gwendolyn McCaffrey McReynolds Heritage Fund

Jimmie Joe McKinley Heritage Fund
Edith Louise Mitchell Heritage Fund
Lloyd Freeman Mitchell Heritage Fund
Snowdy Clifton and Lillian Walkup Mitchell Heritage Fund
Rev. Charles and Paulette Morrow Endowment
Virginia Sue Williamson Morrow Heritage Fund
Anne Elizabeth Swain Odom Heritage Fund
Martha Sue Parr Heritage Fund
Florence Pennewill Heritage Fund
Morris and Ruth Pepper Endowment
Publishing House Endowment
Mable Magrill Rundell Trust
Samuel Callaway Rundell Heritage Fund
Paul and Mary Jo Schnorbus Heritage Fund
Roy and Mary Seawright Shelton Heritage Fund
Shiloh CPC Ellis County Texas Endowment
Hinkley and Vista Smartt Heritage Fund
John William Sparks Heritage Fund
Irvin Scott and Annie Mary Draper Swain Heritage Fund
F. P. Waits Historical Trust

Respectfully submitted,
Rick White, President
Susan Knight Gore, Archivist

THE REPORT OF THE BOARD OF TRUSTEES OF MEMPHIS THEOLOGICAL SEMINARY

Introduction

Memphis Theological Seminary of the Cumberland Presbyterian Church is the only seminary of the Cumberland Presbyterian Church. Our history is traced back through the Cumberland Presbyterian Theological Seminary in McKenzie to the organization of the graduate School of Theology at Cumberland University and the Theological Department at Bethel College, both of which began in 1852. Those two schools of theology continued the legacy begun in the work of founder Finis Ewing, who educated candidates for the ministry in his home, and many other ministers, who trained young candidates in homes, churches, and on the trail. For one hundred fifty seven years, Cumberland Presbyterians have been providing formal theological education for the church's ministers. For almost two hundred years, the Cumberland Presbyterian Church has valued the importance of an educated ministry.

With the denomination's decision to move its seminary to Memphis in 1964, Memphis Theological Seminary of the Cumberland Presbyterian Church began to serve a larger and more diverse student body. Though students from other denominations were admitted during the McKenzie years, the move to a major metropolitan area opened the opportunity to attract more students from more denominations. Today, Memphis Theological Seminary has one of the most diverse student populations, in terms of denomination and race, of any seminary in the United States. This theological and denominational diversity provides a rich environment for educating pastors, chaplains, Christian educators, and other leaders for the church of Jesus Christ. The sign on our campus that faces Union Avenue reads: "Memphis Theological Seminary: an Ecumenical Mission of the Cumberland Presbyterian Church." Every Cumberland Presbyterian can be proud of the mission our seminary fulfills of educating our own church leaders, and leaders from more than 25 other denominations.

This year we have been celebrating the 50th anniversary of our move to Memphis. We are grateful for the step of faith taken by the MTS Board, the Cumberland Presbyterian General Assembly, and the church as a whole that has enabled our seminary to grow and thrive for the past 50 years.

We, the trustees and administration of Memphis Theological Seminary are privileged to be a part of this legacy, born out of and guided by the ecumenical and evangelical spirit of the Cumberland Presbyterian Church. We look forward to what God has in store for our ministry in the future. With gratitude for God's grace, guidance and provision in the past year, we make the following report to the 185th General Assembly of the Cumberland Presbyterian Church, meeting in Cali, Colombia.

I. BOARD OF TRUSTEES

A. OFFICERS
The following officers were elected by the Board of Trustees to serve during the past academic year: Moderator – Mr. Tim Orr (Cumberland Presbyterian, Dyersburg, Tennessee); Vice-moderator – Mrs. K. C. Warren (Presbyterian Church USA laywoman, Memphis, Tennessee); Secretary – Ms. Pat Meeks (Cumberland Presbyterian elder, Bartlett, Tennessee); Treasurer – Mrs. Cassandra Price-Perry (Vice President of Operations and CFO, MTS).

B. BOARD REPRESENTATIVE
Reverend Kevin Brantley (Cumberland Presbyterian, Cumberland Presbytery) was elected to serve as the Board's representative to this meeting of the General Assembly.

C. MEETINGS
The Board has met twice since the last meeting of General Assembly: October 2-3, 2014 and February 12-13, 2015. It is scheduled to meet one more time before the meeting of General Assembly, on May 15, 2015. In addition to full Board meetings, standing committees meet on a regular schedule between Board meetings, usually by conference call.

Members of our Board of Trustees devote significant time and resources to their work on behalf of the seminary. By rule of the General Assembly, thirteen of the twenty-four members are Cumberland Presbyterians. The other eleven members of the Board represent six different denominations.

D. EXPIRATION OF TERMS

The terms of eight of twenty-four members of the Board of Trustees expire each year. Six of the eight whose terms expire this year are eligible to succeed themselves and have agreed to serve another three year term: Reverend Kevin Brantley (Cumberland Presbyterian, Greensburg, Kentucky); Mr. Mark Maddox (Cumberland Presbyterian, Dresden, Tennessee); Mrs. Sondra Roddy (Cumberland Presbyterian, Clarksville, Tennessee); Mr. Takayoshi (Ted) Shirai (Cumberland Presbyterian, Yokohama, Japan), Rev. Dr. Melvin Charles Smith (Baptism, Memphis, Tennessee); and Ms. Litisha Towns (Baptist, Memphis, Tennessee). All have served faithfully and contributed greatly to the life of the seminary. We are grateful for their willingness to continue serving if re-elected.

One trustee submitted his resignation in February: Mr. David Reed (United Methodist, Martin, Tennessee). Two trustees are ineligible for re-election, having served three terms on the board. Both have served as officers, and have given significant service to MTS: Reverend Jody Hill (Cumberland Presbyterian, Corinth, Mississippi), and Mrs. Jan Holmes (Cumberland Presbyterian, Lubbock, Texas).

RECOMMENDATION 1: That the General Assembly express its gratitude to Reverend Jody Hill, Mrs. Jan Holmes, and Mr. David Reed for their faithful service to Memphis Theological Seminary and the Cumberland Presbyterian Church.

E. "MINISTRY FOR THE REAL WORLD"

The 183rd General Assembly approved a recommendation from our Board granting us permission to engage in a major capital campaign for Memphis Theological Seminary. The quiet phase of the campaign is continuing and we are raising funds for the purposes of building a new chapel, building our endowments, and securing the financial future of MTS. We encourage all Cumberland Presbyterians to pray for the success of this program as we work to secure the long term fiscal health of Memphis Theological Seminary.

II. ADMINISTRATION

A. PRESIDENT

Daniel J. (Jay) Earheart Brown, Ph.D., became the seventh President of Memphis Theological Seminary August 1, 2005. Jay had served on the faculty of MTS since August, 1997, having previously served as a pastor in Nashville, Tennessee, and Lexington, Kentucky. He is a life-long Cumberland Presbyterian and son of a Cumberland Presbyterian minister. He is a graduate of Bethel College (B.A.), Memphis Theological Seminary (M.Div.), and Union Theological Seminary in Richmond, Virginia (Ph.D.). He will complete his tenth year in this position at the end of the current academic year.

B. VICE PRESIDENT OF ACADEMIC AFFAIRS/DEAN

Reverend R. Stan Wood, D.Min., was appointed to serve as Interim Vice President of Academic Affairs and Dean in May, 2010. Dr. Wood had previously served MTS as Clara Scott Associate Professor of Ministry and Director of the D.Min. Program. He is an ordained minister in the Cumberland Presbyterian Church in America and currently serves as Pastor of the Mt. Tabor CPCA in Jackson, Tennessee.

C. VICE PRESIDENT OF ADVANCEMENT

In July 2014, Mrs. Cathi Johnson resigned her position as Vice President for Advancement to take a position with the Pink Palace Museum of Memphis. In October 2014, Dr. Keith Gaskin began his work as our new Vice President for Advancement. He is a Presbyterian layman with over 20 years of experience in advancement work, having most recently worked for Mississippi State University and the University of Alabama.

Keith has brought to his work at MTS a proven track record of higher education fundraising, a commitment to the mission of MTS, and the ability to manage and build on the efforts of those who have gone before him. The Board of Trustees is confident that Dr. Gaskin will be able to help us continue to improve our Advancement program at MTS.

D. VICE PRESIDENT OF OPERATIONS/CFO

Mrs. Cassandra Price-Perry began work with MTS in August 2010 as Vice President of Operations and Chief Financial Officer. She is a Certified Public Accountant with over 20 years of experience in business and accounting. Cassandra is an active laywoman in her Roman Catholic Church in Southaven, Mississippi. She has received high praise from our auditors and our Board for her work over the past four plus years.

E. Chief Information Officer

Reverend Cory Williams began work with MTS in 2009 as Director of Information Technology. He is an ordained minister in West Tennessee Presbytery of the Cumberland Presbyterian Church as serves in a part time position as Pastor of the Brunswick Cumberland Presbyterian Church in Shelby County, Tennessee. Following as reorganization last year, Cory was promoted to Chief Information Officer, with a broadened role in supervising our recruiting and marketing efforts, as well as providing oversight to the Library with its information services.

III. INSTRUCTION

A. Degree Programs

Memphis Theological Seminary offers four degree programs and three certificate programs, including the certificate offered through the Program of Alternate Studies. The Master of Divinity is the basic degree program for persons preparing for ordained ministry in many denominations. It continues to be our largest degree program, with over 70% of students enrolled. The M.Div. requires 87 semester hours and takes three years of full-time study to complete.

The Master of Arts (Religion) degree is an academic degree for persons seeking to pursue further graduate studies. The M.A.R. requires 42 semester hours and takes two years of full-time study to complete. This degree program has been revised to focus on the academic study of Christianity.

The Doctor of Ministry degree is a professional degree designed for pastors and other ministers who have at least three years of full-time work in ministry after their M.Div. and who want to engage in further theological reflection on the practice of ministry. The D.Min. is designed around five two-week residencies, in January and July, and the implementation of and report on a major project in ministry.

In the spring of 2013, we awarded our first new degree in several years: the Master of Arts in Youth Ministry (MAYM). Through our partnership with the Center for Youth Ministry Training in Brentwood, Tennessee, and the new certificate program in youth ministry through the Cumberland Presbyterian Church, we have 33 students enrolled in this degree program.

Our Board has approved, and we are in the application process with our accrediting bodies to begin a new degree program: the Master of Arts in Christian Ministry. This degree will consist of 42 hours and will allow students to specialize in Christian Education, rural ministry, urban ministry, or children and family ministry. We hope to be approved during the 2015-16 school year to award the MACM.

Certificate programs include: Program of Alternate Studies of the Cumberland Presbyterian Church, Drug and Alcohol Addiction Counseling Certificate, James Netters Certificate in Ministry, and the Certificate in Wesleyan Studies.

At Commencement in May of 2014, Memphis Theological Seminary awarded the Master of Arts in Youth Ministry degree to three graduates. Seven persons were awarded the Master of Arts (Religion) degree. Forty persons were awarded the Master of Divinity degree, and seventeen were awarded the Doctor of Ministry degree. Of these sixty-seven graduates, sixteen were Cumberland Presbyterians.

Cumberland Presbyterian Master of Arts (Religion) graduate was:
Margaret McFerrin Williams, West Tennessee Presbytery

Cumberland Presbyterian Master of Divinity graduates were:
Larry B. Buchanan, Covenant Presbytery
Garrett Alan Burns, Arkansas Presbytery
SeungMan Ezra Choi, East Tennessee Presbytery
Thomas C. Clark, Columbia Presbytery
Lisa Kay Cook, Nashville Presbytery
Judith M. Dulaney, West Tennessee Presbytery
Jennifer L. Hayes, Grace Presbytery
Brittany Paige Meeks, West Tennessee Presbytery
Jason Edward Mikel, Murfreesboro Presbytery
Dennis Wayne Morrison, Covenant Presbytery
Jennifer Muthoni Muraya, West Tennessee Presbytery
Steven Rogers, West Tennessee Presbytery
Blake Stephens, Murfreesboro Presbytery
April Ann Watson, Covenant Presbytery

Cumberland Presbyterian Doctor of Ministry graduate:
  Tiffany Hall McClung

B. Faculty

For the current academic year, Memphis Theological Seminary has eleven full-time teaching faculty and four administrative faculty members who teach part-time. In addition, the seminary curriculum is greatly enhanced by the work of twenty-five to thirty adjunct professors, most of whom are active in pastoral or other ministries.

Members of the MTS faculty continue to publish books and articles both for the academy and the church. Many faculty members preach in area churches on a regular basis, deliver lectures for local churches and judicatories, deliver papers at academic conferences, and write articles for a wide range of readers.

Under the leadership of VP/Dean Wood, the faculty is currently engaged in a major curriculum review and re-visioning process.

C. Enrollment

Total enrollment in Memphis Theological Seminary for the fall term was 406. We experienced a significant increase in the number of Cumberland Presbyterian students this year. Our largest denomination represented in the student body continues to be the United Methodist Church, with 25% of total enrollment in degree programs. Cumberland Presbyterians are the second largest denomination represented in the student body.

We continue to work to recruit Cumberland Presbyterian students, and to lift up the call of God to ordained ministry in the church. We call on all Cumberland Presbyterians to pray that God will continue to call men and women to the office of ministry, and that they will be well prepared through our educational institutions to lead growing and vibrant congregations in the ministry of Jesus Christ to the world.

The following chart shows statistics on our fall 2014 enrollment.

Memphis Theological Seminary
Quick Facts
Fall 2014

Take a moment to learn about MTS!

406 Enrolled in Degree and Certificate Programs

29 Denominations
Being Represented This Semester

Top 4 of 29 In Graduate Programs

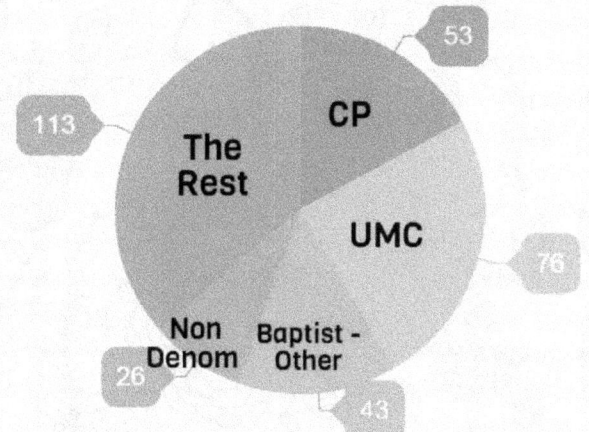

- CP: 53
- The Rest: 113
- UMC: 76
- Baptist - Other: 43
- Non Denom: 26

DID YOU KNOW?

15 Full Time Faculty

12 Adjunct Faculty

Student Faculty Ratio of 16:1

Enrollment By Program

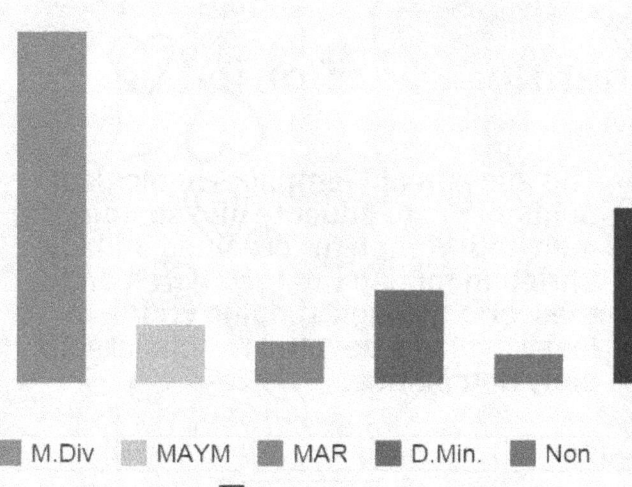

M.Div ■ MAYM ■ MAR ■ D.Min. ■ Non ■ Certificate

We offer several programs and graduate degrees.

- Master of Divinity
- Master of Arts in Youth Ministry
- Doctor of Ministry
- Methodist House of Studies
- Drug/Alcohol Addiction Counseling Program
- Netters Certificate in Congregational Ministry
- Certificate in Advanced CP Studies
- Pastoral Care Specialist and Pastoral Counseling Certificate Training

We Are Diverse

Our Youngest Student is 21

Our Oldest is 83

The Average Age is 44

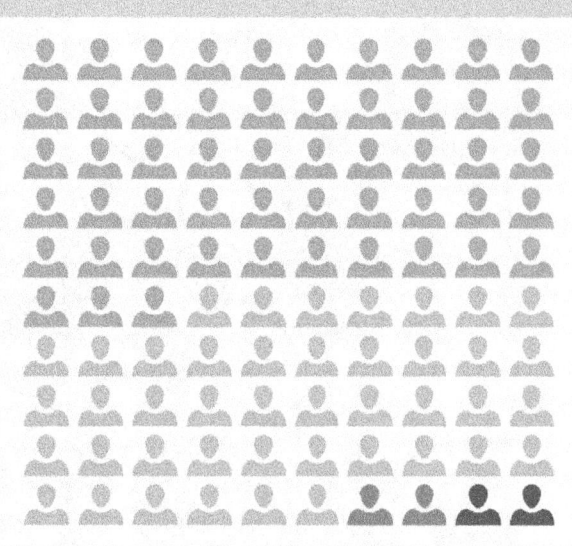

■ African American ■ Caucasian ■ Hispanic ■ Asian

We come from as close as Memphis and the surrounding region and as far as the UK, Africa, Asia and South America

You Might Also Like To Know

Our Library holdings include over 85,000 book and another 16,000+ Periodicals

We award over $2.5 Million Dollars in Federal Student loans each year!

There is an additional $103,235 in scholarships awarded for Fall 2014 alone!

44.4 % Female

55.5 % Male

Practical   Authentic   Spirit-Led

We are fully accredited by:

Association of Theological Schools (ATS)

Southern Association of Colleges and Schools (SACS)

The University Senate of the United Methodist Church

The mission of Memphis Theological Seminary is to educate and sustain men and women for ordained and lay Christian ministry in the church and the world through shaping and inspiring lives devoted to scholarship, piety and justice.

D. PROGRAM OF ALTERNATE STUDIES

The Program of Alternate Studies continues to help the Cumberland Presbyterian Church serve the world by preparing women and men for ordained ministry who have been hindered from the traditional route. It is the perfect corollary to MTS, our excellent seminary. Our denomination is one which values an educated clergy and is willing to be led by the Spirit to meet contextual needs.

1. Ministers from Other Traditions

One of the burgeoning areas for PAS in recent years is the preparation of ordained ministers coming into the denomination from other communions seeking to have their ordination recognized. This is a very enriching opportunity. It appears to be a trend that will continue so we are trying to stay abreast of the many issues in order to be a resource for presbytery Probationer Care Committees. There are a wide variety of approaches to preparation out there. It means reviewing each case.

2. Online Courses

We are this track to have all four CP Studies courses available online by the end of this year. To date we have offered CP Theology II and CP History in an asynchronous format allowing students some flexibility as to when they will access and interact with course material within the six-week progressive schedule. The experience has been, by all accounts, a terrific learning experience for both instructor and students. CP Polity and CP Theology I courses are slated to roll-out in the fall. With the geographic distances and sparse student populations, given especially the trend mentioned above, this will be a valuable tool for the presbyteries of the Cumberland Presbyterian Church into the future. We will evaluate fully at the end of the year with our PAS Advisory Council.

3. PAS-COLOMBIA

The Director will be on hand in Cali, Colombia to recognize the third anniversary of PAS-Colombia. It has been an amazing journey of faith and faithfulness. We wish to acknowledge the leadership of Rev. Michele Gentry and the PAS-Colombia Advisory Council with a special presentation at General Assembly. We will continue to develop three or four courses each year for translation and modification for the Colombian CP context.

4. Summer Extension School (SES)

The three blocks of SES will be July 11-25 at Bethel University. Graduation will be on Saturday July 11 at 11:00 am with Dr. Walter Butler, President of Bethel University, as commencement speaker. We have a terrific schedule of summer course offerings for regular PAS students and for anyone who wishes to enlighten themselves in areas of theological studies or ministry. Access the PAS page on the MTS Website, visit us on Facebook, or call the office for details.

The joint course taken by MDiv students AND PAS students will be ReVangelism taught by Dr. Michael Qualls July 21-25. This practical course will help students:

1) examine the Biblical/theological rationale for the enterprise of making disciples,
2) develop a "missional ecclesiology" that affirms the critical role of the local congregation in contextualizing the gospel,
3) learn to provide strategic leadership for congregations which bear faithful witness in the cultural context of postmodern pluralistic America,
4) explore practical tools and methodologies currently employed in holistic, healthy churches that are welcoming communities of faith.

The Pastoral Development Ministry Team offers scholarships to "retreat" at Bethel that coincide with the last block of SES. We invite auditors to any of our classes.

5. Pete Palmer Recognized

Reverend Pete Palmer was driven by a quest for knowledge. After graduating from seminary he continued to attend PAS every summer to audit courses until, at summer school last year he suffered a fall that resulted in his death at the age of 87. In honor of that kind of desire we are establishing the Pete Palmer Endowment for the Program of Alternate Studies. The proceeds will be used to help pay tuition for students. It will fulfill Pete's wishes and will continue his learning legacy long after his final flight.

E. ACCREDITATION

Memphis Theological Seminary holds dual accreditation by the Association of Theological

Schools in the United States and Canada (ATS), and the Southern Association of Colleges and Schools (SACS). Every ten years, member schools go through an extensive process of re-accreditation review. We are also approved by the University Senate of the United Methodist Church for educating ministers for that denomination.

Our last accreditation visit occurred in 2008, at which time we were fully affirmed for the next ten years by both accrediting bodies.

IV. FACILITIES

A. LEADERSHIP
Since the summer of 2014, our facilities and safety department has been ably led by Mr. Andy Santucci and a dedicated staff of facilities technicians. Mr. Santucci came to MTS after many years of experience with Memphis Light, Gas and Water, and Baptist Memorial Hospital in Memphis.

B. COMMUTER HOUSING
MTS began to convert its student housing from individual rentals to commuter housing in the 1998. Currently, MTS provides commuter housing, with very reasonable nightly rates, for about fifty students each week of the regular term. The need for such commuter housing has continued to grow, as has income from such rentals. Our ability to serve students from about a 250 mile radius around Memphis, through block scheduling of classes and provision of affordable commuter housing, has had a significant impact on the growth of the student body over the past ten years.

C. CAMPUS WORK GROUPS
We have been blessed in recent years by adult and youth work groups who have come to MTS during the summer months to help repair and maintain our campus housing. Groups have come from Trilla, Illinois, Greeneville, Tennessee, Florence, Alabama, Bowling Green, Kentucky, and Collierville, Tennessee, and the youth from West Tennessee Presbytery to volunteer their time in a variety of areas. We encourage work groups who would be willing to help the seminary in this way to contact Mr. Greg Spencer in the Facilities Office, or Mrs. Cathi Johnson in the Advancement Office of the seminary.

D. SAFETY
The Office of Safety of MTS continues to explore ways to enhance the safety of our students in the context of our urban campus. Through the use of lighting, security officers, secure locks, and well articulated safety plans, the seminary seeks to provide a safe environment for students and visitors to our campus.

During past four years, MTS has contracted with a local security company to provide regular patrols around our neighborhood. This additional safety measure has been well received by our students and by our neighbors. We continue to seek ways to provide a safe environment for our campus community.

V. ADVANCEMENT AND FINANCE

A. BUDGET
Our Board of Trustees will approve a budget for the 2014-2015 academic year at its May meeting. Copies of that budget will be provided at the meeting of General Assembly.

After two years of significant budget reductions in the worst of the recession, we have begun to restore some of the cuts as income has improved the past two years. We continue to be very conservative in our budget planning as we work to recover from the effects of the recession. We were able to give modest raises to our employees next year, after four years of flat or reduced compensation. Our employees deserve much credit for hanging in with us through some tough economic times.

B. SCHOLARSHIPS AND GRANTS
We continue to cultivate relationships with foundations whose mission closely aligns with ours. In the previous year we have received Grant funding from the Assisi Foundation of Memphis, the Wilson Family Foundation, and the Eli Lilly Endowment of Indianapolis, Indiana.

Persons and churches are encouraged to consider funding scholarships for our students so that they can pursue their callings without taking on educational debt.

C. ENDOWMENTS

Our current endowment for MTS stands a little over $9 million. Those endowed funds support operations, scholarships, faculty work, and the library operations, among other elements of our overall work. We regularly talk to donors and prospective donors about gifts to endowed funds for the future work of MTS.

D. ESTATE GIFTS

MTS has been notified of two estate gifts that we will be receiving in the near future. We are deeply grateful for these two men and their commitment to the ministry of MTS:

Dr. Virgil Todd, former Professor of Old Testament, former Moderator of the General Assembly, and lifelong Cumberland Presbyterian minister.

Reverend Walter (Pete) Palmer, M.Div. class of 2000, of Tulsa, Oklahoma. Pete was a faithful donor to the work of MTS and the Program of Alternate Studies for many years.

E. SEMINARY SUNDAY

We have many churches in our denomination, and in other denominations we serve who recognize Seminary Sunday in their local churches. This provides time for education of members about the work of MTS and the Program of Alternate Studies and provides an opportunity for members to make a special one-time gift to support the work of the seminary. Please contact the seminary for more information on how you can recognize Seminary Sunday in your local church, and to request a speaker for the occasion.

RECOMMENDATION 2: That the General Assembly encourage all churches to recognize and support Seminary Sunday.

F. ANNUAL FUND

Memphis Theological Seminary could not operate without the faithful contribution of its alumni and friends. Annual Fund contributions help us keep the cost of tuition down, so that students do not leave seminary with a large burden of debt to have to pay during their early years in ministry. Annual Fund contributions have grown steadily over the past fifteen years, as income from Our United Outreach has declined.

In some respects, the income we receive from OUO puts us in a better position than many theological seminaries, whose income from denominational sources has declined significantly over the past twenty years. Our income from OUO has remained relatively steady and over that time period. However, as a percentage of our total income, OUO has fallen from almost 20% to about 3% of our operating budget. We are grateful for the commitment of Cumberland Presbyterians to the ministry of MTS, and all our common ministries, expressed so tangibly through giving to Our United Outreach.

At the same time, we do not expect income from denominational contributions to increase significantly in the future. This means that we are required to put more time and energy into fund raising than ever before. We are grateful for the many alumni who have made a financial contribution to our ministry this year. We are also grateful for all the faithful laypersons who have given to the Annual Fund because they know the importance of an educated ministry to the life and health of our denomination.

G. AUDIT REPORT

The auditing firm of Zoccola Kaplan, P.C. has audited the books of Memphis Theological Seminary for the 2013-2014. The audit was unqualified, and noted several significant improvements in the financial position of MTS. Copies of that report have been filed with the office of the Stated Clerk.

Respectfully submitted,
Tim Orr, Moderator of the Board of Trustees
Daniel J. Earheart-Brown, President
Michael Qualls, Director of the Program of Alternate Studies

THE REPORT OF THE
OUR UNITED OUTREACH COMMITTEE

The 2009 General Assembly established a denominational Our United Outreach Committee to be made up of 12 voting representatives, one from each Synod and the rest from the church programs and institutions. Executives from the church programs and institutions participate on the Committee as advisory members. This Committee meets annually unless there is a needed called meeting.

A goal of the Our United Outreach Committee is to encourage ALL churches to contribute to Our United Outreach. Approximately 30 percent of the churches do not give anything with a high percentage of other churches not giving at the 10 percent level. This past year, 2014, the budgeted goal for Our United Outreach was $2,900,000 – 88% giving was achieved. While this was an admirable achievement, the Committee seeks to involve ALL churches with Our United Outreach giving and at a greater level of giving.

I. OUR UNITED OUTREACH FUNDS ALLOCATION

The Our United Outreach Committee met April 24, 2015, to allocate the Our United Outreach funds for the 2016 year. The Our United Outreach allocation basis for 2016 is $2,800,000.

The 2012 General Assembly had two funding requests which affected the allocation process beginning in 2014. One of these requests has been completed. One of these two requests still affects the funding process in 2016. This is that $3,500 a year for three years—2014, 2015, 2016—be budgeted out of Our United Outreach funds for the use of the Evaluation Committee when doing agency evaluations.

The 2013 General Assembly had one funding request from the Unification Task Force which was for $20,000 a year starting in 2014 but has been increased to $30,000 for 2016.

These requests, along with the Development Coordinator's salary/benefits, have been approved as guaranteed amounts and are deducted from the goal amount prior to allocation purposes.

RECOMMENDATION 1: We ask General Assembly that the following allocation for incoming 2016 for Our United Outreach funds be adopted:

The allocation is to be as follows:	$2,800,000.00		
Development Coordinator		92,044.00	
Evaluation Committee		3,500.00	
Contingency		14,000.00	
Unification Task Force		30,000.00	
	Sub-total	139,544.00	
(Amount to be allocated)	$2,660,456.00		
Ministry Council	$1,330,228.00		50%
Bethel University	133,023.00		5%
Children's Home	79,814.00		3%
Stewardship	159,627.00		6%
General Assembly Office	212,836.00		8%
Memphis Theological Seminary/ Program of Alternate Studies	186,231.00		7%
Historical Foundation	79,814.00		3%
Shared Services	452,278.00		17%
(Next four items total 1%)			
Comm. on Chaplains	10,296.00		.387%
Judiciary Committee	9,710.00		.365%
Theology/Social Concerns	3,618.00		.136%
Nominating Committee	2,981.00		.112%
	$2,660,456.00		
Our United Outreach Goal	$2,800,000.00		

From the agencies listed above, all should be self-explanatory except maybe Shared Services. Maintenance, utilities, mowing, trash pick-up, pest extermination, and custodial are all examples of Shared Services for agencies sharing the Cumberland Presbyterian Center.

II. OUR UNITED OUTREACH EDUCATION

It is important that all within the bounds of the Cumberland Presbyterian Church be educated on the importance of Our United Outreach and the many benefits these funds provide. While OUO funds help provide for the staffing and operation of the Cumberland Presbyterian Church Center, funds also help feed children, provide camps, and help educate future leaders. Many of the programs and facilities here in Colombia, are in part funded through Our United Outreach.

The Our United Outreach Committee members are enthusiastic in their approach to the development of total participation in this program of the church.

Respectfully submitted,
Ron Gardner, Chairperson
Reverend Lanny Johnson, Vice-Chairperson
Sharon Resch – Secretary
and the Our United Outreach Committee

THE REPORT OF THE COMMISSION ON MILITARY CHAPLAINS AND PERSONNEL

The Commission on on Military Chaplains and Personnel represents the Cumberland Presbyterian Church on the Presbyterian Council for Chaplains and Military Personnel (PCCMP). The commission does its work through the Council which has its headquarters in Washington D.C. and represents also the Cumberland Presbyterian Church in America, Presbyterian Church (USA) and the Korean Presbyterian Church Abroad. The Cumberland Presbyterians who are members of the Commission for the Cumberland Presbyterian Church and hence the broader group known as the PCCMP include the Reverend Mary McCaskey Benedict, the Reverend Cassandra Thomas, the Reverend Lowell G. Roddy, and Stated Clerk the Reverend Michael Sharpe.

I. REPRESENTATION

The term of the Reverend Mary McCaskey Benedict expires in 2016. For 2015, one of the four PCCMP Executive Board positions is filled by CPC member: the Reverend Cassandra O. Thomas as Secretary. The Reverend Mary McCaskey Benedict is now the Chairperson of the Personnel Committee. In 2014, the Reverend Lowell G. Roddy stepped down as Chair of the Council. In February 2015, he submitted his resignation from the council due to health concerns. Lowell served the council with great effectiveness and will be missed. Council staff and members lauded his long standing pastoral care, wise counsel and compassionate ministry. The Chair of the PCCMP is now the Reverend Donna Weddle (PCUSA) and the vice-chair is the Reverend Jung-Soo Park, (PCUSA).

II. RESPONSIBILITY OF THE PCCMP

1. Provide ecclesiastical endorsement for chaplains of the United States Armed Forces who are serving on active duty or in the Reserves/National Guard. The PCCMP also endorses chaplains for the Department of Veterans Affairs. In addition, the PCCMP endorses PCUSA teaching elders into chaplaincy positions with the Civil Air Patrol and the Federal Bureau of Prisons.
2. Provide pastoral support for chaplains and their families.
3. Provide a unified and influential voice for member denominations to the National Council on Ministry to the Armed Forces in matters relating to the ministry and welfare of PCCMP-endorsed clergy.
4. Provide representation to denominational agencies and ecumenical bodies with respect to matters relating to United States military personnel, veterans and their families.
5. Promote closer communications between chaplains and denominational judicatories.
6. Carry out other duties as may be requested by the member denominations.

III. ANNUAL PCCMP MEETING

The annual meeting of the PCCMP takes place in the fall, with representatives of the member denominations in attendance. In 2014, the Council met in Nashville, Tennessee. In 2015, the Council will meet in the CPC office complex in Memphis. During this meeting, the Council discusses and takes action as necessary on business that comes to its attention during the year. The 2014 meeting was the first conducted under the leadership of the PCCMP's new director, the Reverend Dr. Lawrence P. Greenslit, a 27-year Navy veteran who is a teaching elder in the PCUSA. The previous director, the Reverend Ed Brogan, retired in May 2014.

Sometimes, candidates for ecclesiastical endorsement will come before the Interview Committee at this meeting, though this did not happen in 2014. Generally, candidates are required to submit an application, school transcripts, proof that their presbytery approves their seeking this call, and letters of reference. After the documents are gathered, candidates are interviewed personally to determine if they should be endorsed for active duty or service with the Reserve/National Guard and/or Veteran's Administration (VA). A recommendation for each candidate is then submitted to the Council. If they are approved by the Council, then they make application to the various branches of service. The PCCMP maintains sound working relations with the Chief of Chaplains for each branch of the ministry and the VA. In addition, work is being done to provide support to Civil Air Patrol chaplains of the PCCMP Presbyterian members and for the PCUSA, oversight to those seeking to be chaplains for the Federal Department of Justice. Of note for clergy interested in applying to be chaplains in the Navy, a new policy requires two years of post-ordination pastoral experience as part of their package submission.

IV. SUPPORT FOR THE COUNCIL

The Council receives financial support from the four denominations, as well as individuals, judicatories, and churches. The current economic challenges in our country are creating a need to redesign how to minister to our chaplains and their families. We will be faithful stewards as we care for our chaplains and their families.

The Cumberland Presbyterian Churches support this ministry by taking an annual Memorial Day Offering. The PCCMP has also developed resources (a 2½ minute video and a bulletin insert) for congregations that may wish to conduct an offering on Four Chaplains Sunday, which is traditionally held on the first Sunday in February. Congregations may conduct a special offering at a time it deems convenient, such as the Sundays closest to Independence Day or Veteran's Day. In this way, CPC congregations can show support for all men and women, who serve or have served in the United States Armed Services, Reserves, Guard, VA, and CAP, as well as their families. The offerings are sent to the General Assembly Stated Clerk and are then forwarded to the Council for its outreach, mission, and maintenance efforts. The Commission would like to express its deepest appreciation to all churches that collected offerings for the PCCMP during 2014 and 2015 to date. All Cumberland Presbyterian Churches are urged to consider their involvement in this vital ministry to God, country, and Presbyterians.

V. CUMBERLAND PRESBYTERIAN CHAPLAINS

We are proud to say that our denomination has a total of 8 men or women currently involved in various forms of chaplaincy around the world, *1 pending active duty compliance and 3 chaplain candidates. There are 4 full-time chaplains with the VA.

	Active Duty	Reserves
Army	3	2
Air Force	1	1
Navy	*1 pending	

	VA	National Guard	Chaplain Candidates
Full time	4	1	3
Part time	0		

Please remember to pray for those servings in this important ministry and their loved ones. Names and addresses are included in the Yearbook of the Cumberland Presbyterian Church.

Anyone desiring more information can check the CPC website: www.cumberland.org/ccmp or the PCCMP website: www.pccmp.org.

Respectively Submitted,
Reverend Cassandra Thomas
Reverend Mary McCaskey Benedict

THE REPORT OF THE
PERMANENT JUDICIARY COMMITTEE

The Judiciary Committee met February 27, 2015 in Huntsville, Alabama. Present were Harry Chapman, Sherry Ladd, Charles Dawson, Andy McClung, Robert Rush, Kimberly Silvus, Wendell Thomas, and Felicia Walkup. Also attending were Jaime Jordan, legal counsel, and Mike Sharpe, Stated Clerk of General Assembly. Annetta Camp was excused.

I. ORGANIZATION OF THE COMMITTEE

Kimberly Silvus was elected chairperson. Wendell Thomas was elected vice-chairperson. Andy McClung was elected secretary.

II. GENERAL ASSEMBLY REFERRAL

The 184th General Assembly instructed this committee to work with the Missions Ministry Team of the denominational Ministry Council to develop an amendment that would constitutionally empower the Missions Ministry Team to develop churches and pastors outside the United States. A subcommittee is currently working with representatives from the Missions Ministry Team to achieve this goal.

III. REVIEW OF SYNODICAL MINUTES

The committee reviewed the actions of Synod of Great Rivers, Synod of the Midwest, Mission Synod, Synod of the Southeast, and Tennessee Synod. With one universal exception, the minutes were well organized, in good order, and in proper form.

The one universal exception is that the synods, although reviewing their constituent presbyteries' minutes, have no record of reviewing, in particular, ministers' ordinations within the presbyteries.

This committee encourages each synod to commit specific time and effort to reviewing its constituent presbyteries' ordinations (see Cumberland Presbyterian Digest 8.5b Interpretive 1892, 1972, and 8.5b Advisory, 1964).

Respectfully submitted,
The Judiciary Committee

THE REPORT OF THE NOMINATING COMMITTEE

The Nominating Committee consists of a minister and a lay person from each synod, preferably from different presbyteries. Members may serve a three year term, but cannot succeed themselves. Cumberland Presbyterian members of any board or committee can be re-elected to the same board after a two year absence. Ecumenical representatives may be re-elected to the same board after a one year absence. With the exception of the Nominating Committee any person elected to serve on a denominational entity may serve three consecutive terms. Filling an unexpired term counts as one term, thus members of any entity do not always serve nine years before completing eligibility on a board/agency.

The members of the various Ministry Teams are no longer elected by the General Assembly, but are to be appointed by the Ministry Council.

*Ecumenical Representative   +Cumberland Presbyterian Church in America

The Committee submits the following list of nominees:

I. BOARD OF DIRECTORS, GENERAL ASSEMBLY CORPORATION

Ms. Calotta Edsel, First Church, Olive Branch, MS, West Tennessee Presbytery, for a three-year term.
Reverend Norlan Scrudder, Red River Presbytery, Mission Synod, for a three-year term.

II. MINISTRY COUNCIL

Mr. Ken Bean, West Tennessee Presbytery, Great Rivers Synod, for a three-year term.
Reverend Phillip Layne, Tennessee-Georgia Presbytery, Synod of the Southeast, for a three-year term.
Reverend Paula Louder, Nashville Presbytery, Tennessee Synod, for a three-year term.
Reverend Ron McMillan, West Tennessee Presbytery, Great Rivers Synod, for a three-year term.
Ms. Patricia Smith, Cumberland Presbytery, Synod of the Midwest, for a three-year term.
Mr. Caleb Davis, Youth Advisory Member, Trinity Presbytery, Mission Synod, for a one-year term.
Ms. Emily Mahoney, Youth Advisory Member, Murfreesboro Presbytery, Tennessee Synod, for a
    one-year term.

III. HISTORICAL FOUNDATION

Reverend Lisa Oliver, Murfreesboro Presbytery, Tennessee Synod, for a three-year term.
Dr. Sidney Swindle, Christ Church, Grace Presbytery, Synod of the Southeast, for a three-year term.

IV. MEMPHIS THEOLOGICAL SEMINARY

Reverend Kevin Brantley, Cumberland Presbytery, Synod of the Midwest, for a three-year term.
*Ms. Nancy Cole, an ecumenical partner, for a two-year unexpired term.
Reverend Kevin Henson, Red River Presbytery, Mission Synod, for a three-year term.
Reverend Linda Howell, Grace Presbytery, Synod of Southeast, for a three-year term.
Mr. Mark Maddox, Dresden Congregation, West Tennessee Presbytery, Synod of Great Rivers,
    for a three-year term.
Ms. Sondra Roddy, Nashville Presbytery, Tennessee Synod, for a three-year term.
Mr. Takayoshi Shirai, Japan Presbytery, Mission Synod, for a three-year term.
*Reverend Melvin Charles Smith, an ecumenical partner, for a three-year term.
*Ms. Latisha Towns, an ecumenical partner, for a three-year term.

V. BOARD OF STEWARDSHIP, FOUNDATION AND BENEFITS

Mr. Andrew Frazier, Camden Congregation, West Tennessee Presbytery, Synod of Great Rivers,
    for a three-year term.
Mr. James Shannon, Germantown Congregation, West Tennessee Presbytery, Synod of Great Rivers,
    for a three-year term.
Mr. Michael St. John, White Oak Pond Congregation, Missouri Presbytry, Synod of Great Rivers,
    for a three-year term.

VI. COMMISSION ON CHAPLAINS AND MILITARY PERSONNEL

Reverend Tony Janner, West Tennessee Presbytery, Synod of Great Rivers, for a three-year term.

VII. JUDICIARY

Reverend Annetta Camp, West Tennessee Presbytery, Synod of Great Rivers, for a three-year term.
Ms. Kimberly Silvus, Clarksville Congregation, Nashville Presbytery, Tennessee Synod, for a three-year term.
Mr. Bill Tally, Robert Donnell Presbytery, Synod of the Southeast, for a three-year term.

VIII. NOMINATING

Reverend Thomas Campbell, Arkansas Presbytery, Synod of Great Rivers, for a three-year term.
Ms. Heather Morgan, Murfreesboro Presbytery, Tennessee Synod, for a three-year term.

IX. OUR UNITED OUTREACH COMMITTEE

Mr. Randy Weathersby, Hope Presbytery, Synod of the Southeast, for a three-year term.
Ms. Robin Wills, Murfreesboro Presbytery, Tennessee Synod, for a three-year term.

X. UNIFIED COMMITTEE ON THEOLOGY AND SOCIAL CONCERNS

Mr. David Phillips-Burk, West Tennessee Presbytery, Synod of Great Rivers, for a three-year term.
Reverend George Estes, Presbytery del Cristo, Mission Synod, for a three-year term.
Reverend Shelia O'Mara, Presbytery del Cristo, Mision Synod, for a three-year term.

THE REPORT OF THE PLACE OF MEETING COMMITTEE

The The Place of Meeting Committee consists of the Moderator, a representative of the Cumberland Presbyterian Women's Ministry, and the Stated Clerk who serves as the chairperson. The representative of the Cumberland Presbyterian Women's Ministry is the Convention Coordinator.

The 165th General Assembly, "authorized the committee to select meeting places up to five years in the future and that preference be given that keeps, insofar as possible, the General Assembly and the Convention of Cumberland Presbyterian Women's Ministry, and guest rooms in one facility. It is recognized that these places are hard to find and may cost some additional monies. The place of meeting committee will use its best judgment." The 173rd General Assembly approved exploring the use of college campuses and very large conference centers in addition to hotels/convention centers. When the Office of the General Assembly receives an invitation from a congregation or a presbytery, the Stated Clerk makes a site visit. If adequate facilities are discovered, a follow up visit is made by the Stated Clerk, the Assistant to the Stated Clerk, and the Convention Coordinator of the Cumberland Presbyterian Women's Ministry.

Unless the General Assembly sets aside Bylaw 14.02 Standing Rules 1 to allow for a different meeting time, the annual meeting is the third or the fourth week of June.

Commissioners, delegates to Conventions, and visitors are encouraged to stay at the General Assembly/Convention hotel, to assure meeting the contracted room block. Hotel contracts also include a commitment on food and beverages, thus it is important for boards/agencies to continue to sponsor special meal functions. The luncheons/dinners provide opportunities for the sponsoring agencies/boards to keep the church informed about their respective programs, thus enhancing support.

I. INFORMATION ABOUT FUTURE GENERAL ASSEMBLIES

There has been some initial communications with the Chandler Congregation, Bethel University and Choctaw Presbytery (hosted jointly with some additional Oklahoma Congregations in Red River Presbytery) about the possibility of hosting a meeting of the General Assembly.

Bethel University has extended an invitation. The Convention Coordinator, Moderator, Stated Clerk will make plans for an official site visit to the campus this fall along with leadership from the Cumberland Presbyterian Church in America. Continued discussions with the leadership of the Cumberland Presbyterian Church in America regarding joint meetings of the General Assemblies in 2017 and 2018 may also impact future meeting locations.

It is helpful to continue scheduling a few years in advance of the meeting to assure that adequate hotel/convention space is available. If a congregation or a presbytery is interested in hosting the General Assembly/Convention, the Office of the General Assembly will provide information on hosting responsibilities. Hosting the General Assembly/Convention is a service to the Church, allowing the Church to celebrate the good ministries occurring within a particular presbytery, and provides persons within a presbytery the opportunity to participate more fully in the annual meeting.

In the event that no invitation is received in a particular year or a situation arises requiring a change of venue for a particular year, the Corporate Board will be responsible for selecting a place of meeting.

II. SCHEDULE OF FUTURE GENERAL ASSEMBLIES

186th   Nashville, Tennessee   June 20-24, 2016

III. FUTURE INVITATIONS

Bethel University has extended an invitation to host General Assembly. The Convention Coordinator of the Cumberland Presbyterian Women's Ministry, the Moderator and the Stated Clerk will schedule an official site visit this fall to the campus, to determine whether there is adequate facilities (lodging and meeting space) at Bethel to accommodate a joint meeting of the CPC and CPCA Assemblies.

IV. SCHEDULE OF MEETINGS BY PRESBYTERIES

The following schedule shows the annual meetings and the year that the General Assembly last met in the bounds of a particular presbytery.

Chattanooga	2014	East Tennessee	2003
Murfreesboro	2013	Covenant	2002
Hope & Robert Donnell	2012	del Cristo	2001
Missouri	2011	Cumberland	2000
Nashville	2010	Tennessee-Georgia	1998
West Tennessee	2009	Robert Donnell	1996
Japan	2008	Nashville	1995
Arkansas	2007	North Central	1980
Grace	2006	Trinity	1969
Columbia	2005	Hope	1961
Red River	2004	Murfreesboro	1956

Respectfully submitted,
Michael G. Sharpe
Pam Phillips Burk
Lisa Anderson

THE REPORT OF THE UNIFIED COMMITTEE ON THEOLOGY AND SOCIAL CONCERNS

I. MEETING AND OFFICERS

The Unified Committee on Theology and Social Concerns met at the Cumberland Presbyterian Church in America Denominational Center on October 10-11, 2014 and by teleconference on March 27, 2015. The following officers were elected during the fall meeting: Joy Wallace (CPCA) and Reverend Byron Forester (CPC) Co-Chairs; and Reverend Nancy Fuqua (CPCA), Secretary.

II. EXPIRATION OF TERMS

The Committee notes that the terms of service for the Reverend George Estes, Mr. David Phillips-Burk and Reverend Shelia O'Mara all expire in 2015, but each are eligible to be reelected.

III. GENERAL ASSEMBLY REPRESENTATIVES

The committee elected David Phillips-Burke to serve as the representative to the meeting of the CPC General Assembly in Cali, Colombia.

IV. GENERAL ASSEMBLY REFERRAL

The 184th General Assembly directed the Unified Committee on Theology and Social Concerns "to study the scriptures references for Section 3.08 of the 1984 Confession of Faith to see if could be further clarified or strengthened by the addition of John 14:6 or other scripture references."

The committee studied the scriptural passage John 14:6, both as a group and individually. A subcommittee of the Unified Committee on Theology and Social Concerns also met via video conference with representatives from the Theology and Social Concerns Committee of Grace Presbytery, to discuss their concerns regarding this referral.

The committee concluded that the additional passage is not needed to further clarify nor strengthen Section 3.08 of the Confession of Faith.

V. STUDY PAPERS

The Committee presents the following paper "Come, Let Us Reason Together, Being Faithful in the Midst of Conflict" for consideration by the General Assemblies.

"COME LET US DISAGREE TOGETHER"
BEING FAITHFUL IN THE MIDST OF CONFLICT

The following statement might qualify as a perfect illustration of an understatement: "Christians have disagreed passionately *with each other* throughout our history." Truth is, we have frequently disagreed *forcefully* with each other, so much so that oftentimes when we look back on our history, we are dismayed by the behavior of our forebears and wonder how followers of Jesus could be so hate-filled in their responses to one another. Perhaps, then, one source of agreement among us today would be that we wish not to follow in *these* footsteps left by past believers.

Such a desire is not so easily carried out, however, when we still disagree passionately among ourselves. As this paper is being written, any number of issues divides Christians in many churches, including some CP and CPCA churches. Since we know there were causes of conflict in the past and believe there likely will be new ones in the future, the Joint Commission on Theology and Social Concerns has chosen to ask Cumberland Presbyterians via this paper to give attention to the issue of conflict itself (rather than any specific source of conflict). The Commission's concern is this: What will we do *when* we disagree over theology and social concerns? How are we to be faithful to Jesus in the midst of conflict with others who are following Jesus differently from us?

There are a number of fruitful arenas wherein we might seek answers to these questions. For example, there are good studies on the process of conflict resolution from which church folk can benefit. In this paper the Commission proposes that we turn to our foundational document, to Holy Scripture, and allow Paul's first letter to the Corinthian believers to help us. First Corinthians is an excellent text for our concerns because the new community of believers to whom Paul was writing was embroiled in conflict (see 1 Cor. 1:11). Furthermore, they were treating one another badly as they disagreed among themselves (see, as an example, 11:20-22). Examining Paul's counsel to them, therefore, should be instructive for us for those times when we find ourselves in conflict.

After some background information regarding the circumstances surrounding 1 Corinthians, we will examine two passages within the letter. The first, 1:18-31, gives Paul's opening response to the conflict among Corinthian believers. The second, 12:12-27, presents Paul's discussion of "the body of Christ" as part of his response to one conflict among them, a concern over spiritual gifts. The lessons gained from these texts can then allow us to consider how we might respond faithfully to one another in the midst of conflict.

The Background of the Writing of 1 Corinthians

Since every biblical text was written by a real human being to other real human beings living in a certain time and place, the more we know about these people, their times, and their places, the better we may read these texts. We begin our study of 1 Corinthians then by noting that Paul, an apocalyptic Jew who believed that Jesus of Nazareth was the Jewish Messiah who had come to launch the Messianic Age, arrived in the Greco-Roman city of Corinth (located in what we now call Greece) sometime near 50 CE and successfully "planted a church" there. Both the city of Corinth and the believers who responded to Paul's preaching shape the story which unfolds from this point.

The great Greek city of Corinth was conquered by the Romans in 146 BCE, showing the rest of Greece the price of opposing Rome's interests. Julius Caesar re-founded the city in 44 BCE. Sitting astride a narrow isthmus (in what is now southern Greece) between the sea lanes leading to Italy on one side and Asia on the other, the city's commercial, political, and military advantages virtually demanded its re-establishment. When Rome decided to do so, it hastily recruited such people as former slaves (called freedpersons), displaced peasants, and unemployed military veterans to re-populate the city. Scholars have referred to these new Corinthians as a chaotic mixture of "dislocated, deracinated individuals, the most successful of whom had good reason to cast off unpleasant reminders" of their former lives.[1] The seaports brought much commerce to the city as well as settlers from around the Mediterranean world eager to participate in a booming economy. This commerce, in turn, created a prosperous banking system so that great personal wealth was generated for the new Corinthians, among whom was formed a "local ruling class of self-made women and men"[2] loyal to the ways of the emperor. Such opportunities were not available to most people in the Roman Empire. So Corinth was a new (though old) Roman city with new opportunity, new money, new people, new leaders, etc. Its environment was chaotic and competitive. The city has been compared to San Francisco during the gold rush days.

The new community of Jesus followers which Paul called into being reflected the diversity in the city: these believers were Jew and Gentile, male and female, high-born, slave, and every socio-economic class in between. Some of them apparently also reflected the competitiveness of the city in their dealings with fellow believers. While in Ephesus during his so-called "Third Missionary Journey" (about the year 53 CE), Paul got news that "issues" had arisen among Corinthian believers which had led to factions and infighting among them. Some of these issues were no doubt due to the challenges of relating to one another (e.g., slaves and non-slaves, men and women, etc., were unaccustomed to relating to one another). Others were the result of cultural differences (e.g., Greco-Roman folk struggling with Jewish apocalyptic thinking), and others simply to being so new at following Jesus. Ethical and theological debates were bound to occur in such a setting. But Paul seems to have perceived that there was one particular issue lying beneath many of the problems surfacing among the Corinthian faithful: Some of the believers considered themselves wise, spiritual, and superior to others in the community (see e.g., 1 Cor 3:18, 4:6-8). Impressed with their own spirituality, they treated other believers as "less than" themselves. Such a status-seeking spirituality would have been at home in the culture of Corinth, but it was wrecking the new Christian community there as believers sought to "beat down" those who disagreed with them. Paul wrote the letter we call 1 Corinthians to address this situation.

1 Corinthians 1:18-31

After greeting the Corinthian saints (1:1-4) and offering his opening prayer (1:4-9), Paul turns to his reason for writing as he calls the believers to turn aside from the "schisms" (1:10) which he has heard are plaguing them (1:11-12). At 1:18 he is ready to begin his theological rationale for calling them to unity with the passage we Christians often call "The Foolishness of the Cross." Here is a text worth exploring.

The focus of this text is knowing God. We should remember the biblical understanding of "know," which, as one seminary professor once said, isn't "head knowledge" (see Gen. 4:1). There is a world of difference between *knowing* as the intellectual acquisition of facts (for ex., knowing that 2 + 2 = 4), and *knowing* your spouse, your sibling, your best friend, or God, etc. Paul is concerned about the latter kind of knowing (see 1 Cor. 13:12).

One key aspect of Paul's discussion in the text is *wisdom*. We do not, Paul says, know God through wisdom (v 21). Indeed, God has made foolish "the wisdom of the world" (v. 20) even as God's wisdom seems like foolishness to unbelievers (v. 18). The repetition of the idea of wisdom suggests that it had become an issue among Corinthian believers. Perhaps they valued persuasive arguments or deducible logic as was found in the great Greek philosophical traditions. Whatever they favored, Paul called it the "wisdom of the world" and declared that it was not the way to know God.

We can note that, while deducible logic had not held a lofty place in many Jewish traditions, some Jews had their own form of proving to others that they understood God better: signs. The great acts of God in Jewish history, particularly those associated with the Exodus, were signs which made God known

But Paul insists we know God through neither wisdom nor signs. The central claim he makes in this passage is:

> A For Jews demand signs and Greeks seek wisdom,
>
> > B But we preach Christ who was crucified,
>
> A' A scandal to Jews and foolishness to Greeks... (vv 22-23).

These two verses are arranged (above) in a *chiasm*, a rhetorical technique commonly used by speakers in an oral culture to make their presentations clear and memorable to their hearers. In our literary culture, both writers and speakers commonly present their primary points at the end of their compositions. But orators in oral cultures often arrive at the climactic moment in the middle of their speeches and then finish by repeating the main tenets of the argument so as to drive the primary point home. Paul has shaped his presentation in this part of his letter (which would have been read aloud, making it oral communication though it was written) so that his central and climactic claim is in v. 23a: *we preach Christ crucified*. Neither the wisdom of the world (for Greeks) nor signs (for Jews) enable us to know God, but Paul preached Christ crucified which is the wisdom and power of God (for both Jewish and Greek believers).[3]

So, Paul claims, we know God through the crucified Jesus. To appreciate his claim we need first to forget 2000 years of veneration of the cross. We need to forget the gold cross necklaces many of us wear and the beautiful crosses which adorn many of our sanctuaries. In the first century Roman Empire crucifixion was not only a horribly painful way to die. It was also a most shameful and degrading way to die. The Corinthians who first heard Paul preach would likely have thought that only misguided and pathetic fools who thought they could challenge Rome without a massive army behind them were crucified. Such fools ended up dead with their idiocy displayed for all to see. In just such a fool, Paul says, we know God.

But how is this so? If Jesus was the Messiah of God, how did he end up on the wrong end of Roman crucifixion? The Christian story is that Jesus' crucifixion shows us the depth and breadth of God's love. Jesus came to announce God's love for the whole creation (John 3:16). As he touched lepers, ate with tax collectors and sinners, and healed blind beggars and the daughters of Syro-Phoenician women he threatened the order established by its rulers wherein some were favored and sat on top of the world, while others were unclean, outcast, and beneath anyone's concern. Everybody else figured out their place in between and behaved accordingly. But Jesus' life showed that he considered no one unworthy of God's favor. Then, when the rulers told him to stop his nonsense, he loved the people too much to do so. When the rulers said they'd kill him if he didn't stop, he still loved them too much to do so. And when they finally set out to stop him violently, he even loved his enemies too much to respond with violence against them. Consequently, while many people look at the crucified Jesus and see only a loser, others see the breadth and depth of God's love. For them, therefore, the cross makes known that God is about loving, not about winning. The God of Jesus is *not like* the God of Rome. Jesus' followers know God as the God who is love.

This understanding of Paul's claim fits well with his assertion later in the letter that "love never fails" (1 Cor. 13:8) and that "faith, hope, and love abide, these three, but the greatest of these is love" (13:13). Furthermore, Paul's claims in 1 Corinthians fit well with the central place given to love by other New Testament writers. The writers of the Synoptic Gospels understood Jesus to have taught that the greatest commandments are love God with all you are and love your neighbor as yourself (Mark 12:28-34; Matthew 22:35-40; Luke 10:25-28). The writer of John understood Jesus to have said, "This is my commandment that you love one another as I have loved you. No one has greater love than this, to lay down one's life for one's friends. You are my friends…" (15:12-14a). The writer of 1 John famously wrote,

> Beloved, let us love one another, for love is from God, and everyone who loves has been born from God and knows God. The one who does not love does not know God because God is love. In this the love of God is revealed among us, that God sent his only begotten son into the world so that we might live through him (4:8-9).

So, to the Corinthians who considered themselves superior to other believers, to a community wracked by competition and conflict, Paul wrote that the greatest of those things which are eternal is love, and that in the cross of Jesus we know God (and the depth and breadth of God's love). Against the backdrop of the rest of the New Testament we understand that God loved us so much that God sent Jesus to live out God's love, and Jesus' love was so strong that he continued to love even as he was unjustly condemned precisely because he loved. The God whose children the Corinthians claimed to be was all about love. Thus the Corinthians should be as well. If they won all the arguments and triumphed in all the conflicts but did not love one another, Paul insisted, they would be nothing (paraphrasing 1 Cor. 13:1-3).

The Joint Commission on Theology and Social Concerns can think of no reason to assume that Paul would not give the same counsel to Cumberland Presbyterians when we disagree. Thus, if we win all the arguments and triumph in all our conflicts but do not love one another, Paul would tell us we are nothing. We hasten to add here that this counsel does not mean that Paul would tell us to give up our convictions or to be silent about them. Certainly no one can accuse Paul of yielding his convictions or not speaking out about them! Rather, Paul's counsel calls us to hold to and advocate for our convictions *while* we love others who hold different convictions as strongly as we hold ours. But this task is not at all easy. Let us, therefore, ask Paul for some advice on how we might live out his counsel.

1 Corinthians 12:12-27

Having offered his theological rationale for calling Corinthian believers to unity, Paul turns his attention to conflicts which have threatened their unity such as perceived competition between himself and Apollos, lawsuits among believers, troubling sexual practices, and eating meat sacrificed to idols. As chapter 12 gets underway he is ready to address yet another area of contention among them: "Now concerning spiritual gifts, brothers and sisters," he begins (12:1a). In chapter 14 we will discover that some Corinthian believers were particularly impressed by the gift of speaking in tongues. In a context where some believers considered themselves spiritually superior to others, tongue speaking was likely coveted because it was "showy," thus, proving the speaker to be very spiritual (at least in the minds of some). These believers' efforts to show off their tongue speaking were seriously disrupting worship times. But before addressing spiritual gifts in the context of worship in chapter 14, Paul will first lay a theological foundation for understanding spiritual gifts generally. As he does so, he gives us the beloved image of the church as the "body of Christ," an image which speaks to our concern for loving one another when we disagree.

In the first part of chapter 12 Paul focuses on the *source* of the gifts: there are varieties of gifts, services, and activities but the same Spirit, the same Lord, the same God is the source of them all (12:4-6). After reviewing some of this variety among the gifts (12:8-10), he returns to the *one* source of them all: "All of these are activated by one and the same Spirit" (12:11a). His point is clear: if the Spirit is the originator, giver, and activator of all the gifts, then how can we consider the recipients of some gifts to be worthy of greater esteem than others as if they (rather than the Spirit) were responsible for them? Furthermore, how can we consider some gifts to be less needed than others?

With his point about the *one* true source of the gifts now made, Paul is ready in verse 12 to address differences among the gifts. If the one Spirit is the source of all the gifts, why is there such a variety among the gifts? The answer, Paul says, is because believers are the "body of Christ" (12:12-13). And the body "does not consist of one member but of many" (12:14). Paul elaborates on this point at length. Hands and feet, though very different, are both part of the body (12:15). If all the body were an eye, then how could it hear (12:17)? Heads need feet, eyes need hands (12:23). We treat some parts of the body differently than other parts (more protective of some parts, more open with other parts, 12:23-24). But all these different parts together make up one body (12:20). Indeed, the different parts are necessary in order to be a body. If everyone is a hand, we don't have a body. We just have a bunch of hands (12:19). Consequently, the different parts need each other, which creates mutuality and interdependence among the parts (12:26). So it is with Christ, Paul says. "For in the one Spirit we were all baptized into one body—Jews or Greeks, slaves or free—and we were all made to drink of one Spirit" (12:13).

An implication of the particular claim Paul makes in verse 13 is that difference is not limited to spiritual gifts. Here Paul mentions diversity in ethnicity (Jews or Greeks) and socio-economic class (slaves or free). In other contexts he mentions diversity in gender (Gal. 3:28), in theological perspective (Gal. 2:6-9), even in eating practices and observance of special days (Rom. 14:1-6). Clearly the early believers were quite a "motley crew." Just as clearly Paul accepted the diversity, even appreciated it.

One implication of Paul's teaching for our current discussion is this: diversity among us is *a necessity* if we would be the Body of Christ. We can—and according to Paul, we *should*—recognize and appreciate our differences rather than fear them or try to hide, fix, or eliminate them. For only when there is variety among us do we have the opportunity to be the body of Christ.

We can illustrate Paul's point by reflecting on our history. If Martin Luther had not disagreed with the Catholic Church over indulgences (and other points as well), then there may not have been a badly needed Reformation of the Church (not only did Protestantism come into being, but the Catholic Church was also reformed through these events). If English Separatists had not disagreed with the idea of a state church, then freedom of religion might not be one of the treasured freedoms of the American landscape. If abolitionists had not disagreed with mainline churches over slavery, it might have taken us even longer to exorcise that demon from our midst. If Louisa Woosley had not disagreed with the Church's position on the ordination of women, then the Cumberland Presbyterian Church might have been as slow as others to recognize that God calls whom God chooses regardless of race, gender, ethnicity, or anything else that we have used to prohibit someone's ordination. In each of these cases the Church struggled with the disagreements. No claim is made here that coping with difference is easy. But in each of these cases the Church was reformed, transformed, deepened, and enriched because of those who voiced different perspectives and those who dared to hear them rather than remove them from the community. Consequently, our differences have enabled us to come closer to being the Body of Christ than before we disagreed. Our history shows us how right Paul was on this point: "For just as the body is one and has many members, and all the members of the body, though many, are one body, so it is with Christ" (12:12).

So, our "different members" enable us to be the Body of Christ as Paul encouraged us to be. He rarely got upset over differences. Instead, he got upset when believers who differed with one another treated one another badly. As an example, he disagreed with Corinthian believers who believed that eating meat sacrificed to idols was no big deal (1 Cor 10:18-20). But he was upset with them because they did not care that their behavior was hurtful to others (1 Cor. 8:9-13). We shouldn't be surprised, then, that he follows the discussion of the body of Christ in 1 Corinthians 12 with these words: "If I speak in the tongues of mortals and of angels, but do not have love, I am a noisy gong or a clanging symbol" (1 Cor. 13:1). And so we find ourselves right back to the significance of love in the lives of believers.

Practically Speaking

With this examination of Paul's counsel to believers in Corinth who disagreed with each other in our minds, we can now ask ourselves, what we can learn for the times when we disagree with each other. Cumberland Presbyterians will benefit by discussing this question and seeking answers together. The Joint Commission on Theology and Social Concerns offers the following suggestions for consideration in our conversations.

Paul tells the Corinthians that we know God through the foolishness of the cross, which, in that culture, indicates that God is concerned with loving, not winning. Later in the letter he declares that love never ends and is the greatest of the things which abide forever.

Paul's teaching is echoed throughout the New Testament. We Cumberland Presbyterians would do well to recognize anew the central and foundational importance of love in the Gospel of Jesus Christ.

Paul insists that diversity among us isn't just inevitable; it's also necessary if we are to be the Body of Christ (rather than a collection of hands or ears or feet). Christians in general and Cumberland Presbyterians in particular are different from one another in how we look, believe, worship, and act (and likely in other ways). When we are different, we are bound to have conflict. It's simply going to happen. And it's usually not much fun. Conflict isn't, however, always a sign that something is wrong. It might indicate that we're embracing diversity rather than avoiding it, which means we are striving to be the Body of Christ.

Finally, if we focus anew on "God is love," and that the cross reveals God to be more concerned with loving than "winning, and if we embrace the diversity which allows us to be the body of Christ, then perhaps we'll find ourselves able to *disagree together* rather than having our disagreements tear us apart. We may find that we can hold our convictions deeply, advocate for them passionately, AND love those who disagree with us at the same time. We may discover that loving is more important than winning. In so doing, we can bear a great witness to our world that we are indeed children of God whom we came to know in Christ crucified.

Joint Commission on Theology and Social Concerns
CP and CPCA Churches

Rev. Mitzi Minor, PhD
Professor of New Testament
Memphis Theological Seminary

---

[1] Richard A. Horsley and Neil Asher Silberman, *The Message and the Kingdom: How Jesus and Paul Ignited a Revolution and Transformed the Ancient World* (Minneapolis: Fortress Press, 1997), 164.

[2] This descriptive phrase is from Horsley and Silberman, *The Message and the Kingdom*, 163.

[3] All of 1:18-31 can be arranged in a chiasm as a number of scholars have shown. While their chiasms differ slightly, all of them have v 23a in the center. "We preach Christ crucified" is clearly the center of the passage.

RECOMMENDATION 1: That the General Assemblies accept this paper as study paper and that it be used to initiate thought and discussion within the Cumberland Presbyterian Church and the Cumberland Presbyterian Church in America.

RECOMMENDATION 2: That the Office of the General Assembly of both denominations make this paper available to churches through the stated clerks of the presbyteries.

The paper, "Illegal, Undocumented, or Unauthorized Immigrant…Commonly Used Terms; Which Is Right?" by Reverend Johan Daza, is being reviewed by the committee. The committee discussed ways to raise awareness of the impact of the use of the terminology "illegal" versus "undocumented" or "unauthorized" and to assist persons and congregations with information and resources on obtaining documentation.

The Committee invites the submission of Reflection or Position Papers on current issues that individuals or groups feel called to address. A Guide to the Process of Writing Papers is available on the website (www.cumberland.org/uctsc).

VI. WORKS IN PROGRESS

The Permanent Committee is currently discussing theological reflections on the following concerns: "Homelessness" – a paper by authored by Reverend Seila O'Mara and Reverend Byron Forester, which explores the root cause of homelessness, what the Christian Response to this social concern should be, and how some Cumberland Presbyterian Churchees are currently ministering to our sisters and brothers who live on the streets. Other topics under discussion include: Racial Profiling: Domestic Abuse, Cost of Medical Care, and Child Abuse, Discrimination Issues (racial, gender, age).

The Permanent Committee would like to commend the work done by the Women's Ministry of the Cumberland Presbyterian Church in the area of "Human Trafficking". The Committee will partner with the Coordinator for Women's Ministry to provide an ongoing focus on this issue and resources for the annual Domestic Violence and Human Trafficking Awareness Sunday observances.

VII. UNIFICATION EFFORTS

It is the hope of the Committee that presbyteries and local churches that have not yet read the study paper Reflections On A Divided Church will do so and will find opportunities to participate in the following action steps that have been approved by both General Assemblies:

1. That local congregations where the churches have overlapping boundaries to organize joint activities between the CPC and CPCA to provide opportunities to build better relationships between the two churches such as holding joint activities through worship, pulpit exchange, times of fellowship, revivals, VBS, and discussion of the papers produced by this committee.

2. That presbyteries of the CPC and CPCA might also consider ways that committees boards and agencies might begin working together. Committees on ministry and missions, Christian education committees, and camping programs would all benefit from joint interaction. Examples of ways presbyteries can work together include having advisory members participate in the other denomination's meetings, workshops, projects for the Cumberland Presbyterian Women, working together on local, regional, and even denominational mission efforts including Habitat for Humanity, and raising money for disaster areas around the world.

The committee also recommends utilizing the resource from Reverend Andy McClung, CPC & CPCA, Siblings in Faith.

Respectfully Submitted,
Unified Committee on Theology and Social Concerns

THE REPORT OF THE UNIFICATION TASK FORCE

I. MEETING AND OFFICERS

The Unification force of the Cumberland Presbyterian Church in America (CPCA) and the Cumberland Presbyterian Church (CPC) met on November 13, 2014 in Nashville, Tennessee. Officers elected at the meeting were Joy Warren (CPC) and William Robinson (CPCA), co-chairs; Craig White (CPCA) and Jay Earheart-Brown (CPC), secretaries. Members of the UTF include Jay Earheart-Brown (CPC), Elton Hall (CPCA), Arthur Haywood (CPCA), Lynne Herring (CPCA), William Robinson (CPCA), Anthony Hollis (CPCA), Steve Mosley (CPC), Perryn Rice (CPCA/CPC), Robert Rush (CPC), Leon Cole (CPCA), Gloria Villa-Diaz (CPC), Mitchell Walker (CPCA), Joy Warren (CPC), Craig White (CPCA) and Mike Sharpe (CPC). Current CPC Moderator Lisa Anderson was present for this meeting. Current CPCA Moderator Leon Cole serves as a member of the UTF.

II. SUMMARY OF MEETING

During the November meeting we spent time reviewing the activities taking place throughout both denominations regarding unification. The workshop at the General Assembly meeting in Chattanooga provided feedback from hundreds of attendees. The fall Ministry Council meeting also provided many responses to the Proposed Plan of Union recommended for study by both Assemblies. The UTF received letters from individuals containing responses to the Proposed Plan, and UTF members reported on many of the meetings taking place regionally in the US regarding unification.

We would like to highlight the fact that much work is being done by West Tennessee Presbytery (CPC) and New Hopewell Presbytery (CPCA), as evidenced by their Joint Summit on Unification last fall. These presbyteries have a joint committee on unification. Our impressions so far from feedback and information on hand are that in general both denominations feel we have a theological basis for union. Because there are questions and concerns about some challenges presented in the Proposed Plan, the UTF earnestly desires feedback and suggestions for solutions from the bodies of both denominations. We remind everyone that the requested deadline for feedback is July 1, 2015.

At this meeting, we also began planning regional events to be held during 2015. The goal of these events is to share worship, fellowship, and a meal with brothers and sisters in Christ. The UTF strongly feels that relationship building is strengthening true unity between our denominations and among our local churches. The discussion regarding unity is awakening a celebration of our connectional nature.

Education and communication through face to face meetings are vital aspects of the work of the UTF. We are thankful to all those who have extended invitations to the UTF and have gathered to study various aspects of the unification discussion. In order to continue this momentum, the UTF suggests presence of unification advocates at meetings on all judicatorial levels and funding from both denominations.

RECOMMENDATION 1: That the Unification Task Force be given time at Summer and Fall 2015 and Spring 2016 presbytery and synod meetings to present updates on unification and to communicate feedback on the plan for union.

RECOMMENDATION 2: That joint clusters of churches also schedule a time for a presentation on unification by a member of the task force, unification advocates, and/or other leaders within both denominations.

RECOMMENDATION 3: That the General Assembly increase its funding for 2016 to $30,000 to support the programming and travel of the Unification Task Force, legal fees, and subsequent implementation costs that may be incurred.

RECOMMENDATION 4: That clergy, elders and laity make all efforts to attend a regional meeting if geographically possible.

Respectfully submitted,
Unification Task Force

THE REPORT OF BOARD OF TRUSTEES OF BETHEL UNIVERSITY

Bethel University is completing its 172nd year of operation. The University continues to educate people from all walks of life. This year, Bethel University served students from states all across our United States and 23 foreign countries as well. Since Day 1 of Bethel's existence in McLemoresville, Tennessee, to today in McKenzie, Tennessee and its satellite campuses, the University has been associated and aligned with the Cumberland Presbyterian Church.

Bethel University's mission is this: "To create opportunities for members of the learning community to develop to their highest potential as whole persons – intellectually, spiritually, socially and physically – in a Christian environment." That is the standard we operate by.

Bethel University is proud to be affiliated with the Cumberland Presbyterian Church. It is a covenant relationship approved by both entities and one that looks to carry us into the next 172 years. Our ties are strong as Bethel tries to help in the education of future and current leaders of the Cumberland Presbyterian Church.

Bethel University is under the accreditation of the Southern Association of College and Schools, Commission on Colleges and several state and national groups.

Bethel University currently has 24 Board of Trustee Members. 17 of our current Board of Trustees are Cumberland Presbyterians. Our Board members are:

Chairman Judge Ben Cantrell – Nashville, Tennessee
Mr. Jeff Amrein - Prospect, Kentucky
Dr. Larry A. Blakeburn – Dyersburg, Tennessee
Mr. Mike Cary – Huntington, Tennessee
Ms. Lisa Cole – Nashville, Tennessee
Dr. Army Daniel – Huntsville, Alabama
Mr. Ladd Daniel – Houston, Texas
Mr. Chet Dickson – Houston, Texas
Mr. Bill Dobbins – Franklin, Tennessee
Mr. Charlie Garrett – Jackson, Tennessee
Reverend Elton C. Hall, Jr. – Hewitt, Texas
Reverend Mark S. Hester – Friendsville, Tennessee
Ms. Charlene Jones – McKenzie, Tennessee
Mr. Art Laffer, Nashville, Tennessee
Ms. Dewana Latimer – Humboldt, Tennessee
Reverend Eugene Leslie – Olive Branch, Mississippi
Dr. Robert Low – Springfield, Missouri
Reverend Nancy McSpadden – St. Peters, Missouri
Mr. Bobby Owen – Franklin, Tennessee
Dr. Ed Perkins – McKenzie, Tennessee
Mr. Ken Quinton – Sturgis, Kentucky
Mr. Ben Surber – McKenzie, Tennessee
Reverend Rob Truitt – Burns, Tennessee
Reverend Bob Watkins – Sun City, Arizona

The current President of Bethel University is Walter Butler. He is a Bethel graduate for both his undergraduate degree and his Master of Business Administration. His wife, three sons and one daughter-in-law are also Bethel graduates. He became Bethel University's 40th President on August 1, 2014, after serving one year as Interim President. The Bethel University Cabinet is:

Dr. Dale Henry – Vice President for Development
Ms. Nancy Bean – Vice President for College of Arts and Sciences
Ms. Kelly Sanders Kelley – Vice President for College of Professional Studies
Mr. Roland Colson – Vice President for College of Public Service
Dr. Joe Hames – Vice President for Health Sciences
Dr. Phyllis Campbell – Chief Academic Officer

Mr. Steve Perryman – Treasurer
Mr. David Huss – Director of Business Affairs

Enrollment for Fall of 2014 was 5,906 students compared to 5,825 students for Fall of 2015. The breakdown and comparisons for the two years are as follows:

	August 26, 2013	August 28, 2014
College of Arts & Sciences		
Dual Enrollment	63	151
Master of Arts in Education Face to Face	68	43
Master of Arts in Education Online	426	306
Roane State	14	7
Undergraduate	1439	1298
College of Health Science		
Bachelor of Science in Nursing	(included in COAS Undergraduate)	39
Master of Science in Physician Assistant Studies	90	88
RN to BSN (online)	7	24
College of Public Service		
Master of Science in Criminal Justice	151	117
Criminal Justice	999	901
Master of Arts in Conflict Resolution	139	137
School of University Studies	75	91
Associates	-----	-----
College of Professional Studies		
Master of Arts in Business Administration	551	605
Undergraduate Face to Face (Success)	819	1106
Undergraduate Online (Success online)	984	993
Grand Total for Enrollment	5825	5906

As of March, 2015, applications for the Fall, 2015, class of Arts & Sciences looks strong. We have over 250 more applications than at this same date last year. Our acceptances are also up.

If you live in Tennessee, you have heard of Tennessee Promise this year. It is an initiative passed this year by The Tennessee General Assembly to guarantee a free community college education for any current and future high school senior. Bethel University worked to become a part of this program and became one of only six bachelor granting institutions to be included in this bill. Bethel University felt strongly that this is part of our mission.

Bethel University's students are its strengths. Accolades are way too numerous to list, but a partial listing may give you an idea of our students.

* 100% pass rate on the Nursing Licensing exam for our graduates for 2nd year in a row.
* Chief Ranger Shane Petty began working in Tennessee State Parks as a teenager and continued in State Parks working his way through high school and college. He earned his Master's Degree in Criminal Justice from Bethel. Chief Ranger Petty oversees all law enforcement operations within the 55 state parks. He graduated from TLETA at the top of his class in 1989 and has been a member of the visiting faculty since 1998.
* The College of Public Service exists to provide a variety of online programs for working professionals that do not have the time to attend traditional university classes. Bethel University's online format has allowed thousands of working professionals to keep their job while they complete their college degrees. Now as these students graduate, we begin to see many promoted to top ranking positions within their fields. Approximately 70% of our graduates either receive promotions are significant increases in their incomes due to their graduate degrees.
* Tennessee State Representative Barrett Rich said he is proud that his degree from Bethel afforded him the opportunities to serve in his current role. "I was in law enforcement and then later became a Farm Bureau agent." "Because I chose this route, I did not have time to attend college when most people my age were going to school. The non-traditional program I went through at Bethel really helped. The program

I went through was extremely writing intensive, which has helped me tremendously in my work at the legislature, and it was also vital during my attendance at law school." Rich also said that without Bethel's degree and their commitment to non-traditional students, he would have never had the opportunity to earn his Doctor of Jurisprudence.

* Tennessee Highway Patrol Captain Jessie Brooks says Bethel's Online Criminal Justice Program has played a big part in getting him to where he is today. He was promoted to Captain of the Chattanooga District after receiving his Bachelor's Degree, Summa Cum Laude, in Criminal Justice from Bethel University. Captain Brooks has since begun working toward his Master Degree at this time.

* Kevin Genovese is the Director of Statewide Transportation for the Tennessee Department of Correction. He is a 42 year old single father of two boys and will say to anyone "never give up, because anything is possible". Mr. Genovese received his Bachelor's and Master's from Bethel University.

* Jackson Deputy Chief of Police Barry Michael in December 2011 graduate summa Cum Laude with his bachelor's degree in Bethel's first graduating class of the College of Criminal Justice (now the college of Public Service). Chief Michael's message to others with regrets about college…."We are all busy and have many things going on in our lives, but if you truly want to get a college degree, no matter what your season in life, then it can happen. I am proof of that." He obviously credits Bethe University for his success.

* Gerald McAllister is the Warden at Northeast Correctional Facility in Mountain City. He served as the Superintendent of the Department of Correction's Training Academy for several years as well. Warden McAllister received his Bachelor's and his Master's Degree from Bethel University. He claims that until getting his degrees from Bethel, he had little promotional opportunity within the department. He strongly advocates for those in corrections to obtain the college degree.

* Bethel University has the largest online Criminal Justice Program in Tennessee.
* Bethel University has the largest MBA program in the state of Tennessee.
* Our Women's basketball team is ranked #5 (NAIA) in the nation.
* Our men's basketball team is ranked in the top 25.
* Our hockey team is going to regionals.
* Our number of Cumberland Presbyterian students has risen almost 100% since hiring a recruiter for Cumberland Presbyterian students. Our hope and our efforts are to increase that number dramatically in the next few years. We are The Cumberland Presbyterian University and want to be the University of Choice for Cumberland Presbyterians.
* Our Dual Enrollment numbers in the fall of 2014 were almost double what we had the entire year last year. We are signing a number of new schools up for our Dual Enrollment classes for 2015-2016. As of January 15, 24% of our high school senior dual enrollment students have applied to Bethel for the remainder of their undergraduate work.
* We have completed a student lounge for students in the Vera Low Center for Student Enrichment.
* We hosted the District and Regional high school basketball tournaments in Crisp Arena.
* We are offering courses for our students to go to the Colegio Americano in Colombia and assist students there with English or to work in whatever capacity is needed in or around the Colegio.
* A Harlem Globetrotter is enrolled in the MAEd program.
* Some Renaissance students did back-up for professional gospel singer Mark Lowry for the new CD he is recording.

On our Development side of the University, we will always seem to have to ask for funds. Whether Endowment funds to be used for certain projects or unrestricted funds to help in daily needs, we must work daily in this effort. Our current projects include raising money for The Cumberland Chapel. We have approximately ½ of this raised or committed. We need The Chapel! We recently had donor pledge money for a new football fieldhouse. Their generosity will pay for ½ of the cost. We will not start on this or other projects until the money is in the bank. Bethel needs lights for our baseball, softball and soccer fields. Bethel needs new stadium seats and dugouts for our baseball field. These are huge needs for us.

Bethel is undergoing, this year, a $3.1 million renovation to the Library (Burroughs Learning Center). It will (upon completion) qualify as a safe shelter during storms. This project was made possible by a Federal grant of which Bethel's match is 12%. The completion will be no later than April 2016.

Our last two years of audited financials are enclosed. They show two strong financial years.

Continue to pray for Bethel University. Continue to support Bethel University and send us names of prospective students. We pray daily for The Cumberland Presbyterian Church.

Bethel Forevermore

THE REPORT OF THE BOARD OF TRUSTEES OF THE CUMBERLAND PRESBYTERIAN CHILDREN'S HOME

The 2015 Cumberland Presbyterian Children's Home Report to the 185th General Assembly of the Cumberland Presbyterian Church.

I am grateful for your interest. I invite you to look beneath the facts and the figures in this report. They attempt to quantitatively describe the incarnation of God's transforming grace in the lives touched by the people who live and work at the Cumberland Presbyterian Children's Home. We strive to be good stewards of your gifts and donations to us. Many of you come to our campus to visit and work. Most of you send money to pay for the expensive work of ending the cycle of abuse and neglect by bringing healing and hope to children and families. All of you support our mission with your prayers and your commitment of time and energy to support the work. Thank you and God bless you.

I. OVERVIEW

Our 111 year ministry at the Children's Home serves children and families in different ways:
- Children's Residential Care,
- Children's Emergency Shelter Care,
- Single Parent Family Services, and
- Cumberland Family Services Counseling.

In the 21st Century, we focus our ministry on ending the maltreatment of children. Child abuse and neglect not only injure children, but impact the lives and families of adults who were once abused. We must stop the cycle of harm, a harm that can be measured in many ways.

Foremost, I believe we are called to this redemptive ministry by God. God has called us to feed, clothe, teach, and love the little, the last, the lost and the least.

The harm also creates a toll in human tragedy correlated with crime, addiction, unemployment, incarceration, broken relationships, mental and emotional dysfunction, ill health, violence and self destructive actions. The cost to society is numbing.

So Cumberland provides a safe, nurturing and loving residence where children and families can live and grow. It also provides tools for healing and health through counseling and parenting training. And most importantly, the Children's Home enacts Christ's command to serve in His name. Here are some numbers to give you a flavor of the scope of our ministry.

Cumberland helps children and families in residential and nonresidential programs.
- In its residential programs, Cumberland served 125 children and 14 single parents.
- Over 1,729 additional children and families were served through intake and referral services, counseling sessions, or classes in our nonresidential programs.
- Cumberland held over 2,648 separate counseling sessions.

In all, 1,930 lives were touched with healing and hope by the Cumberland Presbyterian Children's Home during 2014.

Mission

In response to Christ's love and example, we serve children and families by providing healing and hope.

Campus

Cumberland's 17acre campus in Denton, Texas, includes three residential cottages for children and teens and 8 apartments for single parent families. Other features include the Parr Family Resource Building, which houses the Library and Technology Center, therapy rooms, meeting facilities and staff offices. The campus is also home to the GilbertParr Activities Building, which houses Cumberland's recreational facilities and a chapel, the 250seat Lela Stricklen Hall.

Corporate entity and governance

Cumberland is a nonprofit corporation incorporated under the laws of the state of Texas. Cumberland is taxexempt under IRS Code section 501(c)(3). Cumberland is governed by a board of 18 Trustees. The Cumberland Board of Trustees hired the President, CEO & General Counsel to manage the agency.

Trustees: There are currently 17 trustees: ten Cumberland Presbyterians and seven ecumenical partners (the Board is in the process of filling a vacated seat).

Ecumenical Partners: Caroline Booth, John O'Carroll, Charles Harris, Knight Miller, Kay Goodman, Tiffany Smith and Baron Smith.
Cumberland Presbyterians: Mamie Hall, Reverend Melissa Knight, Patricia Huff, Reverend Don Tabor, Richard Dean, Mickey Shell, Reverend Lisa Anderson, Ruby Letson, Reverend Alfonso Marquez and Patricia Long.
Officers: Chair—Richard Dean; ViceChair—Patricia Long; Secretary—Patricia Huff.
Leadership: President, CEO & General Counsel: Reverend Richard A. Brown, Esq., LCCA
Vice President, Programs: Dr. Jennifer Livings, LPCS
Vice President & CFO: Warren Nagumo
Vice President of Development: Larry Brown
Interim Chaplain: Reverend Katie Klein

Organizational Structure

Because our mission calls us to a ministry of service, we have adopted the following "Pyramid of Care©" as an organizational structure. Rather than organizing from the top down, we wish to follow in Christ's example of servant leadership. We place the people we serve, both in residential care and in non-residential care, at the top of the pyramid.

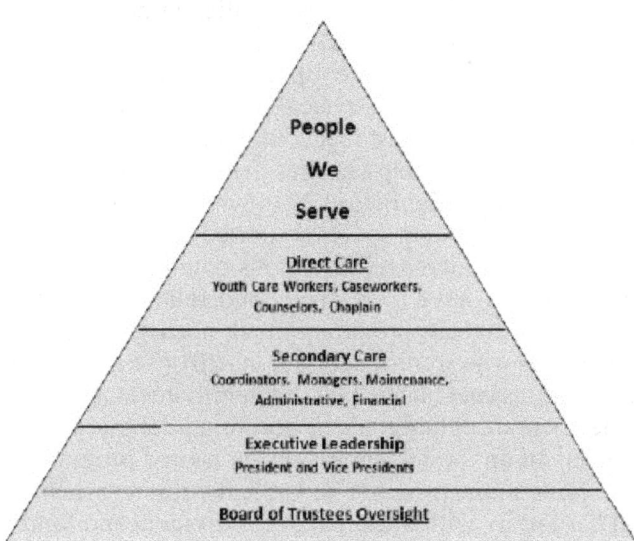

II. OUTCOMES

In our efforts to serve families and children, Cumberland looks for quantitative ways to measure our work. Beginning in 2010, Cumberland contracted with a third party to create an unbiased and verifiable method of measuring outcomes. This process helps us constantly improve our programs and maintain accountability with our donors and service partners.

Below are a few of the positive outcomes from our study covering the calendar year 2014.

Continuum of Care in Cumberland's Culture Cumberland Family Services: We provide counseling services to our campus residents as well as clients from the community through our program called Cumberland Family Services ("CFS"). CFS has seen a significant increase in revenue over the past year. In 2014, Cumberland Family Services generated a revenue of approximately $114,000. We provided approximately 2,700 counseling hours in 2014.

We had a lot of success working and collaborating with community partners. In 2014, major community leaders provided trainings focused on children and adolescent mental health at our very own Lela Stricklen Hall. Our community wishes to address mental health issues and is open to discussing the overwhelming need to close the gap that exists for individuals who are unable to access quality mental health. Systems are changing in response to these pressing issues and our community understands that addressing mental health challenges takes us all working together. Our therapists will no longer have to justify the need for counseling services for our foster youth due to changes in the Mental Health Parity Act.

The use of sliding fee scale and acceptance of certain types of insurance will allow us to further dive into mental health treatment options and work from different modalities with greater ease. In addition to our future goals, we currently have more therapists providing clinical supervision to graduate and postgraduate students which strengthens our visibility.

Helping children and families deal with mental health issues is paramount for CFS. The crisis is national in scope. For instance, in Texas, approximately every 8 minutes a child is abused or neglected and approximately 30% of those children are under the age of three. Frequently, abuse and neglect survivors struggle with mental and emotional stability accompanied by a mental health diagnosis. According to the National Alliance of Mental Illness, 7.5 million children may be affected by mental illness and almost two thirds of individual's diagnosed with mental health issues do not seek treatment. Since one in three females and one in six males experience some form of sexual abuse, the likelihood that CFS will provide services to clients with these issues is alarming. In 2014, we made a conscious decision to increase our knowledge base and treatment options to help survivors of abuse and trauma by becoming trained in trauma focused counseling methods.

Single Parent Family Program: The Single Parent Family Program ("SPF") served 41 adults and children in 2014. We are providing more outreach and aftercare services to these families than ever before. The need to serve families in crisis and families on the verge of needing serious intervention to keep their family together continues to be a need of our community at large. Based on reports from Denton ISD Social Work team, they have identified at least 800 homeless families in our city of 113,000, families that have minor children attending Denton ISD schools. Based on research of the Denton County Homeless Coalition, individuals experiencing homelessness reported the top three reasons for being homeless: unemployment, inability to afford stable housing, and mental or physical health issues. Our program changes in 2015 will continue to address struggles such as these as we feel confident that we will be able to increase our service delivery to continue striving for our goal to help families in crisis achieve lasting changes.

Our SPF program helped multiple families in 2014 with many successes and challenges throughout the year. Many of the clients who are achieving success reported increased abilities to manage their finances, an overall reduction in their stress, and increases in various coping skills. Overall, the community in our SPF circle has grown stronger as they have developed solid relationships with one another and reliable relationships with Cumberland staff that are providing much needed services. The family listed below is just an example among many clients who were successful in 2014. Since this family entered our program approximately 6 months ago, Cumberland has helped this family meet a variety of goals including:

- Helped the client meet her goals of becoming debt free and starting a savings account
- Signed the client up for a Cumberland sponsored program where she can purchase a laptop to use while in the program and take it with her when she successfully graduates
- Provided her family with much needed individual and family counseling
- Supported her goals of setting healthy limits with her family while incorporating strong parenting practices
- Increased stability for the family overall to heal from past abuse and trauma

We are happy when we have successful cases; but we see areas for improvement. The program overall is in continued need of stronger business practices and case management services which is why we are moving forward with a SPF program redesign in 2015. Our hope is to identify areas of improvement that will assist us in helping our clients make lasting changes that have a larger impact on the family as a whole.

General Residential Operation: We are proud of the work we have done in 2014 with our foster youth. We served 98 children in our programs in 2014. We had two residents graduate high school this past year. Both young adults are living Independent Living Programs and choose to live locally in Denton.

Both are attending college and received much needed life skills training provided by our onstaff Life Skills Specialist for many months before launching into the real world.

We have seen a decrease in direct care staff turnover in 2014. If staff are no longer with us, it is due to them being experienced enough to be eligible to work in more advanced positions in social work or other related fields. We are highly selective in our hiring and staffing patterns to ensure we are providing the best care to our kids. We have multiple staff attending graduate school which speaks to the high levels of competency of individuals we have on staff.

Overall, we are proud of the job we are doing. We have seen dramatic increases in our ability to manage a team. Our managers gained valuable experience this past year and our staff are stepping into their roles like never before. We are enrolling our kids in a variety of extracurricular activities. In hopes to provide as close to a normal experience as possible, we are ensuring the kids have their basic needs met as well as meeting many of their wants. In addition, we have increased stability overall in how we designed our program implementation.

Running a General Residential Operation ("GRO") comes with many questions. Simply, we are spending more on the kid's welfare and benefit across the board. We acknowledge the challenge ahead of us as we strive to meet our mission. We had many successes in 2014, but a few stories specifically stand out since we last met in September:

• When we heard our sibling group of 4 was going to be adopted by a couple in our community, a CPS adoption planning meeting was held to assess the children's needs and the adoptive family. Cumberland staff advocated for our children and we went in heavy to this meeting with 2 therapists, 2 Youth Care Workers, and one Cottage Manager. The response from the CPS adoption committee was overwhelming. We received such a warm welcome and it was apparent that our advocacy went above and beyond to ensure that our kids were going to be taken care of in their adoptive home. Overall, the committee was impressed by our professionalism and advocacy. This sibling group was successfully adopted and we played a large role in ensuring our children transitioned into a safe and loving home.

• When one of our cottage managers was on an outing with a resident, our child asked "what is the saddest thing in the world ever." Our staff responded with a great response and simply stated "I do not know." Our child followed up with, "I know, when we go places and go out to eat, seeing all the other families makes me sad because it just is not fair." Our cottage manager reflected back on her sadness and how difficult that must be to see. In resilient response, our child stated, "it's okay because I kind of have my own family here and that makes me happy too." Of course, we thanked her and gave a hug.

III. GIVING

Cumberland Presbyterian Children's Home exists today because of the commitment Cumberland Presbyterian individuals and congregations have made in giving every year and through planned gifts. In her will, Miss Victoria Jackson of Bowling Green, Kentucky, created a home for widows and orphans. Her final act of generosity has allowed thousands of lives to be touched by this ministry. For the past 111 years, many faithful and forward thinking people have blessed the children's home, including the increasingly needed family services, with annually recurring and estate gifts.

We are grateful that more than half of CP churches made direct gifts to the children's home this last year. Through these reliable annual gifts and the endowment built from planned giving, Cumberland Presbyterian Children's Home can keep the church's promise to do more than house, clothe and feed our children. The opportunities for spiritual growth and practical life skills for children and families would not exist without the continued prayers and support from the women and men of Cumberland Presbyterian Churches.

We promise to be good stewards of what you give. When you do your own kitchen table bookkeeping, you know that costs for basic goods increase. We never take the sacrifice you are making for granted. Thank you for helping us keep up with the high cost of providing the one on one relationship building that true change requires, especially when we are focused upon vulnerable and traumatized children and families.

We strive to fulfill the mission to which we believe we have been called. The Cumberland Presbyterian Children's Home does not warehouse residents. We seek to enrich the lives of children, teens and families who have been trapped in the cycle of abuse and neglect like so many children and families in our community and yours. Through your donations, we provide direct care to vulnerable children and families.

We also strive to create a model for care that can be duplicated in homes and campuses anywhere. How can we not take care of the need in front of us? But how can we limit our reach to just the need in front of us? We partner with you to become Christ's tender and caring touch to His traumatized children in whatever place and circumstance. Thank you for your generous giving.

IV. FINANCIAL

Expenses

Based on the unaudited 2014 Financial Statements, Cumberland spent just over $2.5 million bringing healing and hope to children and families. Expenses break down into the following categories:

Residential Childcare	41%
Emergency Shelter Childcare	31%
Cumberland Family Services	9%
Single Parent Family	8%
Administrative	6%
Fundraising	5%

NOTE: 89% of our costs provided care to our residents and clients.

Income

Again based on the unaudited 2014 Financial Statements, Cumberland derived just over $2.1 million in operational income from the following sources:

$ 549,789	Contributions	25.8%
$ 657,640	Service Compensation	30.8%
$ 36,927	Planned Gifts	1.7%
$ 215,000	Grants	10.1%
$ 557,991	Investment Income	26.2%
$ 64,452	OUO	3.0%
$ 51,528	Other	2.4%
$2,133,327	Total	100.0%

NOTE: The fee for service we receive in Service Compensation covers only a fraction of what it takes to enrich the lives of our cottage residents. Your gifts and contributions make it possible for traumatized youth to make a new beginning.

V. STRATEGIC PLAN

With a history of innovation, the Cumberland Board of Trustees has developed a Strategic Vision and a 10 year Strategic Plan. The strategic vision looks to a selfsustaining, fullystaffed ministry in our current location. This vision also sees the replication of our existing programs in other locations, and the vision recognizes the possibility of new programs serving children and families. The 10 year Strategic Plan will work toward fulfilling the vision by improving programs, expanding our outreach and creating sustainability.

Strategic Vision
1. SelfSustaining, fullystaffed agency in Denton, Texas.
2. Replication of our programs.
3. Work toward complete social service ministry for children and families.

2012-2022 Strategic Objectives Program Development
• Cumberland will examine, continue to improve on, and strive for excellence in the existing programs as well as add at least one new, selfsustaining program to the agency's continuum of care.
• Cumberland's Denton campus will be a beautiful fullyfunctioning, synergistic model for other multiple program agencies. Cumberland will replicate one or more of its programs in at least one new geographic location.

Outreach Development
• Cumberland will develop reciprocal professional relationships with institutions such as hospitals, area churches, social service agencies, Bethel University, Memphis Theological Seminary, Texas Woman's University and University of North Texas combining relevant research and mature faith ensuring the long-term sustainability of social service ministry. Cumberland will develop relationships at the highest level with the Texas Department of Family and Protective Services by serving on committees and boards at the state and local level.
• Cumberland will be a significant provider of social services to children and families in Texas and will be the primary social service resource to the Cumberland Presbyterian denomination.

Agency Development
- Cumberland will have a minimum operating budget of $2.5 million with contributions accounting for no more than 20% of the income, be fully staffed for optimum programming outcomes in all locations, and have a total endowment valued at more than $10.2 million.
- Cumberland will become a selfgoverning agency within a covenant, but not legal relationship, with the General Assembly of the Cumberland Presbyterian Church. The Board of Trustees will meet a minimum of three times per year and become more active in resource development, i.e. recruiting major donors, planned giving, forming relationships with businesses, participating in special events and making gifts of their own that indicate significant support for the agency.

VI. PRESIDENT'S MESSAGE

Dear Cumberland Presbyterian Church,
    RE: Laboratory for Transforming Lives

A Cumberland distinctive, evident from February 1810 in Dickson County, Tennessee and throughout the history of the denomination as well as the history of the Children's Home, might be aptly translated into 21st Century social science vernacular: we are a laboratory for transforming lives. While this expression may not be as warm, evocative or directly religious as other descriptions, it offers us a way of understanding nothing short of incarnation. God becomes flesh among us.

One insight from a year of listening and observing ministry to traumatized children and families confirms our Cumberland Presbyterian history, instincts and vision. We distinguish ourselves from other children's home and family service providers by our commitment to results grounded on our theology and philosophy of care.

Commitment plays such a vital role. Whatever budget stress we have is miniscule compared to what we would spend if we paid our staff what they are worth. They work here in part because they want to change the world one relationship at a time.

And our staff believes the Cumberland Presbyterian Children's Home mirrors that passion. We are unapologetically faith based. In part, that means we have options that a forprofit or even a nonfaithbased nonprofit do not have. If we had to increase shareholder profits or if we were limited to programs that paid for themselves, our options and our hands would be tied. Instead, we can choose a course because we believe it is right rather than because it is expedient.

Such a value should not be confused with sloth, ignorance or taking the easy path. On the contrary, we press ourselves to excel and yet know that all of our efforts are not sufficient. We trust God. We trust even as we seek to be faithful stewards. We seek that balance between faith and stewardship.

So to remind you about the distinctive approach Cumberland Presbyterian Children's Home has been implementing throughout its 111 year history, I will conclude with a list of current day characteristics which separate us from all the other group homes, family service providers and counseling clinics. If we only produce results like everyone else, we will decline and become irrelevant. Here is a descriptive list of some Cumberland distinctives incarnated at the Children's Home.

Kid Resilience

Michael Ungar, Ph.D. is CoDirector of the Resilience Research Centre. He is also a Killiam Professor of Social Work, University Research Professor, and Professor, in the School of Social Work at Dalhousie University.

Dr. Ungar's work does not question why so many at risk kids fail. His research focuses on why any succeed. What are the variables that help kids live fully and happily, even in atrisk environments? The correlation between Dr. Ungar's research results and Cumberland's trauma informed practices are striking.

Extended Family Model of Care

Most group homes use some variation of a house parent caregiver structure in order to save money on labor. Is that the best way? Research in Kid Resilience, for instance, suggests another approach, an approach which Cumberland has already incorporated into its Extended Family Model. Limits, consequences, an opportunity to learn from mistakes, structure and multiple healthy relationships with adult role models are some of the variables that set us apart. Many of you grew up as I did. Some of most important lessons were learned from relatives and friends so close I called them relatives. A community of faith becomes the training ground for growing healthy and happy persons.

Big Data

The world of nonprofits is a world where there are never enough resources to meet the ever growing need. So how do you apply the resources to just the right variable in just the right way at just the right time? Marketing and advertising research, as well as the entry of Big Data into the world of social science, are already revolutionizing the way service is provided.

Presentations by Cook Children's Hospital and Devereux Service Group, a leading national behavioral health care provider, show the way in which Big Data application to social service increases good outcomes and lowers costs.

Research: University of North Texas, Texas Woman's University and Bethel University

We are performing well. We obtain good results. But to help as many people as possible and attract the resources to do the work, we need to systematically study what we do and what difference it makes. But we need not reinvent the wheel. There are already institutions that perform research projects.

Pyramid of Care

When you apply strength focused principles to management and leadership, the Pyramid of Care is born. The people we serve are at the top of the pyramid. Driving resources and decision making to the highest level of the pyramid multiplies effective problem solving, increases job satisfaction, unleashes latent resources from the workforce and treats people in a way consistent with Judeo Christian values about human nature and grace.

Strength Focused Approach

As Strength Focused theory and practice become more prevalent and tested, its value in the therapy room as well as the board room, in the home as well as the school room, and on the playground as well as in the workroom will become increasingly evident and its results impossible to ignore. This approach is not Pollyanna or a shallow "power of positive thinking." It is consistent with theological principles as well as practically effective, whether with intractable problems in Milwaukee where Solution Focused Brief Therapy began or in England's nursing community or in corporate think tanks. Cumberland's therapy, parenting education and management goal embraces the Strength Focused Approach and distinguishes the children's home from other organizations.

Spiritual Enrichment

Cumberland is responsible for the physical, emotional, social, intellectual and spiritual development of the foster children who live on campus. The State of Texas requires that. Our 111 year history with the Cumberland Presbyterian Church, our 2,000 year history with Christianity and our 6,000 year old history within the Judeo Christian tradition instruct and inspire us to treat our residents, clients and one another in light of our spiritual lives.

Cumberland does not abide a shallow veneer of religiosity, but it does seek to live out a life of service based on a grateful response to God's grace, particularly revealed in Christ's love and example. When we become the hands, mind and backbone of God's incarnation amid the lives of traumatized children and families, God's transforming grace changes lives.

Thank you for the privilege of carrying on the spirit of the work which was begun more than a century ago. Those forefathers and foremothers looked around at the need surrounding them. Their hearts were broken with compassion by what they saw. Then they rolled up their sleeves and grabbed what was handy to make a real difference in real ways in the lives of real people. We try to carry on that tradition every day at the Children's Home.

Respectfully Submitted,
Reverend Richard A. Brown, Esq.,
LCCA President, CEO & General Counsel

MEMORIALS / RESOLUTION

I. MEMORIAL FROM CUMBERLAND PRESBYTERY

WHEREAS, the Church of Jesus Christ, the teachings of our Lord, the principles of the Bible; and the Christian Faith and lifestyle, are under attack by an increasingly diverse group of liberal, secular, agnostic, atheistic, and pagan propagandists; and

WHEREAS, under the influence and relentless anti-Christian polemic of these entities and their promoters, a growing majority of Americans are abandoning the precepts of the Bible and making lifestyle choices that are diametrically opposed to the Word of God; and

WHEREAS an estimated 57,000,000 babies have been aborted since Roe vs Wade in 1973 and this number is increasing by more than 1.2 million babies each year; and

WHEREAS the 2013 National Health Interview Survey conducted by the Centers for Disease Control and Prevention reported that 4. 7 % of the adult population of the United States, or more than 14.5 million Americans, identified themselves as gay, lesbian, or bi-sexual; and

WHEREAS same sex marriages are now legal in thirty-seven states and Washington D. C. and the number of same-sex marriages are increasing dramatically across the nation; and

WHEREAS a 2013 study by the Bowling Green State University's National Center for Marriage and Family Research reports that traditional marriages have declined by 60% since 1970 which is a leading factor in the decimation of the nuclear family in American society; and

WHEREAS the national debate regarding euthanasia, or physician assisted suicide, is still emerging in popular thought, five states have adopted legislation that approves the action on some level and 71% of Americans have expressed limited support for physicians being allowed to assist terminal patients to die with dignity and without pain; and

WHEREAS applications have already been filed with the FDA to approve a variety of treatments and therapies for diabetes, neuro degenerative disorders, spinal cord injuries, and heart disease using embryonic stem cells; and

WHEREAS our Lord Jesus Christ established His Church to be the advocate of His teachings and the principles of the Bible to the world; and

WHEREAS He commanded the Church to disciple all nations, incorporate them into the Church by the sacrament of baptism, and teach them to observe all His commandments:

THEREFORE BE IT RESOLVED, That the General Assembly of the Cumberland Presbyterian Church shall order its proper agencies to formulate appropriate responses to these issues based upon Christian compassion and Biblical morality.

I certify that this is a true copy of a memorial adopted by Cumberland Presbytery on March 21, 2015.
Signed Darrell Pickett, Presbytery

GENERAL ASSEMBLY AGENCIES

I. OFFICE OF THE GENERAL ASSEMBLY

A. GENERAL ASSEMBLY OFFICE

	Revised 2015	Proposed 2016
INCOME		
Our United Outreach	$212,201	$212,836
Endowments/Interest	20,000	20,000
Interest on Cash Funds Management	2,500	2,500
Sales of yearbook/digest	2,000	2,000
Our United Outreach Committee	7,000	7,000
TOTAL INCOME	**$243,701**	**$244,336**
EXPENSE		
ECUMENICAL RELATIONS		
World Communion of Reformed Churches	$ 6,000	$ 6,000
CANAAC	2,000	2,000
Ecumenical Travel	1,000	1,000
Sub-Total	$ 9,000	$ 9,000
LIAISON WITH CHURCH		
General Assembly Meeting	$ 10,000	$ 10,000
Preliminary Minutes	5,000	5,000
GA Minutes/Mailing	500	500
Yearbook/Mailing	2,500	2,500
Travel/Moderator	8,500	8,500
Travel/Stated Clerk & Staff	8,500	8,500
Sub-Total	$ 35,000	$ 35,000
OFFICE		
Computer Supplies	$ 2,000	$ 2,000
Equipment/Supplies	2,500	2,500
Postage	2,000	2,000
Sub-Total	$ 6,500	$ 6,500
PERSONNEL		
Salaries/Housing	$139,420	$139,420
FICA (Asst to Stated Clerk)	4,300	4,300
Retirement	6,800	6,800
Health Insurance	30,000	30,000
Disability Insurance/Worker's Compensation	800	800
Sub-Total	$181,320	$181,320
STATED CLERK'S CONFERENCE/BOARD EXPENSE/ COMMITTEE EXPENSE		
Legal Fees / Clerk's Conference	$ 1,963	$ 1,963
Corporate Board Expense	2,000	2,000
Our United Outreach Committee	7,000	7,000
Sub-Total	$ 10,963	$ 10,963
TOTAL EXPENSE	**$242,783**	**$242,783**
From Reserves	$ 918	$ 1,553

B. GENERAL ASSEMBLY COMMISSIONS AND COMMITTEES

	Revised 2015	Proposed 2016
INCOME		
Contingency	$ 2,425	$ 2,425
Nominating Committee	2,629	2,629
Commission on Chaplains	8,934	8,934
Judiciary Committee	8,423	8,423
Theology and Social Concerns Committee	3,140	3,140
TOTAL INCOME	**$ 25,551**	**$ 25,551**

	Revised 2015	Proposed 2016
EXPENSE		
Contingency	$ 2,425	$ 2,425
Nominating Committee	2,629	2,629
Commission on Chaplains	8,934	8,934
Judiciary Committee	8,423	8,423
Theology and Social Concerns Committee	3,140	3,140
TOTAL EXPENSE	**$25,551**	**$ 25,551**

II. MINISTRY COUNCIL

	Revised 2015	Proposed 2016
INCOME		
Endowments		
Grants	$ 10,000	$ 21,511
ILP Transfers		
MMT Budget Reserve Fund: out ILP	456,064	529,579
DMT Contingency Fund: in Wells Fargo	-	9,620
Contributions/Gifts		
Teacher of the Year	200	200
Patron Membership (DMT)	100	100
Christian Education Season Offering	100	100
DMT - General	12,000	12,000
MC - General	52,784	52,784
CMT - General	2,524	-
Our United Outreach		
OUO Income	1,200,000	1,201,000
In lieu of Our United Outreach	13,482	13,440
Children's Fest	9,900	9,900
CP Magazine Subscriptions	30,000	30,000
Cumberland Presbyterians Resources	135,336	109,260
CPWM Convention	12,000	12,000
CPWM Convention Offering	250	250
CPWM General	1,000	1,000
CPWM Sales Merchandise	700	700
CPYC	57,800	57,800
Encounter	105,000	105,000
Faith Out Loud	9,000	9,000
Family Week: Brochure Fees	200	200
Global Missions Interns and Consultants: out ILP	18,000	18,000
Global Social Action: Out ILP	21,000	21,000

	Revised 2015	Proposed 2016
Intersections	$ 2,763	$ 2,763
Ministers Conference	10,269	3,554
Missionary Setup	104,500-	104,500
Missionary Support	335,334	357,884
New Program Initiatives - DMT	6,000	-
New Exploration Iniative - NCD	105,000	105,000
NPI: Children's CP Curriculum	6,000	6,000
Presbyteries/Councils	116,800	-
Program Planning Calendar Sales (Planning Calendar)	8,000	8,000
The Forum	4,500	4,500
Youth Evangelism Conference	26,000	26,000
TOTAL INCOME	**$2,872,439**	**$2,832,645**

EXPENSES

Ministry Council Administration Salaries

	Revised 2015	Proposed 2016
Salaries	$ 805,888	$ 803,484
Clergy Housing Allowance	149,092	149,100
Health Insurance	131,544	137,832
Retirement	42,073	40,968
FICA	35,863	35,688
Insurance/Disability	3,256	3,372

Ministry Council Administration General Expenses

	Revised 2015	Proposed 2016
Annual Credit Card Fees	$ 3,516	$ 3,516
Computer Equipment	4,000	-
Computer Software (Wufoo, Adobe, BaseCamp)	19,770	19,770
CPCA Partnership	3,700	3,700
Educational Publications for Distribution	3,000	3,000
Employee Events	3,942	2,500
Employee Recognition	4,000	4,000
Government Fees (annual reports)	40	40
Legal	2,000	2,000
P & C Insurance	-	19,090
Staff Resource Materials	6,000	6,000
Subscriptions/Membership	150	150
Telephone/Internet	624	624
Temporary Help	25,925	26,098
MC/Elected Team Member Recognition	1,340	1,340
Office Supplies	9,300	9,300
Postage	6,432	6,432
Professional Development	6,000	-

	Revised 2015	Proposed 2016
Beth-El Farmworker	$ 40,500	$ 40,500
Birthplace Shrine Chaplaincy: Chaplain's Stipend	3,750	-
CarShare Program	4,296	-
Children's Fest	19,900	19,900
Church Women United	1,300	1,300
Clergy Crisis Support: Distribution	6,000	6,000
Coalition of Applachian Ministry	12,700	12,700
Congregational Expenses	6,600	3,000
CP Magazine		
CP Magazine: Printing	66,850	60,798
Cumberland Presbyterian Resources	50,500	50,500
CPWM General	7,100	7,100
CPWM Sales Merchandise	2,530	2,530
CPWM Convention	17,400	17,400
CPWM Offering	250	250
CPYC	60,558	60,558
Cross-Culture Immigrant Leadership Training	4,000	4,000
Ecumenical Stewardship Center	9,000	4,500
Ecumenical Youth Ministry Staff Team Partnership	500	500
Encounter	38,012	38,012
Faith in 3D - Partnership	5,000	5,000
Faith Out Loud	3,152	3,152
Family Week	2,700	2,700
General Assembly	31,867	28,700
General Consultants	16,800	9,600
Global Mission Interns and Consultants	18,000	18,000
Global Social Action	21,000	21,000
Intersections	7,992	7,992
Leadership Referral Services	2,100	1,752

	Revised 2015	Proposed 2016
Ministers Conference	$ 13,940	$ 10,225
Ministers Encouragement & Recognition	3,818	3,818
Ministers Retreat	1,000	1,000
Missionary Messenger	73,624	73,636
Missionary Setup	104,500	104,500
Missionary Support	335,244	357,884
National Farm Worker	3,500	3,500
New Church Development (NCD) Subsidies	181,134	161,084
New Exploraation Initiative	105,000	105,000
New Program Iniatives	12,000	12,000
NPI - CPWM Girls and Young Women Council	6,500	6,500
NPI - CP Learning Circles	12,000	12,000
PREP Staff Expenses	996	996
Presbyterial Expenses	5,400	3,000
Presbyterian Youth Triennium	10,000	10,000
Presbyteries/Councils	116,800	101,833
Program Planning Calendar	6,600	6,600
Project Vida	8,500	8,500
Prostestant Church Owned Pub Assoc (DMT)	200	200
Staff Meetings	900	900
Support Ministries	1,000	1,000
The Event	5,000	5,000
The Forum	14,000	14,000
Third Age Ministry	500	500
Travel (includes elected member travel)	75,232	82,971
Web Development/Maintenance	6,000	1,200
Young Adult Conference	6,000	6,000
Young Adult Ministry	6,000	6,000
Youth Evangelism Conference	23,350	23,350
Youth Ministry Planning Council - UBCD	4,000	4,000
TOTAL EXPENSES	**$2,870,550**	**$2,832,645**
Surplus/(Deficit)	$ 1,889	$ 0

III. BOARD OF STEWARDSHIP

	Revised 2015	Proposed 2016
INCOME		
Contributions		
Contributions/Gifts	$ 2,000	$ 2,000
ILP Contributions	2,000	20,000
Endowment Contributions	25,000	25,000
Total Contributions	**29,000**	**47,000**
Our United Outreach	150,000	135,000
Investment Earnings		
Endowment Earnings	80,000	80,000
ILP Earnings	18,000	18,500
Endowment WF Income	17,000	32,000
Total Investment Earnings	**115,000**	**130,500**
Service Fees		
Management Fees - Acct Coordinator	1,600	1,600
Management Fees	50,000	50,000
Total Service Fees	**51,600**	**51,600**
TOTAL INCOME	**$345,600**	**$ 364,100**
EXPENSE		
Salaries		
Salaries	$181,703	$ 206,420
Housing Allowance	21,000	21,000
Total Salaries	**202,703**	**227,420**
Benefits		
Health Insurance	75,000	75,000
Retirement	10,135	10,389
FICA	9,025	9,251
Insurance/Disability	5,000	800
Total Benefits	**99,160**	**95,440**
Events		
Conference/Events	500	500
Tax Guide for Ministers	3,100	3,700
Total Events	**3,600**	**4,200**
Board Expense		
Board/Agency Travel	12,500	12,500
Board/Agency Recognition	550	600
Total Board Expense	**13,050**	**13,100**
Resource Purchases		
Subscriptions	100	100
Total Resources Purchases	**100**	**100**
Contracted Services		
Legal	500	500
Temporary Help	500	500
Total Contracted Services	$ **1,000**	$ **1,000**
Professional Development		
Subscriptions & Membership	2,000	1,000
Total Professional Development	**2,000**	**1,000**
Payment/Subsidies		
ESC Stewardship Expense	2,000	2,000
ILP Withdrawal	2,000	2,500
Endowment Distribution	2,000	2,000
Total Payments/Subsidies	**6,000**	**6,500**
Equipment		
Office Equipment	537	800
Computer Equipment	1,500	2,000
Computer Maintenance	150	150

	Revised 2015	Proposed 2016
Computer Software	$ 500	$ 500
Total Equipment	**2,687**	**3,450**
Supplies		
Computer Supplies	500	500
Office Supplies	2,500	2,500
Total Supplies	**3,000**	**3,000**
Postage/Shipping		
Postage	2,700	2,000
Shipping	500	300
Total Postage/Shipping	**3,200**	**2,300**
Employee Recognition		
Employee Recognition	1,200	1,000
Total Employee Recognition	**1,200**	**1,000**
Travel		
Staff Travel	7,500	5,000
Total Travel	**7,500**	**5,000**
Miscellaneous		
Miscellaneous	300	490
Total Miscellaneous	**300**	**490**
Organization		
Organizational Expense	100	100
Total Organization	**100**	**100**
TOTAL EXPENSE	**$345,600**	**$ 364,100**

IV. HISTORICAL FOUNDATION

	Revised 2015	Proposed 2016
INCOME		
Our United Outreach	$ 79,575	$ 79,575
Endowments	48,500	49,000
Gifts	9,000	11,000
ILP Earnings	5,550	5,550
Denomination Day Offering	5,000	5,000
TOTAL INCOME	**$ 147,625**	**$ 150,125**
EXPENSE		
Salaries	$ 85,450	$ 87,702
FICA / Retirement	14,542	14,940
Health, LTD, Dental & Vision Insurance	9,199	10,034
Board Travel	5,000	5,000
Legal Fees	200	200
Continuing Education	1,000	1,000
Subscriptions/Memberships	2,000	2,000
Archival Equipment	2,000	2,000
Computer Supplies	500	500
Office Supplies	2,000	2,000
Postage	300	300
Acquisitions	8,000	8,000
Birthplace Shrine	4,000	4,000
Employee Recognition	600	600
Staff Travel	7,000	7,000
Denomination Day Project	5,000	5,000
TOTAL EXPENSE	**$ 146,591**	**$ 150,076**

	Revised 2015	Proposed 2016

V. MEMPHIS THEOLOGICAL SEMINARY

REVENUE

Student Tuition Fees	$2,926,825	$2,778,340
Investment	379,280	336,668
Gifts and Grants	1,326,325	1,647,093
Other Revenues	93,919	137,285
TOTAL REVENUES	**$4,726,349**	**$4,899,386**

EXPENSES

Business Office	$ 337,750	$ 348,955
Dean's Office	145,295	139,670
Chapel	44,487	46,167
Formation For Ministry	117,311	122,830
Financial Leadership Ministry	76,325	88,023
Educational Development Committee	17,250	17,250
Advancement Office	314,617	326,186
Doctor of Ministry	66,920	64,270
Facilities	556,818	568,322
Faculty	916,026	945,299
Summer Classes	37,600	37,600
January Classes	11,000	11,000
Financial Aid	64,199	64,872
Information Technology	194,015	201,572
Library	220,958	318,204
President's Office	264,250	261,350
Admissions	155,485	156,527
Student Services	80,161	86,641
Registrar & Institutional Research	130,692	132,000
Public Relations	85,849	90,010
Communications	38,544	37,670
Student Housing	124,280	124,280
Certificate & Continuing Education	40,390	41,230
Student Government	3,255	3,255
Theology & Arts	23,288	42,688
Scholarships	562,473	473,946
Program of Alternate Studies	130,476	138,551
Depreciation	233,317	233,317
TOTAL EXPENSES	**$4,993,031**	**$5,121,685**
Increase (Decrease) in Net Assets	(266,682)	(222,299)

	Revised 2015	Proposed 2016

VI. SHARED SERVICES

	Revised 2015	Proposed 2016
REVENUE		
Our United Outreach	$ 450,926	452,278
TOTAL REVENUES	**$ 450,926**	**$ 452,278**
EXPENSES		
Salaries	$ 48,601	$ 49,767
Health Insurance	23,940	25,137
Retirement	2,430	2,488
FICA	3,718	3,807
Accounting Coordinator	1,600	1,600
Audit	20,000	21,000
Payroll Service	8,200	8,500
Bank Charges	15,000	17,500
Technology System Consultants - EMS	18,000	18,000
Software Maintenance Agreement - Blackbaud	13,200	14,140
Building & Maintenance	12,000	42,000
Pest Control	840	840
Lawn & Ground Maintenance	18,000	18,500
Lawn Treatment	1,500	1,500
Loan Interest	3,000	500
Computer Loan	38,049	15,000
Utilities - Building 1	23,552	27,750
Utilities - Building 2	15,701	20,097
Janitorial Service	8,100	8,100
Security System Monitoring	1,100	1,100
Trash Collection	1,850	1,850
Telephone/Internet	7,500	7,500
Heating & AC Maintenance Agreement	5,000	5,000
Insurance/Liability	34,000	11,140
Office Equipment Maintenance	13,000	13,000
Computer Maintenance	3,000	3,000
Office Supplies	2,500	2,500
Postage	750	750
Employee Events	1,000	1,000
TOTAL EXPENSE	$ 345,131	$ 343,066
Surplus/Deficit	$ 105,795	$ 109,212

The Proceedings of the
ONE HUNDRED EIGHTY-FIFTH GENERAL ASSEMBLY
of the
CUMBERLAND PRESBYTERIAN CHURCH
session held in
CALI, COLOMBIA
June 20 - 26, 2015

At Cali, Colombia, South America and within the facilities of the Colegio Americano, there the twentieth day of June in the year of our Lord, Two Thousand Fifteen, at the appointed hour of three o'clock in the afternoon, Minister and Elder Commissioners from the various presbyteries, youth advisory delegates and visitors assembled.

FIRST DAY – SATURDAY – JUNE 20, 2015

WELCOME AND OPENING WORSHIP

In the Chapel of the Colegio Americano, the one hundred eighty-fifth General Assembly, the Convention of Cumberland Presbyterian Women's Ministry, and visitors gathered for worship at 3:00 p.m. The Reverend Jairo Rodriguez welcomed the gathering on behalf of Andes and Cauca Valley presbyteries. Following the Call to Worship, Psalm 98:1-3 by Athala Jaramillo, Women's Ministry President, and the singing of the hymn, "How Great Thou Art," Reverend Rodriguez introduced Dignitaries including Elder Leon Cole, Moderator of the Cumberland Presbyterian Church in America; Reverend Lisa Anderson, current Moderator of the Cumberland Presbyterian Church; Reverend Manual Vargas, Association of Christian Churches in Cali, and City Council Member, Sr. Jose Fernando Gil.

Following the introductions, worship continued led by the Reverend Jairo Rodriguez, the Reverend Boyce Wallace, Sr. Guillermo Arguello, and the Reverend Rich Shugert, and with Special Music by the Bethel Quartet. Sra. Javiel Rodriguez served as Translator. The Reverend Lisa Anderson, Moderator, presented the sermon, "Holy Confusion." The Closing Prayer was given by the Reverend Jairo Lopez, after which a fifteen minute break was announced.

THE ASSEMBLY IS CONSTITUTED

The Moderator, the Reverend Lisa Anderson, called the assembly to order at 5:20 pm. Reverend Takehiko Miyai, Japan Presbytery, prayed the constituting prayer. On motion, the program was adopted.

The Reverend Stephanie Brown, Red Presbytery, presented the Report of the Credentials Committee. There were forty-eight (48) ministers, forty three (43) elders, for a total of ninety-one (91) commissioners present at 5:20 p.m. There were seventeen (17) Youth Advisory Delegates present. On motion, the report of the Credentials Committee was concurred in, marked Appendix "A" and filed.

ASSEMBLY BUSINESS

Moderator Anderson declared the floor open for nominations for the office of Moderator of the One Hundred Eighty-fifth General Assembly. The Reverend Michele Gentry, previously endorsed by Andes Presbytery, was nominated by Elder Rene Porras, Andes Presbytery.

ELECTION OF MODERATOR

A motion was made that nominations cease and the body move to elect. By election, Moderator Anderson declared that the Reverend Michele Gentry, Andes Presbytery, to be the Moderator of the one hundred eighty-fifth General Assembly of the Cumberland Presbyterian Church. The Reverend Robert Watkins, North Central Presbytery, informed the assembly of Moderator Gentry's qualifications and ministry experience.

Elder Porras escorted Moderator Gentry to the podium. Retiring Moderator Lisa Anderson placed the Moderator's cross on Reverend Gentry, and presented her the gavel.

Moderator Gentry thanked the Assembly for the opportunity to serve the Cumberland Presbyterian Church. She introduced her husband, Dr. Adoniran Correal to the body.

VICE-MODERATOR ELECTED

Moderator Gentry opened the floor for nominations for Vice-Moderator. The Reverend Kip Rush, Nashville Presbytery, was nominated. By election, the Reverend Kip Rush was elected as Vice-Moderator of the one hundred eighty-fifth General Assembly of the Cumberland Presbyterian Church.

PRESENTATION BY STATED CLERK

The Stated Clerk, Michael Sharpe, invited retiring Moderator, Lisa Anderson, to the podium and presented her with a replica of the Moderator's cross and a gavel representing the one used in the one hundred eighty-fourth General Assembly of the Cumberland Presbyterian Church. The Stated Clerk thanked Reverend Anderson for her dedication and tireless travel cross the denomination during her tenure. The assembly responded with a standing ovation.

Reverend Anderson thanked her husband, The Reverend Barry Anderson, granddaughter Lily, the congregation of Colonial Cumberland Presbyterian Church, Memphis, Tennessee, and the assembly for allowing her to serve as moderator.

COMMUNICATIONS

The Stated Clerk, Michael Sharpe announced that there were no communications.

GREETINGS FROM THE CUMBERLAND PRESBYTERIAN CHURCH IN AMERICA

Moderator Gentry recognized Elder Leon Cole, Moderator of the Cumberland Presbyterian Church in America. Elder Cole brought greetings to the assembly in the name of the Cumberland Presbyterian Church in America and expressed his delight in attending the proceedings. He briefly addressed the challenges facing the Cumberland Presbyterian family of churches.

PROGRAM OF ALTERNATE STUDIES PRESENTATION

The Reverend Dr. Michael Qualls, Director of the Program of Alternate Studies spoke of the founding of the Cumberland Presbyterian Church as a movement whose Founding Fathers found a "new way" to present the Gospel on the Frontier. Moving ahead 200 years later, the Cumberland Presbyterian work in Colombia needed to discover a "new way" to bring theological education to the women and men seeking to serve the church as clergy. In 2012, Andes and Cauca Valley presbyteries began a Program of Alternate Studies to serve Candidates for the Ministry in this area. Dr. Qualls presented a plaque of appreciation to Moderator Gentry who serves as the first Dean of PAS. Dr. Qualls also introduced Consuelo Gutierrez who has completed her PAS studies and will be the first graduate of PAS Colombia.

COMMISSIONER RESOLUTIONS

The Reverend Fred Polacek, Minister Commissioner from Nashville Presbytery, presented a resolution to the assembly dealing with the Retirement Program administered by the Board of Stewardship, Foundations, and Benefits. Following the presentation of the resolution, Moderator Gentry announced that the resolution was received to be referred to the appropriate committee at a later time.

CORRECTIONS TO THE PRELIMINARY MINUTES

The Stated Clerk reported that a copy of all corrections to the preliminary minutes were handed out to all commissioners during orientation and would be reflected in the final printing of the minutes.

COMMITTEE APPOINTMENTS AND REFERRALS

REFERRALS TO COMMITTEES

Referrals to the Committee on Children's Home and Historical Foundation

Page	Report
86	The Report of the Board of Trustees of the Historical Foundation
127	The Report of the Board of Trustees of the Cumberland Presbyterian Children's Home

Referrals to the Committee on Higher Education

Page	Report
95	The Report of the Board of Trustees of Memphis Theological Seminary
124	The Report of the Board of Trustees of Bethel University

Referrals to the Committee on Judiciary

Page	Report
108	The Report of the Permanent Committee on Judiciary

Referrals to the Committee on Chaplains/Missions/Pastoral Development

Page	Report
38	The Report of the Ministry Council (shaded sections only)
106	The Report of the Commission on Military Chaplains and Personnel

Referrals to the Committee on Ministry Council/Communication/Discipleship

Page	Report
38	The Report of the Ministry Council, except shaded sections which are referred to Chaplains/Missions/Pastoral Development

Referrals to the Committee on Stewardship/Elected Officers

Page	Report
31	The Report of the Moderator
32	The Report of the Stated Clerk
60	The Report of the Board of Stewardship, Foundation and Benefits
104	The Report of the Our United Outreach Committee
111	The Report of the Place of Meeting Committee
135	Line Item Budgets Submitted by General Assembly Agencies
	Resolution presented by Reverend Fred Polacek, Minister Commissioner, Nashville Presbytery

Referrals to the Committee on Theology and Social Concerns

Page	Report
113	The Report of the Unified Committee on Theology and Social Concerns
123	The Report of the Unification Task Force
134	Memorial from Cumberland Presbytery

INTRODUCTION OF BOARD/AGENCY REPRESENTATIVES

The Stated Clerk introduced the following Board/Agency Representatives:

Bethel University   Dr. Walter Butler

Commission on Chaplains	Rev. Cassandra Thomas
Children's Home	Dr. Richard Brown
Historical Foundation	Rev. Tommy Jobe
Memphis Theological Seminary	Rev. Kevin Brantley
Stewardship	Sylvia Hall
Theology and Social Concerns	Rev. Gloria Vila-Diaz (CPC)
	Elder Leon Cole (CPCA)

RECESS

On Motion, the General Assembly of the Cumberland Presbyterian Church recessed at 6:10 p.m.

THE EVENING PROGRAM

The General Assembly, the Convention of Cumberland Presbyterian Women's Ministry, and visitors participated in a reception to honor the past Moderator, the Reverend Lisa Anderson and the newly elected Moderator, the Reverend Michele Gentry with a reception on the grounds of the Colegio Americano.

SECOND DAY – SUNDAY – JUNE 21, 2015

The General Assembly and visitors began their day travelling by bus in groups to the local Cumberland Presbyterian Churches in Cauca Valley Presbytery for worship. Following worship, all enjoyed fellowship and lunch provided by the host churches.

At 4:00 p.m., current Missionaries, former Missionaries and their families gathered for a reunion and time of remembering.

At 5:00 p.m., Clergy Women gathered for fellowship and programing.

At 6:30 p.m., the General Assembly, CPWM, and visitors were invited to gather for "*A Night of Memories/Sharing*" which included the signing of hymns, reading scripture and a program that included current and former Missionaries or family members and descendants sharing stories about life on the Colombian Missions Field as the church celebrates 90 years of Mission Work in Colombia.

THIRD DAY – MONDAY – JUNE 22, 2015

The General Assembly and visitors began the day with a devotional led by Ms. Noriko Matsumoto, Japan Presbytery. The scripture reading was Matthew 3:16-17. The message was "*Serve and Proclaim*." There were forty-seven (47) ministers, forty one (41) elders for a total of eighty-eight (88) commissioners, and sixteen (16) youth advisory delegates present at 8:45 a.m.

Following the devotional, necessary announcements were made and copies of a Resolution submitted by the Reverend Fred Polacek, Nashville Presbytery, were distributed. Commissioners were then dismissed to committee work until 5:00 p.m.

Other events that were scheduled for the day included a concert by the Bethel University Quartet at 2:00 p.m. and a Unification (CPC/CPCA) Presentation/Q & A at 4:00 p.m.

At 7:00 p.m. the General Assembly, CP Women's Ministry and visitors gathered for a service of worship and Holy Communion, which included an offering for the CP Women's Ministry project, "*Set Them Free*." This service was a celebration of 90 years of Mission and Ministry in Colombia. Included in the service were moving prayers, joyful singing, a moving message and the celebration of the Lord's Supper. The Reverend John Jairo Correa, Pastor of Cumberland Presbyterian Church in Armenia brought the message, "*Let us Serve as Jesus Did*." The Reverend Lynn Thomas served as translator for the sermon. Elder Takeshi Yohena, Japan Presbytery, presented a touching reading written by Yoshimasa Nina, Moderator of Japan Presbytery. Special music was provided by the Bethel University Quartet and the Praise Group from Renacer.

Those who helped serve Communion were: Reverend Virginia Espinoza, USA, Choctaw Nation; Reverend John Lo, South Korea; Reverend Takechiko Miyal, Japan; Reverend Ella Hung, Hong Kong; Reverend Luz Dary Guerrero, Mexico; Reverend Socorro Delgado, Guatemala; Mr. Leon Cole, Cumberland Presbyterian Church in America; Reverend So Li Wong, Hong Kong; Reverend Sergio Betancur; Reverend Sol Maria Sanchez; Reverend Luciria Aguirre; Reverend Wilfrido Quinonez; Reverend Ricardo Castaneda; Reverend Luz Maria Heilbron; Reverend Diana Valdez; Reverend Juan Esteban Blanon.

Following the singing of "*Happy Birthday*" to the Colombian Cumberland Presbyterian Church and the Benediction, worship participants were treated to birthday cake.

FOURTH DAY – TUESDAY – JUNE 23, 2015

The General Assembly and visitors began the day with a devotional led by Mr. Caleb Rhodes, Youth Advisory Delegate from Missouri Presbytery, translated by Benjamin Diaz, Youth Advisory Delegate, Trinity Presbytery. *"Being Authentic"* was the title of the devotional with Acts 4:34-5-6 as the scripture. The Memorial Roll of Ministers was read. The roll includes those ministers that have died during the past year.

IN MEMORY OF MINISTERS LOST BY DEATH

NAME	PRESBYTERY	AGE	DATE
Brodeur, Evelyn M.	Robert Donnell	91	12/02/14
Chang, John	del Cristo		03/08/14
Chesnut, Walter	Cumberland	98	12/26/14
Cravens, Marvin	Missouri	86	08/02/14
Denton, Clyde M.	Columbia	72	06/27/14
Drylie, James T	West Tennessee	75	02/14/15
Fajardo, Jose	Red River	101	02/21/15
Gerard, Eugene "Stan"	Covenant	82	04/26/15
Hester, J. David	East Tennessee	83	07/31/14
Leslie, Eugene	West Tennessee	83	03/10/15
Matlock, Joe	del Cristo		02/26/15
McGregor, David	Columbia	86	01/23/14
McKee, Margaret	West Tennessee	87	11/06/14
Morgan, Jerry	Red River		09/19/14
Palmer, Walter (Pete)	Red River	87	07/26/14
Powell, Omer Thomas	Cumberland	90	01/30/15
Rapson, Tim <Candidate>	Tennessee-Georgia		03/30/14
Rodriguez, Paul	Cauca Valley		03/10/14
Todd, Virgil	Nashville	93	10/20/14
White, Bobby	Cumberland		??
Wilkins, Marvin E.	Columbia	65	04/01/14

Special music was provided by Divino Redentor Women's Choir who performed two traditional songs brought from Africa.

The Stated Clerk invited all from the Colegio Americano who have made our General Assembly visit to Colombia possible to move to the stage area and say their names. Appreciation was expressed by the body for their hard work, hospitality and help. Appreciation was also shown to the committee that has been working and planning for 3 years for this event.

CALL TO ORDER

The Moderator, Reverend Michele Gentry, called the assembly to order at 9:23 a.m. There were forty-eight (48) ministers, thirty-nine (40) elders for a total of 88 commissioners, and thirteen (13) youth advisory delegates present as of 9:23 a.m.

ANNOUNCEMENTS

The Moderator announced procedures for presenting reports. Youth will cast an unbinding vote before the minister and elder commissioners vote.

PARLIMENTARIAN APPOINTED

The Moderator appointed the Reverend Dr. Jay Earhart-Brown, President of MTS, as Parliamentarian.

ASSEMBLY BUSINESS

THE REPORT OF THE NOMINATING COMMITTEE

The Report of the Nominating Committee was presented by Nancy Bean who was given permission to address the body by vote as she is not a member of the body. There being no other nominations, the Moderator closed nominations and the body proceeded to elect. By vote, all named in the Nominating Committee Report were elected to their respective offices.

THE REPORT OF THE COMMITTEE ON
CHILDREN'S HOME AND HISTORICAL FOUNDATION

The Report of the Committee on Children's Home and Historical Foundation was presented by Reverend Susan Parker, Hope Presbytery. The report was read by YAD's Wendy Keiser, Nashville Presbytery; Charli Uhlrich, North Central Presbytery; and Jacob Perkey, Red River Presbytery. Motion was made that the report be concurred in and the recommendation be adopted. Motion passed. The report was marked "B" and filed.

PRESENTATION

The Moderator recognized Elder Baker Thompson, Covenant Presbytery. Mr. Baker's great grandfather was David Moorman McAnulty, Moderator of the Ninety-Third General Assembly of the Cumberland Presbyterian Church. Mr. Baker spoke of his family's early involvement in the Cumberland Presbyterian Church and his great grandfather's support of the Cumberland Presbyterian Church's work in Colombia and how proud he would be to see the work today.

THE REPORT OF THE
MINISTRY COUNCIL/COMMUNICATION/DISCIPLESHIP COMMITTEE

The Report of the Ministry Council/Communications/Discipleship Committee was presented by Mike Davis, Red River Presbytery. The report was read by YAD, John Lorick, Robert Donnell Presbytery. Motion was made that the report be concurred in and the recommendations be adopted. Motion passed. The report was marked "C" and filed.

THE REPORT OF THE COMMITTEE ON JUDICIARY

The Report of the Committee on Judiciary was presented by Reverend Joseph Butler, Murfreesboro Presbytery. The report was read by YAD Logan Reed, Red River Presbytery. Motion was made that the report be concurred in and the recommendation be adopted. Motion passed. The report was marked "D" and filed.

RECESS

The Moderator declared a 15 minute recess.
The Moderator called the meeting to order at 10:36 a.m.

THE REPORT OF THE COMMITTEE ON STEWARDSHIP/ELECTED OFFICIALS

The Report of the Committee on Stewardship/Elected Officials was presented by Edwardo Montoya, North Central Presbytery. The report was read by YADs Arianna Whaley, Murfreesboro Presbytery, and Miles Bray, Arkansas Presbytery. Motion was made that the report be concurred in and the recommendations be adopted. Motion passed with one abstention. The report was marked "E" and filed.

THE REPORT OF THE COMMITTEE ON
CHAPLAINS/MISSIONS/PASTORAL DEVELOPMENT

The Report of the Committee on Chaplains/Missions/Pastoral Development was presented by Reverend Charles McCaskey, Murfreesboro Presbytery. Reverend McCaskey noted an editorial change that the last line of the second paragraph under A. should be deleted. The report was read by YADs Jessica Bane, Nashville Presbytery; Benjamin Diaz, Trinity Presbytery; and Fumika Satoh, Japan Presbytery.
Motion was made to concur in the report and adopt the recommendations. A motion was made

to divide the question and consider Recommendation 5 separately from other recommendations. Motion passed. Following discussion, Recommendation 5 was denied.

Motion made to add the words "USA Federal" to Recommendation 1 to make it read, "That the Cumberland Presbyterian Church authorize the Stated Clerk of the denomination to designate the Presbyterian Council for Chaplains and Military Personnel as the official endorsing agency of the Cumberland Presbyterian Church for those seeking to serve as chaplains in the USA Federal prison setting. Motion passed.

On vote, Recommendation 1, as amended, Recommendations 2-4 and 6-11 were approved. The report was marked "F" and filed.

RECESS

The Moderator declared a recess for lunch.

MEETING RECONVENES

The Moderator called the meeting back to order at 2:00 p.m.

Stated Clerk Mike Sharpe made necessary announcements and reported that Ms. Jessica Preston had fallen ill. Reverend Terra Sisco offered a prayer for healing for Ms. Preston. Reverend Dennis Preston, Cumberland Presbytery, was excused for this session.

Moderator Gentry also made announcements about the use of microphones.

THE REPORT OF THE COMMITTEE ON THEOLOGY AND SOCIAL CONCERNS

The Report of the Committee on Theology and Social Concerns was presented by Reverend Kip Rush, Nashville Presbytery. Rev. Rush commended the Cumberland Presbyterian Women's Ministry for their work with social issues.

The Report was read by YADs Tanner Lindsey, Cumberland Presbyterian; William Moss, Murfreesboro Presbytery; and Kelsey Hayes, Covenant Presbytery. Motion made to concur with the report and adopt its recommendations. Motion made to divide the question and consider Recommendation 10 separately. Motion passed. On vote Recommendation 10 was denied.

By vote the report was concurred in and Recommendations 1-9 and 11 adopted.

Reverend Lisa Anderson addressed the body to congratulate the YADs on their resolve and bravery to face tough issues

REPORT OF THE COMMITTEE ON HIGHER EDUCATION

Moderator Gentry asked Vice Moderator Kip Rush to take the gavel to enable her to participate with the Committee on Higher Education.

The Report of the Committee on Higher Education was presented by Reverend George Estes, del Cristo Presbytery. The report was read by Reverend Estes and Reverend Doy Daniels, West Tennessee Presbytery; and YADs Caleb Rhodes, Missouri Presbytery; and Hunter Webster, West Tenneessee Presbytery. Motion was made to concur in the report and adopt its recommendations.

Nancy Bean was given permission to speak to the body by consent. She reported that Bethel University is participating in the Tennessee Promise Program which provides two years of college for all qualified students in the state of Tennessee. This has increased enrollment and given students more opportunities for education.

By vote report was conurred and the recommendations adopted.

In compliance with the report, standing applause was given for the PAS—Colombia Program.

THE MODERATOR RETURNED TO THE PODIUM

RESOLUTION OF GRATITUDE

A Resolution of Gratitude was presented by the Reverend Tommy Jobe, Murfreesboro Presbytery, expressing gratitude to our Colombian Hosts. The Body responded with a hearty, standing, round of applause. On vote, the body accepted the resolution and directed that it be placed in the minutes.

Resolution of Gratitude

This resolution is presented to the 185th General Assembly by Minister Commissioner from Murfreesboro Presbytery, Reverend Tommy Jobe,

The 185th General Assembly takes this opportunity to express its deepest and heartfelt thanks to the one hundred and ninety seven (197) Colombians who formed the nine (9) committees who have worked tirelessly to plan, prepare for, and provide for, lead and expedite the assembly and convention. Years of preparation have made possible the most memorable and inspiring General Assembly I have experienced in fifty-seven (57) years.

We are grateful to the Organizing Committee of twenty-six (26) people led by their chair, Elder Jairo Lopez; Missionaries, Boyce and Beth Wallace; Ms. Adriana, Rector/Principle of Colegio Americano; Mr. Guillermo Arguello, Administrator of Colegio Americano; Reverend Michelle Gentry, Moderator of Del Presbiterio de Los Andes; and Lucinia Aguirre, Moderator of Presbiterio del Valle.

Other committees include: Colegio Americano personnel (28) primary personnel (21), secondary personnel (52), administrative personnel (33), general service personnel (19), transportation personnel (9), apprentices (7), and airport transportation personnel (2), with twenty (20) assistants. May God be praised for such dedication. Thanks also to all those who served as translators during the week.

The 185th General Assembly was inspired and challenged by our Colombian sisters and brothers as we joined together to celebrate 90 years of Cumberland Presbyterian ministry in Colombia. Each worship service was unique and uplifting, beginning with the opening worship led by Reverend Jairo Rodriguez and Reverend Boyce Wallace. Our thanks to the retiring moderator, Reverend Lisa Anderson for her inspiring message.

We have truly been blessed by the music of the Bethel Quartet from Bethel University, Nicole Newman, Chase Davis, John Holton and Nick Conder, under the direction of Matthew Holt, who also accompanied the sound engineer, Daniel Howell. We are grateful for the words of welcome from Cali City Councilman, Sr. Jose Fernando Gil, and from Reverend Manual Vargas with the Association of Christian Churches in Cali. Our special thanks to Reverend John Jairo Correa, pastor of the Armenia Church for his most challenging message at the service of celebration on Monday evening and Reverend Lynn Thomas who served as interpreter.

Special thanks to the Praise Group from Renacer Church for their wonderful presentation. Thanks also to the singers and instrumentalists who led at the worship service. The Night of Memories shared on Sunday evening will long be kept in our hearts as we looked back on 90 years on missionary service. We were touched deeply by the missionaries and their families as they shared their special memories.

We are thankful to the Divino Redentor Women's choir for bringing the moving culture of Guape to us in song and music on Tuesday morning.

The 185th General Assembly is grateful to Reverend Lisa Anderson for her diligent and dedicated service to the church at-large this past year, and to Vice Moderator, Reverend Paula Louder for her service. We wish to thank the staff of the General Assembly Office for their dedication and going the 2nd mile in this challenging year with assembly being held in another country: to Stated Clerk, Reverend. Michael Sharpe; Engrossing Clerk, Reverend Vernon Sansom, Mrs. Elizabeth Vaughn, Assistant to the Stated Clerk; Mrs. Laurie Sharpe and Mrs. Gloria Villa Diaz, who served as a volunteers; for their tireless work and leadership to make this a most successful week.

We give thanks to each commissioner and youth advisory delegate for your dedicated service on each committee, and special thanks to each chair and vice chair for your leadership.

We are grateful to Elder Leon Cole for representing the Cumberland Presbyterian Church in America and for serving on the Unification Task Force with dedicated leadership.

Thanks also to our moderator, Reverend Michele Gentry, and our vice moderator, Reverend Kip Rush, for leading us in this very dynamic session of General Assembly.

The 185th General Assembly is most special because of the warm, joyous, outreaching, loving hospitality of the members of the churches of Cauca Valley and Andes Presbyteries who have welcomed us with open arms. Muchas Gracias!

Most of all we thank Almighty God for the wind of the Spirit in our midst.

Respectfully submitted, Reverend Tommy Jobe, Minister Commissioner to the 185th General Assembly of the Cumberland Presbyterian Church held June 19-26, 2015, Cali, Columbia, South America.

PRESENTATION

A presentation was made by the Reverend Kip Rush promoting the 186th General Assembly meeting in Nashville, Tennessee to meet concurrently with the Cumberland Presbyterian Church in America.

Moderator Gentry introduced some of the PAS-Colombia students to the Assembly explaining that some are current students and some are graduates. The body showed their support and appreciation with standing applause.

READING OF THE MINUTES

The printed minutes for Saturday were distributed with the committee reports, and the minutes for Sunday, Monday and Tuesday were read. On motion, the minutes were approved as corrected.

ADJOURNMENT

Motion was made to adjourn to meet in Nashville, Tennessee on June 20-24, 2015. Motion passed. Closing Prayer was given by Youth Advisory Delegate, John Lorick, Robert Donnell Presbytery, at 4:10 p.m.

FIFTH DAY – WEDNESDAY – JUNE 24, 2015

Wednesday was a day of sight-seeing and optional tours for General Assembly commissioners, youth advisory delegates and visitors.

SIXTH DAY – THURSDAY – JUNE 25, 2015

Thursday was a day of sight-seeing and optional tours for General Assembly commissioners, youth advisory delegates and visitors.

CLOSING WORSHIP

At 6:30 p.m. on Thursday night, the General Assembly commissioners, youth advisory delegates and visitors gathered for the closing worship of the 185th meeting of the General Assembly. Choruses were led by the local praise group from Central Church. The following statement was included in the worship bulletin:

In the General Assembly, we have celebrated the work of missionaries from the United States in Colombia. That era has passed and we are sending Colombian missionaries to other countries. Tonight, we want to recognize some of them who are present with us and give them a short time to talk about their work.

Presentations by Colombian missionaries in other countries were given by Carlos and Luz Dary Rivera, Anay Ortega, and Fhanor and Socorro Pejendino.

The following is a list of missionaries presented at worship or named:
        Guatemala: Fhanor & Socorro Pejendino and Anay Ortega
        México: Carlos & Luz Dary Rivera
        United States: Milton Ortiz, Johan Daza, and Edward Montoya
            Director Missions Ministry Team , Milton & Francia Ortiz
            Transcultural Ministries USA , Johan & Erin Daza
            Houston, Texas: Ruben Dario & Cecilia Albarracin and Fredy &
                Gloria Villa Diaz and David Andres Montoya, Sirve como candidato
            Fort Lauderdale, Florida: Omar & Virginia Yarce
            Miami, Florida: Luciano & Atala Jaramillo and Wilfredo Mora, Pastor
            Atlanta, Georgia: Mabe & Ivan Garcia
            Chicago, Illinois: Jeremias & Ester Aros and Eduardo & Claudia Montoya
            Boston, Massachusetts: Ricardo y Josefina Sanchez

After the closing prayer, worshippers were dismissed with a greater understanding of the global nature of the Cumberland Presbyterian Church, and a greater understanding of our oneness in Christ.

AUDITED FINANCIAL STATEMENTS OF

THE AGENCIES OF
THE CUMBERLAND PRESBYTERIAN
CHURCH CENTER

DECEMBER 31, 2014

THE AGENCIES OF
THE CUMBERLAND PRESBYTERIAN CHURCH CENTER

TABLE OF CONTENTS
DECEMBER 31, 2014

	PAGE
Independent Auditor's Report	1
Combined Statement of Financial Position	2
Combined Statement of Activity	3
Combined Statement of Cash Flows	4
Individual Statements of Financial Position	
Our United Outreach	5
General Assembly Corporation	6
Ministry Council	7
Shared Services	8
Historical Foundation	9
Board of Stewardship, Foundation, and Benefits	10
Small Church Loan Program	11
Insurance Program	12
Ministerial Aid	13
Investment Loan Program	14
Retirement Fund	15
Endowment Program	16
Individual Statements of Activity	
Our United Outreach	17
General Assembly Corporation	18
Ministry Council	19
Shared Services	20
Historical Foundation	21
Board of Stewardship, Foundation, and Benefits	22
Small Church Loan Program	23
Insurance Program	24
Ministerial Aid	25
Investment Loan Program	26
Retirement Fund	27
Endowment Program	28
Notes to Financial Statements	29 - 42

To the General Assembly Corporation
The Agencies of The Cumberland Presbyterian Church Center
Memphis, Tennessee

INDEPENDENT AUDITOR'S REPORT

We have audited the accompanying combined financial statements of The Agencies of The Cumberland Presbyterian Church Center, which comprise the combined statement of financial position as of December 31, 2014, and the related combined statements of activities and cash flows for the year then ended, and the related notes to the financial statements.

Management's Responsibility for the Financial Statements

Management is responsible for the preparation and fair presentation of these financial statements in accordance with accounting principles generally accepted in the United States of America; this includes the design, implementation, and maintenance of internal control relevant to the preparation and fair presentation of financial statements that are free from material misstatement, whether due to fraud or error.

Auditor's Responsibility

Our responsibility is to express an opinion on these financial statements based on our audit. We conducted our audit in accordance with auditing standards generally accepted in the United States of America. Those standards require that we plan and perform the audit to obtain reasonable assurance about whether the financial statements are free from material misstatement.

An audit involves performing procedures to obtain audit evidence about the amounts and disclosures in the financial statements. The procedures selected depend on the auditor's judgment, including the assessment of the risks of material misstatement of the financial statements, whether due to fraud or error. In making those risk assessments, the auditor considers internal control relevant to the entity's preparation and fair presentation of the financial statements in order to design audit procedures that are appropriate in the circumstances, but not for the purpose of expressing an opinion on the effectiveness of the entity's internal control. Accordingly, we express no such opinion. An audit also includes evaluating the appropriateness of accounting policies used and the reasonableness of significant accounting estimates made by management, as well as evaluating the overall presentation of the financial statements.

We believe that the audit evidence we have obtained is sufficient and appropriate to provide a basis for our audit opinion.

Opinion

In our opinion, the combined financial statements referred to above present fairly, in all material respects, the individual and combined financial position of The Agencies of The Cumberland Presbyterian Church Center as of December 31, 2014, and the changes in their net assets and their cash flows for the year then ended in accordance with accounting principles generally accepted in the United States of America.

FOUTS & MORGAN
Certified Public Accountants

Memphis, Tennessee
June 4, 2015

THE AGENCIES OF THE CUMBERLAND PRESBYTERIAN CHURCH CENTER

COMBINED STATEMENT OF FINANCIAL POSITION
DECEMBER 31, 2014

ASSETS

Cash	$ 452,095
Due from other agencies, boards, and divisions	6,059,625
Accounts receivable	10,174
Interest and dividends receivable, net of allowance for uncollectible interest	92,014
Health insurance tax credit receivable	17,592
Securities and investments	
Cash and cash equivalents	4,833,147
Mortgage backed securities	7,484,557
Bond mutual funds	7,903,441
Closed-end bond funds	3,483,770
Equity mutual funds	3,293,443
Real estate investment trusts	5,158,190
Private investment entities	55,611,839
Real estate	90,573
Inventory - at lower of cost or market	1,371
Prepaid expenses	6,704
Loans receivable, net of allowance for loan losses	11,582,642
Buildings and land	2,760,412
Furniture and equipment	156,745
Less: Accumulated depreciation	(613,771)
Total Assets	$ 108,384,563

LIABILITIES AND NET ASSETS

Liabilities:	
Accounts payable	$ 3,257
Accrued expenses	296
Notes payable to individual investors	1,323,811
Unearned subscriptions	14,008
Due to other agencies, boards, and divisions	6,380,098
Funds held in trust for others	32,904
Depository accounts held for church organizations	9,391,498
Total liabilities	17,145,872
Net Assets:	
Unrestricted	8,278,247
Temporarily restricted	1,830,548
Permanently restricted	57,381,446
Net assets available for benefits, at fair value	23,748,450
Total net assets	91,238,691
Total Liabilities and Net Assets	$ 108,384,563

See accompanying notes.

THE AGENCIES OF
THE CUMBERLAND PRESBYTERIAN CHURCH CENTER

COMBINED STATEMENT OF ACTIVITY
FOR THE YEAR ENDED DECEMBER 31, 2014

	Unrestricted	Temporarily Restricted	Permanently Restricted	Net Assets Available for Benefits	Totals
Revenues, gains, and other support:					
Contributions and gifts	$ 4,600,862	$ 1,150,751	$ 3,092,559	$ -	$ 8,844,172
Insurance program premium revenue	2,143,075	-	-	-	2,143,075
Endowment earnings	-	-	522,008	-	522,008
Interest and dividend income	123,835	59,982	14,833	135,275	333,925
Management service fees	51,116	-	-	(22,266)	28,850
Registration fees	85,443	-	-	-	85,443
Sales and subscription income	211,499	-	-	-	211,499
Net realized and unrealized gain on investments	471,205	-	2,754,888	1,153,146	4,379,239
Rental income	9,682	-	-	-	9,682
Other income	110,978	-	-	-	110,978
Participant retirement contributions	-	-	-	713,181	713,181
Net assets released from restriction	4,557,680	(2,287,819)	(2,269,861)	-	-
Total revenues, gains, and other support	12,365,375	(1,077,086)	4,114,427	1,979,336	17,382,052
Provision for loan losses	-	-	-	-	-
Net revenues, gains, and other support - after provision	12,365,375	(1,077,086)	4,114,427	1,979,336	17,382,052
Expenses:					
Our United Outreach	517,336	-	-	-	517,336
General Assembly Corporation	462,282	-	-	-	462,282
Ministry Council	5,192,663	-	-	-	5,192,663
Shared Services	396,133	-	-	-	396,133
Historical Foundation	175,484	-	-	-	175,484
Board of Stewardship, Foundation and Benefits	286,698	-	-	-	286,698
Small Church Loan Program	54,323	-	-	-	54,323
Insurance Program	2,265,153	-	-	-	2,265,153
Ministerial Aid	1,179,406	-	-	-	1,179,406
Investment Loan Program	70,862	-	-	-	70,862
Retirement Fund	-	-	-	1,091,877	1,091,877
Endowment Program	-	-	2,748,401	-	2,748,401
Total expenses	10,600,340	-	2,748,401	1,091,877	14,440,618
Change in net assets	1,765,035	(1,077,086)	1,366,026	887,459	2,941,434
Net assets at beginning of year	6,513,212	2,907,634	56,015,419	22,860,991	88,297,256
Net assets at end of year	$ 8,278,247	$ 1,830,548	$ 57,381,445	$ 23,748,450	$ 91,238,690

See accompanying notes.

THE AGENCIES OF
THE CUMBERLAND PRESBYTERIAN CHURCH CENTER

COMBINED STATEMENT OF CASH FLOWS
FOR THE YEAR ENDED DECEMBER 31, 2014

Cash flows from operating activities	
Combined change in net assets	$ 2,941,435
Adjustments to reconcile combined change in net assets to net cash used in operating activities:	
Depreciation	65,289
Net realized/unrealized (gain) loss on investments - Investment Loan Program	(418,670)
Net realized/unrealized (gain) loss on investments - Retirement Fund	(1,153,150)
Net realized/unrealized (gain) loss on investments - Endowment Program	(2,754,293)
(Increase) decrease in operating assets:	
Due from other agencies, boards, and divisions	(11,219)
Accounts receivable	2,457
Interest and dividends receivable	(908)
Health insurance tax credit receivable	26,924
Prepaid assets	(282)
Increase (decrease) in operating liabilities:	
Accounts payable	886
Accrued expenses	250
Unearned subscriptions	2,333
Due to other agencies, boards, and divisions	3,737
Funds held in trust for others	399
Notes payable to individual investors	533,176
Depository accounts held for church organizations	53,321
Net cash provided by (used in) operating activities	(708,315)
Cash flows from investing activities	
Proceeds from sale of investments:	
Endowment Program	6,353,665
Retirement Fund	3,225,131
Investment Loan Program	2,878,388
Purchase of investments:	
Endowment Program	(7,065,146)
Retirement Fund	(2,959,972)
Investment Loan Program	(2,945,057)
Loan principal payments received	1,008,738
Net cash provided by (used in) investing activities	495,747
Net increase (decrease) in cash	(212,568)
Cash at the beginning of the year	664,663
Cash at the end of the year	$ 452,095

See accompanying notes.

THE AGENCIES OF
THE CUMBERLAND PRESBYTERIAN CHURCH CENTER
OUR UNITED OUTREACH
STATEMENT OF FINANCIAL POSITION
DECEMBER 31, 2014

ASSETS

Endowment earnings receivable	$ 28,798
Endowments - held by Endowment Program	2,582,202
Total Assets	$ 2,611,000

LIABILITIES AND NET ASSETS

Liabilities:	
Cash borrowed from other agencies, boards, and divisions	$ 10,445
Due to outside church organizations	39,367
Total liabilities	49,812
Net Assets:	
Unrestricted	(21,014)
Permanently restricted	2,582,202
Total net assets	2,561,188
Total Liabilities and Net Assets	$ 2,611,000

See accompanying notes.

THE AGENCIES OF
THE CUMBERLAND PRESBYTERIAN CHURCH CENTER
GENERAL ASSEMBLY CORPORATION
STATEMENT OF FINANCIAL POSITION
DECEMBER 31, 2014

ASSETS

Endowment earnings receivable	$ 5,553
Health insurance tax credit receivable	9,318
Inventory	1,371
Due from other agencies, boards, and divisions	231,504
	247,746
Endowments - held by Endowment Program	465,139
Total Assets	$ 712,885

LIABILITIES AND NET ASSETS

Liabilities:	
Accounts payable	$ 1,094
Cash borrowed from other agencies, boards, and divisions	206,481
Due to other agencies, boards, and divisions	13,207
Funds held in trusts for others	32,904
Total liabilities	253,686
Net Assets:	
Unrestricted	(5,940)
Permanently restricted	465,139
Total net assets	459,199
Total Liabilities and Net Assets	$ 712,885

See accompanying notes.

THE AGENCIES OF
THE CUMBERLAND PRESBYTERIAN CHURCH CENTER
MINISTRY COUNCIL
STATEMENT OF FINANCIAL POSITION
DECEMBER 31, 2014

ASSETS

Cash	$ 91,038
Accounts receivable	9,398
Endowment earnings receivable	158,390
Health insurance tax credit receivable	879
Due from other agencies, boards, and divisions	2,116,367
Securities and investments	
Real estate	51,818
	2,427,890
Endowments - held by Endowment Program	16,402,306
Total Assets	$ 18,830,196

LIABILITIES AND NET ASSETS

Liabilities:	
Accounts payable	$ 140
Accrued expenses	31
Unearned subscriptions	14,008
Total liabilities	14,179
Net Assets:	
Unrestricted	768,000
Temporarily restricted	1,645,711
Permanently restricted	16,402,306
Total net assets	18,816,017
Total Liabilities and Net Assets	$ 18,830,196

See accompanying notes.

THE AGENCIES OF
THE CUMBERLAND PRESBYTERIAN CHURCH CENTER
SHARED SERVICES
STATEMENT OF FINANCIAL POSITION
DECEMBER 31, 2014

ASSETS

Cash	$	23,826
Accounts receivable		624
Buildings and land		2,760,412
Less: accumulated depreciation		(457,026)
Furniture and equipment		156,745
Less: accumulated depreciation		(156,745)
Total Assets	$	2,327,836

LIABILITIES AND NET ASSETS

Liabilities:		
Accrued expenses	$	265
Due to other agencies, boards, and divisions		46,211
Total liabilities		46,476
Net Assets:		
Unrestricted		2,281,360
Total Liabilities and Net Assets	$	2,327,836

See accompanying notes.

THE AGENCIES OF
THE CUMBERLAND PRESBYTERIAN CHURCH CENTER
HISTORICAL FOUNDATION
STATEMENT OF FINANCIAL POSITION
DECEMBER 31, 2014

ASSETS

Cash	$	48,669
Endowment earnings receivable		16,721
Health insurance tax credit receivable		1,326
Due from other agencies, boards, and divisions		179,182
Securities and investments		
Real estate		38,755
		284,653
Endowments - held by Endowment Program		1,497,784
Total Assets	$	1,782,437

LIABILITIES AND NET ASSETS

Net Assets:		
Unrestricted	$	60,810
Temporarily restricted		184,837
Permanently restricted		1,536,790
Total net assets		1,782,437
Total Liabilities and Net Assets	$	1,782,437

See accompanying notes.

THE AGENCIES OF
THE CUMBERLAND PRESBYTERIAN CHURCH CENTER
BOARD OF STEWARDSHIP, FOUNDATION, AND BENEFITS
STATEMENT OF FINANCIAL POSITION
DECEMBER 31, 2014

ASSETS

Endowment earnings receivable	$	21,955
Health insurance tax credit receivable		6,069
Due from other agencies, boards, and divisions		484,998
		513,022
Endowments - held by Endowment Program		1,979,004
Total Assets	$	2,492,026

LIABILITIES AND NET ASSETS

Liabilities:		
Cash borrowed from other agencies, boards, and divisions	$	47,825
Net Assets:		
Unrestricted		465,197
Permanently restricted		1,979,004
Total net assets		2,444,201
Total Liabilities and Net Assets	$	2,492,026

See accompanying notes.

THE AGENCIES OF
THE CUMBERLAND PRESBYTERIAN CHURCH CENTER
SMALL CHURCH LOAN PROGRAM
STATEMENT OF FINANCIAL POSITION
DECEMBER 31, 2014

ASSETS

Interest receivable, net of allowance for uncollectible interest	$ 808
Loans receivable, net of allowance for loan losses	125,341
Due from other agencies, boards, and divisions	291,439
Total Assets	$ 417,588

LIABILITIES AND NET ASSETS

Net Assets:	
Permanently restricted	$ 417,588
Total net assets	417,588
Total Liabilities and Net Assets	$ 417,588

See accompanying notes.

THE AGENCIES OF
THE CUMBERLAND PRESBYTERIAN CHURCH CENTER
INSURANCE PROGRAM
STATEMENT OF FINANCIAL POSITION
DECEMBER 31, 2014

ASSETS

Cash	$ 146,479
Accounts receivable	152
Prepaid expenses	6,704
Due from other agencies, boards, and divisions	2,159,181
Total Assets	$ 2,312,516

LIABILITIES AND NET ASSETS

Liabilities:	
Accounts payable	$ 1,190
Net Assets:	
Unrestricted	2,311,326
Total Liabilities and Net Assets	$ 2,312,516

See accompanying notes.

THE AGENCIES OF
THE CUMBERLAND PRESBYTERIAN CHURCH CENTER
MINISTERIAL AID
STATEMENT OF FINANCIAL POSITION
DECEMBER 31, 2014

ASSETS

Cash	$	75,959
Endowment earnings receivable		13,899
Due from other agencies, boards, and divisions		305,427
		395,285
Endowment Funds - held by Endowment Program		3,008,443
Total Assets	$	3,403,728

LIABILITIES AND NET ASSETS

Net Assets:		
Unrestricted	$	395,285
Permanently restricted		3,008,443
Total net assets		3,403,728
Total Liabilities and Net Assets	$	3,403,728

See accompanying notes.

THE AGENCIES OF
THE CUMBERLAND PRESBYTERIAN CHURCH CENTER
INVESTMENT LOAN PROGRAM
STATEMENT OF FINANCIAL POSITION
DECEMBER 31, 2014

ASSETS

Interest and dividends receivable, net of allowance for uncollectible interest	$ 33,032
Securities and investments	
Cash equivalents	1,483,321
Bonds and mortgage backed securities	7,484,557
Loans receivable, net of allowance for loan losses	7,434,313
Total Assets	$ 16,435,223

LIABILITIES AND NET ASSETS

Liabilities:	
Accounts payable	$ 833
Notes payable to individual investors	1,323,811
Due to other agencies, boards, and divisions	3,695,858
Depository accounts held for church organizations	9,391,498
Total liabilities	14,412,000
Net Assets:	
Unrestricted	2,023,223
Total Liabilities and Net Assets	$ 16,435,223

See accompanying notes.

THE AGENCIES OF
THE CUMBERLAND PRESBYTERIAN CHURCH CENTER
RETIREMENT FUND
STATEMENT OF FINANCIAL POSITION
DECEMBER 31, 2014

ASSETS

Interest and dividends receivable, net of allowance for uncollectible interest	$ 15,833
Securities and investments	
Cash and cash equivalents	955,951
Bond mutual funds	2,479,788
Closed-end bond funds	1,194,077
Equity mutual funds	1,094,752
Real estate investment trusts	1,205,975
Private investment entities	16,802,074
Total Assets	$ 23,748,450

LIABILITIES AND NET ASSETS

Net Assets:	
Net assets available for benefits, at fair value	$ 23,748,450
Total net assets	23,748,450
Total Liabilities and Net Assets	$ 23,748,450

See accompanying notes.

THE AGENCIES OF
THE CUMBERLAND PRESBYTERIAN CHURCH CENTER
ENDOWMENT PROGRAM
STATEMENT OF FINANCIAL POSITION
DECEMBER 31, 2014

ASSETS

Cash equivalents	$ 330,875
Due from other agencies, boards, and divisions	46,211
Interest and dividends receivable, net of allowance for uncollectible interest	42,341
Securities and investments	
Cash equivalents	2,393,875
Bond mutual funds	5,423,653
Closed-end bond funds	2,289,693
Equity mutual funds	2,198,691
Real estate investment trusts	3,952,215
Private investment entities	38,809,765
Loans receivable, net of allowance for loan losses	4,022,988
	59,510,307
Less: net endowment assets of The Agencies of The Cumberland Presbyterian Church Center, as reflected on separate statements of financial position	(25,934,878)
Total Assets	$ 33,575,429

LIABILITIES AND NET ASSETS

Liabilities:	
Due to other agencies, boards, and divisions	$ 2,585,455
Net Assets:	
Permanently restricted:	
Cumberland Presbyterian Children's Home	6,916,026
Discipleship Ministry Team	2,109,007
Missions Ministry Team	13,915,514
Memphis Theological Seminary	9,829,219
Board of Stewardship, Foundation, and Benefits	1,979,004
Our United Outreach	2,582,202
General Assembly Corporation	465,139
Communications Ministry Team	115,523
Pastoral Development Ministry Team	262,263
The Historical Foundation	1,497,784
Ministerial Aid	3,008,442
Bethel University	3,035,061
Other designated persons and organizations	11,209,668
Total net assets	56,924,852
Less: net endowment assets of The Agencies of The Cumberland Presbyterian Church Center, as reflected on separate statements of financial position	(25,934,878)
Total Liabilities and Net Assets	$ 33,575,429

See accompanying notes.

THE AGENCIES OF
THE CUMBERLAND PRESBYTERIAN CHURCH CENTER
OUR UNITED OUTREACH
STATEMENT OF ACTIVITY
FOR THE YEAR ENDED DECEMBER 31, 2014

	Unrestricted	Temporarily Restricted	Permanently Restricted	Totals
Revenues, gains, and other support:				
Contributions	$ 2,422,589	$ -	$ 89,612	$ 2,512,201
Endowment earnings	-	-	21,387	21,387
Income from oil royalties	31,125	-	-	31,125
Net realized and unrealized gain on investments	-	-	119,663	119,663
Net assets released from restriction	116,947	-	(116,947)	-
	2,570,661	-	113,715	2,684,376
Expenses:				
Distribution to other agencies, boards, and divisions of The Cumberland Presbyterian Church:				
Bethel University	115,747	-	-	115,747
Board of Stewardship	138,897	-	-	138,897
Commission on Chaplains	8,102	-	-	8,102
Committee on Theology and Social Concern	2,836	-	-	2,836
Committee on Judiciary	7,639	-	-	7,639
Communications Ministry Team	256,208	-	-	256,208
Contingency Fund	2,199	-	-	2,199
Cumberland Presbyterian Children's Home	69,449	-	-	69,449
Discipleship Ministry Team	285,684	-	-	285,684
Evaluation Committee	3,500			3,500
General Assembly Council	185,196	-	-	185,196
Historical Foundation	69,449	-	-	69,449
Legal Expense	25,000			25,000
Memphis Theological Seminary	162,047	-	-	162,047
Ministry Council	137,630	-	-	137,630
Missions Ministry Team	376,377	-	-	376,377
Nominating Committee	2,373	-	-	2,373
OGA - Contingency Loan	119,993	-	-	119,993
Pastoral Development Ministry Team	101,576	-	-	101,576
Shared Service (Accounting)	61,250	-	-	61,250
Shared Service (Computer Tech)	67,007	-	-	67,007
Shared Service (Maintenance/Operations)	195,787	-	-	195,787
Shared Service (Old Building)	62,556	-	-	62,556
Shared Service (OUO Committee)	85,942	-	-	85,942
Unification Task Force	20,000			20,000
Property tax	5,094	-	-	5,094
	2,567,538	-	-	2,567,538
Change in net assets	3,123	-	113,715	116,838
Net assets at beginning of year	(24,137)	-	2,468,487	2,444,350
Net assets at end of year	$ (21,014)	$ -	$ 2,582,202	$ 2,561,188

See accompanying notes.

THE AGENCIES OF
THE CUMBERLAND PRESBYTERIAN CHURCH CENTER
GENERAL ASSEMBLY CORPORATION
STATEMENT OF ACTIVITY
FOR THE YEAR ENDED DECEMBER 31, 2014

	Unrestricted	Temporarily Restricted	Permanently Restricted	Totals
Revenues, gains, and other support:				
Our United Outreach	$ 192,698	$ -	$ -	$ 192,698
Contributions and gifts	227,276	-	-	227,276
Endowment earnings	21,929	-	-	21,929
Interest income	4,305	-	-	4,305
Other income	79,853	-	-	79,853
Net realized and unrealized gain on investments	-	-	22,055	22,055
Net assets released from restriction	23,481	-	(23,481)	-
	549,542	-	(1,426)	548,116
Expenses:				
Conferences and events	47,606	-	-	47,606
Employee benefits	38,444	-	-	38,444
Equipment maintenance	1,634	-	-	1,634
Grants made	130,971	-	-	130,971
Office expense	2,118	-	-	2,118
Payroll taxes	4,665	-	-	4,665
Planning team expense	90	-	-	90
Postage and shipping	1,364	-	-	1,364
Printing and publications	1,535	-	-	1,535
Retirement	9,098	-	-	9,098
Salaries	208,416	-	-	208,416
Supplies	1,285	-	-	1,285
Travel	15,056	-	-	15,056
Total expenses	462,282	-	-	462,282
Change in net assets	87,260	-	(1,426)	85,834
Net assets at beginning of year	(93,200)	-	466,565	373,365
Net assets at end of year	$ (5,940)	$ -	$ 465,139	$ 459,199

See accompanying notes.

THE AGENCIES OF
THE CUMBERLAND PRESBYTERIAN CHURCH CENTER
MINISTRY COUNCIL
STATEMENT OF ACTIVITY
FOR THE YEAR ENDED DECEMBER 31, 2014

	Unrestricted	Temporarily Restricted	Permanently Restricted	Totals
Revenues, gains, and other support:				
Our United Outreach	$ 1,262,558	$ -	$ -	$ 1,262,558
Contributions	-	1,126,681	1,067,640	2,194,321
Endowment earnings	99,584	-	134,368	233,952
Gifts - designated	458,655	-	-	458,655
Gifts - undesignated	219,264	-	-	219,264
Interest income	16,372	54,449	-	70,821
Registration fees	85,443	-	-	85,443
Rental income	9,682	-	-	9,682
Sales of materials, literature, etc.	176,821	-	-	176,821
Subscription income	34,678	-	-	34,678
Net realized and unrealized gain on investments	-	-	752,473	752,473
Net assets released from restrictions	2,899,467	(2,258,649)	(640,818)	-
	5,262,524	(1,077,519)	1,313,663	5,498,668
Expenses:				
Automobile expenses	20,085	-	-	20,085
Computer expenses	19,052	-	-	19,052
Conferences and events	176,828	-	-	176,828
Consulting fees	50,938	-	-	50,938
Contract labor	27,048	-	-	27,048
Dues and subscriptions	1,838	-	-	1,838
Employee benefits	178,185	-	-	178,185
Equipment maintenance	651	-	-	651
Grants made	2,897,441	-	-	2,897,441
Interest expense	35	-	-	35
Legal fees	3,802	-	-	3,802
Miscellaneous expense	14,890	-	-	14,890
Missionary support	331,899	-	-	331,899
Office expense	346	-	-	346
Payroll taxes	37,765	-	-	37,765
Postage and shipping	46,234	-	-	46,234
Printing and publications	169,388	-	-	169,388
Purchases for resale	49,066	-	-	49,066
Relocation expenses	5,774	-	-	5,774
Rent expense	510	-	-	510
Retirement	40,884	-	-	40,884
Salaries	891,775	-	-	891,775
Supplies	14,565	-	-	14,565
Telephone	4,493	-	-	4,493
Training expenses	3,152	-	-	3,152
Travel expenses	206,019	-	-	206,019
Total expenses	5,192,663	-	-	5,192,663
Change in net assets	69,861	(1,077,519)	1,313,663	306,005
Net assets at beginning of year	698,139	2,723,230	15,088,643	18,510,012
Net assets at end of year	$ 768,000	$ 1,645,711	$ 16,402,306	$ 18,816,017

See accompanying notes.

THE AGENCIES OF
THE CUMBERLAND PRESBYTERIAN CHURCH CENTER
SHARED SERVICES
STATEMENT OF ACTIVITY
FOR THE YEAR ENDED DECEMBER 31, 2014

	Unrestricted	Temporarily Restricted	Permanently Restricted	Totals
Revenues, gains, and other support:				
Our United Outreach	$ 386,600	$ -	$ -	$ 386,600
Gifts	121,594	-	-	121,594
	508,194	-	-	508,194
Expenses:				
Accounting fees	22,585	-	-	22,585
Bank fees	19,945	-	-	19,945
Computer expenses	1,363	-	-	1,363
Consulting fees	40,251	-	-	40,251
Depreciation expense	65,289	-	-	65,289
Employee benefits	22,794	-	-	22,794
Equipment maintenance	16,765	-	-	16,765
Insurance expense	31,567	-	-	31,567
Interest expense	6,306	-	-	6,306
Miscellaneous expense	25,318	-	-	25,318
Occupancy expenses	75,462	-	-	75,462
Office expense	110	-	-	110
Payroll taxes	3,631	-	-	3,631
Postage and shipping	700	-	-	700
Retirement	2,373	-	-	2,373
Salaries	47,462	-	-	47,462
Supplies	1,464	-	-	1,464
Telephone	12,748	-	-	12,748
Total expenses	396,133	-	-	396,133
Change in net assets	112,061	-	-	112,061
Net assets at beginning of year	2,169,299	-	-	2,169,299
Net assets at end of year	$ 2,281,360	$ -	$ -	$ 2,281,360

See accompanying notes.

THE AGENCIES OF
THE CUMBERLAND PRESBYTERIAN CHURCH CENTER
HISTORICAL FOUNDATION
STATEMENT OF ACTIVITY
FOR THE YEAR ENDED DECEMBER 31, 2014

	Unrestricted	Temporarily Restricted	Permanently Restricted	Totals
Revenues, gains, and other support:				
Our United Outreach	$ 69,449	$ -	$ -	$ 69,449
Contributions and gifts	12,486	24,070	19,399	55,955
Endowment earnings	-	-	12,524	12,524
Interest income	-	5,533	-	5,533
Net realized and unrealized gain on investments	-	-	70,329	70,329
Net assets released from restriction	94,396	(29,170)	(65,226)	-
	176,331	433	37,026	213,790
Expenses:				
Archival acquisitions	31,346	-	-	31,346
Archival equipment	2,371	-	-	2,371
Birthplace shrine	4,217	-	-	4,217
Computer equipment and supplies	3,557	-	-	3,557
Conferences and events	50	-	-	50
Contract labor	2,255	-	-	2,255
Dues and subscriptions	2,091	-	-	2,091
Employee benefits	9,083	-	-	9,083
Insurance expense	1,472	-	-	1,472
Miscellaneous expense	689	-	-	689
Payroll taxes	6,222	-	-	6,222
Postage and shipping	284	-	-	284
Printing and publications	3,074	-	-	3,074
Purchases for resale	2,618	-	-	2,618
Rent expense	40	-	-	40
Retirement	7,626	-	-	7,626
Salaries	81,334	-	-	81,334
Supplies	2,361	-	-	2,361
Training expenses	362	-	-	362
Travel expenses	14,432	-	-	14,432
Total expenses	175,484	-	-	175,484
Change in net assets	847	433	37,026	38,306
Net assets at beginning of year	59,963	184,404	1,499,764	1,744,131
Net assets at end of year	$ 60,810	$ 184,837	$ 1,536,790	$ 1,782,437

See accompanying notes.

THE AGENCIES OF
THE CUMBERLAND PRESBYTERIAN CHURCH CENTER
BOARD OF STEWARDSHIP, FOUNDATION AND BENEFITS
STATEMENT OF ACTIVITY
FOR THE YEAR ENDED DECEMBER 31, 2014

	Unrestricted	Temporarily Restricted	Permanently Restricted	Totals
Revenues, gains, and other support:				
Our United Outreach	$ 138,897	$ -	$ -	$ 138,897
Contributions and gifts	17,038	-	20,200	37,238
Endowment earnings	(12,200)	-	16,512	4,312
Interest income	14,455	-	-	14,455
Management service fees	51,116	-	-	51,116
Net realized and unrealized gain on investments	-	-	92,773	92,773
Net assets released from restriction	85,788	-	(85,788)	-
	295,094	-	43,697	338,791
Expenses:				
Computer expenses	507	-	-	507
Contract labor	330	-	-	330
Dues and subscriptions	1,797	-	-	1,797
Employee benefits	66,756	-	-	66,756
Grants made	1,650	-	-	1,650
Miscellaneous	30	-	-	30
Payroll taxes	6,809	-	-	6,809
Postage and shipping	1,653	-	-	1,653
Printing and publications	3,643	-	-	3,643
Relocation expenses	22	-	-	22
Retirement	8,485	-	-	8,485
Salaries	169,698	-	-	169,698
Stewardship fees	2,000	-	-	2,000
Stewardship materials and events	155	-	-	155
Supplies	2,538	-	-	2,538
Travel and board meetings	20,625	-	-	20,625
Total expenses	286,698	-	-	286,698
Change in net assets	8,396	-	43,697	52,093
Net assets at beginning of year	456,801	-	1,935,307	2,392,108
Net assets at end of year	$ 465,197	$ -	$ 1,979,004	$ 2,444,201

See accompanying notes.

**THE AGENCIES OF
THE CUMBERLAND PRESBYTERIAN CHURCH CENTER
SMALL CHURCH LOAN PROGRAM
STATEMENT OF ACTIVITY
FOR THE YEAR ENDED DECEMBER 31, 2014**

	Unrestricted	Temporarily Restricted	Permanently Restricted	Totals
Revenues, gains, and other support:				
Contributions	$ -	$ -	$ 54,323	$ 54,323
Interest income	-	-	14,833	14,833
Net assets released from restriction	54,323	-	(54,323)	-
	54,323	-	14,833	69,156
Expenses:				
Distribution to other agencies, boards, and divisions of The Cumberland Presbyterian Church:				
Investment Loan Program	54,323	-	-	54,323
	54,323	-	-	54,323
Change in net assets	-	-	14,833	14,833
Net assets at beginning of year	-	-	402,755	402,755
Net assets at end of year	$ -	$ -	$ 417,588	$ 417,588

See accompanying notes.

THE AGENCIES OF
THE CUMBERLAND PRESBYTERIAN CHURCH CENTER
INSURANCE PROGRAM
STATEMENT OF ACTIVITY
FOR THE YEAR ENDED DECEMBER 31, 2014

	Unrestricted	Temporarily Restricted	Permanently Restricted	Totals
Revenues, gains, and other support:				
Premium revenue	$ 2,143,075	$ -	$ -	$ 2,143,075
Contributions	1,121,960	-	-	1,121,960
Interest income	12,153	-	-	12,153
Net realized gain on investments	896	-	-	896
Net unrealized gain on investments	51,639	-	-	51,639
	3,329,723	-	-	3,329,723
Expenses:				
Insurance premiums	2,238,488	-	-	2,238,488
Payroll taxes	1,786	-	-	1,786
Postage and shipping	359	-	-	359
Retirement	1,168	-	-	1,168
Salaries	23,352	-	-	23,352
Total expenses	2,265,153	-	-	2,265,153
Change in net assets	1,064,570	-	-	1,064,570
Net assets at beginning of year	1,246,756	-	-	1,246,756
Net assets at end of year	$ 2,311,326	$ -	$ -	$ 2,311,326

See accompanying notes.

THE AGENCIES OF
THE CUMBERLAND PRESBYTERIAN CHURCH CENTER
MINISTERIAL AID
STATEMENT OF ACTIVITY
FOR THE YEAR ENDED DECEMBER 31, 2014

	Unrestricted	Temporarily Restricted	Permanently Restricted	Totals
Revenues, gains, and other support:				
Endowment earnings	$ -	$ -	$ 32,462	$ 32,462
Interest income	8,783	-	-	8,783
Net realized and unrealized gain on investments	-	-	184,657	184,657
Net assets released from restriction	1,173,965	-	(1,173,965)	-
	1,182,748	-	(956,846)	225,902
Expenses:				
Ministerial aid	1,178,356	-	-	1,178,356
Retirement resident distribution	1,050	-	-	1,050
Total expenses	1,179,406	-	-	1,179,406
Change in net assets	3,342	-	(956,846)	(953,504)
Net assets at beginning of year	391,943	-	3,965,289	4,357,232
Net assets at end of year	$ 395,285	$ -	$ 3,008,443	$ 3,403,728

See accompanying notes.

THE AGENCIES OF
THE CUMBERLAND PRESBYTERIAN CHURCH CENTER
INVESTMENT LOAN PROGRAM
STATEMENT OF ACTIVITY
FOR THE YEAR ENDED DECEMBER 31, 2014

	Unrestricted	Temporarily Restricted	Permanently Restricted	Totals
Revenues, gains, and other support:				
Interest income	$ 498,197	$ -	$ -	$ 498,197
Interest expense	(430,430)	-	-	(430,430)
Net interest income	67,767	-	-	67,767
Net gain (loss) on investments	418,670	-	-	418,670
	486,437	-	-	486,437
Expenses:				
Accounting fees	5,321	-	-	5,321
Legal fees	2,266	-	-	2,266
Management fee	51,127	-	-	51,127
Miscellaneous expense	6,712	-	-	6,712
Office expenses	2,078	-	-	2,078
Postage and shipping	3,094	-	-	3,094
Supplies	264	-	-	264
Total expenses	70,862	-	-	70,862
Change in net assets	415,575	-	-	415,575
Net assets at beginning of year	1,607,648	-	-	1,607,648
Net assets at end of year	$ 2,023,223	$ -	$ -	$ 2,023,223

See accompanying notes.

THE AGENCIES OF
THE CUMBERLAND PRESBYTERIAN CHURCH CENTER
RETIREMENT FUND
STATEMENT OF ACTIVITY
FOR THE YEAR ENDED DECEMBER 31, 2014

	Net Assets Available for Benefits
Additions to Net Assets attributed to:	
Investment income:	
Interest and dividend income	$ 135,275
Management service fees	(22,266)
Net realized gain on investments	34,072
Net unrealized gain on investments	1,119,074
Net investment income	1,266,155
Contributions:	
Contributions by participants	713,181
	1,979,336
Deductions from Net Assets attributed to:	
Disbursements to participants	1,091,877
	1,091,877
Change in plan assets available for benefits	887,459
Net assets available for benefits at beginning of year	22,860,991
Net assets available for benefits at end of year	$ 23,748,450

See accompanying notes.

THE AGENCIES OF
THE CUMBERLAND PRESBYTERIAN CHURCH CENTER
ENDOWMENT PROGRAM
STATEMENT OF ACTIVITY
FOR THE YEAR ENDED DECEMBER 31, 2014

	Unrestricted	Temporarily Restricted	Permanently Restricted	Totals
Changes in Permanently Restricted Net Assets:				
Revenues, gains, and other support:				
Contributions	$ -	$ -	$ 3,092,559	$ 3,092,559
Interest and dividend income	-	-	522,008	522,008
Net realized gain on investments	-	-	34,911	34,911
Net unrealized gain on investments	-	-	2,719,977	2,719,977
	-	-	6,369,455	6,369,455
Expenses:				
Distribution for designated purposes	-	-	2,592,957	2,592,957
Distribution of earnings	-	-	2,377,045	2,377,045
Other expenses	-	-	48,258	48,258
	-	-	5,018,260	5,018,260
Change in net assets	-	-	1,351,195	1,351,195
Net assets at beginning of year	-	-	55,573,657	55,573,657
Net assets at end of year	$ -	$ -	$ 56,924,852	$ 56,924,852
Represented by funds held in trust for others:				
Bethel University	$ -	$ -	$ 3,035,061	$ 3,035,061
Cumberland Presbyterian Children's Home	-	-	6,916,026	6,916,026
Memphis Theological Seminary	-	-	9,829,219	9,829,219
Other designated persons and organizations	-	-	11,209,668	11,209,668
	-	-	30,989,974	30,989,974
Represented by funds held for The Agencies of The Cumberland Presbyterian Church Center:				
Discipleship Ministry Team	-	-	2,109,007	2,109,007
Missions Ministry Team	-	-	13,915,514	13,915,514
Board of Stewardship, Foundation, and Benefit	-	-	1,979,004	1,979,004
Our United Outreach	-	-	2,582,202	2,582,202
General Assembly Corporation	-	-	465,139	465,139
Communications Ministry Team	-	-	115,523	115,523
Pastoral Development Ministry Team	-	-	262,263	262,263
The Historical Foundation	-	-	1,497,784	1,497,784
Ministerial Aid	-	-	3,008,442	3,008,442
	-	-	25,934,878	25,934,878
Net assets at end of year	$ -	$ -	$ 56,924,852	$ 56,924,852

See accompanying notes.

THE AGENCIES OF
THE CUMBERLAND PRESBYTERIAN CHURCH CENTER

NOTES TO FINANCIAL STATEMENTS
DECEMBER 31, 2014

Note A - Nature of Activities and Significant Accounting Policies

Nature of Activities - By the covenant of Abraham and his descendants according to faith, God has established the church in the world through His Son Jesus Christ. This household of faith, the universal church, consists of all those persons in every nation and every age who confess Jesus Christ as Lord and Savior and who respond to His call for discipleship. The church in the world never exists for herself alone, but to glorify God and work for reconciliation through Christ. Christ claims the church and gives her the word and sacraments in order to bring God's grace and judgment to persons.

The General Assembly is the highest judicatory of this church and represents in one body all the particular churches thereof. It bears the title of the General Assembly of the Cumberland Presbyterian Church and constitutes the bond of union, peace, correspondence, and mutual confidence among all its churches and judicatories. The Agencies of The Cumberland Presbyterian Church Center have been established by the General Assembly and in 2000 it caused the Cumberland Presbyterian Church General Assembly Corporation to be formed. The Agencies consist of the following entities:

Cumberland Presbyterian Church General Assembly Corporation
Ministry Council of the Cumberland Presbyterian Church, Inc.
Board of Stewardship, Foundation, and Benefits of the Cumberland Presbyterian Church, Inc.
Historical Foundation of the Cumberland Presbyterian Church and the Cumberland Presbyterian Church in America

Contributions - Contributions received are recorded as unrestricted, temporarily restricted, or permanently restricted, depending on the existence and/or nature of any donor restrictions.

Support that is restricted by the donor is reported as an increase in unrestricted net assets if the restriction expires in the reporting period in which the support is recognized. All other donor restricted support is reported as an increase in temporarily or permanently restricted net assets depending on the nature of the restriction. When a restriction expires, temporarily restricted net assets are reclassified to unrestricted net assets.

Donated Equipment and Services - Donated equipment is reflected as contributions in the accompanying financial statements at their estimated values at the date of receipt. No equipment was donated to the Center during the year ended December 31, 2014. No amounts have been reflected in the statements for donated services because they did not meet the criteria for recognition under FASB ASC 958-605-25.

Use of Estimates - The preparation of financial statements in conformity with generally accepted accounting principles requires management to make estimates and assumptions that affect the reported amounts of assets and liabilities and disclosure of contingent assets and liabilities at the date of the financial statements and the reported amounts of revenues and expenses during the reporting period. Actual results could differ from these estimates.

NOTES CONTINUED

Note A - Nature of Activities and Significant Accounting Policies - Continued

The Cumberland Presbyterian Church Investment Loan Program, Inc.'s notes receivable will consist of loans made to congregations, governing bodies, church organizations, and other qualifying related entities. The ability of each borrower to repay its loan generally depends upon the contributions received from its members. The number of members of each congregation and its revenue is likely to fluctuate.

The Program must rely on the borrower's or guarantor's continued financial viability for repayment of loans. If a borrower or guarantor experiences a decrease in contributions or revenues, payments on that loan may be adversely affected. Even though the loans are collateralized by real estate, realization of the appraised value upon default is not assured and is dependent upon the local economic conditions of the borrower. Therefore, the determination of the adequacy of the allowance for notes receivable losses is based on estimates that are particularly susceptible to significant changes in the economic environment and market conditions for the geographic areas where the borrowers are located.

While management uses available information to recognize losses on notes receivable, further reductions in the carrying amounts of notes receivable may be necessary based on changes in the economic conditions for the geographic area of the borrowers. It is therefore reasonably possible that the estimated losses on notes receivable may change materially in the near term. However, the amount of the change that is reasonably possible cannot be estimated.

Promises to Give - Unconditional promises to give are recognized as revenue or gains in the period received and as assets or decreases of liabilities depending on the form of the benefits received. Conditional promises to give are recognized when the conditions on which they depend are substantially met. The Center has no promises to give at December 31, 2014.

Inventory - Inventories are stated at the lower of cost or market. Cost is determined using the average cost method.

Depreciation - In years past, Shared Services has recorded property and equipment as assets and depreciated them. Depreciation of property and equipment was computed using the straight-line method over the estimated useful lives of the assets. Purchases of equipment after 1996 are not capitalized, but expensed when purchased; therefore, no depreciation expense has been recorded for items acquired in 1997 and thereafter. The difference between the cost of fixed assets expensed and depreciation expense that would be recorded is immaterial. In 2008, the Center purchased land and two incomplete office buildings. The cost of these plus the construction costs necessary to complete the new Center were capitalized and are being depreciated over an estimated useful life of 39 years. In 2009, the Shared Services agency purchased a large amount of computer equipment and capitalized these costs. The computer equipment purchased is being depreciated over an estimated useful life of four years.

Property and Equipment - Property and equipment is recorded at historical cost. Donated property and equipment is recorded at fair market value at the date of donation. Such donations are reported as unrestricted support unless the donor has restricted the donated asset to a specific purpose. Assets donated with explicit restrictions regarding their use and contributions of cash that must be used to acquire property and equipment are reported as restricted support. Absent donor stipulations regarding how long those donated assets must be maintained, the Center reports expirations of donor restrictions when the donated or acquired assets are placed in service as instructed by the donor. The Center re-classes temporarily restricted net assets to unrestricted net assets at that time.

NOTES CONTINUED

Note A - Nature of Activities and Significant Accounting Policies - Continued

Investments - Investments are stated at fair value. Investments in private investment entities are valued based on the Center's proportional share of the net asset valuations reported by the general partners of the underlying entities. The reported values of all other investments (with the exception of notes receivable) are measured by quoted prices in active markets. Realized and unrealized gains and losses are reflected in the statement of activities. (See Note L)

The Center's investments include various types of securities in various companies within various markets. Investment securities are exposed to several risks, such as interest rate, market and credit risks. Due to the risks associated with certain investment securities, it is at least reasonably possible that changes in the values of investment securities will occur in the near term and those changes could materially affect the amounts reported in the Center's combined financial statements.

Fair Value Measurements - Fair value under accounting principles generally accepted in the United States of America is defined as the price that would be received to sell an asset or paid to transfer a liability in an orderly transaction between market participants at the measurement date. Generally accepted accounting principles establishes a three-tier fair value hierarchy that prioritizes the inputs used to measure fair value. These tiers include: Level 1, defined as observable inputs such as quoted prices available in active markets for identical assets or liabilities; Level 2, defined as pricing inputs other than quoted prices in active markets that are either directly or indirectly observable; and Level 3, defined as unobservable inputs about which little or no market data exists, therefore requiring an entity to develop its own assessment about the assumptions the market participants would use in pricing an asset or liability.

Income Tax Status - The Center is a not-for-profit organization exempt from federal income taxes under Internal Revenue Code (IRC) Section 501 (c)(3). Thus, no provision for federal income taxes has been made. The Center has a defined contribution retirement plan which is qualified under Internal Revenue Code Section 403 (b); no provision for income taxes has been included in the Plan's financial statements.

Cash and Cash Equivalents - For purposes of the statement of cash flows, all highly liquid investments with a maturity of three months or less are considered to be cash equivalents. However, cash and cash equivalents reported as securities and investments by the Endowment Program, Investment Loan Program and Retirement Fund are considered investments for purposes of the statement of cash flows.

Loans Receivable and Allowance for Losses - Loans receivable are stated at unpaid principal balances, less the allowance for notes receivable losses. Inter-agency loans are shown as due to/from other agencies, boards, and divisions.

The allowance for loans receivable is maintained at a level which, in management's judgment, is adequate to absorb credit losses inherent in the loans receivable portfolio. The amount of the allowance is based on management's evaluation of the collectability of the portfolio, including the nature of the portfolio, credit concentrations, trends in historical loss experience, economic conditions, and other risks inherent in the portfolio. Although management uses available information to recognize losses on notes receivable, because of uncertainties associated with the various local economic conditions of the borrowers and collateral values, it is reasonably possible that a material change could occur in the allowance for notes receivable in the near term. However, the amount of the change that is reasonably possible cannot be estimated. When considered necessary, the allowance is increased by a charge to expense and reduced by actual charge-offs, net of recoveries.

NOTES CONTINUED

Note B - Retirement Plan

General - The Cumberland Presbyterian Church Retirement Plan Number Two is available to certain employees of the Church and its agencies. All agencies, boards, and divisions match each employee's contribution up to five percent of the employee's salary. The total retirement contribution expense for The Agencies of The Cumberland Presbyterian Church Center for 2014 was $68,466.

The Plan obtained its latest determination letter on January 31, 1972, in which the Internal Revenue Service stated that the Plan, as then designed, was in compliance with the applicable requirements of the Internal Revenue Code. The Plan has been amended since receiving the determination letter. However, the Plan administrator and the Plan's tax counsel believe that the plan is currently designed and being operated in compliance with the applicable requirements of the Internal Revenue Code. The Plan is a "church plan" and is, therefore, not subject to ERISA.

Eligibility - Employees who are 18 years of age are immediately eligible to participate in the plan.

Vesting - Participants are immediately 100% vested in their accounts.

Investments - The Plan's investments are held by a bank-administered trust fund. The trust is the funding vehicle for the Plan, and all contributions are made to the trust. The cost and market value of the Plan's investments at December 31, 2014, are as follows:

	Cost	Market Value
Total	$ 19,101,091	$ 23,748,450

Note C - Endowment Program

The Endowment Program includes assets of The Agencies of The Cumberland Presbyterian Church Center and the assets of other agencies, boards, and divisions.

The Program's investments, other than notes receivable, real estate, and certificates of deposit, are held by a bank-administered trust fund. The costs and market value of the Program's investments held in trust at December 31, 2014, are as follows:

	Cost	Market Value
Total	$ 45,152,471	$ 55,098,335

The Center has interpreted the Uniform Prudent Management of Institutional Funds Act ("UPMIFA") requiring a portion of a donor restricted endowment of perpetual duration be classified as permanently restricted assets. The amount of the endowment that must be retained permanently is in accordance with explicit donor stipulations as outlined in their respective trust agreements.

NOTES CONTINUED

Note C - Endowment Program - Continued

The primary objective of these endowments is to provide a balance between capital appreciation, preservation of capital, and current income. This is a long-term goal designed to maximize returns without undue risk. The Board of Stewardship has set distribution rates with certain beneficiaries of the Endowment Program.

Unless otherwise stated in the donor agreement, the Board of Stewardship shall select the investment portfolio where the endowments will be invested as described in the Investment Policy of the Center. The Investment Policy of the Center outlines the asset allocations, permissible investments, and objectives of the portfolios.

Endowment Net Asset Composition by Type of Fund as of December 31, 2014:

	Permanently Restricted	Total
Donor-restricted endowment funds	$ 56,924,852	$ 56,924,852
Total funds	$ 56,924,852	$ 56,924,852

Changes in Endowment Net Assets for the year ended December 31, 2014:

	Permanently Restricted	Total
Endowment net assets, beginning of year	$ 55,573,657	$ 55,573,657
Investment return	3,228,638	3,228,638
Contributions	3,092,559	3,092,559
Withdrawal of principal balances	-	-
Appropriation of endowment assets for expenditures	(4,970,002)	(4,970,002)
Endowment net assets, end of year	$ 56,924,852	$ 56,924,852

Description of Amount Classified as Permanently Restricted Net Assets (Endowment Only):

Permanently Restricted Net Assets -

The portion of perpetual endowment funds that is required to be retained permanently either by explicit donor stipulation or by UPMIFA	$ 56,924,852
Total endowment funds classified as permanently restricted net assets	$ 56,924,852

NOTES CONTINUED

Note D - Investment Loan Program

Nature of Activities - On March 19, 1999, the State of Tennessee approved the charter for the Cumberland Presbyterian Church Investment Loan Program, Inc., a subsidiary corporation of the Board of Stewardship, Foundation and Benefits of the Cumberland Presbyterian Church, Inc. The Program is designed to allow participants to help provide the loans needed to finance the growth of Cumberland Presbyterian congregations in the 21st century.

1. It provides building loans secured by first mortgages to congregations, presbyteries, and church agencies.

2. It allows congregations, presbyteries, church agencies, and individual members of the Cumberland Presbyterian Church to invest their funds in interest bearing accounts from which withdrawals can be made "on demand" replacing the function of the Cash Funds Management Program.

3. All participants have the opportunity to invest funds for specific terms (such as three years or five years) in order to receive a higher rate of interest. A prospectus outlines the added investment options offered.

Securities and Investments - The cost and market values of Investment Loan Program investments at December 31, 2014, are as follows:

	Cost	Market Value
Total	$ 9,258,141	$ 8,967,878

Notes Payable to Individual Investors - Notes payable to individual investors are made through a general offering in the states of Kentucky, New Mexico, Tennessee, and Texas to eligible individual investors and must be purchased in minimum face amounts of $500. All notes payable to individual investors shown in these financial statements are Adjustable Rate Ready Access Notes. Adjustable Rate Ready Access Notes are payable on demand and pay an adjustable interest rate that may be adjusted each month. Additions of principal may be made to Adjustable Rate Ready Access Notes at any time. Withdrawals from Adjustable Rate Ready Access Notes may be made at any time and are payable upon written request of the investor; however, the Program reserves the right to require the investor to provide up to thirty (30) days written notice of any intended withdrawal before such withdrawal is made. Both additions to and withdrawals from Adjustable Rate Ready Access Notes must be made in minimum amounts of $250. The Program may review certain factors, such as investment gap analysis, loan demand, cash flow needs, and the current policy of the Federal Reserve, before establishing each month's rate of interest.

The notes are non-negotiable and may be assigned only upon the Program's written consent. The notes are unsecured and of equal priority with all other current indebtedness of the Program.

NOTES CONTINUED

Note D - **Investment Loan Program** - Continued

Depository Accounts Held for Church Organizations - The Cumberland Presbyterian Church Investment Loan Program, Inc. accepts depository accounts in which church organizations may place funds with the Program, in minimum amounts of $500. All depository accounts shown in these financial statements are Adjustable Rate Ready Access accounts. Like the Program's notes, depository accounts are general obligations of the Program, are unsecured and not insured, and are of equal priority with all other current indebtedness of the Program including notes. The interest rate on the depository accounts is adjusted pursuant to the policies of the Cumberland Presbyterian Church Investment Loan Program, Inc. as they may be adopted from time to time by its Board of Directors. The Cumberland Presbyterian Church Investment Loan Program, Inc. may terminate any depository account upon sixty (60) days written notice to the church organization.

Loans Receivable - Amounts that have been loaned are included on the Statement of Financial Position as loans receivable. There are 23 loans outstanding at December 31, 2014.

Loans receivable are collectible primarily through monthly payments based on up to a twenty-five year amortization period. Interest rates, as determined by the board, are based on the Prime Interest Rate as reported in the Wall Street Journal plus 2.5% per annum. On loans originated for $500,000 or less, the interest rate will be adjusted triennially. On loans originated for more than $500,000, the interest rate will be adjusted annually for the term of the loan.

The composition of loans is as follows:

Loans receivable (secured by real estate)	$ 8,470,313
Less: allowance for loan losses	(1,036,000)
	$ 7,434,313

A summary of changes in the allowance for loan losses is as follows:

Balance at beginning of year	$ 1,036,000
Provision charged to operations	-
Loans charged off	-
Recoveries	-
Balance at end of year	$ 1,036,000

Estimated receipts of principal payments for the five years subsequent to 2014 are:

Year ending December 31,	Amount
2015	$ 389,236
2016	403,003
2017	422,680
2018	443,161
2019	935,179
Thereafter	4,841,054
	$ 7,434,313

NOTES CONTINUED

Note E - Funds Held in Trust

The Discipleship Ministry Team leader of the Ministry Council is responsible for certain funds held in trust for outside groups. Funds invested by the executive director in Investment Loan Program amounted to the following as of December 31, 2014:

P.R.E.M. $ 227,745

The General Assembly Corporation is responsible for funds held in trust for certain committees and commissions. These funds are shown as liabilities in the Statement of Financial Position of the General Assembly Corporation. Activity in these funds for the year ended December 31, 2014, is as follows:

	Nominating Committee	Committee on Judiciary	Non-USA Moderator Travel Fund
Balance January 1, 2014	$ 6,181	$ 3,605	$ 5,847
Our United Outreach	2,373	7,639	-
Contributions	-	3,356	-
Disbursements	(2,512)	(11,698)	-
Balance December 31, 2014	$ 6,042	$ 2,902	$ 5,847

	Committee on Theology and Social Concerns	Commission on Chaplains
Balance January 1, 2014	$ 15,002	$ 7,718
Our United Outreach	2,836	8,102
Contributions	3,089	50
Disbursements	(5,958)	(6,877)
Balance December 31, 2014	$ 14,969	$ 8,993

Note F - Insurance Program

The Cumberland Presbyterian Group Health and Life Insurance Program is a fully insured, experience-rated plan with a policy year ending on the last day of February. Any excess of premium over medical claims and other plan expenses is retained by the insurer; excess losses are no longer carried forward as a charge against the experience for subsequent policy years, as in the past, but must be absorbed by the insurer. The plan is the responsibility of the Board of Stewardship, Foundation, and Benefits.

The plan has one Investment Loan Program account and one account in the Endowment Program. Both are used as a stabilization reserve to provide some protection against unexpected medical claims volatility. The balance at December 31, 2014 of the Investment Loan Program account is $83,051. The balance at December 31, 2014 of the Endowment Program account is $2,076,130.

NOTES CONTINUED

Note G - Concentrations of Credit Risk Arising from Cash Deposits in Excess of Insured Limits

The Center maintains its cash balances in a financial institution located in Memphis, Tennessee. The balances are insured by the Federal Deposit Insurance Corporation up to $250,000 as of December 31, 2014. At various times there were balances that exceeded these FDIC limits. Cash and cash equivalents classified as securities and investments are items held in equities backed by the Federal Government. These equities, while backed by the Federal Government, are not insured by the Federal Deposit Insurance Corporation.

Note H - Real Estate

Real estate assets of both the Ministry Council and the Historical Foundation are held for investment and are therefore not depreciated. These assets amounted to the following at December 31, 2014:

Property Location	Ministry Council	Historical Foundation	Total
San Francisco, California	$ 51,818	$ -	$ 51,818
Birthplace Shrine Chapel, Dickson County, Tennessee	-	21,500	21,500
McAdow Home, Dickson County, Tennessee	-	17,255	17,255
Total	$ 51,818	$ 38,755	$ 90,573

Note I - Leases

The Ministry Council leases three copiers and two postage machines for use in its offices. Lease payments for the year ended December 31, 2014, totaled $12,185. The minimum lease payments for the next five years ended December 31 are as follows:

2015	$	11,090
2016		10,288
2017		7,716
2018		-
2019		-
Thereafter		-
	$	29,094

NOTES CONTINUED

Note J - Combined Statement of Activities Expenses

The total expenses of various Agencies are included in the Combined Statement of Activities as follows:

Expense Description	Agencies
Our United Outreach	Our United Outreach
General Assembly Corporation	General Assembly Corporation
Ministry Council	Ministry Council
Shared Services	Shared Services
Historical Foundation	Historical Foundation
Board of Stewardship, Foundation and Benefits	Board of Stewardship, Foundation, and Benefits
Small Church Loan Program	Small Church Loan Program
Insurance Program	Insurance Program
Ministerial Aid	Ministerial Aid
Investment Loan Program	Investment Loan Program
Retirement Fund	Retirement Fund
Endowment Program	Endowment Program

Costs originating from Shared Services (formerly Central Services - made up of Building and Maintenance, Computer Services Division, and Central Accounting Division) are now funded by Our United Outreach appropriations instead of being charged to the various applicable agencies based on usage.

Inter-agency revenue and expense items for Our United Outreach and endowment earnings have been eliminated on the combined statement of activity.

Note K - Fair Value Measurements

Prices for closed-end bond funds and equity mutual funds are readily available in the active markets in which those securities are traded, and the resulting fair values are categorized as level 1.

Prices for mortgage backed securities, bond mutual funds, and real estate investment trusts are determined on a recurring basis based upon inputs that are readily available in public markets or can be derived from information available in publicly quoted markets and are categorized as level 2.

NOTES CONTINUED

Note K - Fair Value Measurements - Continued

There is limited or no observable data for the prices of private investment entities that are held by the Center and the resulting fair values of these securities are categorized as level 3.

Fair values of assets measured on a recurring basis at December 31, 2014 are as follows:

	Fair Value	Quoted Prices In Active Market for Identical Assets (Level 1)	Significant Other Observable Inputs (Level 2)	Significant Unobservable Inputs (Level 3)
December 31, 2014				
Mortgage backed securities	$ 7,484,557	$ -	$ 7,484,557	$ -
Bond mutual funds	7,903,441	-	7,903,441	-
Closed-end bond funds	3,483,770	3,483,770	-	-
Equity mutual funds	3,293,443	3,293,443	-	-
Real estate investment trusts	5,158,190	-	5,158,190	-
Private investment entities	55,611,839	-	-	55,611,839
Total	$ 82,935,240	$ 6,777,213	$ 20,546,188	$ 55,611,839

Because of the multiple number and complexity of the calculations necessary, management does not believe it is practicable to estimate fair value of loans receivable, net of allowance for loan losses. Therefore, no adjustment has been made to the net carrying value of $11,582,642 listed on the Combined Statement of Financial Position.

NOTES CONTINUED

Note K - Fair Value Measurements - Continued

The following table provides information related to the previously mentioned investments that are valued based primarily on net asset value at December 31, 2014:

	Fair Value	Unfunded Commitments	Redemption Frequency (If Currently Eligible)	Redemption Notice Period
Private Investment Entities				
GT Emerging Markets (QP), L.P.	$ 5,667,363	None	Annual	90 Days
GT Offshore Fund, Ltd. (Class A)	8,119,681	None	Annual	90 Days
GT Offshore Fund, Ltd. (Class B)	10,463,118	None	Annual	90 Days
GT ERISA Fund, Ltd. (Class A)	3,492,991	None	Annual	90 Days
GT ERISA Fund, Ltd. (Class B)	4,551,867	None	Annual	90 Days
GT Real Assets, L.P.	1,055,084	None	Annual	90 Days
GT Special Opportunities III, L.P.	1,607,100	None	see note	see note
Midland Intl Equity QP Fund, L.P.	8,765,111	None	Quarterly	60 Days
Midland U.S. QP Fund, L.P.	11,889,524	None	Quarterly	60 Days
	$ 55,611,839			

The GT Special Opportunities III, L.P. provides for an annual redemption upon 90 days notice after an initial lock-up period of eighteen months.

The following table summarizes fair value by fund for investments in private investment entities that are valued based primarily on net asset value at December 31, 2014:

	Retirement Fund	Endowment Program	Total Fair Value
Private Investment Entities			
GT Emerging Markets (QP), L.P.	$ 1,723,248	$ 3,944,115	$ 5,667,363
GT Offshore Fund, Ltd. (Class A)	-	8,119,681	8,119,681
GT Offshore Fund, Ltd. (Class B)	-	10,463,118	10,463,118
GT ERISA Fund, Ltd. (Class A)	3,492,991	-	3,492,991
GT ERISA Fund, Ltd. (Class B)	4,551,867	-	4,551,867
GT Real Assets, L.P.	327,440	727,644	1,055,084
GT Special Opportunities III, L.P.	481,315	1,125,785	1,607,100
Midland Intl Equity QP Fund, L.P.	2,648,109	6,117,002	8,765,111
Midland U.S. QP Fund, L.P.	3,577,104	8,312,420	11,889,524
	$ 16,802,074	$ 38,809,765	$ 55,611,839

NOTES CONTINUED

Note K - Fair Value Measurements - Continued

Assets measured at fair value on a recurring basis using significant unobservable inputs (Level 3):

Fair value at beginning of year	$ 52,250,400
Investments and distributions, net	290,000
Realized/unrealized gains (losses)	3,071,439
Fair value at end of year	$ 55,611,839

Gains and losses (realized and unrealized) for Level 3 assets included in net assets for the year are reported as follows:

On the Combined Statement of Activity, under Revenues, gains, and other support:

Permanently restricted net assets:	
Endowment program	$ 2,149,226
Net assets available for benefits:	
Retirement fund	922,213
Total net assets	$ 3,071,439

These investments without readily determinable values comprise approximately 50% of total assets at December 31, 2014.

All assets have been valued using a market approach.

A description of the Private Investment Entities and the investment objectives is as follows:

GT Emerging Markets (QP), L.P. - This fund is organized as a "fund of funds" which seek to achieve long-term capital appreciation through investments in limited partnerships, off-shore corporations, open-end mutual funds, closed-end mutual funds, commingled trust funds, and separately managed accounts that invest primarily in "emerging markets." Investments may also be made in industrialized nations such as the United States and Japan.

GT Offshore Fund, Ltd. / GT ERISA Fund, Ltd. - These are open-ended "umbrella" funds, incorporated as exempted companies in the Cayman Islands with multiple classes of Shares. Each class of share is separately valued and pursues its own clearly defined investment objective(s) and strategy(ies). These funds overall investment objectives are as follows:

Class A is broadly diversified among multiple investment managers and multiple investment strategies. The strategies employed may include multi-strategy arbitrage, capital structure arbitrage, distressed debt, long/short equity or niche financing.

Class B seeks to achieve a superior rate of return exceeding that of the MSCI World Index with less volatility while minimizing market risk through a hedged approach. The primary investment strategy will be a long/short equity strategy. This class is broadly diversified among multiple investment managers and multiple long/short equity strategies.

NOTES CONTINUED

Note K - Fair Value Measurements - Continued

GT Real Assets, L.P. - This fund is organized as a "fund of funds" investment vehicle that will pool and invest funds, generally through "Managed Investment Vehicles," for the purpose of generating attractive risk-adjusted returns by opportunistically investing in a broad spectrum of resources, real assets, and other investment strategies.

GT Special Opportunities, III, L.P. - This fund is organized as a "fund of funds" investment vehicle that will pool and invest funds, generally through "Managed Investment Vehicles," for the purpose of achieving a superior rate of return. The fund focuses on a very limited number of investment strategies that are considered to be opportunistic based upon prevailing market conditions. At times, the fund may only invest in one strategy and do so in a non-diversified manner, perhaps with only a single manager. The strategies sought by the fund will often be niche-focused. Accordingly, the risk level for the fund is anticipated to be extremely high.

Midland International Equity QP Fund, L.P. - This is an international equity fund which seeks to identify listed companies selling at a discount to intrinsic net worth on liquid stock exchanges of non-U.S. countries. The focus of this fund is long-term capital appreciation. This fund seeks to outperform the MSCI EAFE Index, net of fees and taxes, over a full market cycle.

Midland U.S. QP Fund, L.P. - This fund's objective is to outperform the broad U.S. equity market, defined as the Russell 3000 Index, net of fees and taxes over a full market cycle. The fund seeks to compound capital at attractive rates through direct and indirect long-term ownership of publicly traded businesses domiciled in the United States.

Note L - Securities and Investments

Securities and investments at December 31, 2014 are as follows:

	Ministry Council	Historical Foundation	Investment Loan Program	Retirement Fund	Endowment Program	Total
Cash and cash equivalents	$ -	$ -	$ 1,483,321	$ 955,951	$ 2,393,875	$ 4,833,147
Mortgage backed securities	-	-	7,484,557	-	-	7,484,557
Bond mutual funds	-	-	-	2,479,788	5,423,653	7,903,441
Closed-end bond funds	-	-	-	1,194,077	2,289,693	3,483,770
Equity mutual funds	-	-	-	1,094,752	2,198,691	3,293,443
Real estate investment trusts	-	-	-	1,205,975	3,952,215	5,158,190
Private investment entities	-	-	-	16,802,074	38,809,765	55,611,839
Real estate	51,818	38,755	-	-	-	90,573
	$ 51,818	$ 38,755	$ 8,967,878	$ 23,732,617	$ 55,067,892	$ 87,858,960

Note M - Subsequent Events

Subsequent events were evaluated through June 4, 2015, which is the date the financial statements were available to be issued.

BETHEL UNIVERSITY

**FINANCIAL STATEMENTS
AND OTHER INFORMATION**

JULY 31, 2014 AND 2013

BETHEL UNIVERSITY

Table of Contents

	Page
INDEPENDENT AUDITOR'S REPORT	1 - 2
FINANCIAL STATEMENTS	
Statements of Financial Position	3
Statements of Activities	4 - 5
Statements of Cash Flows	6 - 7
Notes to Financial Statements	8 - 31
OTHER INFORMATION	
Schedule of Expenditures of Federal Awards	32
Notes to Schedule of Expenditures of Federal Awards	33
INDEPENDENT AUDITOR'S REPORT ON INTERNAL CONTROL OVER FINANCIAL REPORTING AND ON COMPLIANCE AND OTHER MATTERS BASED ON AN AUDIT OF FINANCIAL STATEMENTS PERFORMED IN ACCORDANCE WITH *GOVERNMENT AUDITING STANDARDS*	34 - 35
INDEPENDENT AUDITOR'S REPORT ON COMPLIANCE FOR THE MAJOR PROGRAM AND ON INTERNAL CONTROL OVER COMPLIANCE REQUIRED BY OMB CIRCULAR A-133	36 - 38
SCHEDULE OF FINDINGS AND QUESTIONED COSTS	39 - 42

Independent Auditor's Report

The Board of Trustees
Bethel University
McKenzie, Tennessee

Report on the Financial Statements

We have audited the accompanying financial statements of Bethel University (the "University"), which comprise the statements of financial position as of July 31, 2014 and 2013, and the related statements of activities and cash flows for the years then ended, and the related notes to the financial statements.

Management's Responsibility for the Financial Statements

Management is responsible for the preparation and fair presentation of these financial statements in accordance with accounting principles generally accepted in the United States of America; this includes the design, implementation, and maintenance of internal control relevant to the preparation and fair presentation of financial statements that are free from material misstatement, whether due to fraud or error.

Auditor's Responsibility

Our responsibility is to express an opinion on these financial statements based on our audits. We conducted our audits in accordance with auditing standards generally accepted in the United States of America and the standards applicable to financial audits contained in *Government Auditing Standards*, issued by the Comptroller General of the United States. Those standards require that we plan and perform the audit to obtain reasonable assurance about whether the financial statements are free from material misstatement.

An audit involves performing procedures to obtain audit evidence about the amounts and disclosures in the financial statements. The procedures selected depend on the auditor's judgment, including the assessment of the risks of material misstatement of the financial statements, whether due to fraud or error. In making those risk assessments, the auditor considers internal control relevant to the entity's preparation and fair presentation of the financial statements in order to design audit procedures that are appropriate in the circumstances, but not for the purpose of expressing an opinion on the effectiveness of the entity's internal control. Accordingly, we express no such opinion. An audit also includes evaluating the appropriateness of accounting policies used and the reasonableness of significant accounting estimates made by management, as well as evaluating the overall presentation of the financial statements.

The Board of Trustees
Bethel University

We believe that the audit evidence we have obtained is sufficient and appropriate to provide a basis for our audit opinion.

Opinion

In our opinion, the financial statements referred to above present fairly, in all material respects, the financial position of Bethel University as of July 31, 2014 and 2013, and the changes in its net assets and its cash flows for the years then ended in accordance with accounting principles generally accepted in the United States of America.

Other Matters

Other Information

Our audit was conducted for the purpose of forming an opinion on the financial statements as a whole. The accompanying schedule of expenditures of federal awards, as required by Office of Management and Budget Circular A-133, *Audits of States, Local Governments*, and *Non-Profit Organizations*, is presented for purposes of additional analysis and is not a required part of the financial statements. Such information is the responsibility of management and was derived from and relates directly to the underlying accounting and other records used to prepare the financial statements. The information has been subjected to the auditing procedures applied in the audit of the financial statements and certain additional procedures, including comparing and reconciling such information directly to the underlying accounting and other records used to prepare the financial statements or to the financial statements themselves, and other additional procedures in accordance with auditing standards generally accepted in the United States of America. In our opinion, the information is fairly stated, in all material respects, in relation to the financial statements as a whole.

Other Reporting Required by Government Auditing Standards

In accordance with *Government Auditing Standards*, we have also issued our report dated October 15, 2014, on our consideration of the University's internal control over financial reporting and on our tests of its compliance with certain provisions of laws, regulations, contracts, and grant agreements and other matters. The purpose of that report is to describe the scope of our testing of internal control over financial reporting and compliance and the results of that testing, and not to provide an opinion on internal control over financial reporting or on compliance. That report is an integral part of an audit performed in accordance with *Government Auditing Standards* in considering the University's internal control over financial reporting and compliance.

Crosslin & Associates, P.C.

Nashville, Tennessee
October 15, 2014

BETHEL UNIVERSITY
STATEMENTS OF FINANCIAL POSITION

ASSETS

	July 31, 2014	July 31, 2013
Cash and cash equivalents	$ 1,058,990	$ 879,267
Perkins loan cash	76,644	112,743
Receivables:		
Contributions, net (Note B)	2,752,506	4,768,311
Students, net of allowances of $2,396,395 and $1,851,395 respectively	5,942,697	4,949,281
Perkins loans, net of allowances of $233,504 and $223,290, respectively	270,453	266,751
Other	83,724	106,500
Note receivable	7,998,454	8,200,000
Inventories	273,836	280,849
Prepaid expenses and deposits	153,446	127,786
Investments (Note C)	3,233,407	3,395,719
Beneficial interest in assets held by others (Note D)	3,692,558	3,489,347
Property, buildings, and equipment:		
Land	705,511	711,511
Buildings and improvements	66,437,520	62,460,515
Equipment, furniture and automobiles	7,906,415	7,906,789
Library books	1,284,514	1,284,514
Property held under capital leases (Note F)	5,893,443	5,508,296
Construction in progress	1,027,314	1,092,977
	83,254,717	78,964,602
Less: Accumulated depreciation	(25,218,406)	(20,387,270)
Total property and equipment, net	58,036,311	58,577,332
Total assets	$ 83,573,026	$ 85,153,886

LIABILITIES AND NET ASSETS

	2014	2013
Liabilities:		
Accounts payable and student account deposits	$ 6,483,151	$ 7,104,700
Accrued payroll and benefits	523,136	886,993
Deferred tuition revenue	6,708,638	11,192,236
Annuities payable	-	707
Debt (Note E)	44,715,695	44,125,905
Obligations under capital leases (Note F)	464,140	535,935
Advances from the federal government	411,781	411,781
Total liabilities	59,306,541	64,258,257
Net Assets:		
Unrestricted	10,458,902	6,166,553
Temporarily restricted (Notes G and H)	3,701,005	4,853,004
Permanently restricted (Notes G and H)	10,106,578	9,876,072
Total net assets	24,266,485	20,895,629
Total liabilities and net assets	$ 83,573,026	$ 85,153,886

See accompanying notes to financial statements.

BETHEL UNIVERSITY
STATEMENTS OF ACTIVITIES

	Year Ended July 31, 2014			
	Unrestricted	Temporarily Restricted	Permanently Restricted	Total
Revenue, gains and other support:				
Regular tuition and fees	$ 56,246,891	$ -	$ -	$ 56,246,891
Degree completion tuition	12,353,628	-	-	12,353,628
Institutional scholarships and grants	(12,958,497)	-	-	(12,958,497)
Net tuition and fees	55,642,022	-	-	55,642,022
Bookstore income	1,984,512	-	-	1,984,512
Private gifts and contracts	4,089,036	1,049,022	27,294	5,165,352
Investment income	166,742	157,674	-	324,416
Unrealized gain on beneficial interests in assets held by others	-	-	203,212	203,212
Auxiliary fund revenues	7,225,816	-	-	7,225,816
Government grants	463,486	-	-	463,486
Other income	1,133,336	-	-	1,133,336
Net assets released from restrictions	2,358,695	(2,358,695)	-	-
Total revenue, gains and other support	73,063,645	(1,151,999)	230,506	72,142,152
Expenses:				
Education and general:				
Instruction	40,725,673	-	-	40,725,673
Academic support	1,327,251	-	-	1,327,251
Student services	7,609,265	-	-	7,609,265
Institutional support	12,853,939	-	-	12,853,939
Auxiliary enterprises	6,255,168	-	-	6,255,168
Total expenses	68,771,296	-	-	68,771,296
Net increase (decrease) in net assets	4,292,349	(1,151,999)	230,506	3,370,856
Net assets, beginning of year	6,166,553	4,853,004	9,876,072	20,895,629
Net assets, end of year	$ 10,458,902	$ 3,701,005	$ 10,106,578	$ 24,266,485

	Year Ended July 31, 2013			
Unrestricted	Temporarily Restricted	Permanently Restricted	Total	
$ 54,394,364	$ -	$ -	$ 54,394,364
12,693,723	-	-	12,693,723
(14,330,903)	-	-	(14,330,903)
52,757,184	-	-	52,757,184
2,200,323	-	-	2,200,323
11,225,480	3,705,081	35,077	14,965,638
150,116	137,643	-	287,759
-	-	280,535	280,535
7,623,967	-	-	7,623,967
421,791	-	-	421,791
1,388,519	-	-	1,388,519
1,174,051	(1,174,051)	-	-
76,941,431	2,668,673	315,612	79,925,716
41,178,333	-	-	41,178,333
1,069,385	-	-	1,069,385
7,429,354	-	-	7,429,354
13,438,273	-	-	13,438,273
8,587,106	-	-	8,587,106
71,702,451	-	-	71,702,451
5,238,980	2,668,673	315,612	8,223,265
927,573	2,184,331	9,560,460	12,672,364
$ 6,166,553	$ 4,853,004	$ 9,876,072	$ 20,895,629

See accompanying notes to financial statements.

- 5 -

BETHEL UNIVERSITY
STATEMENTS OF CASH FLOWS

	Year ended July 31,	
	2014	2013
CASH FLOWS FROM OPERATING ACTIVITIES:		
Increase in net assets	$ 3,370,856	$ 8,223,265
Adjustments to reconcile change in net assets to net cash provided by operating activities		
Non-cash:		
Allowance for doubtful student accounts, contributions and Perkins loans receivable	(580,609)	543,859
Disposal of property and equipment	445,549	-
Unrealized (gain) loss on investments and beneficial interests in assets held by others	(527,627)	(568,296)
Non-cash contributions	(3,185,000)	-
Gain on the change in fair value of interest rate swap	(125,533)	(166,961)
Depreciation	4,949,999	6,010,614
(Increase) decrease in:		
Perkins loan cash	36,099	18,482
Contributions receivable	3,151,628	(1,740,706)
Student accounts receivable	(1,538,416)	1,667,761
Perkins loans receivable	(13,916)	(19,939)
Other receivables	22,776	(106,500)
Inventories	7,013	(59,796)
Prepaid expenses and deposits	(25,660)	85,087
Increase (decrease) in:		
Accounts payable and student account deposits	(504,429)	(868,416)
Accrued payroll and benefits	(363,857)	241,584
Deferred tuition revenue	(4,483,598)	2,245,843
Contributions restricted for long-term investments	(27,294)	(35,077)
Total adjustments	(2,762,875)	7,247,539
Net cash provided by operating activities	607,981	15,470,804
CASH FLOWS FROM INVESTING ACTIVITIES:		
Withdrawal of investments, net	486,728	1,940,010
Payments received on note receivable	201,546	-
Payment of accounts payable for property, buildings and equipment	(117,120)	(4,026,603)
Purchases of property, buildings and equipment	(452,780)	(4,235,419)
Net cash provided by (used in) investing activities	118,374	(6,322,012)
CASH FLOWS FROM FINANCING ACTIVITIES:		
Payments on annuity obligations	(707)	-
Proceeds from notes payable and line-of-credit	4,244,473	26,183,740
Payments on notes payable and line-of-credit	(4,360,750)	(31,156,240)
Repayments of capital lease obligations	(456,942)	(3,708,112)
Contributions restricted for long-term investments	27,294	35,077
Changes in advances from the federal government	-	(1,261,992)
Net cash used in investing activities	(546,632)	(9,907,527)

See accompanying notes to financial statements.

BETHEL UNIVERSITY
STATEMENTS OF CASH FLOWS - Continued

	Year ended July 31,	
	2014	2013
Net increase (decrease) in cash and cash equivalents	179,723	(758,735)
Cash and cash equivalents at beginning of year	879,267	1,638,002
Cash and cash equivalents at end of year	$ 1,058,990	$ 879,267
Supplemental disclosures of cash flow information:		
Interest paid	$ 3,409,897	$ 2,405,667
Non-cash financing and investing activities:		
Purchases of property and equipment	4,854,527	6,148,260
Amount financed through capital leases, accounts payable, debt, or received through donations	(4,401,747)	(1,912,841)
Total paid for property and equipment	$ 452,780	$ 4,235,419

See accompanying notes to financial statements.

BETHEL UNIVERSITY
NOTES TO FINANCIAL STATEMENTS
JULY 31, 2014 AND 2013

A. SUMMARY OF SIGNIFICANT ACCOUNTING POLICIES

Organization and Business Purpose

Bethel University (the "University") is a private, residential, coeducational University affiliated with the Cumberland Presbyterian Church, dedicated primarily to educating students in the liberal arts and science while also offering select pre-professional programs, a graduate teacher education program, a masters of business administration program, and an online criminal justice program. In addition to its traditional academic programs, the University also offers a degree-completion program. The University is accredited by the Commission on Universities of the Southern Association of Universities and Schools and its education emphasizes academic excellence, high achievement, intellectual and personal integrity, and participation in community life. Its Christian heritage finds expression in commitment to the values of personal growth, justice, community, and service.

Accrual Basis and Financial Statement Presentation

The financial statements of the University have been prepared on the accrual basis of accounting.

The University classifies its revenue, expenses, gains, and losses into three classes of net assets based on the existence or absence of donor-imposed restrictions. Net assets of the University and changes therein are classified as follows:

Unrestricted net assets - Net assets that are not subject to donor-imposed stipulations.

Temporarily restricted net assets - Net assets subject to donor-imposed stipulations that may or will be met either by actions of the University and/or the passage of time.

Permanently restricted net assets - Net assets subject to donor-imposed stipulations that are required to be maintained permanently by the University. Generally, the donors of these assets permit the University to use all or part of the income earned on related investments for general or specific purposes.

The amount for each of these classes of net assets is displayed in the statements of financial position and the amount of change in each class of net assets is displayed in the statements of activities.

BETHEL UNIVERSITY
NOTES TO FINANCIAL STATEMENTS
JULY 31, 2014 AND 2013

A. SUMMARY OF SIGNIFICANT ACCOUNTING POLICES - Continued

Use of Estimates in the Preparation of Financial Statements

The preparation of financial statements in conformity with accounting principles generally accepted in the United States of America requires management to make assumptions that affect the reported amounts of assets and liabilities, disclosure of contingent assets and liabilities at the date of the financial statements and the reported amounts of revenues and expenses during the reporting period. The more significant areas include the recovery period for property and equipment, the allocation of certain operating expenses to functional categories, the collection of contributions receivable and the adequacy of the allowance for doubtful student receivables. Management believes that such estimates have been based on reasonable assumptions and that such estimates are adequate. Actual results could differ from those estimates.

Contributions

The University reports gifts of cash and other assets as restricted support if they are received with donor stipulations that limit the use of the donated assets. When a donor restriction expires, that is, when a stipulated time restriction ends or the purpose of the restriction is accomplished, temporarily restricted net assets are reclassified to unrestricted net assets and reported in the statement of activities as net assets released from restrictions. The University has elected to report contributions received with donor-imposed restrictions as an increase to unrestricted net assets if the restrictions are met in the same fiscal year that the contributions are received.

The University reports gifts of land, equipment and other assets as unrestricted support unless explicit donor stipulations specify how the donated assets must be used. Gifts of long-lived assets with explicit restrictions that specify how the assets are to be used and gifts of cash or other assets that must be used to acquire long-lived assets are reported as restricted support. Absent explicit donor stipulations regarding how long the long-lived assets must be maintained, the University reports expirations of donor restrictions when the donated or acquired long-lived assets are placed in service.

Contribution of services are recognized if the services received (a) create or enhance non-financial assets or (b) require specialized skills, provided by individuals possessing those skills and would typically need to be purchased if not provided by donation.

In the event a donor makes changes to the nature of a restricted gift which affects its classification among the net asset categories, such amounts are reflected as reclassifications in the statements of activities.

BETHEL UNIVERSITY
NOTES TO FINANCIAL STATEMENTS
JULY 31, 2014 AND 2013

A. SUMMARY OF SIGNIFICANT ACCOUNTING POLICIES - Continued

Perkins Loan - Cash

As required by federal regulations, cash related to the Federal Perkins Loan Program is maintained in a separate bank account.

Student Accounts Receivable

The University records accounts receivable at their estimated net realizable value. An allowance for doubtful accounts is recorded based upon management's estimate of uncollectible accounts determined by analysis of specific student balances and a general reserve based upon agings of outstanding balances. Past due balances and delinquent receivables are charged against the allowance when they are determined to be uncollectible by management.

Notes Receivable - Students

Notes receivable from students at July 31, 2014 and 2013, totaled $270,453 and $266,751, respectively, net of allowances of $233,504 and $223,290, respectively. Student loans are granted by the University under the federally funded Perkins loan program. These funds are disbursed based upon the demonstration of financial need on the Perkins loan, at which time the loan will also begin accruing interest. Perkins loan amounts are then repaid through a third party billing service. Student loans are considered past due when payment has not been received within 30 days. At both July 31, 2014 and 2013, student loans represented 0.32% of total assets.

The allowance for doubtful accounts is established based on prior collection experience and current economic factors which, in management's judgment, could influence the ability of loan recipients to repay the amounts per the loan terms. Loan balances are written off only when they are deemed to be permanently uncollectible.

Contributions Receivable

Contributions receivable are recorded at their estimated fair value using a discount rate commensurate with the rate on U.S. Government Securities whose maturities correspond to the maturities of the contributions. Contributions receivable are considered to be either conditional or unconditional promises to give. A conditional contribution is one which depends on the occurrence of a specified uncertain future event to become binding on the donor. Conditional contributions are not recorded as revenue until the condition is met, at which time they become unconditional. Unconditional contributions are recorded as revenue at the time verifiable evidence of the promise to give is received.

BETHEL UNIVERSITY
NOTES TO FINANCIAL STATEMENTS
JULY 31, 2014 AND 2013

A. SUMMARY OF SIGNIFICANT ACCOUNTING POLICIES - Continued

Inventories

Inventories consist primarily of books and supplies and are stated at the lower of cost or market. Cost is determined using the average cost method.

Investments

Investments in marketable equity securities with readily determinable fair values and investments in debt securities are stated at their fair values in the statements of financial position. Fair value of investments is determined based on quoted market prices or using Level 2 or 3 inputs as described in Note I. All gains and losses (both realized and unrealized) and other investment income are reported in the statements of activities.

Property and Equipment

Property and equipment are recorded at cost at the date of acquisition or fair value at the date of donation in the case of gifts. Depreciation on property and equipment is calculated on the straight-line method over estimated useful lives of 20-70 years for buildings and improvements, 18 months - 10 years for equipment, furniture, and library books, 5 years for automobiles, and 20 years for other property. Property held under capital leases is being depreciated on the straight-line method based on the shorter of the estimated useful life of the property to the University or the life of the capital lease. Repairs and renovations that do not add value or extend the life of the assets are expensed as incurred. Depreciation and operation and maintenance charges are allocated to appropriate functional expense categories.

The estimate to complete construction in progress is $300,000 as of July 31, 2014.

Deferred Revenue

Deferred revenue consists primarily of charges and cash receipts collected prior to year-end for services rendered after year-end. These receipts pertain to upcoming tuition and fees.

Advances from the Federal Government for Student Loans

The Perkins Loan Program is a campus-based program providing revolving loan funds for financial assistance to eligible postsecondary school students based on financial need. The Department of Education provides funds along with the University which are used to make loans to eligible students at low interest rates. Refundable government advances for Perkins at both July 31, 2014 and 2013 totaled $411,781.

BETHEL UNIVERSITY
NOTES TO FINANCIAL STATEMENTS
JULY 31, 2014 AND 2013

A. SUMMARY OF SIGNIFICANT ACCOUNTING POLICIES - Continued

Derivative Instruments

The University accounts for its derivative instruments under Financial Accounting Standards Board Accounting Standards Codification (ASC) 815, *Derivatives and Hedging*, which establishes accounting and reporting standards requiring that derivative instruments be recorded in the statements of financial position at estimated fair value. Changes in a derivative's fair value are included in the statements of activities as a component of the change in net assets in the period of change. As described in Note E, the University has interest rate swap agreements which are considered to be derivative instruments. The University's interest rate risk management strategy is to stabilize cash flow requirements by maintaining interest rate swap contracts to convert certain variable-rate debt to a fixed rate.

Advertising Costs

Advertising costs are expensed as incurred and totaled approximately $1,554,126 and $1,296,474 for the years ended July 31, 2014 and 2013, respectively.

Tax Status

The University is exempt from Federal income taxes under 501(a) of the Internal Revenue Code ("IRC") as an organization described in IRC Section 501(c)(3). Accordingly, no provision for income taxes has been made in the accompanying financial statements. The University is not classified as a private foundation.

The University accounts for the effect of any uncertain tax positions based on a more likely than not threshold to the recognition of the tax positions being sustained based on the technical merits of the position under examination by the applicable taxing authority. If a tax position or positions are deemed to result in uncertainties of those position, the unrecognized tax benefit is estimated based on a cumulative probability assessment that aggregates the estimated tax liability for all uncertain tax positions. Tax positions for the University include, but are not limited to, the tax-exempt status and determination of whether certain income is subject to unrelated business income tax; however, the University has determined that such tax positions do not result in an uncertainty requiring recognition.

BETHEL UNIVERSITY
NOTES TO FINANCIAL STATEMENTS
JULY 31, 2014 AND 2013

A. SUMMARY OF SIGNIFICANT ACCOUNTING POLICIES - Continued

Fair Value Measurements

Assets and liabilities recorded at fair value in the statements of financial position are categorized based on the level of judgment associated with the inputs used to measure their fair value. Related disclosures are included in Note I. Level inputs, as defined by Financial Accounting Standards Board Accounting Standards Codification ("ASC") 820, *Fair Value Measurements and Disclosures*, are as follows:

Level 1 - Values are unadjusted quoted prices for identical assets and liabilities in active markets accessible at the measurement date.

Level 2 - Inputs include quoted prices for similar assets or liabilities in active markets, quoted prices from those willing to trade in markets that are not active, or other inputs that are observable or can be corroborated by market data for the term of the instrument. Such inputs include market interest rates and volatilities, spreads and yield curves.

Level 3 - Certain inputs are unobservable (supported by little or no market activity) and significant to the fair value measurement. Unobservable inputs reflect the University's best estimate of what hypothetical market participants would use to determine a transaction price for the asset or liability at the reporting date.

Classification of Expenses

Expenses are classified functionally as a measure of service efforts and accomplishments. Direct expenses incurred for a single function are allocated entirely to that function. Joint expenses applicable to more than one function are allocated on the basis of objectively summarized information or management estimates.

Reclassifications

Certain reclassifications have been made to the 2013 financial statements in order for them to conform to the 2014 presentation.

B. CONTRIBUTIONS RECEIVABLE

Contributions receivable at July 31, 2014 and 2013 consist of the following:

	2014	2013
Contributions receivable (present value)	$ 2,920,096	$ 6,071,724
Less: allowance for doubtful contributions	(167,590)	(1,303,413)
	$ 2,752,506	$ 4,768,311

BETHEL UNIVERSITY
NOTES TO FINANCIAL STATEMENTS
JULY 31, 2014 AND 2013

B. CONTRIBUTIONS RECEIVABLE - Continued

Expected maturities of contributions receivable at July 31, 2014 are as follows:

Fiscal Year Ending July 31,	Amount
2015	$ 1,006,487
2016	339,310
2017	353,827
2018	332,077
2019	328,577
Thereafter	686,423
Total expected contributions	3,046,701
Less: allowance for net present value using a weighted average discount rate of 1.00%	(126,605)
Present value of contributions receivable	$ 2,920,096

C. INVESTMENTS

The investments of the University are principally administered by the University or by the Board of Stewardship of the Cumberland Presbyterian Church, Inc. (the "Board"). The funds administered by the Board are co-mingled with funds of other agencies of the Church. The University's portion represents approximately 6% and 5% of the funds administered by the Board at July 31, 2014 and 2013, respectively. The investments of the University are invested as follows:

	2014	2013
Administered by the Board:		
Marketable equity and debt securities	$3,072,565	$2,865,236
Administered by the University:		
Marketable equity and debt securities	4,044	76,967
Certificates of deposits (partially pledged in 2013, see Note E)	99,941	428,567
Other	56,857	24,949
	$3,233,407	$3,395,719

- 14 -

BETHEL UNIVERSITY
NOTES TO FINANCIAL STATEMENTS
JULY 31, 2014 AND 2013

D. BENEFICIAL INTEREST IN ASSETS HELD BY OTHERS

Beneficial interest in assets held by others represents arrangements in which a donor establishes and funds a perpetual trust administered by an individual or organization other than the University. The fair value of perpetually held trusts in which the University had a beneficial interest as of July 31, 2014 and 2013, was $3,692,558 and $3,489,347, respectively. The University records these trusts at estimated fair value. Income distributed to the University from the beneficial interest assets is temporarily restricted for scholarships.

E. DEBT

The University has the following debt obligations at July 31, 2014 and 2013:

	2014	2013
Note payable to Regions Bank, payable in monthly installments of $25,737 including interest of 4.79% through July 17, 2015, with a final payment of $1,396,516 due August 17, 2015; collateralized by certain real property.	$ 1,627,008	$ 1,852,033
Note payable to Regions Bank, payable in monthly installments of $25,936 including interest of 4.79% through July 17, 2015, with a final payment of $2,636,959 due August 17, 2015; collateralized by certain real property.	2,807,181	2,979,452
Note payable to Regions Bank, payable in monthly installments of $10,108 including interest of 4.18% through February 28, 2016; collateralized by certain real property.	697,028	787,135
Step down revolver credit agreement with Regions Bank, bearing interest of 6.35%. Monthly principal payments of $26,000 plus accrued interest are due through March 15, 2015, at which time all unpaid principal and interest are due; collateralized by substantially all real property.	4,444,146	4,679,146

BETHEL UNIVERSITY
NOTES TO FINANCIAL STATEMENTS
JULY 31, 2014 AND 2013

E. DEBT - Continued

	2014	2013
Notes payable to various financial institutions, with interest incurred at rates ranging from 3.29% to 5.5%. Certain notes are unsecured with the remaining notes collateralized by certificates of deposit, specified real estate, or specified equipment.	5,364	7,590
Bond bearing interest at the greater of 3.25% or a variable per annum rate based on LIBOR plus certain basis points (6.12% at July 31, 2014), payable in monthly principal payments of $26,389 plus interest through April 4, 2015, with a final payment of $3,203,965 due May 4, 2015; collateralized by certain real property.	3,430,556	3,747,222
Credit loan totaling $2,000,000 with Regions Bank, bearing interest at 6.25%, payable in equal monthly principal and interest payments with a maturity date of August 16, 2016; collateralized by certain real property.	914,037	1,309,006
Bond bearing interest at a variable per annum rate based on LIBOR plus certain basis points (5.32% at July 31, 2014), payable in monthly principal and interest payments through July 28, 2016, with a final payment of $1,558,366 due August 30, 2016; collateralized by certain real property.	1,830,167	1,945,910
Bond bearing interest at a variable per annum rate based on LIBOR plus certain basis points (4.99% at July 31, 2014), payable in monthly principal and interest payments through July 28, 2016, with a final payment of $1,551,166 due September 16, 2016; collateralized by certain real property.	1,830,167	1,945,910

BETHEL UNIVERSITY
NOTES TO FINANCIAL STATEMENTS
JULY 31, 2014 AND 2013

E. DEBT - Continued

	2014	2013
Bond bearing interest at a variable per annum rate based on LIBOR plus certain basis points (3.33% at July 31, 2014), payable in monthly principal and interest payments through July 28, 2016, with a final payment of $1,561,066 due September 1, 2016; collateralized by certain real property.	1,830,167	1,945,910
Bond bearing interest at a variable per annum rate based on LIBOR plus certain basis points (5.00% at July 31, 2014), payable in monthly principal and interest payments through July 28, 2016, with a final payment of $1,562,902 due September 15, 2016; collateralized by certain real property.	1,830,167	1,945,910
Demand line-of-credit totaling $220,000 with McKenzie Banking Company, bearing interest at 2.80% payable on demand with a stated maturity date of February 23, 2014; paid in full during 2014.	-	202,635
Line-of-credit totaling $2,000,000 with Farmers and Merchants Bank, bearing interest at 6% with the full principal payment due on January 29, 2015; collateralized by accounts receivable.	1,237,711	975,810
Note payable to City of Paris, bearing interest at 0%, with monthly payments of $8,663 of principal due beginning on September 30, 2014, through final maturity on September 30, 2022 upon which the remaining principal balance will be paid.	831,600	-
Line-of-credit totaling $500,000 with First Bank, bearing interest at 4.5%, maturing on August 1, 2015; collateralized by real property.	188,610	476,755

BETHEL UNIVERSITY
NOTES TO FINANCIAL STATEMENTS
JULY 31, 2014 AND 2013

E. DEBT - Continued

	2014	2013
Note payable at Carroll County Bank & Trust, bearing interest at 6.4%, with the full principal balance maturing on October 21, 2014; paid in full on August 28, 2014.	400,100	-
Note payable to Carroll County Bank & Trust, bearing interest at 6.4% with the full principal balance paid in August 2014.	300,100	-
Debt agreement through the City of Paris, Tennessee, bearing interest at SIFMA rate, plus 180 basis points (5% at July 31, 2014) and a trustee fee of $125. Interest payments are due monthly through June 1, 2026. Principal amounts totaling $6,500,000 are due in varying amounts ranging from $330,000 to $625,000 annually beginning June 1, 2013 through 2026. This amount was paid in full in August 2013.	-	288,363
Note payable to a related party private company totaling $16,666,000, bearing interest at one year LIBOR plus 7%, payable in monthly installments of interest only. Starting on August 31, 2013, and continuing until January 31, 2015; principal payments due in monthly installments of $308,629, with the remaining balance due at final maturity on July 1, 2019. (See Note R).	16,666,000	16,666,000
Line-of-credit with a related party private company totaling $5,000,000, bearing interest at one year LIBOR plus 9%, payable in monthly installments of interest only starting on August 31, 2013, and continuing until August 31, 2015; at which time the outstanding balance is due.	3,600,000	2,000,000
	44,470,109	43,754,787
Interest rate swap	245,586	371,118
	$44,715,695	$44,125,905

BETHEL UNIVERSITY
NOTES TO FINANCIAL STATEMENTS
JULY 31, 2014 AND 2013

E. DEBT - Continued

The anticipated maturities of the University's notes payable are as follows:

Fiscal Year Ending July 31,	Amount
2015	$14,638,789
2016	14,313,142
2017	7,582,656
2018	3,807,506
2019	3,807,506
Thereafter	320,510
	$44,470,109

Interest Rate Swap

During fiscal year 2011, the University entered into interest rate swap agreements with Regions Bank having an original notional amount of $6,337,500 to reduce the risk associated with debt interest rate fluctuations on portions of the Special Project bonds payable. During fiscal year 2012, the notional amount was increased to $8,450,000 in line with the related bonds payable. The University does not engage in trading these derivatives. The financial instruments are used to manage interest rate risk. The notional amounts are being amortized over the life of the agreements and at July 31, 2014 and 2013, the remaining amounts totaled $7,320,669 and $7,783,640, respectively. The interest rate swap agreements provide for the University to receive interest at a variable rate of 63.456% of LIBOR plus 321 basis points and to pay a fixed monthly interest rate of 5.32% expiring in August 2016.

Gains or losses on the derivatives are included as a component of the change in unrestricted net assets in the statement of activities. The University's interest rate risk management strategy is to stabilize cash flow requirements by maintaining the interest rate swap contracts to convert certain variable-rate debt to fixed rate. The fair value of the derivative was a liability at July 31, 2014 and 2013, totaling $245,586 and $371,118, respectively.

Interest Expense

For the years ending July 31, 2014 and 2013, Bethel University incurred interest expense of $3,409,897 and $2,405,667, respectively.

BETHEL UNIVERSITY
NOTES TO FINANCIAL STATEMENTS
JULY 31, 2014 AND 2013

E. DEBT - Continued

Compliance with Covenants

Certain loan agreements contain various covenants and establish certain financial ratios. The University was not in compliance with certain covenants and ratios at July 31, 2014. However, the University is in the process of and management expects to obtain the appropriate waivers.

F. OBLIGATIONS UNDER CAPITAL LEASES

The University has entered into capital lease agreements for certain computer equipment relating to the University's notebook computer program. The agreements expire at various dates through April 2016. Equipment under capital lease at July 31, 2014 and 2013, totaled $516,827 and $1,669,460, net of accumulated depreciation of $5,376,616 and $3,838,836, respectively.

Minimum future lease payments under capital leases as of July 31, 2014, are as follows:

Fiscal Year Ending July 31,	Amount
2015	$ 409,097
2016	59,881
	468,978
Less: Amount representing interest	(4,838)
Present value of net minimum lease payments	$ 464,140

Interest rates on capitalized leases range from 3.20% to 4.37% and are imputed based on the lessor's implicit rate of return.

G. TEMPORARILY AND PERMANENTLY RESTRICTED NET ASSETS

At July 31, 2014 and 2013, temporarily restricted net assets are available for the following purposes:

	2014	2013
Scholarships	$ -	$ 84,693
Contributions and other	3,701,005	4,768,311
	$3,701,005	$4,853,004

BETHEL UNIVERSITY
NOTES TO FINANCIAL STATEMENTS
JULY 31, 2014 AND 2013

G. TEMPORARILY AND PERMANENTLY RESTRICTED NET ASSETS - Continued

At July 31, 2014 and 2013, permanently restricted net assets are as follows:

	2014	2013
Beneficial interest in assets held by others	$ 3,692,558	$3,489,348
Student loan fund	3,965	3,965
Endowments	6,410,055	6,382,759
	$10,106,578	$9,876,072

The endowments represent nonexpendable funds that are subject to restrictions requiring the principal to be invested and only the income used as specified by the donors. The student loan fund consists of funds subject to donor restrictions related to loan requirements.

Net assets were released from donor restrictions by incurring expenses satisfying the restricted purposes. The following is a summary of the assets released from restrictions for the years ended July 31, 2014 and 2013:

	2014	2013
Institutional support expenditures	$1,958,645	$ 654,580
Scholarship and grant expenditures	23,218	55,466
Endowment expenditures	376,832	464,005
	$2,358,695	$1,174,051

BETHEL UNIVERSITY
NOTES TO FINANCIAL STATEMENTS
JULY 31, 2014 AND 2013

H. ENDOWMENT

The University's endowment consists of individual donor-restricted funds established for a variety of purposes. As required by U.S. generally accepted accounting principles, net assets associated with endowment funds are classified and reported based on the existence or absence of donor-imposed restrictions.

Interpretation of Relevant Law

The Board of Trustees of the University has interpreted the applicable state laws as requiring the preservation of the original gift as of the gift date of the donor-restricted endowment funds absent explicit donor stipulations to the contrary. As a result of this interpretation, the University classified as permanently restricted net assets (a) the original value of gifts donated to the permanent endowment, (b) the original value of subsequent gifts to the permanent endowment, and (c) accumulations to the permanent endowment made in accordance with the direction of the applicable donor gift instrument at the time the accumulation is added to the fund. The remaining portion of the donor-restricted endowment fund that is not classified in permanently restricted net assets is classified as temporarily restricted net assets until those amounts are appropriated for expenditure by the University in a manner consistent with the standard of prudence prescribed by applicable state laws. In accordance with applicable state laws, the University, considers the following factors in making a determination to appropriate or accumulate donor-restricted endowment funds:

- The duration and preservation of the fund
- The purposes of the University and the donor-restricted endowment fund
- General economic conditions
- The possible effect of inflation and deflation
- The expected total return from income and the appreciation of investments
- Other resources of the University
- The investment policies of the University

BETHEL UNIVERSITY
NOTES TO FINANCIAL STATEMENTS
JULY 31, 2014 AND 2013

H. ENDOWMENT - Continued

Changes in Endowment Net Assets

	Temporarily Restricted	Permanently Restricted	Total
Endowment net assets, August 1, 2012	$ 387,837	$ 9,560,460	$ 9,948,297
Investment return:			
Investment income	137,643	-	137,643
Net appreciation (realized and unrealized)	-	280,535	280,535
Total investment return	137,643	280,535	418,178
Contributions	23,218	35,077	58,295
Appropriation of endowment assets for expenditure (scholarships)	(464,005)	-	(464,005)
Endowment net assets, July 31, 2013	84,693	9,876,072	9,960,765
Investment return:			
Investment income	157,674	-	157,674
Net appreciation (realized and unrealized)	-	203,212	203,212
Total investment return	157,674	203,212	360,886
Contributions	-	27,294	27,294
Appropriation of endowment assets for expenditure (scholarships)	(242,367)	-	(242,367)
Endowment net assets, July 31, 2014	$ -	$10,106,578	$10,106,578

Return Objectives and Risk Parameters

The University has adopted investment and spending policies for endowment assets that attempt to provide a predictable stream of funding to programs supported by its endowment while seeking to maintain the purchasing power of the endowment assets. Endowment assets include those assets of donor-restricted funds that the University must hold in perpetuity or for a donor-specified period(s). Under this policy, as approved by the Board of Trustees, the endowment assets are invested with an overall total return objective as established for each time horizon: 1) Short Term, 2) Intermediate, and 3) Long Term according to the funding needs of the University. The returns will be compared with the generally accepted indices, i.e., the S&P 500, certain Bond Indices,

BETHEL UNIVERSITY
NOTES TO FINANCIAL STATEMENTS
JULY 31, 2014 AND 2013

H. ENDOWMENT - Continued

and MSCI EAFE stock indices, and an index of U.S. Treasury Bills depending on the time horizon in place. At July 31, 2014 and 2013, the endowment assets consist of investments in certificates of deposit, marketable debt and equity securities, beneficial interests in assets held by others.

Strategies Employed for Achieving Objectives

To satisfy its rate-of-return objectives, the University relies on a total return strategy in which investment returns are achieved through both capital appreciation (realized and unrealized) and current yield (interest and dividends). The University targets an investment allocation based on the three time horizons described above and that places emphasis on diversification of assets within prudent risk constraints.

Spending Policy and How the Investment Objectives Relate to Spending Policy

During fiscal year 2009, the University's Board of Trustees adopted a spending policy, which is based on the "Total Return" concept of determining the amount available for distribution. Total Return takes into consideration all of the elements of long-term investment return. The appropriate spending amount is based on the projected long-term Total Return of the funds, less an estimate of future inflation. The goal of the Total Return approach is to provide for a level of current income that protects the future purchasing power of the fund, thereby providing for increasing amounts of future income. The University anticipates that this percentage will be in the range of 3 to 5% of market value based on historical measurements of Total Return and Inflation. The market value of the fund will be noted each year on a specific date and a three-year rolling average market value will be established. The rolling three-year market value will be multiplied by the approved spending percentage which will be set annually.

BETHEL UNIVERSITY
NOTES TO FINANCIAL STATEMENTS
JULY 31, 2014 AND 2013

I. FAIR VALUES OF FINANCIAL INSTRUMENTS

Required disclosures concerning the estimated fair values of financial instruments are presented below. The estimated fair value amounts have been determined based on the University's assessment of available market information and appropriate valuation methodologies. The following table summarizes required fair value disclosures under ASC 825, *Financial Instruments*, and measurements at July 31, 2014 and 2013 for the assets and liabilities measured at fair value on a recurring basis under ASC 820, *Fair Value Measurements and Disclosures*:

	Carrying Amount	Estimated Fair Value	Measured at Fair Value	Fair Value Measurements Using		
				Level 1	Level 2	Level 3
July 31, 2014						
Assets:						
Investments:						
Cash and cash equivalents	$ 155,592	$ 155,592	$ 155,592	$155,592	$ -	$ -
Certificates of deposits	99,941	99,941	99,941	99,941	-	-
Bond funds	361,924	361,924	361,924	-	361,924	-
Equity funds:						
Mutual Funds	76,552	76,552	76,552	76,552	-	-
U.S. Equities	13,154	13,154	13,154	13,154	-	-
Total Equity Funds	89,706	89,706	89,706	89,706	-	-
Venture Capital	1,147,582	1,147,582	1,147,582	-	-	1,147,582
Other Limited Partnerships	1,378,662	1,378,662	1,378,662	-	-	1,378,662
Total Investments	$ 3,233,407	$ 3,233,407	$3,233,407	$345,239	$361,924	$2,526,244
Beneficial interests in trusts	3,692,558	3,692,558	3,692,558	-	3,692,558	-
Liabilities:						
Notes payable and long-term obligation	45,179,835	50,241,843	-	-	-	-

- 25 -

BETHEL UNIVERSITY
NOTES TO FINANCIAL STATEMENTS
JULY 31, 2014 AND 2013

I. FAIR VALUES OF FINANCIAL INSTRUMENTS - Continued

Required disclosures concerning the estimated fair values of financial instruments are presented below. The estimated fair value amounts have been determined based on the University's assessment of available market information and appropriate valuation methodologies. The following table summarizes required fair value disclosures under ASC 825, *Financial Instruments*, and measurements at July 31, 2014 and 2013 for the assets and liabilities measured at fair value on a recurring basis under ASC 820, *Fair Value Measurements and Disclosures*:

	Carrying Amount	Estimated Fair Value	Measured at Fair Value	Fair Value Measurements Using		
				Level 1	Level 2	Level 3
July 31, 2013						
Assets:						
Investments:						
Cash and cash equivalents	$ 71,054	$ 71,054	$ 71,054	$ 71,054	$ -	$ -
Certificates of deposits	428,567	428,567	428,567	428,507	-	-
Bond funds	514,345	514,345	514,345	-	514,345	-
Equity funds:						
Mutual Funds	67,237	67,237	67,237	67,287	-	-
U.S. Equities	12,985	12,985	12,985	12,985	-	-
Total Equity Funds	80,222	80,222	80,222	80,222	-	-
Venture Capital and Other Limited Partnerships	2,005,402	2,005,402	2,005,402	-	-	2,005,402
Other miscellaneous	296,129	296,129	296,129	296,129	-	-
Total Investments	$3,395,719	$3,395,719	$3,395,719	$863,904	$516,808	$2,015,007
Beneficial interests in trusts	3,489,347	3,489,347	3,489,347	-	3,489,347	-
Liabilities:						
Notes payable and long-term obligation	44,661,840	49,665,811	-	-	-	-

- 26 -

BETHEL UNIVERSITY
NOTES TO FINANCIAL STATEMENTS
JULY 31, 2014 AND 2013

I. FAIR VALUES OF FINANCIAL INSTRUMENTS - Continued

Changes in Level 3 assets are as follows:

	Fair Value Measurements Using Significant Unobservable Inputs (Level 3)	
	2014	2013
Beginning Balance	$2,015,007	$1,239,142
Purchases and sales, net	362,245	696,570
Unrealized gain	148,992	79,295
Ending Balance	$2,526,244	$2,015,007

The following methods and assumptions were used to estimate the fair value of each class of financial instruments:

Cash equivalents, receivables, accounts payable and accrued payroll and benefits, deferred revenue and advances from the Federal government for student loans

The carrying values of these items approximate their fair values due to the short maturities of these instruments.

Investments

Fair values are based on quoted market prices, where available, and Level 2 and 3 inputs. The carrying amounts and the fair values of the University's investments are presented in Note C.

Notes payable and obligations under capital leases

For fixed rate debt, fair value was estimated using discounted cash flow analyses based on the University's current incremental borrowing rates for similar types of borrowing arrangements.

J. FUND RAISING ACTIVITIES

The University conducts fund raising activities each year. The total cost of these activities for fiscal years 2014 and 2013, was $1,032,705 and $712,179, respectively.

BETHEL UNIVERSITY
NOTES TO FINANCIAL STATEMENTS
JULY 31, 2014 AND 2013

K. RETIREMENT PLAN

The University's full-time employees may participate in either a retirement plan which is administered by the Cumberland Presbyterian Board of Finance or the TIAA/CREF Plan, which is a national pension plan. Payments are made to the plans by withholding five percent of the employee's salary with the University in the past paying a matching amount. During 2014, the University ceased all matching contributions. Total matching contributions were made by the University for fiscal years 2014 and 2013, of $-0- and $242,434, respectively.

L. CONCENTRATION OF RISKS

Concentration of Risk

The University generates revenue predominantly from tuition and fees, investment income, gifts, auxiliary enterprises and contributions. In planning and budgeting during a fiscal year, significant reliance is placed on meeting tuition, gift, auxiliary, investment earnings and contribution goals in order for the University to sustain successful operations. In the event that enrollment or gifts and contributions significantly decrease in any one year, operations could be adversely affected.

Financial instruments that potentially subject the University to concentrations of credit risk and market risk consist principally of cash equivalents, investments, and student receivables.

The University, in connection with its activities, grants credit to students that involves, to varying degrees, elements of credit risk. The maximum accounting loss from credit risk is limited to the amounts that are recognized in the accompanying statements of financial position as student accounts receivable at July 31, 2014 and 2013.

The University also has two bank deposits in excess of those insured under regulatory insurance limits.

BETHEL UNIVERSITY
NOTES TO FINANCIAL STATEMENTS
JULY 31, 2014 AND 2013

M. OPERATING LEASES

The University leases office space for satellite campuses relating to its degree-completion program. These leases expire at various dates through fiscal year 2020. Minimum future rental payments under non-cancelable operating leases as of July 31, 2014 are as follows:

Fiscal Year Ending July 31,	Amount
2015	$ 2,644,818
2016	2,643,279
2017	2,262,655
2018	2,244,992
2019	2,117,835
Thereafter	49,147
	$11,962,726

Rent expense under the non-cancelable operating leases totaled $2,599,490 and $953,964 for the years ended July 31, 2014 and 2013, respectively.

On July 31, 2013, the University entered into a sale-leaseback agreement with a related party for a building in Paris, Tennessee. The purchasor entered into a note receivable with the University for $8,200,000, which approximated the carrying value of the building, and therefore, no gain or loss was recognized. The purchasor will be paying the note receivable over 30 years at an interest rate of 2%. The University will lease the building for six years with monthly payments of $120,275. The note receivable totaled $7,998,454 at July 31, 2014.

BETHEL UNIVERSITY
NOTES TO FINANCIAL STATEMENTS
JULY 31, 2014 AND 2013

N. FUNCTIONAL ALLOCATION OF EXPENSES

During the years ended July 31, 2014 and 2013, the University allocated the cost of certain professional fees and the operation and maintenance of physical plant, including depreciation expense of $4,949,999 and $6,010,614, respectively, over the cost of providing instruction, research, academic support, institutional support and auxiliary enterprises as follows:

	2014	2013
Instruction	$3,439,442	$3,979,934
Academic support	112,973	103,809
Student services	647,686	721,192
Institutional support	1,094,102	1,304,498
Auxiliary enterprises	532,428	833,579
Total operation and maintenance of physical plant	$5,826,631	$6,943,012

O. LITIGATION AND CONTINGENCIES

The University is a defendant in legal actions from time to time in the normal course of operations. It is not currently possible to state the ultimate liability, if any, in these matters. In the opinion of management, any resulting liability from these actions will not have a material adverse effect on the financial position of the activities of the University.

P. RELATED PARTY TRANSACTIONS

During fiscal years 2014 and 2013, the University had an agreement with a company owned by a member of the University's faculty. Under the agreement, the company developed and is maintaining the University's online masters of business administration program. Specifically, the company is responsible for developing course work, producing lectures and graphic presentations, and maintaining student records. Fees under the agreement are $300 per student, per course and the agreement has no contractual expiration. Total fees incurred during fiscal years 2014 and 2013 were $7,535,299 and $7,635,564, respectively.

During fiscal years 2013, the University contracted with a company owned by a member of the Board of Trustees. Under the contract, the company was responsible for the construction of certain University buildings. Total charges incurred and capitalized during the fiscal year 2013 was $1,106,656. There were no expenses incurred with the vendor during 2014.

BETHEL UNIVERSITY
NOTES TO FINANCIAL STATEMENTS
JULY 31, 2014 AND 2013

P. RELATED PARTY TRANSACTIONS - Continued

The University entered into a note payable and a line-of-credit with a private company owned by a member of the Board of Trustees. Total outstanding balances during fiscal year 2014 and 2013 were $20,266,000 and $18,666,000 respectively (See Note E).

The University entered into a leasing arrangement with a related party as described in Note M.

Q. SUBSEQUENT EVENTS

The University has evaluated subsequent events through October 15, 2014, the issuance date of the University's financial statements, and has determined that there are no subsequent event requires disclosure.

OTHER INFORMATION

BETHEL UNIVERSITY
SCHEDULE OF EXPENDITURES OF FEDERAL AWARDS
YEAR ENDED JULY 31, 2014

Federal Grantor/Pass-through Grantor/ Program or Cluster Title	Federal CFDA Number	Federal Expenditures
U.S. Department of Education - Direct Awards		
Student Financial Assistance - Cluster: (1)		
Federal Direct Student Loans Program (Note C)	84.268	$64,748,698
Federal Perkins Loan Program (Note B)	84.038	44,602
Federal Work-Study Program	84.033	139,664
Federal Supplemental Educational Opportunity Grants Program	84.007	262,380
Federal Pell Grant Program	84.063	15,405,822
Teacher Education Assistance for University and Higher Education Grant	84.379	45,597
Total Student Financial Assistance - Cluster		80,646,763
U.S. Department of Education - Pass-through Program from:		
Special Education: Grants to States Tennessee Teachers Assistants Grant	84.027A	78,353
Total Expenditures of Federal Awards		$80,725,116

(1) Tested as a major program

See independent auditor's report.

BETHEL UNIVERSITY
NOTES TO SCHEDULE OF EXPENDITURES OF FEDERAL AWARDS
YEAR ENDED JULY 31, 2014

A. BASIS OF PRESENTATION

The accompanying schedule of expenditures of federal awards is presented in accordance with the requirements of OMB Circular A-133, *Audits of States, Local Governments, and Non-Profit Organizations*, on the accrual basis of accounting consistent with the basis of accounting used by the University in the preparation of its financial statements.

B. FEDERAL PERKINS LOAN PROGRAM - CFDA #84.038

The outstanding loan balance for the Federal Perkins Loan Program at July 31, 2014 was $270,453, net of the allowance for uncollectible loans of $233,504. Total loan disbursements for the program for the year ended July 31, 2014, were $44,602. These disbursements include expenditures such as loans to students, repayments of fund capital, and administrative expenditures.

C. FEDERAL DIRECT LOANS PROGRAM - CFDA #84.268

During the fiscal year ending July 31, 2014, the University processed $64,748,698 of new loans under the Federal Direct Loans program (which includes subsidized and unsubsidized Stafford Loans, Parents' for Undergraduate Students, and Supplemental Loans for Students)

D. MATCHING FUNDS

The University provided matching funds of $87,460 for the Federal Supplemental Educational Opportunity Grants program and $46,555 for the Federal Work Study program during the fiscal year ended July 31, 2014.

CROSSLIN & ASSOCIATES
CERTIFIED PUBLIC ACCOUNTANTS

Independent Auditor's Report on Internal Control Over
Financial Reporting and on Compliance and Other Matters
Based on an Audit of Financial Statements Performed in
Accordance with *Government Auditing Standards*

The Board of Trustees
Bethel University
McKenzie, Tennessee

We have audited, in accordance with the auditing standards generally accepted in the United States of America and the standards applicable to financial audits contained in *Government Auditing Standards* issued by the Comptroller General of the United States, the financial statements of Bethel University (the "University"), which comprise the statements of financial position as of July 31, 2014, and the related statements of activities and cash flows for the year then ended, and the related notes to the financial statements, and have issued our report thereon dated October 15, 2014.

Internal Control Over Financial Reporting

In planning and performing our audit of the financial statements, we considered the University's internal control over financial reporting (internal control) to determine the audit procedures that are appropriate in the circumstances for the purpose of expressing our opinion on the financial statements, but not for the purpose of expressing an opinion on the effectiveness of the University's internal control. Accordingly, we do not express an opinion on the effectiveness of the University's internal control.

A *deficiency in internal control* exists when the design or operation of a control does not allow management or employees, in the normal course of performing their assigned functions, to prevent, or detect and correct misstatements on a timely basis. A *material weakness* is a deficiency, or a combination of deficiencies, in internal control such that there is a reasonable possibility that a material misstatement of the entity's financial statements will not be prevented, or detected and corrected on a timely basis. A *significant deficiency* is a deficiency, or a combination of deficiencies, in internal control that is less severe than a material weakness, yet important enough to merit attention by those charged with governance.

The Astoria • 3803 Bedford Avenue, Suite 103 • Nashville, Tennessee 37215 • phone: 615-320-5500 • fax: 615-329-9465 • www.crosslinpc.com
An Independent Member of The BDO Alliance USA

The Board of Trustees
Bethel University

Our consideration of the internal control was for the limited purpose described in the first paragraph of this section and was not designed to identify all deficiencies in internal control that might be material weaknesses or significant deficiencies. Given these limitations, during our audit we did not identify any deficiencies in internal control that we consider to be material weaknesses. However, material weaknesses may exist that have not been identified.

Compliance and Other Matters

As part of obtaining reasonable assurance about whether the University's financial statements are free from material misstatement, we performed tests of its compliance with certain provisions of laws, regulations, contracts, and grant agreements, noncompliance with which could have a direct and material effect on the determination of financial statement amounts. However, providing an opinion on compliance with those provisions was not an objective of our audit, and accordingly, we do not express such an opinion. The results of our tests disclosed no instances of noncompliance or other matters that are required to be reported under *Government Auditing Standards*.

Purpose of this Report

The purpose of this report is solely to describe the scope of our testing of internal control and compliance and the results of that testing, and not to provide an opinion on the effectiveness of the University's internal control or on compliance. This report is an integral part of an audit performed in accordance with *Government Auditing Standards* in considering the University's internal control and compliance. Accordingly, this communication is not suitable for any other purpose.

Crosslin & Associates, P.C.

Nashville, Tennessee
October 15, 2014

Independent Auditor's Report on Compliance For The Major
Program and on Internal Control Over Compliance
Required by OMB Circular A-133

The Board of Trustees
Bethel University
McKenzie, Tennessee

Report on Compliance for Each Major Federal Program

We have audited Bethel University's (the "University") compliance with the types of compliance requirements described in the *OMB Circular A-133 Compliance Supplement* that could have a direct and material effect on the University's major federal program for the year ended July 31, 2014. The University's major federal program is identified in the summary of auditor's results section of the accompanying schedule of findings and questioned costs.

Management's Responsibility

Management is responsible for compliance with the requirements of laws, regulations, contracts, and grants applicable to its federal programs.

Auditor's Responsibility

Our responsibility is to express an opinion on compliance for each of the University's major federal programs based on our audit of the types of compliance requirements referred to above. We conducted our audit of compliance in accordance with auditing standards generally accepted in the United States of America; the standards applicable to financial audits contained in *Government Auditing Standards*, issued by the Comptroller General of the United States; and OMB Circular A-133, *Audits of States, Local Governments, and Non-Profit Organizations*. Those standards and OMB Circular A-133 require that we plan and perform the audit to obtain reasonable assurance about whether noncompliance with the types of compliance requirements referred to above that could have a direct and material effect on a major federal program occurred. An audit includes examining, on a test basis, evidence about the University's compliance with those requirements and performing such other procedures as we considered necessary in the circumstances.

We believe that our audit provides a reasonable basis for our opinion on compliance for each major federal program. However, our audit does not provide a legal determination of the University's compliance.

The Board of Trustees
Bethel University

Opinion on Each Major Federal Program

In our opinion, the University complied, in all material respects, with the types of compliance requirements referred to above that could have a direct and material effect on its major federal program for the year ended July 31, 2014.

Other Matters

The results of our auditing procedures disclosed an instance of noncompliance, which is required to be reported in accordance with OMB Circular A-133 and which is described in the accompanying schedule of findings and questioned costs as item CF 14-1. Our opinion on the major federal program is not modified with respect to these matters.

The University's response to the noncompliance findings identified in our audit is described in the accompanying schedule of findings and questioned costs. The University's response was not subjected to the auditing procedures applied in the audit of compliance and, accordingly, we express no opinion on the response.

Report on Internal Control Over Compliance

Management of the University is responsible for establishing and maintaining effective internal control over compliance with the types of compliance requirements referred to above. In planning and performing our audit of compliance, we considered the University's internal control over compliance with the types of requirements that could have a direct and material effect on each major federal program to determine the auditing procedures that are appropriate in the circumstances for the purpose of expressing an opinion on compliance for each major federal program and to test and report on internal control over compliance in accordance with OMB Circular A-133, but not for the purpose of expressing an opinion on the effectiveness of internal control over compliance.

Accordingly, we do not express an opinion on the effectiveness of the University's internal control over compliance.

Our consideration of internal control over compliance was for the limited purpose described in the preceding paragraph and was not designed to identify all deficiencies in internal control over compliance that might be material weaknesses or significant deficiencies and therefore, material weaknesses or significant deficiencies may exist that were not identified. However, as discussed below, we identified certain deficiencies in internal control over compliance that we consider to be a significant deficiency.

The Board of Trustees
Bethel University

A deficiency in internal control over compliance exists when the design or operation of a control over compliance does not allow management or employees, in the normal course of performing their assigned functions, to prevent, or detect and correct, noncompliance with a type of compliance requirement of a federal program on a timely basis. A material weakness in internal control over compliance is a deficiency, or combination of deficiencies, in internal control over compliance, such that there is a reasonable possibility that material noncompliance with a type of compliance requirement of a federal program will not be prevented, or detected and corrected, on a timely basis. We noted no deficiencies in internal control over compliance that we consider to be material weaknesses. However, material weaknesses may exist that have not been identified.

A significant deficiency in internal control over compliance is a deficiency, or a combination of deficiencies, in internal control over compliance with a type of compliance requirement of a federal program that is less severe than a material weakness in internal control over compliance, yet important enough to merit attention by those charged with governance. We consider the deficiency in internal control over compliance described in the accompanying schedule of findings and questioned costs as item CF 14-1 to be a significant deficiency.

The University's response to the internal control over compliance findings identified in our audit is described in the accompanying schedule of findings and questioned costs. The University's response was not subjected to the auditing procedures applied in the audit of compliance and, accordingly, we express no opinion on the response.

The purpose of this report on internal control over compliance is solely to describe the scope of our testing of internal control over compliance and the results of that testing based on the requirements of OMB Circular A-133. Accordingly, this report is not suitable for any other purpose.

Crosslin + Associates, P.C.

Nashville, Tennessee
October 15, 2012

BETHEL UNIVERSITY
SCHEDULE OF FINDINGS AND QUESTIONED COSTS
YEAR ENDED JULY 31, 2014

I. SUMMARY OF INDEPENDENT AUDITOR'S RESULTS

   Financial Statements

   Type of auditor's report issued: Unmodified

   Internal control over financial reporting:

   - Material weakness(es) identified?   ___Yes _X_ No
   - Significant deficiency(ies) identified?   ___Yes _X_ None Reported

   Noncompliance material to financial statements
   noted?   ___Yes _X_ No

   Federal Awards

   Internal control over major program:

   - Material weakness(es) identified?   ___Yes _X_ No
   - Significant deficiency(ies) identified?   _X_ Yes ___ No

   Type of auditor's report issued on compliance for
   major program: Unmodified

   Any audit findings disclosed that are required
   to be reported in accordance with
   section 510(a) of Circular A-133?   _X_ Yes ___ No

- 39 -

BETHEL UNIVERSITY
SCHEDULE OF FINDINGS AND QUESTIONED COSTS
YEAR ENDED JULY 31, 2014

I. SUMMARY OF INDEPENDENT AUDITOR'S RESULTS - Continued

Major Program:

CFDA Number	Name of Federal Program	Amount Expended
SFA Cluster:		
84.063	Federal Pell Grant Program	$15,405,822
84.268	Federal Direct Student Loans Program (new loans processed)	64,748,698
84.038	Federal Perkins Loan Program	44,602
84.007	Federal Supplemental Educational Opportunity Grants Program	262,380
84.033	Federal Work Study Program	139,664
84.038	Perkins Loans ($503,957 outstanding balance of loans)	-
84.379	TEACHER Education Assistance for College and Higher Education Grant	45,597

Dollar threshold used to distinguish between type A
and type B programs $300,000

Auditee qualified as low-risk auditee   __Yes X No

II. FINANCIAL STATEMENT FINDINGS

None reported.

BETHEL UNIVERSITY
SCHEDULE OF FINDINGS AND QUESTIONED COSTS
YEAR ENDED JULY 31, 2014

III. FINDINGS AND QUESTIONED COSTS FOR FEDERAL AWARDS

ITEM #LF 14-1

STUDENT DEPOSITS/CASH MANAGEMENT

Criteria, Condition, Context, Cause and Effect

The balance of student account deposits that related to excess financial aid (those amounts exceeding tuition), exceeded the total balance of student financial aid cash on hand. These funds were being temporarily used for operational purposes. Per the 2013-2014 Federal Student Aid Handbook, as the trustee of these funds, use of these funds outside of the intended purpose is not allowed.

Recommendation and Benefits

While these funds, which represent credit balances on the student accounts, were being properly issued to the student within the 14 day period as required by the Department of Education, the funds are not allowed to be used for any other purpose. Prudent policy would be to maintain these funds in a separate account until these credit refunds are issued to the students. This will allow the University to better monitor its operational cash position and ensure compliance with DOE regulations related to student financial aid.

Management's Response

Although funds were not in a separate account, funds were available to make all student refunds in the required time frame. Bethel University is changing its practice and will leave the funds in a separate account until a student's funds are issued within the 14 day period. This change, in Bethel's handling of student accounts, will be effective October 15, 2014.

BETHEL UNIVERSITY
SCHEDULE OF FINDINGS AND QUESTIONED COSTS
YEAR ENDED JULY 31, 2014

The University had no prior audit findings related to the testing of its federal award programs.

**CUMBERLAND PRESBYTERIAN
CHILDREN'S HOME**

FINANCIAL STATEMENTS
AND
AUDITORS' REPORT

DECEMBER 31, 2014

CUMBERLAND PRESBYTERIAN CHILDREN'S HOME

TABLE OF CONTENTS

	Page
Independent Auditors' Report	1
Statement of Financial Position	3
Statement of Activities	4
Statement of Cash Flows	5
Statement of Functional Expenses	6-7
Notes to the Financial Statements	8-14
Supplemental Information	
Schedule of Board of Stewardship Endowments	16-17

Members:
AMERICAN INSTITUTE OF
CERTIFIED PUBLIC
ACCOUNTANTS
TEXAS SOCIETY OF CERTIFIED
PUBLIC ACCOUNTANTS

HANKINS, EASTUP, DEATON, TONN & SEAY
A PROFESSIONAL CORPORATION
CERTIFIED PUBLIC ACCOUNTANTS

902 NORTH LOCUST
P.O. BOX 977
DENTON, TX 76202-0977
TEL. (940) 387-8563
FAX (940) 383-4746

Independent Auditors' Report

Cumberland Presbyterian Children's Home
Denton, Texas

We have audited the accompanying financial statements of Cumberland Presbyterian Children's Home (a nonprofit organization), which comprise the statement of financial position as of December 31, 2014 and the related statements of activities and cash flows for the year then ended, and the related notes to the financial statements.

Management's Responsibility for the Financial Statements

Management is responsible for the preparation and fair presentation of these financial statements in accordance with accounting principles generally accepted in the United States of America; this includes the design, implementation, and maintenance of internal control relevant to the preparation and fair presentation of financial statements that are free from material misstatement, whether due to fraud or error.

Auditor's Responsibility

Our responsibility is to express an opinion on these financial statements based on our audit. We conducted our audit in accordance with auditing standards generally accepted in the United States of America. Those standards require that we plan and perform the audit to obtain reasonable assurance about whether the financial statements are free of material misstatement.

An audit involves performing procedures to obtain audit evidence about the amounts and disclosures in the financial statements. The procedures selected depend on the auditor's judgment, including the assessment of the risks of material misstatement of the financial statements, whether due to fraud or error. In making those risk assessments, the auditor considers internal control relevant to the entity's preparation and fair presentation of the financial statements in order to design audit procedures that are appropriate in the circumstances, but not for the purpose of expressing an opinion on the effectiveness of the entity's internal control. Accordingly, we express no such opinion. An audit also includes evaluating the appropriateness of accounting policies used and the reasonableness of significant accounting estimates made by management, as well as evaluating the overall presentation of the financial statements. We believe that the audit evidence we have obtained is sufficient and appropriate to provide a basis for our audit opinion.

Opinion

In our opinion, the financial statements referred to above present fairly, in all material respects, the financial position of Cumberland Presbyterian Children's Home as of December 31, 2014, and the changes in its net assets and its cash flows for the year then ended in accordance with accounting principles generally accepted in the United States of America.

Hankins, Eastup, Deaton, Tonn & Seay

Hankins, Eastup, Deaton, Tonn & Seay
Denton, Texas
June 18, 2015

Page left blank intentionally

CUMBERLAND PRESBYTERIAN CHILDREN'S HOME

STATEMENT OF FINANCIAL POSITION
DECEMBER 31, 2014

ASSETS:

Cash and cash equivalents	$ 294,294
Due from Board of Stewardship	79,286
Other receivables	53,866
Prepaid expenses	13,746
Land, buildings and equipment, net	4,032,047
Other long-term investments	10,552,992
TOTAL ASSETS	**$15,026,231**

LIABILITIES AND NET ASSETS:

Liabilities:	
Accounts payable and accrued liabilities	$ 110,598
Total Liabilities	110,598
Net Assets:	
Unrestricted	7,392,485
Temporarily restricted	63,081
Permanently restricted	7,460,067
Total Net Assets	14,915,633
TOTAL LIABILITIES AND NET ASSETS	**$15,026,231**

See Accompanying Notes to the Financial Statements.

CUMBERLAND PRESBYTERIAN CHILDREN'S HOME

STATEMENT OF ACTIVITIES
FOR THE YEAR ENDED DECEMBER 31, 2014

	Unrestricted	Temporarily Restricted	Permanently Restricted	Total
Revenues, Gains and Other Support:				
Contributions and grants	$ 748,353	$ 10,000	$ 45,944	$ 804,297
CPS revenue	498,609	-	-	498,609
Other program fees	118,779	-	-	118,779
Denominational support	65,766	-	-	65,766
Income on long-term investments	393,675	283	188	394,146
Oil and gas royalties	17,804	-	-	17,804
Realized gains on investments	3,545	-	73,873	77,418
Unrealized gains on investments	2,628	738	-	3,366
Special events	29,712	-	-	29,712
Rents	34,232	-	-	34,232
Gain on sale of fixed assets	20,590	-	-	20,590
Other	1,276	-	-	1,276
Subtotal	1,934,969	11,021	120,005	2,065,995
Net assets released from Restrictions	4,000	(4,000)	-	-
Total Revenue, Gains and Other Support	1,938,969	7,021	120,005	2,065,995
Expenses and Losses:				
Expenses:				
Program services:				
Children's residential program	1,198,138	-	-	1,198,138
Emergency shelter program	851,500	-	-	851,500
Single parent family program	210,641	-	-	210,641
Cumberland family services	235,064	-	-	235,064
Management and general	177,329	-	-	177,329
Fundraising	170,741	-	-	170,741
Total Expenses	2,843,413	-	-	2,843,413
Losses:				
Unrealized losses on investments	-	-	36,991	36,991
Total Expenses and Losses	2,843,413	-	36,991	2,880,404
Change in net assets	(904,444)	7,021	83,014	(814,409)
Net assets at beginning of year	8,327,458	56,060	7,377,053	15,760,571
Prior period adjustment	(30,529)	-	-	(30,529)
Net assets at end of year	$ 7,392,485	$ 63,081	$ 7,460,067	$14,915,633

See Accompanying Notes to the Financial Statements.

CUMBERLAND PRESBYTERIAN CHILDREN'S HOME

STATEMENT OF CASH FLOWS
FOR THE YEAR ENDED DECEMBER 31, 2014

Cash Flows from Operating Activities:	
Change in net assets	$ (814,409)
Adjustments to reconcile change in net assets to net cash provided by operating activities:	
Depreciation	213,357
(Increase) Decrease in receivables	(912)
(Increase) Decrease in prepaid expenses	6,766
Increase (Decrease) in accounts payable/accrued liabilities	62,597
Realized gains on investments	(77,418)
Unrealized gains on investments	(3,366)
Unrealized losses on investments	36,991
Contributions restricted for long-term investment	(45,944)
Net Cash Provided (Used) by Operating Activities	(622,338)
Cash Flows from Investing Activities:	
Purchase of fixed assets	123,175
Purchase of investments (net)	(1,724,404)
Net gains (losses) on investments	43,793
Net Cash Provided (Used) by Investing Activities	(1,557,436)
Cash Flows from Financing Activities:	
Proceeds from contributions restricted for investment in endowment	45,944
Net Cash Provided by Financing Activities	45,944
Net Increase (Decrease) in Cash and Cash Equivalents	(2,133,830)
Cash and Cash Equivalents at Beginning of Year	2,428,124
Cash and Cash Equivalents at End of Year	$ 294,294
Supplemental Data:	
Interest paid during the year	$ 1,825
Noncash investing activities:	
Unrealized gains on investments	3,366

See Accompanying Notes to the Financial Statements.

CUMBERLAND PRESBYTERIAN CHILDREN'S HOME

STATEMENT OF FUNCTIONAL EXPENSES
FOR THE YEAR ENDED DECEMBER 31, 2014

	Program Services			
	Children's Residential Program	Emergency Shelter Program	Single Parent Family Program	Cumberland Family Services
Salaries and Wages	$ 613,612	$ 463,951	$ 119,729	$ 134,695
Employee Benefits	91,536	69,210	17,861	20,093
Payroll Taxes	48,729	36,844	9,508	10,697
Total Salaries and Related Expenses	753,877	570,005	147,098	165,485
Activities and travel	60,076	26,589	1,603	1,241
Clothing and supplies	47,531	24,425	2,523	7,116
Food and dining out	68,707	32,951	899	264
Training and education	7,873	1,962	-	2,874
Medical and dental	4,271	2,156	8,606	-
Other program expenses	-	-	-	1,932
Utilities	58,387	44,146	11,393	12,817
Property, liability insurance	26,677	20,170	5,205	5,856
Repairs and maintenance	37,507	28,359	7,318	8,233
Supplies, postage, printing	11,337	8,572	2,212	2,489
Computer software, maintenance	8,391	6,345	1,637	1,842
Small furniture and equipment	2,818	2,131	550	619
Permits and fees	1,178	890	230	258
Special events expense	-	-	-	-
Vehicle expenses	8,633	6,527	1,684	1,895
General assembly	-	-	-	-
Professional fees	13,399	10,131	2,614	2,941
Public relations/communications	-	-	-	-
Investment management fees	-	-	-	-
Board expense	-	-	-	-
Interest	-	-	-	-
Total Expenses Before Depreciation	1,110,662	785,359	193,572	215,862
Depreciation	87,476	66,141	17,069	19,202
TOTAL EXPENSES	$ 1,198,138	$ 851,500	$ 210,641	$ 235,064

The accompanying notes are an integral part of this statement

	Supporting Services			Total
Total	Fundraising	Administration	Total	Expenses
$ 1,331,987	$ 74,831	$ 89,797	$ 164,628	$ 1,496,615
198,700	11,163	13,396	24,559	223,259
105,778	5,943	7,130	13,073	118,851
1,636,465	91,937	110,323	202,260	1,838,725
89,509	2,755	-	2,755	92,264
81,595	-	-	-	81,595
102,821	-	1,000	1,000	103,821
12,709	-	5,226	5,226	17,935
15,033	-	-	-	15,033
1,932	-	-	-	1,932
126,743	7,120	8,545	15,665	142,408
57,908	3,254	3,904	7,158	65,066
81,417	4,574	5,489	10,063	91,480
24,610	6,991	1,661	8,652	33,262
18,215	1,023	1,229	2,252	20,467
6,118	344	411	755	6,873
2,556	144	172	316	2,872
-	8,002	-	8,002	8,002
18,739	1,053	1,263	2,316	21,055
-	-	8,516	8,516	8,516
29,085	1,634	1,961	3,595	32,680
-	31,242	-	31,242	31,242
-	-	3,429	3,429	3,429
-	-	9,574	9,574	9,574
-	-	1,825	1,825	1,825
2,305,455	160,073	164,528	324,601	2,630,056
189,888	10,668	12,801	23,469	213,357
$ 2,495,343	$ 170,741	$ 177,329	$ 348,070	$ 2,843,413

CUMBERLAND PRESBYTERIAN CHILDREN'S HOME

NOTES TO FINANCIAL STATEMENTS
DECEMBER 31, 2014

NOTE A - SUMMARY OF SIGNIFICANT ACCOUNTING POLICIES

Organization

Cumberland Presbyterian Children's Home (CPCH) is a nonprofit organization originally chartered in Kentucky in 1904 and moved to Denton, Texas in 1932. Its purpose is to provide long-term residential basic child care for children between the ages of 3 and 17. CPCH is licensed to care for up to 40 children. CPCH's primary sources of revenue are income from child care, donations and income from long-term investments.

Basis of Presentation

The accompanying financial statements have been prepared on the accrual basis of accounting in accordance with accounting principles generally accepted in the United States of America. Net assets and revenues, expenses, gains, and losses are classified based on the existence or absence of donor-imposed restrictions. Accordingly, net assets of CPCH and changes therein are classified and reported as follows:

> Unrestricted Net Assets – not subject to donor-imposed restrictions. Unrestricted net assets may be designated for specific purposes by action of the Board of Directors.
>
> Temporarily Restricted Net Assets – subject to donor-imposed stipulations that may be fulfilled by actions of CPCH to meet the stipulations or that become unrestricted at the date specified by the donor.
>
> Permanently Restricted Net Assets – subject to donor-imposed stipulations that they be retained and invested permanently by CPCH to use all or part of the investment return on these net assets for specified or unspecified purposes.

Income Taxes

CPCH is exempt from Federal income taxes under Section 501(c)(3) of the Internal Revenue Code. In addition, CPCH has been determined by the Internal Revenue Service not to be a private foundation within the meaning of Section 509(a)(1) and 170 (b)(1)(A)(vi) of the Code.

Fixed Assets

All acquisitions of property and equipment in excess of $5,000 and all expenditures for repairs, maintenance, or improvements that significantly prolong the useful lives of the assets are capitalized. Prior to 1/1/13 CPCH used an acquisition cost threshold of $1,000 but increased the threshold to $5,000 at that date in order to reduce the administrative costs of recording and tracking items of furniture and equipment. Purchases of property and equipment are recorded at cost. Donations of property and equipment are recorded as support at their estimated fair value at the date of gift. Such donations are reported as unrestricted support unless the donor has restricted the donated asset to a specific purpose. Assets donated with explicit restrictions regarding their use and contributions of cash that must be used to acquire property and equipment are reported as restricted support. Absent donor stipulations regarding how long those donated assets must be maintained, CPCH reports expirations of donor restrictions when the donated or acquired assets are placed in service as instructed by the donor. CPCH reclassifies temporarily restricted net assets to unrestricted net assets at that time. Property and equipment are depreciated using the straight-line method over the estimated useful life of assets.

CUMBERLAND PRESBYTERIAN CHILDREN'S HOME

NOTES TO FINANCIAL STATEMENTS
DECEMBER 31, 2014

The class lives of the more significant items within each property classification are as follows:

Vehicles	5 years
Equipment	5 to 10 years
Furniture and fixtures	5 to 10 years
Buildings	20 to 40 years

Investment Securities

Investments in marketable securities with readily determinable fair values and all investments in debt securities are valued at their fair values in the statement of financial position. Unrealized gains and losses are included in the change in net assets.

Estimates

The preparation of financial statements in conformity with generally accepted accounting principles requires management to make estimates and assumptions that affect the reported amounts of assets and liabilities at the date of the financial statements and the reported amounts of revenues and expenses during the reporting period. Accordingly, actual results could differ from those estimates.

FASB 116 and 117

In accordance with Statement of Financial Accounting Standards ("SFAS") No. 116, *Accounting for Contributions Received and Contributions Made*, contributions received are recorded as unrestricted, temporarily restricted, or permanently restricted support depending on the existence and/or nature of donor restrictions. CPCH reports gifts of cash and other assets as restricted support if they are received with donor stipulations that limit the use of the donated assets. When a donor restriction expires, that is, when a stipulated time restriction ends or purpose restriction is accomplished, temporarily restricted net assets are reclassified to unrestricted net assets and reported in the statement of activities as net assets released from restrictions. Contributions that are restricted by the donor are reported as increases in unrestricted net assets if the restrictions expire in the fiscal year in which the contributions are recognized.

Unconditional promises to give are recorded as revenue when received. Unconditional promises to give that are due within one year are recorded at the face amount of the commitment. Unconditional promises to give that are due beyond one year are not reflected at the face amount of the commitment, but when material are discounted to a present value, or net realizable value, using a 3% discount rate. Unconditional promises to give that are determined to be uncollectible are written off as an expense at that time. At December 31, 2014, CPCH had no outstanding unconditional promises to give.

CPCH reports gifts of land, buildings, and equipment as unrestricted support unless explicit donor stipulations specify how the donated assets must be used. Gifts of long-lived assets with explicit restrictions that specify how the assets are to be used and gifts of cash or other assets that must be used to acquire long-lived assets are reported as restricted support. Absent explicit donor stipulations about how long those long-lived assets must be maintained, CPCH reports expirations of donor restrictions when the donated or acquired long-lived assets are placed in service.

CUMBERLAND PRESBYTERIAN CHILDREN'S HOME

NOTES TO FINANCIAL STATEMENTS
DECEMBER 31, 2014

Contributed Services and Materials

In addition to receiving cash contributions, CPCH occasionally receives in-kind contributions from various donors. It is the policy of CPCH to record the estimated fair market value of certain in-kind donations as an asset or expense in its financial statements, and similarly increase donations by a like amount.

A substantial number of volunteers have donated significant amounts of time to CPCH's programs and supporting services. Contributions of donated services that create or enhance non-financial assets or that require specialized skills, are provided by individuals possessing these skills, and would typically need to be purchased if not provided by donation, are recorded at their fair values in the period received. For the year ended December 31, 2014, there were no amounts recorded for contributed services and materials.

Cash and Cash Equivalents

For purposes of the statement of cash flows, CPCH considers all highly liquid investments with a maturity of three months or less to be cash equivalents.

NOTE B – INVESTMENTS

Investments in equity securities with readily determinable fair values and all investments in debt securities are measured at fair value. All non cash contributions are recorded at fair value at the date of receipt. Stock is recorded at the average of the high and low selling price on the date received. Investments sold are recorded at amount received on the trade date.

Investment income and realized gains and losses are reported as increases in unrestricted net assets unless the donor placed restrictions on the income's use. The change in fair value between years along with realized gains or losses are reflected in the statement of activities in the year of the change.

Some investments are held and managed by the Board of Stewardship, Finance and Benefits of the Cumberland Presbyterian Church, while other investments are held in an investment brokerage account in the name of CPCH, and are managed by investment managers of the brokerage firm. No single investment exceeds five percent of CPCH's net assets.

NOTE C – ENDOWMENTS

CPCH's endowments consist of 87 individual donor-restricted funds established by individual donors for a variety of purposes. Net assets associated with endowments are classified and reported based on the existence or absence of donor-imposed restrictions.

A reconciliation of the beginning and ending balances of endowment funds is as follows:

	Permanently Restricted
Balance, 12/31/13	$6,853,756
Contributions	45,944
Investment gains	73,873
Balance, 12/31/14	$6,973,573

CUMBERLAND PRESBYTERIAN CHILDREN'S HOME

NOTES TO FINANCIAL STATEMENTS
DECEMBER 31, 2014

Funds with Deficiencies

From time to time, the fair value of assets associated with individual donor restricted endowment funds may fall below the level that the donor requires CPCH to retain as a fund of perpetual duration. CPCH did not have any net deficiencies of this nature as of December 31, 2014.

Return Objectives and Risk Parameters

CPCH has adopted investment and spending policies for endowment assets that attempt to provide a predictable stream of funding to programs supported by its endowment while seeking to maintain the purchasing power of the endowment assets. Under this policy, as approved by the board of trustees, the endowment assets are invested in equity securities, fixed-income securities and short-term reserves with asset allocation within defined acceptable ranges, while assuming a moderate level of investment risk. CPCH expects its endowment funds, over time, to provide an average rate of return sufficient to provide operating funds as needed. Actual returns in any given year may vary from this amount.

Strategies Employed for Achieving Objectives

To satisfy its long-term rate-of-return objectives, CPCH relies on a total return strategy in which investment returns are achieved through both capital appreciation (realized and unrealized) and current yield (interest and dividends). CPCH targets a diversified asset allocation that places a greater emphasis on equity-based investments to achieve its long-term return objectives within prudent risk constraints.

Spending Policy and How the Investment Objectives Relate to Spending Policy

CPCH has no written spending policy that commits it to annual distributions from any of the endowment's fund balances. CPCH normally appropriates for distribution each year sufficient earnings needed to fund its operating budget. Accordingly, over the long term, CPCH expects the current spending policy to allow its endowment to continue to grow. This is consistent with CPCH's objective to maintain the purchasing power of the endowment assets held in perpetuity or for a specified term as well as to provide additional real growth through new gifts and investment return.

NOTE D – FAIR VALUE OF FINANCIAL INSTRUMENTS

CPCH's financial instruments, none of which are held for trading purposes, include cash, securities and receivables. CPCH has estimated fair value of financial instruments in accordance with requirements of SFAS No. 157. The estimated fair value amounts have been determined by CPCH, using available market information and appropriate valuation methodologies. However, considerable judgment is necessarily required in interpreting market data to develop the estimates of fair value. Accordingly, the estimates presented herein are not necessarily indicative of the amounts that CPCH could realize in a current market exchange. The use of different market assumptions and estimation methodologies may have a material effect on the estimated fair value amounts. The carrying amount of cash and cash equivalents, and receivables approximated fair market value at December 31, 2014 because of their relatively short maturity and market terms. The fair value of long term investments at December 31, 2014 is determined based on quoted market values for U.S. government securities, fixed income securities and equity securities.

CUMBERLAND PRESBYTERIAN CHILDREN'S HOME

NOTES TO FINANCIAL STATEMENTS
DECEMBER 31, 2014

NOTE D – FAIR VALUE OF FINANCIAL INSTRUMENTS (CONT'D)

Financial instruments are considered Level 1 when their values are determined using quoted prices in active markets for identical assets that the reporting entity has the ability to access at the measurement date. Level 2 inputs are inputs other than quoted prices included within Level 1, such as quoted prices for similar assets in active or inactive markets, inputs other than quoted prices that are observable for the asset, or inputs that are derived principally from or corroborated by observable market data by correlation or other means.

Financial instruments are considered Level 3 when their values are determined using pricing models, discounted cash flow methodologies or similar techniques and at least one significant model assumption or input is unobservable. Level 3 financial instruments also include those for which the determination of fair value requires significant management judgment or estimation.

In accordance with these definitions, the following table represents CPCH's fair value hierarchy for its investments measured at fair value as of December 31, 2014:

	Quoted Prices for Active Markets for Identical Assets (Level 1)	Significant Other Observable Inputs (Level 2)	Total
U.S. Government securities	$ 344,198	$ -	$ 344,198
Equity securities	9,051,001	-	9,051,001
Fixed income securities	-	1,157,793	1,157,793
Total	$9,395,199	$1,157,793	$10,552,992

The estimated fair value of investments was determined by CPCH in accordance with its investment policy. Estimated fair value is determined by CPCH based on a number of factors, including: comparable publicly traded securities, the costs of investments to CPCH, as well as the current and projected operating performance. Changes in unrealized appreciation or depreciation of the investments are recognized as unrealized gains and losses in the statement of activities. Because of the inherent uncertainty of these valuations, the estimated values may differ from the actual fair values that may or may not be ultimately realized.

NOTE E - LAND, BUILDINGS AND EQUIPMENT

Land, buildings and equipment at December 31, 2014 consist of the following:

	Cost	Accumulated Depreciation	Book Value
Land	$ 23,477		$ 23,477
Buildings	5,774,167	$2,282,922	3,491,245
Campus infrastructure	583,513	207,667	375,846
Furniture & equipment	346,640	291,386	55,254
Vehicles	171,761	85,536	86,225
Total	$6,899,558	$2,867,511	$4,032,047

CUMBERLAND PRESBYTERIAN CHILDREN'S HOME

NOTES TO FINANCIAL STATEMENTS
DECEMBER 31, 2014

NOTE F - TEMPORARILY RESTRICTED NET ASSETS

Temporarily restricted net assets are available for the following purposes or periods:

Lena Hart Educational Fund	$ 3,573
Humphrey Scholarship Endowment	768
Walker Trimble Scholarship Fund	1,465
David Long Memorial Fund	207
Sybil V. Cockerham College Fund	1,059
Eleanor Sargeant Endowment	380
Medical clinic	36,000
For periods after December 31, 2014 - term endowment to be received in a future year – Naomi Locke Trust	19,629
Total	$ 63,081

NOTE G - PERMANENTLY RESTRICTED NET ASSETS

Permanently restricted net assets are restricted as follows:

Investments in perpetuity, the income from which is expendable to support any activities of CPCH	$7,460,067
Total	$7,460,067

NOTE H - OTHER LONG-TERM INVESTMENTS

	Total	Unrestricted	Temporarily Restricted	Permanently Restricted
Endowments held by the Board of Stewardship	$ 6,916,804	$ -	$ -	$6,916,804
Mutual funds held by Regions Bank – Laura Harpole Trust	110,851	-	-	110,851
Mutual funds held by Fairfield Natl. Bank - Naomi Locke Trust	19,629	-	19,629	-
Funds held at J P Morgan:				
Lena Hart Educational Fund	6,073	-	3,573	2,500
Humphrey Scholarship Endowment	4,249	-	768	3,481
Walker Trimble Scholarship Fund	9,745	-	1,465	8,280
David Long Memorial Fund	1,207	-	207	1,000
Sibyl V. Cockerham College Fund	3,059	-	1,059	2,000
Eleanor Sargeant Endowment	2,960	-	380	2,580
Operating Reserve	3,108,615	3,072,615	36,000	-
4,000 shares Exxon-Mobil held by CPCH - Jessie DiCarlo Endowment	369,800	-	-	369,800
Total	$10,552,992	$3,072,615	$ 63,081	$7,417,296

CUMBERLAND PRESBYTERIAN CHILDREN'S HOME

NOTES TO FINANCIAL STATEMENTS
DECEMBER 31, 2014

NOTE I – SUBSEQUENT EVENTS

Management evaluates subsequent events through the date of the report, which is the date the financial statements were available to be issued.

NOTE J – COMPONENTS OF INVESTMENT RETURN

Investment return for the year ended December 31, 2014, including interest and dividends on investments and interest earned on cash balances is summarized as follows:

Unrestricted investment return:	
Interest and dividend income:	
Board of Stewardship investments	$ 310,951
JP Morgan investments	47,124
Exxon Mobil stock investment	10,800
Fidelity investments	20,415
Other	4,385
Unrealized gains on investments	2,628
Realized gains on investments	3,545
Total unrestricted investment return	399,848
Restricted investment return:	
Interest income	471
Unrealized gains on investments	738
Unrealized losses on investments	(36,991)
Realized gains on investments	73,873
Total restricted investment return	38,091
Total Investment Return	$ 437,939

NOTE K – BANK LINE OF CREDIT

From time to time CPCH draws on a $200,000 line of credit established at Northstar Bank of Texas for working capital purposes. A total of $625,000 was borrowed and repaid on the line of credit during 2014, with no balance owed at the end of the year. Total interest paid during 2014 on the line of credit was $1,825.

SUPPLEMENTAL SCHEDULE

CUMBERLAND PRESBYTERIAN CHILDREN'S HOME

SCHEDULE OF BOARD OF STEWARDSHIP ENDOWMENTS
DECEMBER 31, 2014

Donor-established Endowments:

	Balance
Merlyn & Joann Kitterman Alexander	$ 1,467
W.A. and Elizabeth Bearden Trust	16,704
Grace Johnson Beasley Memorial Endowment	38,892
Bethlehem CPC Memorial Endowment	6,357
Bridges Scholarship Fund	43,445
J.T. and Dorothy Britt Trust	11,761
Children's Home Endowment	339,277
Lavenia Campbell Cole Trust 20%	21,394
Lavenia Campbell Cole Annuity Endowment	86,884
Lavenia Cole Testamentary Trust 25%	627,247
Mrs. A.L. Colvin Memorial Fund	1,056
John W. and Eva Cox Trust Fund	32,563
Steve Curry Trust	571,605
Daniel Class, First Cumberland Presbyterian Church	33,629
Donnie Curry Davis Memorial	196,789
Mary Elberta Davis Memorial	20,998
Fred and Mattie Mae Dwiggins Memorial Trust	84,313
J.S. Eustis Memorial Trust Fund	13,311
Clester H. Evans, Sr., Trust	22,223
John M. Friedel Trust	22,988
Joyce C. Frisby Memorial Endowment	29,528
Vaughn and Mary Elizabeth Fults Trust	21,205
Garner-Miller Memorial Trust	13,082
James C. and Freda M. Gilbert Endowment	115,704
Henry and Jayne Glaspy Memorial Fund	8,678
Rev. W.J. Gregory Memorial	109,074
Glenn Griffin Endowment	46,500
Rev. and Mrs. Henry M. Guynn Memorial	4,832
Chad Harper Endowment	11,632
Newsome and Imogene Harvey Endowment	2,667
Clarence & Lula Herring Endowment	6,349
Kenneth and Clara Holsopple Trust	56,204
George and Lottie M. Hutchins Trust	1,195,323
Norma K. Johnson Memorial Library	11,996
P.F. Johnson Memorial Endowment	19,913
Robert and Genevie Johnson Endowment	5,052
Mr. and Mrs. Robert L. Johnson	12,548
Violet Louise Jolly Endowment	1,267
Eulava Joyce Memorial Trust	10,470
Ruth Cypert and Harlie Klugler Memorial Fund	21,084
Blanche R. Lake Endowment	15,195
Wade P. Lane/Maude Dorough Memorial Trust	10,001
Adolphus M. Latta Memorial Trust	53,965
Mr. and Mrs. Robert F. Little Endowment Fund	36,554
Charles E. and Addie Mae Lloyd Endowment Fund	23,770
Tony and Ann Martin Endowment	2,512
Mrs. Lucille (Lucy) Mast Endowment	2,554

CUMBERLAND PRESBYTERIAN CHILDREN'S HOME

SCHEDULE OF BOARD OF STEWARDSHIP ENDOWMENTS (CONT'D)
DECEMBER 31, 2014

Donor-established Endowments:

	Balance
W.B. and Azales McClurkan, Sr. Memorial	$ 20,322
Williams J. McCall Memorial Trust	10,470
McEwen Church Trust	8,044
McKinley and Barnett Families Endowment	854,973
J.C. McKinley Endowment	19,826
Velma McKinley Trust	19,826
Mary McKnight Memorial Trust	11,134
Kenneth and Mae Moore Endowment Fund	7,404
Operational Trust Fund	155,785
Bert and Pat Owen Endowment	1,647
Hamilton & Merion Parks Family Trust #3	11,697
Joe Parr Trust Fund	82,323
Martha Sue Parr Endowment	1,681
Mary M. Poole Endowment Fund	1,007,156
Jack and Mary Proctor Memorial Trust Fund	67,153
SQ&K Maurine Proctor Trust	5,948
Mary Acena Prewitt Trust Fund	94,934
Rev. and Mrs. Joe Reed Memorial	2,871
Marguerite D. Richards Endowment	26,745
Agnes Durbin Richardson Trust	31,725
Pat N. & Essie H. Roberts Memorial	61,922
Frances Benefield Roberts Trust Fund	2,453
Rev. and Mrs. John A. Russell Memorial	4,789
John Ann and Mary Shimer	15,764
Rev. W.B. and Lydia Snipes Memorial Trust	19,888
Don M. & Nancy Tabor Endowment Trust	36,172
Townsend Trust Fund	40,414
Hattie A. Wheeless Fund	20,790
Whitfield Family Endowment	12,643
Porter and Hattie S. Williamson Memorial Trust	180,327
Helen Wynn Endowment Fund	11,026
Maxie and Will Young Memorial Endowment	21,828
Dixie Campbell Zinn Memorial Trust	6,562
Total	$ 6,916,804

MEMPHIS THEOLOGICAL SEMINARY OF THE
CUMBERLAND PRESBYTERIAN CHURCH

FINANCIAL STATEMENTS AND REPORT OF INDEPENDENT
CERTIFIED PUBLIC ACCOUNTANTS

JULY 31, 2014

TABLE OF CONTENTS

	PAGE
INDEPENDENT AUDITOR'S REPORT	3
FINANCIAL STATEMENTS	
Statements of Financial Position	6
Statement of Activities	7
Statement of Functional Expenses	9
Statements of Cash Flows	10
NOTES TO FINANCIAL STATEMENTS	11
SUPPLEMENTAL INFORMATION	
Schedule of Expenditures of Federal Awards	21
NON-FINANCIAL SECTION	
Independent Auditor's Report on Internal Control over Financial Reporting and on Compliance and Other Matters Based on an Audit of Financial Statements Performed in Accordance with *Government Auditing Standards*	23
Independent Auditor's Report on Compliance for Each Major Program and on Internal Control over Compliance Required by OMB Circular A-133	25
Schedule of Findings and Questioned Costs	27
Schedule of Prior Year Findings and Questioned Costs	28
Independent Auditors' General Comments	29

CERTIFIED PUBLIC ACCOUNTANTS
ATRIUM 1, 6800 POPLAR AVE., STE. 210
GERMANTOWN, TENNESSEE 38138
(901) 523-8283 (901) 523-8287 FAX
www.zkcpas.com

INDEPENDENT AUDITOR'S REPORT

Board of Trustees
Memphis Theological Seminary of the
    Cumberland Presbyterian Church
Memphis, Tennessee

Report on the Financial Statements

We have audited the accompanying financial statements of Memphis Theological Seminary of the Cumberland Presbyterian Church (the "Seminary"), a nonprofit organization), which comprise the statement of financial position as of July 31, 2014, and the related statements of activities, functional expenses, and cash flows for the year then ended, and the related notes to the financial statements.

Management's Responsibility for the Financial Statements

Management is responsible for the preparation and fair presentation of these financial statements in accordance with accounting principles generally accepted in the United States of America; this includes the design, implementation, and maintenance of internal control relevant to the preparation and fair presentation of financial statements that are free from material misstatement, whether due to fraud or error.

Auditor's Responsibility

Our responsibility is to express an opinion on these financial statements based on our audit. We conducted our audit in accordance with auditing standards generally accepted in the United States of America and the standards applicable to financial audits contained in *Government Auditing Standards*, issued by the Comptroller General of the United States. Those standards require that we plan and perform the audit to obtain reasonable assurance about whether the financial statements are free from material misstatement.

An audit involves performing procedures to obtain audit evidence about the amounts and disclosures in the financial statements. The procedures selected depend on the auditor's judgment, including the assessment of the risks of material misstatement of the financial statements, whether due to fraud or error. In making those risk assessments, the auditor considers internal control relevant to the entity's preparation and fair presentation of the financial statements in order to design audit procedures that are appropriate in the circumstances, but not for the purpose of expressing an opinion on the effectiveness of the entity's internal control. Accordingly, we express no such opinion. An audit also includes evaluating the appropriateness of accounting policies used and the reasonableness of significant accounting estimates made by management, as well as evaluating the overall presentation of the financial statements.

We believe that the audit evidence we have obtained is sufficient and appropriate to provide a basis for our audit opinion.

Opinion

In our opinion, the financial statements referred to above present fairly, in all material respects, the financial position of the Seminary as of July 31, 2014, and the changes in its net assets and its cash flows for the year then ended in accordance with accounting principles generally accepted in the United States of America.

Other Matters

Other Information

Our audit was conducted for the purpose of forming an opinion on the financial statements as a whole. The accompanying schedule of expenditures of federal awards, as required by Office of Management and Budget Circular A-133, *Audits of States, Local Governments, and Non-Profit Organizations*, is presented for purposes of additional analysis and is not a required part of the financial statements. Such information is the responsibility of management and was derived from and relates directly to the underlying accounting and other records used to prepare the financial statements. The information has been subjected to the auditing procedures applied in the audit of the financial statements and certain additional procedures, including comparing and reconciling such information directly to the underlying accounting and other records used to prepare the financial statements or to the financial statements themselves, and other additional procedures in accordance with auditing standards generally accepted in the United States of America. In our opinion, the information is fairly stated, in all material respects, in relation to the financial statements as a whole.

Other Reporting Required by *Government Auditing Standards*

In accordance with *Government Auditing Standards*, we have also issued our report, dated December 10, 2014, on our consideration of the Seminary's internal control over financial reporting and on our tests of its compliance with certain provisions of laws, regulations, contracts, and grant agreements and other matters. The purpose of that report is to describe the scope of our testing of internal control over financial reporting and compliance and the results of that testing, and not to provide an opinion on internal control over financial reporting or on compliance. That report is an integral part of an audit performed in accordance with *Government Auditing Standards* in considering the Seminary's internal control over financial reporting and compliance.

Report on Summarized Comparative Information

We have previously audited the Seminary's 2013 financial statements and our report, dated December 16, 2013, expressed an unmodified opinion on those audited financial statements. In our opinion, the summarized comparative information presented herein as of and for the year ended July 31, 2013, is consistent, in all material respects, with the audited financial statements from which it has been derived.

Zoccola Kaplan, PLLC

Germantown, Tennessee
December 10, 2014

FINANCIAL STATEMENTS

MEMPHIS THEOLOGICAL SEMINARY
OF THE CUMBERLAND PRESBYTERIAN CHURCH
STATEMENTS OF FINANCIAL POSITION
July 31, 2014

ASSETS

	2014	2013
Assets		
Cash and cash equivalents (Notes B5 and E)	$ 472,063	$ 838,001
Cash and cash equivalents, temporarily restricted (Note E)	145,152	215,776
Total cash and cash equivalents	617,215	1,053,777
Investments, at fair value (Notes B3, C, D, and K)		
Unrestricted	1,668,078	1,510,028
Temporarily restricted	2,080,907	1,672,184
Permanently restricted	6,252,462	5,966,473
Total investments	10,001,447	9,148,685
Tuition and fees receivable, net of allowance of $249,147 in 2014 and $234,747 in 2013 (Note E)	176,117	213,992
Pledges receivable, net of discounts on pledges (Note F)	781,776	60,000
Other receivables	8,366	112,522
Capital assets, net of accumulated depreciation (Notes B4 and B8)	3,311,228	3,550,769
Cash value of life insurance	40,280	38,708
Land held for sale (Notes B8 and D)	27,448	81,851
Other assets	31,858	41,147
Total assets	$ 14,995,735	$ 14,301,451

LIABILITIES AND NET ASSETS

	2014	2013
Liabilities		
Accounts payable and accrued expenses (Note K)	$ 291,254	$ 281,652
Prepaid revenue	129,688	204,919
Line of credit (Note G)	270,000	75,000
Notes payable (Notes H and K)	1,607,493	2,399,362
Total liabilities	2,298,435	2,960,933
Net Assets (Note B1)		
Unrestricted	3,404,681	3,426,085
Temporarily restricted	3,040,157	1,947,960
Permanently restricted	6,252,462	5,966,473
Total net assets	12,697,300	11,340,518
Total liabilities and net assets	$ 14,995,735	$ 14,301,451

The accompanying notes are an integral part of these financial statements.

MEMPHIS THEOLOGICAL SEMINARY
OF THE CUMBERLAND PRESBYTERIAN CHURCH
STATEMENT OF ACTIVITIES
For the Years Ended July 31, 2014 and 2013

	2014				2013
	Unrestricted	Temporarily Restricted	Permanently Restricted	Total	Total
Operating Revenues and Support					
Tuition and fees, net of scholarships of $439,462 and $429,993	$ 2,167,591	$ -	$ -	$ 2,167,591	$ 2,069,821
Contributions and grants (Note B2)	525,095	1,320,493	270,594	2,116,182	1,061,510
Other revenue and support	219,443	-	-	219,443	338,107
Net assets released from restrictions	823,793	(823,793)	-	-	-
Total operating revenues and support	3,735,922	496,700	270,594	4,503,216	3,469,438
Expenses (Note B9)					
Educational program services					
Instruction	1,381,442	-	-	1,381,442	1,356,786
Library	186,956	-	-	186,956	240,343
Student services	202,281	-	-	202,281	232,436
Financial leadership for ministry	29,032	-	-	29,032	-
Program for alternative studies	120,423	-	-	120,423	118,169
Academic support	106,331	-	-	106,331	104,631
Supporting services					
Facilities operations	639,184	-	-	639,184	736,143
Institutional support	819,488	-	-	819,488	816,710
Security services	47,973	-	-	47,973	51,624
Development and fundraising	716,535	-	-	716,535	437,598
Total operating expenses	4,249,645	-	-	4,249,645	4,094,440
Increase (decrease) in net assets from operations	(513,723)	496,700	270,594	253,571	(625,002)
Non-operating revenues and expenses					
Investment income (loss) (Notes B3 and D)	492,319	595,497	15,395	1,103,211	1,027,126
Increase (decrease) in net assets	(21,404)	1,092,197	285,989	1,356,782	402,124
Net Assets, beginning of year	3,426,085	1,947,960	5,966,473	11,340,518	10,938,394
Net Assets - end of year	$ 3,404,681	$ 3,040,157	$ 6,252,462	$ 12,697,300	$ 11,340,518

The accompanying notes are an integral part of these financial statements.

MEMPHIS THEOLOGICAL SEMINARY
OF THE CUMBERLAND PRESBYTERIAN CHURCH
STATEMENT OF ACTIVITIES (CONTINUED)
For the Year Ended July 31, 2013

	2013			
	Unrestricted	Temporarily Restricted	Permanently Restricted	Total
Operating Revenues and Support				
Tuition and fees, net of scholarships of $441,283	$ 2,069,821	$ -	$ -	$ 2,069,821
Contributions and grants (Note B2)	643,712	337,756	80,042	1,061,510
Other revenue and support	338,107	-	-	338,107
Net assets released from restrictions	484,628	(484,628)	-	-
Total operating revenues and support	3,536,268	(146,872)	80,042	3,469,438
Expenses (Note B9)				
Educational program services				
Instruction	1,356,786	-	-	1,356,786
Library	240,343	-	-	240,343
Student services	232,436	-	-	232,436
Program for alternative studies	118,169	-	-	118,169
Academic support	104,631	-	-	104,631
Supporting services				
Facilities operations	736,143	-	-	736,143
Institutional support	816,710	-	-	816,710
Security services	51,624	-	-	51,624
Development and fundraising	437,598	-	-	437,598
Total operating expenses	4,094,440	-	-	4,094,440
Increase (decrease) in net assets from operations	(558,172)	(146,872)	80,042	(625,002)
Non-operating revenues and expenses				
Investment income (loss) (Note B3 and D)	539,691	472,364	15,071	1,027,126
Reduction in fair value of land held for sale	-	-	-	-
Increase (decrease) in net assets	(18,481)	325,492	95,113	402,124
Reclassification of net assets (Note L)	119,800	249,861	(369,661)	-
Net Assets, beginning of year	3,324,766	1,372,607	6,241,021	10,938,394
Net Assets - end of year	$ 3,426,085	$ 1,947,960	$ 5,966,473	$ 11,340,518

The accompanying notes are an integral part of these financial statements.

MEMPHIS THEOLOGICAL SEMINARY
OF THE CUMBERLAND PRESBYTERIAN CHURCH
STATEMENT OF FUNCTIONAL EXPENSES
For the Year Ended July 31, 2014
(With Summarized Comparative Financial Information for the Year Ended July 31, 2013)

	Educational Program Services					Supporting Services				
	Instruction	Library	Student Services	Financial Leadership for Ministry	Program for Alternative Studies	Academic Support	Facilities Operations	Institutional Support	Security Services	Development and Fund Raising	2014 Total	2013 Total
Salaries and Wages	$1,084,588	$115,446	$145,553	$11,611	$67,539	$87,963	$98,044	$425,321	$ -	$274,143	$2,310,208	$2,308,071
Benefits	165,660	20,543	26,642	245	7,258	12,822	35,552	87,182	-	45,087	400,991	397,994
Professional Development	10,103	-	3,095	500	-	1,595	-	611	-	45	15,949	12,381
Travel/Auto Expense	2,029	450	4,086	263	6,129	1,161	1,932	6,669	-	11,148	33,867	38,534
Office Supplies and Expense	13,484	48,151	6,700	2,892	988	2,540	3,330	52,799	-	36,205	167,089	178,548
Consultants / Professional	-	-	-	6,945	-	-	-	83,879	-	49,612	138,797	123,259
Student / Special Events	40,241	-	3,766	-	37,782	-	-	34,386	47,973	-	165,787	183,468
Covenant Groups	49,263	-	-	-	-	-	-	-	-	-	49,263	44,021
Repairs and Maintenance	190	-	3,722	-	-	-	48,656	95	-	-	54,184	56,825
Utilities	-	-	5,987	-	-	-	80,829	-	-	-	86,816	86,600
Insurance Expense	-	-	-	-	-	-	90,634	-	-	5,000	95,634	94,348
Property Taxes	-	-	-	-	-	-	24,518	-	-	-	24,518	-
Other Expense	15,884	845	2,730	6,576	727	250	18,678	35,236	-	5,813	86,739	144,983
Interest Expense	-	-	-	-	-	-	-	93,310	-	-	93,310	145,305
Capital Campaign Expense	-	-	-	-	-	-	-	-	-	289,482	289,482	-
Depreciation	-	-	-	-	-	-	237,011	-	-	-	237,011	280,103
	$1,381,442	$186,956	$202,281	$29,032	$120,423	$106,331	$639,184	$819,488	$47,973	$716,535	$4,249,645	$4,094,440

The accompanying notes are an integral part of these financial statements.

MEMPHIS THEOLOGICAL SEMINARY
OF THE CUMBERLAND PRESBYTERIAN CHURCH
STATEMENTS OF CASH FLOWS
For the Year Ended July 31, 2014

	2014	2013
Cash Flows from Operating Activities		
Change in net assets	$ 1,356,782	$ 402,124
Adjustments to reconcile change in net assets to net cash provided by (used in) operating activities:		
Depreciation	237,011	280,103
Bad debt expense	19,648	12,779
Discount on pledges	63,224	-
Changes in operating assets and liabilities:		
(Increase) decrease in assets		
Tuition, fees and other receivables	18,227	(141,128)
Pledges receivable	(785,000)	90,000
Other assets	113,445	(6,128)
Increase (decrease) in liabilities		
Accounts payable and accrued expenses	9,602	(60,519)
Deferred Revenue	(75,231)	204,919
Net cash provided by operating activities	957,708	782,150
Cash Flows from Investing Activities		
Withdrawals from investments	170,376	583,537
Investments of endowment gifts	(270,594)	(80,043)
Net earnings on investments-(reinvested)/distributed	240,112	217,072
Capital (gains) losses on investments	(992,656)	(896,712)
(Increase) decrease in value of land held for sale	(838)	(7,508)
Sale of property held for sale	55,241	-
(Increase) decrease in cash surrender value of life insurance	(1,572)	(2,125)
Sale of property	147,323	749,440
Purchases of property and equipment	(144,793)	(171,295)
Net cash provided by (used for) investing activities	(797,401)	392,366
Cash Flows from Financing Activities		
Increase (decrease) in line of credit	195,000	(324,739)
Principal payments on long term debt	(791,869)	(2,315)
Net cash provided by (used for) financing activities	(596,869)	(327,054)
Net increase (decrease) in cash and cash equivalents	(436,562)	847,462
Cash and cash equivalents, beginning of year	1,053,777	206,315
Cash and cash equivalents, end of year	$ 617,215	$ 1,053,777
Supplemental Disclosure:		
Interest paid	$ 104,107	$ 165,211

The accompanying notes are an integral part of these financial statements.

MEMPHIS THEOLOGICAL SEMINARY
OF THE CUMBERLAND PRESBYTERIAN CHURCH
NOTES TO FINANCIAL STATEMENTS
For the Year Ended July 31, 2014

NOTE A – ORGANIZATION AND PURPOSE

The Memphis Theological Seminary of the Cumberland Presbyterian Church (the "Seminary") is an ecumenical Protestant seminary serving the mid-south region from its campus in Memphis, Tennessee. The Seminary provides postgraduate theological education to clergy and church leaders of the parent denomination and qualified students from other denominations. The Seminary is governed by a Board of Trustees elected by the General Assembly of the Cumberland Presbyterian Church.

NOTE B – SIGNIFICANT ACCOUNTING POLICIES

1. Financial Statement Presentation

   The Seminary prepares its financial statements in accordance with FASB ASC 958-205, *Not-For-Profit Entities Presentation of Financial Statements*. Under FASB ASC 958, the Seminary reports information regarding its financial position and activities according to three classes of net assets: unrestricted net assets, temporarily restricted net assets, and permanently restricted net assets.

   The financial statements are prepared using the accrual basis of accounting.

2. Contributions

   Contributions received by the Seminary are recorded as unrestricted, temporarily restricted, or permanently restricted support depending on the existence and/or nature of any donor restrictions. Temporarily restricted net assets are reclassified to unrestricted net assets upon satisfaction of the time or purpose restrictions.

3. Investment Valuation and Income Recognition

   Investments are reported at fair value. Fair value is the price that would be received to sell an asset or paid to transfer a liability in an orderly transaction between market participants at the measurement date. See Notes C and D for discussion and computation of fair value.

   Unrealized holding gains and losses are included in current year revenue and support as a component of investment income. Realized gains and losses are computed using the specific identification method.

4. Capital Assets

   All acquisitions of property and equipment and expenditures for repairs and maintenance that prolong the useful lives of assets in excess of $1,000 are capitalized at cost. Expenditures for normal repair and maintenance are expensed to operations as they occur. Depreciation is provided through the straight-line method over the assets' estimated useful lives which range from three to ten years for equipment, fifteen years for library books and twenty-five to forty years for buildings. Depreciation expense amounts for the years ended July 31, 2014 and 2013 were $237,011 and $280,103, respectively.

MEMPHIS THEOLOGICAL SEMINARY
OF THE CUMBERLAND PRESBYTERIAN CHURCH
NOTES TO FINANCIAL STATEMENTS (CONTINUED)
For the Year Ended July 31, 2014

NOTE B – SIGNIFICANT ACCOUNTING POLICIES *(Continued)*

Fixed assets are as follows:

	2014	2013
Building and improvements	$ 4,255,844	$ 4,412,187
Furniture and equipment	874,852	842,476
Library books	1,769,930	1,724,046
Vehicles	48,515	48,515
	6,949,141	7,027,224
Less accumulated depreciation	4,234,432	4,030,098
	2,714,709	2,997,126
Land	208,650	208,650
Construction in progress	387,869	344,993
Capital assets, net	$ 3,311,228	$ 3,550,769

5. Cash Equivalents

Cash equivalents are defined as short term, highly liquid investments that are both readily convertible to known amounts of cash and are so near maturity that they present insignificant risk of changes in value because of changes in interest rates.

6. Use of Estimates in the Preparation of Financial Statements

The preparation of financial statements in conformity with generally accepted accounting principles requires management to make estimates and assumptions that affect the amounts reported in the financial statements and accompanying notes. Actual results could differ from those estimates.

7. Income Taxes

The Seminary is a not-for-profit organization that is exempt from income taxes under Internal Revenue Code Section 501 (c) (3) and is also exempt from state income taxes.

8. Donated Property, Equipment and Services

Donations of property and use of property are recorded as support at their estimated fair value at the date of donation. Such donations are reported as unrestricted support unless the donor has restricted the donated asset to a specific purpose. The value of donated property was $0 in 2014.

Donated services are recognized as contributions if the services (a) create or enhance non-financial assets or (b) require specialized skills, are performed by people with those skills, and would otherwise be purchased by the Organization. There were no contributed services recorded for accounting and consulting in 2014.

MEMPHIS THEOLOGICAL SEMINARY
OF THE CUMBERLAND PRESBYTERIAN CHURCH
NOTES TO FINANCIAL STATEMENTS (CONTINUED)
For the Year Ended July 31, 2014

NOTE B – SIGNIFICANT ACCOUNTING POLICIES *(Continued)*

9. Functional Allocation of Expenses

   The cost of providing the various educational programs and supporting services has been summarized on a functional basis in the statement of functional expenses. Accordingly, certain costs have been allocated among the programs and services benefited.

10. Subsequent Events

    The Seminary evaluated all events or transactions that occurred after July 31, 2014 and through December 10, 2014, the date the Seminary approved these financial statements for issuance.

NOTE C – FAIR VALUE MEASUREMENT

The FASB ASC Subtopic 820-10 *Fair Value Measurements,* (formerly SFAS No. 157), defines fair value as the exchange price that would be received for an asset or paid to transfer a liability in the principal or most advantageous market for the asset or liability in an orderly transaction between market participants at the measurement date. SFAS No. 157 established a three-level fair value hierarchy that prioritizes the inputs used to measure fair value. This hierarchy requires entities to maximize the use of observable inputs and minimize the use of unobservable inputs.

The three levels of inputs used to measure fair value are as follows:

- Level 1 – Quoted prices in active markets for identical assets or liabilities.
- Level 2 – Observable inputs other than quoted prices included in Level 1, such as quoted prices for similar assets and liabilities in active markets; quoted prices for identical or similar assets or liabilities in markets that are not active; or inputs that are observable or can be corroborated by observable market data.
- Level 3 – Unobservable inputs that are supported by little or no market activity and that are significant to the fair value of the assets or liabilities. This includes certain pricing models, discounted cash flow methodologies and similar techniques that use significant unobservable inputs.

The estimated fair value of the Seminary's financial instruments has been determined by management using available market information. However, considerable judgment is required in interpreting market data to develop the estimates of fair value. Accordingly, the fair values are not necessarily indicative of the amounts that the Seminary could realize in a current market exchange. The use of different market assumptions may have a material effect on the estimated fair value amounts.

The carrying amounts of cash and cash equivalents, net receivables, cash value of life insurance, payables, accrued liabilities, and debt are a reasonable estimate of their fair value, due to their short term nature, method of computation and interest rates for current debt.

All financial assets that are measured at fair value on a recurring basis (at least annually) have been segregated into the most appropriate level within the fair value hierarchy based on the inputs used to determine the fair value at the measurement date. These assets measured at fair value on a recurring basis are summarized in Note D.

MEMPHIS THEOLOGICAL SEMINARY
OF THE CUMBERLAND PRESBYTERIAN CHURCH
NOTES TO FINANCIAL STATEMENTS (CONTINUED)
For the Year Ended July 31, 2014

NOTE D – INVESTMENTS AND OTHER ASSETS

Nearly all of the Seminary's investments are managed by the Board of Stewards and Benefits of the Cumberland Presbyterian Church, Inc., and maintained in po accounts with other funds. The investments generally originate from gifts and c which separate identifiable investment accounts are created that indicate the sou and/or the purpose for which the funds are to be used. Many of these accounts ar monthly distributions to the Seminary based on one-twelfth of 5% of the rollin; The Board of Stewardship, Foundation and Benefits issues an aggregate amount and charges the applicable accounts for their proportionate share. In addition, th request on an as needed basis, additional distributions that will be used for the pι the account was created.

Accounts subjected to the fair values measurement process consist of the followii

	July 31, 2014		
	Total Fair Value	Quoted Prices in Active Markets for Identical Assets (Level 1)	Significant Other Observable Inputs (Level 2)
Investment securities			
Cash/Cash Equivalents	$ 317,318	$ 317,318	$ -
Money market funds	2,897	2,897	-
U. S. Treasuries	-	-	-
Mortgage/asset - backed securities	-	-	-
Bonds and bond funds	1,656,703	10,205	1,646,498
Common and preferred stocks	127,405	127,405	-
Real estate investment funds	698,638	-	698,638
Mutual funds	231,036	231,036	-
Private investment entities	6,967,450	-	-
Total investments	$ 10,001,447	$ 688,861	$ 2,345,136
Land held for sale	$ 27,448	$ -	$ -

MEMPHIS THEOLOGICAL SEMINARY
OF THE CUMBERLAND PRESBYTERIAN CHURCH
NOTES TO FINANCIAL STATEMENTS (CONTINUED)
For the Year Ended July 31, 2014

NOTE D – INVESTMENTS AND OTHER ASSETS *(Continued)*

	July 31, 2013			
	Total Fair Value	Quoted Prices in Active Markets for Identical Assets (Level 1)	Significant Other Observable Inputs (Level 2)	Unobservable Inputs (Level 3)
Investment securities				
Cash/Cash Equivalents	$ 1,627,077	$ 1,627,077	$ -	$ -
Money market funds	7,747	7,747	-	-
U. S. Treasuries	83,122	83,122	-	-
Mortgage - backed securities	1,112,265	-	1,112,265	-
Bonds and bond funds	1,196,920	10,213	1,186,707	-
Common and preferred stocks	107,152	107,152	-	-
Real estate investment funds	725,050	-	725,050	-
Private Investment entities	4,289,352	-	-	4,289,352
Total investments	$ 9,148,685	$ 1,835,311	$ 3,024,022	$ 4,289,352
Land held for sale	$ 81,851	$ -	$ -	$ 81,851

The private investment entities for the years ended July 31, 2014, are investments entered into by the Board of Stewardship to achieve greater rates of return. They include funds whose inputs used to determine fair value are considered unobservable and are therefore Level 3 inputs.

The carrying value of the above land held for sale is based on expected recoverability at the time of sale. The Seminary uses appraised values and other information available to determine the carrying value. The inputs used to determine fair value are considered unobservable and are therefore Level 3 inputs.

MEMPHIS THEOLOGICAL SEMINARY
OF THE CUMBERLAND PRESBYTERIAN CHURCH
NOTES TO FINANCIAL STATEMENTS (CONTINUED)
For the Year Ended July 31, 2014

NOTE D – INVESTMENTS AND OTHER ASSETS *(Continued)*

Transactions in Level 3 assets for the years ended July 31, 2014 and 2013, were as follows:

	July 31, 2014	July 31, 2013
Private investment entities		
Beginning balance	$ 4,289,352	$ 4,801,086
Additional allocation of investments	380,821	-
Investments/withdrawals, net	465,003	(993,601)
Realized/unrealized gains (losses)	1,832,274	481,867
Ending balance	$ 6,967,450	$ 4,289,352
Land held for sale		
Beginning balance	$ 81,851	$ 74,343
Improvements to land previously received	838	7,508
Sale of Thor Road property	(55,241)	-
Ending balance	$ 27,448	$ 81,851

Non-operating income (loss) from investments was as follows:

	July 31, 2014	July 31, 2013
Investment income	$ 110,933	$ 130,414
Realized investment gains (losses)	(378)	57,519
Unrealized investment gains (losses)	992,656	839,193
Net investment income (loss)	$ 1,103,211	$ 1,027,126

NOTE E – CONCENTRATION OF CREDIT RISK

The Seminary has cash equivalents invested by the Board of Stewardship, Foundation and Benefits. At July 31, 2014, these funds total $145,152 and are not insured by the Federal Deposit Insurance Corporation (FDIC).

In addition, the Seminary maintains cash balances in accounts at a well-established financial institution located in Memphis, Tennessee. These balances are insured by the Federal Deposit Insurance Corporation up to certain limits. At July 31, 2014, the Seminary had uninsured balances of $152,987.

The Seminary's tuition and fees receivable are from students for which the majority receive some form of financial assistance. Management maintains an allowance for uncollectible based on periodic reviews of each individual student's account.

MEMPHIS THEOLOGICAL SEMINARY
OF THE CUMBERLAND PRESBYTERIAN CHURCH
NOTES TO FINANCIAL STATEMENTS (CONTINUED)
For the Year Ended July 31, 2014

NOTE F - PLEDGES RECEIVABLE

Pledges receivable represent pledges from numerous donors to be used for a capital campaign which was initiated in the prior year with a feasibility study with most donations and pledges beginning in the current year. The campaign has three purposes: 1) To help fund the construction of a new free-standing chapel; 2) To fund construction of a new classroom/office building; and 3) To increase endowments. At July 31, 2014, pledges receivable for the capital campaign totaled $845,000. This total amount is discounted by $63,224 using a discount rate of 3.07% which is based on the published 20-year Treasury rate at July 31, 2014. The pledges, net of the discount, are due to be received as follows:

Year Ending July 31,	Amount
2015	$ 44,120
2016	217,110
2017	215,150
2018	191,273
2019	64,472
Thereafter	49,651
Total pledges net of discount	$ 781,776

NOTE G – LINE OF CREDIT

The Seminary has a $400,000 revolving line of credit agreement with a local bank. Borrowings outstanding under the agreement ($270,000 at July 31, 2014) bear interest at the bank's prime rate (3.25 percent at July 31, 2014). The line is guaranteed by the Board of Stewardship, Foundation and Benefits.

MEMPHIS THEOLOGICAL SEMINARY
OF THE CUMBERLAND PRESBYTERIAN CHURCH
NOTES TO FINANCIAL STATEMENTS (CONTINUED)
For the Year Ended July 31, 2014

NOTE H – NOTES PAYABLE

Notes payable consist of the following at July 31, 2014 and 2013:

	2014	2013
Note payable, due in monthly installments at a variable interest (4.75% at July 31, 2013) through November 2016.	$ -	$ 62,536
Note payable, due in monthly installments at a variable interest (4.75% at July 31, 2013) through March 2030.	-	80,153
Note payable, due in monthly installments at a variable interest (4.75% at July 31, 2014) through January 2031.	749,849	771,793
Note payable, due in monthly installments at a variable interest (4.75% at July 31, 2013) through April 2031.	-	108,699
Note payable, due in monthly installments at a variable interest (4.75% at July 31, 2013) through December 2031.	-	121,823
Note payable, due in monthly installments at a variable interest (4.75% at July 31, 2013) through April 2032.	-	118,920
Note payable, due in monthly installments at a variable interest (4.75% at July 31, 2014) through April 2032.	525,860	678,325
Note payable, due in monthly installments through interest (4.75% at July 31, 2014) through April 2033.	255,484	261,046
Note payable, due in monthly installments through interest (4.75% at July 31, 2014) through September 2033.	76,300	196,067
Total notes payable	$ 1,607,493	$ 2,399,362

The notes payable are collateralized by income earned from permanently restricted investments and are payable to the Board of Stewardship, Foundation and Benefits.

Scheduled principal payments required for each of the next five fiscal years and thereafter are as follows:

Year Ending July 31,	Amount
2015	$ 80,408
2016	75,889
2017	79,573
2018	83,437
2019	87,186
Thereafter	1,201,000
Total notes payable	$ 1,607,493

MEMPHIS THEOLOGICAL SEMINARY
OF THE CUMBERLAND PRESBYTERIAN CHURCH
NOTES TO FINANCIAL STATEMENTS (CONTINUED)
For the Year Ended July 31, 2014

NOTE I – RETIREMENT PLAN

The Seminary sponsors a qualified defined contribution retirement plan for eligible employees as defined by the plan under IRC Section 403(b). Employees are eligible to participate in the plan immediately upon hire and contributions to the plan are vested immediately. Each participant in the plan may make voluntary contributions to the plan of up to the lesser of twenty percent (20%) of annual compensation received by the participant during the plan year, or the maximum allowed by law. The Seminary matches participant's contributions to a maximum of 2.5%. Contributions to the plan by the Seminary for the years ended July 31, 2014 and 2013 were $40,603 and $42,406, respectively.

NOTE J - FINANCIAL STATEMENT PRESENTATION

Certain amounts in the July 31, 2013 financial statements have been reclassified to conform to the July 31, 2014 presentation.

NOTE K – RELATED PARTY

The Seminary and the Board of Stewardship are separate corporations but both are affiliated with the Cumberland Presbyterian Church in that the governing board of the Church elects the members of the Board of Trustees of the Seminary and the Board of Stewardship. There are no common board members between the Seminary and the Board of Stewardship. Amounts due to and from the Board of Stewardship are as follows:

	July 31, 2014	July 31, 2013
Due the Board of Stewardship from the Seminary:		
Notes Payable	$ 1,607,493	$ 2,399,362
Accrued Interest	$ 7,570	$ 18,366
Due to the Seminary from the Board of Stewardship:		
Seminary cash held	$ 145,152	$ 215,776
Seminary investments held	$ 9,861,031	$ 9,023,572

SUPPLEMENTAL INFORMATION

MEMPHIS THEOLOGICAL SEMINARY
OF THE CUMBERLAND PRESBYTERIAN CHURCH
SCHEDULE OF EXPENDITURES OF FEDERAL AWARDS
For the Year Ended July 31, 2014

CFDA Number	Federal Grantor / Pass-Through Grantor	2014	2013
84.032	U.S. Department of Education Federal Family Education Loan Program	$ 2,840,781	$ 2,501,924

NON-FINANCIAL INFORMATION

CERTIFIED PUBLIC ACCOUNTANTS
ATRIUM 1, 6800 POPLAR AVE., STE. 210
GERMANTOWN, TENNESSEE 38138
(901) 523-8283 (901) 523-8287 FAX
www.zkcpas.com

INDEPENDENT AUDITOR'S REPORT ON INTERNAL CONTROL OVER FINANCIAL REPORTING AND ON COMPLIANCE AND OTHER MATTERS BASED ON AN AUDIT OF FINANCIAL STATEMENTS PERFORMED IN ACCORDANCE WITH *GOVERNMENT AUDITING STANDARDS*

Board of Trustees
Memphis Theological Seminary
 of the Cumberland Presbyterian Church
Memphis, Tennessee

We have audited, in accordance with the auditing standards generally accepted in the United States of America and the standards applicable to financial audits contained in Government Auditing Standards issued by the Comptroller General of the United States, the financial statements of Memphis Theological Seminary of the Cumberland Presbyterian Church (the "Seminary", a nonprofit organization), which comprise the statement of financial position as of July 31, 2014, and the related statements of activities, and cash flows for the year then ended, and the related notes to the financial statements, and have issued our report thereon dated December 10, 2014.

Internal Control over Financial Reporting

In planning and performing our audit of the financial statements, we considered the Seminary's internal control over financial reporting (internal control) to determine the audit procedures that are appropriate in the circumstances for the purpose of expressing our opinion on the financial statements, but not for the purpose of expressing an opinion on the effectiveness of the Seminary's internal control. Accordingly, we do not express an opinion on the effectiveness of the organization's internal control.

A *deficiency in internal control* exists when the design or operation of a control does not allow management or employees, in the normal course of performing their assigned functions, to prevent, or detect and correct, misstatements on a timely basis. A *material weakness* is a deficiency, or a combination of deficiencies, in internal control, such that there is a reasonable possibility that a material misstatement of the entity's financial statements will not be prevented, or detected and corrected on a timely basis. A *significant deficiency* is a deficiency, or a combination of deficiencies, in internal control that is less severe than a material weakness, yet important enough to merit attention by those charged with governance.

Our consideration of internal control was for the limited purpose described in the first paragraph of this section and was not designed to identify all deficiencies in internal control that might be material weaknesses or significant deficiencies. Given these limitations, during our audit we did not identify any deficiencies in internal control that we consider to be material weaknesses. However, material weaknesses may exist that have not been identified.

Compliance and Other Matters

As part of obtaining reasonable assurance about whether the Seminary's financial statements are free from material misstatement, we performed tests of its compliance with certain provisions of laws, regulations, contracts, and grant agreements, noncompliance with which could have a direct and material effect on the determination of financial statement amounts. However, providing an opinion on compliance with those provisions was not an objective of our audit, and accordingly, we do not express such an opinion. The results of our tests disclosed no instances of noncompliance or other matters that are required to be reported under Government Auditing Standards.

Purpose of this Report

The purpose of this report is solely to describe the scope of our testing of internal control and compliance and the results of that testing, and not to provide an opinion on the effectiveness of the organization's internal control or on compliance. This report is an integral part of an audit performed in accordance with *Government Auditing Standards* in considering the organization's internal control and compliance. Accordingly, this communication is not suitable for any other purpose.

Zoccola Kaplan, PLLC

Germantown, Tennessee
December 10, 2014

CERTIFIED PUBLIC ACCOUNTANTS
ATRIUM 1, 6800 POPLAR AVE., STE. 210
GERMANTOWN, TENNESSEE 38138
(901) 523-8283 (901) 523-8287 FAX
www.zkcpas.com

INDEPENDENT AUDITOR'S REPORT ON COMPLIANCE FOR A MAJOR PROGRAM AND ON INTERNAL CONTROL OVER COMPLIANCE REQUIRED BY OMB CIRCULAR A-133

Board of Trustees
Memphis Theological Seminary
 of the Cumberland Presbyterian Church
Memphis, Tennessee

Report on Compliance for a Major Federal Program

We have audited the Seminary's compliance with the types of compliance requirements described in the *OMB Circular A-133 Compliance Supplement* that could have a direct and material effect on the Memphis Theological Seminary of the Cumberland Presbyterian Church's (the "Seminary") major federal program for the year ended July 31, 2014. The Seminary's major federal program is identified in the summary of auditor's results section of the accompanying schedule of findings and questioned costs.

Management's Responsibility

Management is responsible for compliance with the requirements of laws, regulations, contracts, and grants applicable to its federal program.

Auditor's Responsibility

Our responsibility is to express an opinion on compliance for the Seminary's major federal program based on our audit of the types of compliance requirements referred to above. We conducted our audit of compliance in accordance with auditing standards generally accepted in the United States of America; the standards applicable to financial audits contained in *Government Auditing Standards*, issued by the Comptroller General of the United States; and OMB Circular A-133, *Audits of States, Local Governments, and Non-Profit Organizations*. Those standards and OMB Circular A-133 require that we plan and perform the audit to obtain reasonable assurance about whether noncompliance with the types of compliance requirements referred to above that could have a direct and material effect on a major federal program occurred. An audit includes examining, on a test basis, evidence about the Seminary's compliance with those requirements and performing such other procedures as we considered necessary in the circumstances.

We believe that our audit provides a reasonable basis for our opinion on compliance for each major federal program. However, our audit does not provide a legal determination of the Seminary's compliance.

Opinion on a Major Federal Program

In our opinion, the Seminary complied, in all material respects, with the types of compliance requirements referred to above that could have a direct and material effect on its major federal program for the year ended July 31, 2014.

Report on Internal Control over Compliance

Management of the Seminary is responsible for establishing and maintaining effective internal control over compliance with the types of compliance requirements referred to above. In planning and performing our audit of compliance, we considered the Seminary's internal control over compliance with the types of requirements that could have a direct and material effect on a major federal program to determine the auditing procedures that are appropriate in the circumstances for the purpose of expressing an opinion on compliance for a major federal program and to test and report on internal control over compliance in accordance with OMB Circular A-133, but not for the purpose of expressing an opinion on the effectiveness of internal control over compliance. Accordingly, we do not express an opinion on the effectiveness of the Seminary's internal control over compliance.

A *deficiency in internal control over compliance* exists when the design or operation of a control over compliance does not allow management or employees, in the normal course of performing their assigned functions, to prevent, or detect and correct, noncompliance with a type of compliance requirement of a federal program on a timely basis. A *material weakness in internal control over compliance* is a deficiency, or combination of deficiencies, in internal control over compliance, such that there is a reasonable possibility that material noncompliance with a type of compliance requirement of a federal program will not be prevented, or detected and corrected, on a timely basis. A *significant deficiency in internal control over compliance* is a deficiency, or a combination of deficiencies, in internal control over compliance with a type of compliance requirement of a federal program that is less severe than a material weakness in internal control over compliance, yet important enough to merit attention by those charged with governance.

Our consideration of internal control over compliance was for the limited purpose described in the first paragraph of this section and was not designed to identify all deficiencies in internal control over compliance that might be material weaknesses or significant deficiencies. We did not identify any deficiencies in internal control over compliance that we consider to be material weaknesses. However, material weaknesses may exist that have not been identified.

The purpose of this report on internal control over compliance is solely to describe the scope of our testing of internal control over compliance and the results of that testing based on the requirements of OMB Circular A-133. Accordingly, this report is not suitable for any other purpose.

Zoccola Kaplan, PLLC

Germantown, Tennessee
December 10, 2014

MEMPHIS THEOLOGICAL SEMINARY
OF THE CUMBERLAND PRESBYTERIAN CHURCH
SCHEDULE OF FINDINGS AND QUESTIONED COSTS
For the Year Ended July 31, 2014

SECTION I - SUMMARY OF AUDITOR'S RESULTS

Financial Statements

Type of auditor's report issued:	*Unqualified*
Internal control over financial reporting:	
- Material weakness(es) identified?	____ yes ✓ no
- Significant deficiencies identified that are not considered to be material weaknesses?	____ yes ✓ none noted
- Noncompliance material to financial statements noted?	____ yes ✓ no

Federal Awards:

Internal control over major programs:	
- Material weakness(es) identified?	____ yes ✓ no
- Significant deficiencies identified that are not considered to be material weaknesses?	____ yes ✓ none noted
Type of auditor's report issued on compliance for major program:	*Unqualified*
Any audit findings disclosed that are required to be reported in accordance with section 510(a) of OMB Circular A-133?	____ yes ✓ no

Identification of major programs:

CFDA 84.032	U. S. Department of Education Federal Family Education Loan Program
Threshold for distinguishing type A and B programs:	$300,000
Auditee qualified as low risk auditee:	✓ yes ____ no

SECTION II - FINANCIAL STATEMENT FINDINGS

There are no financial statement findings for the year ended July 31, 2014.

SECTION III - FEDERAL AWARD FINDINGS AND QUESTIONED COSTS

There are no federal award findings or questioned costs for the year ended July 31, 2014.

MEMPHIS THEOLOGICAL SEMINARY
OF THE CUMBERLAND PRESBYTERIAN CHURCH
SCHEDULE OF PRIOR YEAR FINDINGS AND QUESTIONED COSTS
For the Year Ended July 31, 2014

Prior year findings and the current status of these findings is as follows:

Finding 2011-1

Condition: During our review of endowment activity, it was noted that requests for withdrawals from certain endowment funds were made by the Seminary. In several instances, the requests were made from individual endowments where funds were not available. The requests for distribution were granted by the Board of Stewardship causing several individual endowments to have negative balances in temporarily restricted or unrestricted categories. In the aggregate, the amount of temporarily restricted and unrestricted funds is positive; however, the balances in all individual funds should remain positive.

Current Status: Test work for the year ended July 31, 2014, revealed only two instances where the Seminary withdrew from individual endowments in a manner that caused new or increased negative balances in either the temporarily restricted or the unrestricted category. The Seminary has made significant efforts to eliminate withdrawals from funds which do not have sufficient balances to support the withdrawals. One of the instances in the current year was immaterial, and the other instance was related to expenses of the capital campaign which will be replenished by the receipts resulting from the capital campaign. Due to the Seminary's efforts in correcting the condition noted in the past regarding withdrawals from the endowments, this finding is considered cleared.

MEMPHIS THEOLOGICAL SEMINARY
OF THE CUMBERLAND PRESBYTERIAN CHURCH
INDEPENDENT AUDITOR'S GENERAL COMMENTS
For the Year Ended July 31, 2014

Required disclosures related to the auditor:

Name of Lead Auditor:	W. Marcus Rountree, CPA
Firm:	Zoccola Kaplan, PLLC
Firm Address:	6800 Poplar Avenue, Suite 210, Germantown, TN 38138
Firm Telephone Number:	(901) 523-8283
Firm Federal I.D. Number:	62-1152935

APPENDICES

REPORT OF THE CREDENTIALS COMMITTEE
(Appendix A)

The Credentials Committee certifies the list of commissioners on pages 5 and 6 of the Preliminary Minutes with the following changes:

On the part of the Minister Commissioners, Reverend Casey Nicholson, Presbytery of East Tennessee and Reverend Ella Hung, Hong Kong Presbytery are not present. Reverend Chris Franklin has been moved from the Judiciary Committee to the Higher Education Committee.

On the part of Elder Commissioners, Elder Cheong Cheung, Hong Kong Presbytery is not present. Elder Nancy Blake, Presbytery of East Tennessee should be listed as Nancy Franklin.

Enrollment as of 5:20 p.m. is certified as forty-eight (48) ministers, 43 (forty-three) elders for a total of ninety-one (91) Commissions with seventeen (17) Youth Advisory Delegates.

Respectfully submitted,
Reverend Stephanie Brown, Chair
Reverend Brent Wills
Elder Sylvia Hall
Youth Advisory Delegate Benjamin Diaz

REPORT OF THE COMMITTEE ON
CHILDREN'S HOME/HISTORICAL FOUNDATION
(Appendix B)

I. REFERRALS

Referrals to this committee are as follows: The Report of the Board of Trustees of the Cumberland Presbyterian Children's Home and The Report of the Board of Trustees of the Historical Foundation.

II. PERSONS OF COUNSEL

Appearing before this committee were: Reverend Richard Brown, President, CEO and General Counsel of the Cumberand Presbyterian Children's Home; Mr. Mickey Shell, member of the Board of Trustees of the Cumberland Presbyterian Children's Home; Ms. Susan Knight Gore, Executive Director of the Historical Foundation; and Reverend Tommy Jobe, member of the Board of Trustees of the Historical Foundation.

III. THE REPORT OF THE BOARD OF TRUSTEES
OF THE CUMBERLAND PRESBYTERIAN CHILDREN'S HOME

The Report of the Board of Trustees of the Cumberland Presbyterian Children's Home had no recommendations.

RECOMMENDATION 1: That the Report of the Board of Trustees of the Cumberland Presbyterian Children's Home be concurred in.

A. COMMENDATION OF THE STAFF OF THE CHILDREN'S HOME

The committee was impressed with the descriptions of the hard work and excellence of the Children's Home staff. It is clear that they do a difficult and necessary job under sometimes unsupportive and ever-changing legal and social climates and with resources insufficient to their vision, and that they do so with great professionalism and to great effect. For this reason, the committee would like to express our gratitude to the staff of the Children's Home, and, even more, to ask General Assembly to express the gratitude of the Cumberland Presbyterian Church as a whole.

RECOMMENDATION 2: That the General Assembly express its gratitude to the staff of the Cumberland Presbyterian Children's Home for the excellence with which they perform their jobs.

B. SUPPORTIVE ACTIONS BY GENERAL ASSEMBLY

The committee makes the following recommendations in support of the work of the Board of Trustees of the Cumberland Presbyterian Children's Home.

1. Children's Home Sunday

More universal participation in the special offering taken for the Children's Home each April would be beneficial to their ministry. For this reason, the Children's Home produces materials such as bulletin inserts to educate congregations and prepare members for this special offering.

RECOMMENDATION 3: That the General Assembly encourage all its congregations to participate in Cumberland Presbyterian Children's Home Sunday (April 10, 2016) by using the resources provided by the Children's Home to educate their congregations and promote the ministry of the Children's Home.

2. Tours and Work Teams

It is beneficial to both the Children's Home and to the denomination at every level for individuals and groups to become more involved and familiar with their ministry. The Children's Home offers opportunities for work teams, tours, and other volunteer services, so that relationships can be formed and strengthened with the Church at large.

RECOMMENDATION 4: That the General Assembly encourage churches and presbyteries to send teams of youth and adults to visit or volunteer at the Cumberland Presbyterian Children's Home.

IV. REPORT OF THE BOARD OF
TRUSTEES OF THE HISTORICAL FOUNDATION

A. HISTORY INTERPRETATION AND PROMOTIONAL ACTIVITIES

1. 1810 Circle

RECOMMENDATION 5: That Recommendation 1 of the Report of the Board of Trustees of the Historical Foundation, "that the General Assembly make congregations and presbyteries aware of the 1810 Circle and encourage new members to support this endeavor annually," be adopted.

2. Denomination Day Offering

RECOMMENDATION 6: That Recommendation 2 of the Report of the Board of Trustees of the Historical Foundation, "that congregations be encouraged to have a special offering on the Sunday designated as Denomination Day to help support the special project designated for that year," be adopted.

B. PUBLICATIONS

1. Publication Series

RECOMMENDATION 7: That Recommendation 3 of the Report of the Board of Trustees

of the Historical Foundation, "that the General Assembly make presbyteries, congregations, and individuals aware that the Historical Foundation is interested and has funds to publish books on topics concerning the Cumberland Presbyterian Church and Cumberland Presbyterian Church in America," be adopted.

2. Online Promotions

RECOMMENDATION 8: That Recommendation 4 of the Report of the Board of Trustees of the Historical Foundation, "that the General Assembly encourage presbyteries, congregations, and individuals active on the internet to join the Historical Foundation of the CPC & CPCA Facebook group," be adopted.

C. ACQUISITIONS

RECOMMENDATION 9: That Recommendation 5 of the Report of the Board of Trustees of the Historical Foundation, "that the General Assembly encourage all congregations to preserve their session records by depositing them in the Historical Foundation," be adopted.

RECOMMENDATION 10: That Recommendation 6 of the Report of the Board of Trustees of the Historical Foundation, "that the General Assembly instruct each synod and presbytery to deposit their minutes in a timely fashion with the Historical Foundation," be adopted.

RECOMMENDATION 11: That Recommendation 7 of the Report of the Board of Trustees of the Historical Foundation, "that the General Assembly instruct presbyteries to locate the session records when closing a church and then deposit them in the Historical Foundation," be adopted.

D. COMMENDATION OF HISTORICAL FOUNDATION STAFF

The committee was impressed with the dedication displayed by the Historical Foundation staff and Board to the heritage of the Cumberland Presbyterian Church and the Cumberland Presbyterian Church in America. Their efforts in preserving our historical records and artifacts and in educating our churches and individuals about their heritage are to be commended. For that reason, the committee makes the following recommendation:

RECOMMENDATION 12: That the General Assembly express its gratitude to the Historical Foundation for their work in preservation and education of the heritage of the Cumberland Presbyterian Church and Cumberland Presbyterian Church in America.

Respectfully Submitted,
The Committee on the Children's Home/Historical Foundation

REPORT OF THE COMMITTEE ON
MINISTRY COUNCIL/COMMUNICATIONS/DISCIPLESHIP
(Appendix C)

I. REFERRALS

Referral to this committee is as follows: The Report of the Ministry Council, except shaded sections which are referred to Chaplains/Missions/Pastoral Development.

II. PERSONS OF COUNSEL

Appearing before this committee were: Ms. Edith Old, Director of Ministries; Mr Ken Bean, Representative from Ministry Council; Reverend Elinor Brown, Discipleship Ministry Team; Reverend Nathan Wheeler, Coordinator of Youth & Young Adult Ministry; and Mr. Mark Davis, Communications Ministry Team.

III. CONSIDERATION OF REFERRAL

A. REPORT OF THE MINISTRY COUNCIL EXCEPT SHADED SECTIONS

We commend the Ministry Council and their hard work of good stewardship with the funds that God and his church have entrusted to them and make the following recommendations.

RECOMMENDATION 1: That Recommendation 1 of the Report of the Ministry Council, "that the General Assembly amend the Bylaws of The Ministry Council, ARTICLE III, BOARD OF DIRECTORS, AUTHORITY, AND MEETINGS, Section C. Advisory Members "There shall be six Advisory Members to the board of directors, who shall be the Stated Clerk, the Moderator of General Assembly, the Immediate Past Moderator of the General Assembly, and three youth Advisory Members appointed by the member" to remove the Immediate Past Moderator as an Advisory Member, reducing the number of Advisory Members to five (Stated Clerk, Moderator, and three Youth Advisory Members," be adopted.

RECOMMENDATION 2: That Recommendation 8 of the Report of the Ministry Council, "that General Assembly ask every presbytery to appoint a person to serve as a youth and young adult contact person and send this person's name and pertinent information to the discipleship ministry team coordinator of youth and young adult ministry," be adopted.

Respectfully submitted,
The Committee on Ministry Council/Communication/Discipleship

REPORT OF THE COMMITTEE ON JUDICIARY
(Appendix D)

I. REFERRALS

Referral to this committee is as follows: The Report of the Permanent Committee on Judiciary.

II. PERSONS OF COUNSEL

Appearing before this committee were: Reverend Michael Sharpe, Stated Clerk; Reverend Milton Ortiz, Missions Ministry Team, and Elder Leon Cole, moderator of the Cumberland Presbyterian Church in America.

III. CONSIDERATION OF REFERRAL

A. REPORT OF THE PERMANENT COMMITTEE ON JUDICIARY

We reviewed the report of the Permanent Committee on Judiciary. The report of the Permanent Committee had no recommendations. We commend the permanent committee on their work.

RECOMMENDATION 1: We strongly encourage the Committee on Judiciary to have the constitutional amendment referred to them by the 184th General Assembly (which read: *That the Permanent Committee on Judiciary work in concert with the Missions Ministry Team, in development of amendment(s) to the constitution, empowering the Missions Ministry Team (or its successor) to develop new churches outside of the United States.*) ready for the 186th General Assembly to review and vote for referral to the Presbyteries for ratification. Further, if the amendment is not ready, a detailed progress report must be provided to the 186th General Assembly.

With regard to the review of presbytery minutes we concur in the permanent committee's request for the synods to be more diligent in following the Cumberland Presbyterian Digest 8.5b Interpretive 1892, 1973 and 8.5b Advisory, 1964.

8.5b INTERPRETIVE, 1892, 1973.
Whereas, the Constitution of our church prescribes the standard of literary attainment to be reached by licentiates preparatory to ordination and emphatically states that a knowledge of the branches of literature therein enumerated is indispensable to ordination; and whereas, it is the habit of many of our presbyteries to disregard often this requirement of the Constitution, and, by laying hands on men who have not reached the standard required, to thrust into the ranks of the ministry incompetent men; therefore be it
Resolved: That we recommend to this General Assembly that it instruct the synods under its jurisdiction to make careful observation of the work of presbyteries touching this matter, and where presbyteries are found acting in violation of this law of the church to administer to them a severe reprimand and if this fails to correct the evil, to proceed to dissolve said presbytery and distribute their ministers and churches among other presbyteries, according to the wisdom of the synod so acting. 1892, p. 37.
We recommend that synods be instructed to include a statement in their minutes as to whether or not the ordination practices of the presbyteries are in keeping with the directives given in the Assembly of 1968. 1973, p. 180.

Synods to See that Ordination Records Are Complete
8.5b ADVISORY, 1964.
That the synods of the church be instructed to give attention to the examination of presbyterial records to observe that the records of ordination are complete and in order. 1964, pp. 149, 183.

Respectfully submitted,
The Committee on Judiciary

REPORT OF THE COMMITTEE ON STEWARDSHIP/ELECTED OFFICERS
(Appendix E)

Referrals to this committee are as follows: The Report of the Moderator; The Report of the Stated Clerk; The Report of the Board of Stewardship, Foundation and Benefits; The Report of the Our United Outreach Committee; The Report of the Place of Meeting Committee; The Line Item Budgets Submitted by General Assembly Agencies; and the Resolution submitted by Reverend Fred Polacek, Minister Commissioner, Nashville Presbytery.

II. PERSONS OF COUNSEL

Appearing before this committee were: Reverend Robert Heflin, Executive Secretary and Mr. Mark Duck, Coordinator of Benefits from the Board of Stewardship, Foundation and Benefits; Reverend Michael Sharpe, Stated Clerk; and Moderator of the 184th General Assembly, Reverend Lisa Anderson.

We wish to express our appreciation to the persons of counsel for their presentations.

III. CONSIDERATION OF REFERRALS

A. REPORT OF THE MODERATOR

We commend the Moderator, Reverend Lisa Anderson, for her compassionate and insightful leadership, as well as the thoughtfulness of her suggestion. After listening to the Moderator share her observations and points of concern related to the need to improve the knowledge of ministers and congregations on the doctrine, theology and polity of the Cumberland Presbyterian Church, the committee shares the Moderator's concerns. The report was received and the following recommendations are made.

RECOMMENDATION 1: That SUGGESTION 1 of the Report of the Moderator, "that the Cumberland Presbyterian Church renew commitment to study the *Confession of Faith* in churches, Sunday Schools, Bible Studies and small groups. Throughout the year many of the concerns of people in communication have been based on an inadequate and sometimes absent knowledge of the doctrine of the church. The health of our church depends on our study of scripture and our expression of Christianity spelled out in the *Confession of Faith*," be denied.

RECOMMENDATION 2: That the Cumberland Presbyterian Church renew commitment to study the *Confession of Faith* in churches, Sunday schools, Bible studies and small groups. Throughout the year many of the concerns of people in communication have been based on an inadequate and sometimes absent knowledge of the doctrine of the church. The health of our church depends on our study of scripture and our expression of Christianity spelled out in the *Confession of Faith*.

B. REPORT OF THE STATED CLERK

We commend the excellent work of the Stated Clerk, Reverend Michael Sharpe. The Report of the Stated Clerk was received and the following recommendations are made.

RECOMMENDATION 3: That Recommendation 1 of the Report of the Stated Clerk, "that the 185th General Assembly approve the following dates for the 2015-2016 Church Calendar," be adopted.

CHURCH CALENDAR 2015-2016

July-2015
5-10	Cumberland Presbyterian Youth Conference, Bethel, McKenzie, Tennessee
11	Program of Alternate Studies Graduation
11-25	PAS Summer Extension School, Bethel, McKenzie, Tennessee
18	Children's Fest, Bethel, McKenzie, Tennessee
22-26	Ministers Retreat, Bethel, McKenzie, Tennessee
25-28	Children's Fest On the Go, Casa de Fe, Malden, Massachusetts

August-2015
22	MTS Fall Semester Begins
30-Sept 27	Christian Education Season

September-2015
2	MTS Opening Convocation
13	Senior Adult Sunday
20	Christian Service Recognition Sunday
20	International Day of Prayer and Action for Human Habitat

October-2015
	Clergy Appreciation Month
4	Worldwide Communion Sunday
11	Pastor Appreciation Sunday
25	Native American Sunday

November-2015

	Any Sunday Loaves and Fishes Program
1	All Saints Day
1	Stewardship Sunday
6	World Community Day (Church Women United)
8	Day of Prayer for People with Aids and Other Life-Threatening Illnesses
8-11	The Forum, Brenthaven Chuch, Brentwood, Tennessee
15	Bible Sunday
22	Christ the King Sunday
29-Dec 25	Advent in Church and Home

December-2015

	Any Sunday Gift to the King Offering
24	Christmas Eve
25	Christmas Day
27-30	Youth Evangelism Conference, Louisville, Kentucky

January-2016

6	Epiphany
11	Human Trafficking Awareness Day
11	BU Spring Semester Begins
11-12	Stated Clerks' Conference
12-14	Ministers Conference, Brenthaven Church, Brentwood, Tennessee
15	Deadline for receipt of 2015 Our United Outreach Contributions

February-2016

	Black History Month
1	Annual congregational reports due in General Assembly office
7	Denomination Day
7	Historical Foundation Offering
7	Souper Bowl Sunday
10	Ash Wednesday, the beginning of Lent
10–Mar 27	Lent to Easter
14	Our United Outreach Sunday
21	Youth Sunday

March-2016

	Women's History Month (USA)
20	Palm/Passion Sunday
20	One Great Hour of Sharing
24	Maundy Thursday
25	Good Friday
27	Easter
27-April 1	National Farm Workers Awareness Week

April-2016

3-9	Family Week
10	CPCH Sunday
25-26	30-Hour Famine

May-2016

6	Friendship Day (Church Women United)
7	BU Commencement
14	MTS Closing Convocation & Graduation
15	Pentecost
15	Stott-Wallace Missionary Fund Offering
15	World Mission Sunday
30	Memorial Day Offering for Military Chaplains & Personnel for USA churches

June-2016
20-24	General Assembly, Nashville, Tennessee
20-24	CPWM Convention, Nashville, Tennessee
26-July 1	Cumberland Presbyterian Youth Conference, Bethel, McKenzie, Tennessee

July-2016
9	Program of Alternate Studies Graduation
9-23	PAS Summer Extension School, Bethel, McKenzie, Tennessee
19-23	Presbyterian Youth Triennium, Purdue University, Lafayette, Indiana

August-2016
6	BU Commencement
20	MTS Fall Semester Begins
22	BU Fall Semester Begins
28-Sept 25	Christian Education Season
30	BU Spring Convocation

September-2016
3	MTS Opening convocation
11	Senior Adult Sunday
18	Christian Service Recognition Sunday
18	International Day of Prayer and Action for Human Habitat
25	MTS/PAS Sunday

October-2016
	Clergy Appreciation Month
2	Worldwide Communion Sunday
9	Pastor Appreciation Sunday
23	Native American Sunday

November-2016
	Any Sunday Loaves and Fishes Program
1	All Saints Day
4	World Community Day (Church Women United)
6	Stewardship Sunday
6-9	The Forum
13	Day of Prayer for People with Aids and Other Life-Threatening Illnesses
13	Bible Sunday
20	Christ the King Sunday
27-Dec 25	Advent in Church and Home

December-2016
	Any Sunday Gift to the King Offering
10	BU Commencement
24	Christmas Eve
25	Christmas Day

RECOMMENDATION 4: That presbyteries, congregations and individuals should consider the importance of maintaining and reporting accurate statistical reports in a timely manner to General Assembly for accountability and communication concerns.

C. REPORT OF THE BOARD OF STEWARDSHIP, FOUNDATION AND BENEFITS

We commend the Board of Stewardship, Foundation, and Benefits for their diligent work. The Report of the Board of Stewardship, Foundation, and Benefits was received. The committee listened to Reverend Robert Heflin, Executive Secretary, and Mr. Mark Duck, Coordinator of Benefits: from the Board of Stewardship, Foundation and Benefits review the report with enhanced commentary. After a time of questions and answers between committee members and counsel, the committee makes the following recommendations:

RECOMMENDATION 5: That Recommendation 1 of the Report of the Board of Stewardship, Foundation and Benefits, "that to properly answer the 184th General Assembly's inquiry pertaining to what is currently covered by the health insurance benefits and to clarify anything that might be in conflict with the *Confession of Faith* and previous General Assembly statements regarding the sanctity of life, the Board of Stewardship requests to refer the matter to Theology and Social Concerns," be denied.

The committee substituted the following recommendation:

RECOMMENDATION 6: That the Board of Stewardship and the Committee on Theology and Concerns have joint responsibility to properly answer the 184th General Assembly's inquiry pertaining to what is currently covered by the health insurance benefits and to clarify anything that might be in conflict with the *Confession of Faith* and previous General Assembly statements regarding the sanctity of life. The jointly tasked responsibilities along with findings will be reported to the 186th General Assembly.

D. REPORT OF THE OUR UNITED OUTREACH COMMITTEE

Reverend Michael Sharpe, Stated Clerk, provided the Report of the Our United Outreach Committee. We commend the work of the Our United Outreach Committee and the Development Director for their diligent work. We especially commend their work toward debt retirement. Special recognition will be given during the 186th General Assembly of the denomination's debts being paid in full. The committee discussed ways in which presbyteries and congregations could be educated of the importance to turn in statistical reports in a timely manner as well as educate and encourage them to provide in a consistent manner toward the Our United Outreach fund.

RECOMMENDATION 7: That Recommendation 1 of the Report of the Our United Outreach Committee, "that we ask General Assembly that the following allocation for incoming 2016 for Our United Outreach funds," be adopted.

The allocation is to be as follows:	$2,800,000.00	
Development Coordinator		92,044.00
Evaluation Committee		3,500.00
Contingency		14,000.00
Unification Task Force		<u>30,000.00</u>
	Sub-total	139,544.00
(Amount to be allocated)	$2,660,456.00	
Ministry Council	$1,330,228.00	50%
Bethel University	133,023.00	5%
Children's Home	79,814.00	3%
Stewardship	159,627.00	6%
General Assembly Office	212,836.00	8%
Memphis Theological Seminary/	186,231.00	7%
Program of Alternate Studies		
Historical Foundation	79,814.00	3%
Shared Services	452,278.00	17%
(Next four items total 1%)		
Commission on Chaplains	10,296.00	.387%
Judiciary Committee	9,710.00	.365%
Theology/Social Concerns	3,618.00	.136%
Nominating Committee	<u>2,981.00</u>	.112%
	$2,660,456.00	

RECOMMENDATION 8: That Presbyteries, congregations and individuals should consider inviting the Our United Outreach Development Director to meetings to educate constituents on the importance of timely, consistent giving to Our United Outreach funds and explain the diverse ministries, missions, and fiscal needs met by such giving across the denomination.

E. REPORT OF THE PLACE OF MEETING COMMITTEE

We commend the work of the Place of Meeting Committee. The Report of the Place of Meeting Committee was received with calendar corrections. No further actions were required of this committee.

F. LINE ITEM BUDGETS SUBMITTED BY GENERAL ASSEMBLY AGENCIES

The committee reviewed the line item budgetary items. No actions were required of this committee.

G. RESOLUTION SUBMITTED BY REVEREND FRED POLACEK, MINISTER COMMISSIONER, NASHVILLE PRESBYTERY

The 185th General Assembly referred a Commissioner Resolution from Reverend Fred Polacek to the Committee on Stewardship/Elected Officers: The resolution states:

"WHEREAS the Cumberland Presbyterian Church has a Retirement Program ("Plan 2"), administered by the Board of Stewardship, Foundation, and Benefits, and

WHEREAS the Retirement Program includes the provision for disbursements to participants to be counted as a housing allowance and so be tax-free within appropriate guidelines, and

WHEREAS the current investment strategy is a "high level of diversification and a low level of risk" (with no mention of goal for performance/return), and

WHEREAS employers in the public/secular area often provide employees with investment options with varying levels of risk for the employee's 401k or other retirement options, and

WHEREAS some individual participants in the Retirement Program may be willing to utilize an investment strategy that may be described as "low-moderate" or even "moderate" rather than the current "low-risk strategy," and

WHEREAS participants in the Retirement Program, in order to keep the housing allowance provision, must currently take the only investment strategy provided by the Board with no other articulated option:

THEREFORE BE IT RESOLVED that the Board of Stewardship, Foundation and Benefits be directed to provide participants in the Retirement Plan with opportunities to select more than the one investment strategy offered by the Board, and

BE IT FURTHER RESOLVED that the Board of Stewardship, Foundation and Benefits be directed to develop appropriate mechanisms to allow the participants of the Retirement Program more input in the investment strategy decision-making process, and

BE IT FURTHER RESOLVED that the Board of Stewardship, Foundation and Benefits complete these tasks by January 1, 2016.

Respectfully Submitted, Reverend Fred E. Polacek, Minister Commissioner, Nashville Presbytery,"

The committee met with Reverend Fred Polacek, who is a member of the Committee of Stewardship/Elected Officers, to hear his concerns as related to his resolution. The committee also heard from Reverend Robert Heflin, Executive Secretary from the Board of Stewardship, Foundation, and Benefits, regarding the resolution and Reverend Polacek's concerns. After hearing from the two individuals and asking many questions and points of clarification, the committee felt many of the points made in the resolution were addressed and answered during the discussion on the resolution. Reverend Polacek abstained from voting on this issue.

RECOMMENDATION 9: That the resolution submitted by the Reverend Fred Polacek, Minister Commissioner, Nashville Presbytery, be denied.

We encourage all church employees to actively communicate with the Board of Stewardship, Foundation, and Benefits regarding the Retirement Program.

Respectfully submitted:
The Committee on Stewardship/Elected Officers

REPORT OF THE COMMITTEE ON CHAPLAINS/MISSIONS/PASTORAL DEVELOPMENT
(Appendix F)

I. REFERRALS

Referrals to this committee are as follows: The Report of the Ministry Council (shaded sections only) and The Report of the Commission on Military Chaplains and Personnel.

II. PERSONS OF COUNSEL

Appearing before this committee were: Reverend Larry Greenslit, Director Presbyterian Council for Chaplains and Military Personnel; Reverend Cassandra Thomas, representative; Reverend Chuck Brown, Pastoral Development Ministry Team; Reverend Milton Ortiz, Missions Ministry Team; and Reverend Michael Sharpe, Stated Clerk.

III. CONSIDERATION OF REFERRALS

A. REPORT OF THE COMMISSION ON MILITARY CHAPLAINS AND PERSONNEL

We note that we are a global church and as such we need to respect the position, history and nature of the many members of our global church that may not be a part of the United States. We would encourage the Commission on Military Chaplains and Personnel to be aware and identify needs and possibilities for chaplain service in other countries as we continue to be a more global church.

We commend the members that represent us as a part of the Presbyterian Council for Chaplains and Military Personnel.

We encourage the home presbyteries of those chaplains deployed and living outside the bounds of their home presbytery to keep in touch with those chaplains and include them in all information sharing processes.

The endorsement process of chaplains for many communities is important. Since there is an even greater number of people being incarcerated, more and more ministers are seeking a call to ministry in the prison setting. We feel those individuals should have the endorsement of their denomination. We note that the Presbyterian Council for Chaplains and Military Personnel has taken the added responsibility of endorsing ministers to serve in the prison setting, making sure to meet the requirements of such ministry.

RECOMMENDATION 1: That the Cumberland Presbyterian Church authorize the Stated Clerk of the denomination to designate the Presbyterian Council for Chaplains and Military Personnel as the official endorsing agency of the Cumberland Presbyterian Church for those seeking to serve as chaplains in the USA federal prison setting.

We would ask that this General Assembly recognize Reverend Larry Greenslit (an ordained PCUSA minister) and that the Assembly allow Reverend Greenslit the opportunity to address the Assembly about the work of the Presbyterian Council for Chaplains and Military Personnel.

B. REPORT OF THE MINISTRY COUNCIL (SHADED SECTIONS ONLY)

We express excitement to both Reverend Chuck Brown who shared with us plans for the Pastoral Development Ministry Team with plans for Minister's Conferences and leadership development; and Reverend Milton Ortiz who offered plans for many concepts of ministry, especially our cross cultural ministry.

RECOMMENDATION 2: That Recommendation 2 of the Report of the Ministry Council, "that the General Assembly encourage all USA presbyteries to explore opportunities for Cross-Culture church starts within their boundaries," be adopted.

RECOMMENDATION 3: That Recommendation 3 of the Report of the Ministry Council, "that according to the *Confession of Faith* for Cumberland Presbyterians, and the example of Christ, the General Assembly affirms that the Cumberland Presbyterian Church and all its judicatories and agencies are called to minister to all immigrants regardless of their nationality, culture, race, social economics, migration status, and/or political preference, who are coming to live in countries where the Cumberland Presbyterian Church is present," be adopted.

RECOMMENDATION 4: That Recommendation 4 of the Report of the Ministry Council, "that the Mission Ministry Team through the Cross-Culture Ministry USA Program assists the judicatories of the Cumberland Presbyterian Church regarding immigration education and/or resources to embrace ministerial opportunities among communities made up of immigrants within all presbyteries and synods," be adopted.

RECOMMENDATION 5: That Recommendation 5 of the Report of the Ministry Council, "that the Missions Ministry Team engage new immigrants associated with the Cumberland Presbyterian Church in the study of scriptures that ask followers of Christ to obey the laws imposed on society, if not contrary to God's laws, providing theological guidance to Christian immigrants who may not be in compliant legal status," be adopted.

RECOMMENDATION 6: That Recommendation 6 of the Report of the Ministry Council, "that the General Assembly pray that God give us wisdom and leads us as a church into places in the world where God can use the Cumberland Presbyterian Church to show the love and compassion of Jesus Christ," be adopted.

RECOMMENDATION 7: That Recommendation 7 of the Report of the Ministry Council, "that Cumberland Presbyterian Churches everywhere light 19 candles or display 19 Bibles (or some other appropriate symbol) on Mission Sunday (Pentecost Sunday) to recognize the service of these 19 Cumberland Presbyterian Missionaries, and that they set aside special time for prayer for the work of these missionaries who are carrying the light of Christ into our world," be adopted.

RECOMMENDATION 8: That Recommendation 9 of the Report of the Ministry Council, "that each presbytery's Committee on the Ministry urge ministers/leaders who may be open to considering a call to create an online profile (http://ministrycoiuncil.cumberland.org/leadershipreferral)," be adopted.

RECOMMENDATION 9: That Recommendation 10 of the Report of the Ministry Council, "that each presbytery's Board of Missions urge churches who are searching for a pastor to create an online church profile to maximize the effectiveness of the Leadership Referral Services process (http://ministrycouncil.cumberland.org/leadershipreferral)," be adopted.

RECOMMENDATION 10: That Recommendation 11 of the Report of the Ministry Council, "that the General Assembly request that all pastors provide brochures and information about the Stott-Wallace Missionary Offering to their churches, explain the importance of the offering, and invite their church to participate in supporting Cumberland Presbyterian missionaries through this offering," be denied.

RECOMMENDATION 11: That the General Assembly request that all pastors provide brochures and information about the Stott-Wallace Missionary Offering to their churches, explain the importance of the offering, (which helps support Anay Ortega, a layperson from Andes Presbytery; Boyce and Beth Wallace, semi-retired Cumberland Presbyterian missionaries in Cali, Colombia; Carlos and Luz Dary Rivera, who are pastors in Andes Presbytery working in Mexico; D and S, missionaries in Laos; Daniel and Kay Jang, who are church planters in the Philippines; Fhanor and Socorro Pejendino, who are church planters in Guatemala; Glen Watts, a layperson serving in Hong Kong; John and Joy Park, who will deploy to the Philippines as soon as they finish deputation; Kenneth and Delight Hopson in Uganda, Africa; N B, a layperson working with an interdenominational organization in China; and T and T G, who work with an interdenominational mission in Central Asia) and invite their church to participate in supporting Cumberland Presbyterian missionaries through this offering.

Respectfully submitted:
The Committee on Chaplains/Missions/Pastoral Development

REPORT OF THE COMMITTEE ON THEOLOGY & SOCIAL CONCERNS
(Appendix G)

I. REFERRALS

Referrals to this committee are as follows: The Report of the Unified Committee on Theology and Social Concerns, The Report of the Unificaition Task Force and the Memorial from Cumberland Presbytery.

II. PERSONS OF COUNSEL

Appearing before this committee were: Mr. David Phillips-Burk, representative from the Unified Committee on Theology and Social Concerns: Elder Leon Cole, CPCA and Reverend Gloria Villa-Diaz, CPC, representatives of the Unification Task Force.

III. CONSIDERATION OF REFERRALS

A. REPORT OF THE UNIFICATION TASK FORCE

We strongly support unification because we share one confession and should be together as one church body. We commend the work of the Unification Task Force. We recognize that this document is a working document designed for study and discussion over the next year. We encourage every commissioner of the 185th General Assembly to go back to her or his home congregation and presbytery, resolve to study this document and provide feedback to the Unification Task Force. We applaud their efforts to develop a proposal that would allow for ownership on the congregational level. However, we acknowledge that the greatest obstacle to the proposal seems to be a lack of communication at the presbyterial and congregational levels. This can be better accomplished if we all commit to study and discussion concerning this document while supporting the concept. One suggestion is sharing the proposal in the Missionary Messenger, the Cumberland Presbyterian magazine and the Cumberland Flag.

RECOMMENDATION 1: That Recommendation 1 of the Report of the Unification Task Force, "that the Unification Task Force be given time at Summer and Fall 2015 and Spring 2016 presbytery and synod meetings to present updates on unification and to communicate feedback on the plan for union," be denied.

RECOMMENDATION 2: That presbyteries be directed to allow the Unification Task Force sufficient time at Summer, Fall 2015 and Spring 2016 presbytery and synod meetings to present updates on unification and to communicate feedback on the proposal for union.

RECOMMENDATION 3: That Recommendation 2 of the Report of the Unification Task Force, "that joint clusters of churches also schedule a time for a presentation on unification by a member of the task force, unification advocates, and/or other leaders within both denominations," be adopted.

RECOMMENDATION 4: That Recommendation 3 of the Report of the Unification Task Force, "that the General Assembly increase its funding for 2016 to $30,000 to support the programming and travel of the Unification Task Force, legal fees, and subsequent implementation costs that may be incurred," be adopted.

RECOMMENDATION 5: That the General Assembly add an additional $5,000 for 2016 to the Unification Task Force budget to be used for communication purposes, such as informational videos, additional mailings to members, session clerks and clergy, press releases, or any other means to maximize the sharing of information.

RECOMMENDATION 6: That Recommendation 4 of the Report of the Unification Task Force, "that clergy, elders and laity make all efforts to attend a regional meeting if geographically possible," be denied.

RECOMMENDATION 7: That clergy, elders and laity make all efforts to attend a regional meeting.

B. REPORT OF THE UNIFIED COMMITTEE OF THEOLOGY AND SOCIAL CONCERNS

1. General Assembly Referral

We note an editorial change. The representatives from Grace Presbytery mentioned in the General Assembly Referral were not "representatives from the Theology and Social Concerns of Grace Presbytery," but rather an "ad hoc Committee on Universalism from Grace Presbytery." We commend the Unified Committee of Theology and Social Concerns for their study of the questions regarding section 3.08 of the *Confession of Faith* and their affirmation of the Sovereignty of God, the Authority of Scriptures, and the strength of sections 3.08 and 4.08 of the *Confession of Faith*, which clearly states that (3.08) "Jesus Christ, ... is the only hope of reconciliation between God and sinful persons" and (4.08) "that persons rely solely upon God's grace in Jesus Christ for salvation."

2. Study Papers

We commend the Unified Committee on Theology and Social Concerns for their hard work in writing these study papers. We encourage all ministers and presbyteries to spend time with these and use them for study purposes. We do note that there are two titles, one in the report and one on the paper itself. We are assuming (and hoping) that the name for the paper is *"Come Let Us Reason Together, Being Faithful in the Midst of Conflict."* We do ask that the committee make all papers available online in a format that can be searched in a word processor rather than a picture format. Some are in this format but some are not.

RECOMMENDATION 8: That Recommendation 1 of Report of the Unified Committee on Theology and Social Concerns, "that the General Assemblies accept this paper as study paper and that it be used to initiate thought and discussion within the Cumberland Presbyterian Church and the Cumberland Presbyterian Church in America," be adopted.

RECOMMENDATION 9: That Recommendation 2 of Report of the Unified Committee on Theology and Social Concerns, "that the Office of the General Assembly of both denominations make this paper available to churches through the stated clerks of the presbyteries," be adopted.

C. MEMORIAL FROM CUMBERLAND PRESBYTERY

The committee discussed the memorial from Cumberland Presbytery. With the many concerns listed in this memorial and the fact that the Cumberland Presbyterian Church has made statements regarding some of the issues in this memorial, we feel that the best action is to refer it to the appropriate agency.

RECOMMENDATION 10: That the Memorial from Cumberland Presbytery which states:

"WHEREAS, the Church of Jesus Christ, the teachings of our Lord, the principles of the Bible; and the Christian Faith and lifestyle, are under attack by an increasingly diverse group of liberal, secular, agnostic, atheistic, and pagan propagandists; and

WHEREAS, under the influence and relentless anti-Christian polemic of these entities and their promoters, a growing majority of Americans are abandoning the precepts of the Bible and making lifestyle choices that are diametrically opposed to the Word of God; and

WHEREAS an estimated 57,000,000 babies have been aborted since Roe vs Wade in 1973 and this number is increasing by more than 1.2 million babies each year; and

WHEREAS the 2013 National Health Interview Survey conducted by the Centers for Disease Control and Prevention reported that 4.7 % of the adult population of the United States, or more than 14.5 million Americans, identified themselves as gay, lesbian, or bi-sexual; and

WHEREAS same sex marriages are now legal in thirty-seven states and Washington D. C. and the number of same-sex marriages are increasing dramatically across the nation; and

WHEREAS a 2013 study by the Bowling Green State University's National Center for Marriage and Family Research reports that traditional marriages have declined by 60% since 1970 which is a leading factor in the decimation of the nuclear family in American society; and

WHEREAS the national debate regarding euthanasia, or physician assisted suicide, is still emerging in popular thought, five states have adopted legislation that approves the action on some level and 71% of Americans have expressed limited support for physicians being allowed to assist terminal patients to die with dignity and without pain; and

WHEREAS applications have already been filed with the FDA to approve a variety of treatments and therapies for diabetes, neuro degenerative disorders, spinal cord injuries, and heart disease using embryonic stem cells; and

WHEREAS our Lord Jesus Christ established His Church to be the advocate of His teachings and the principles of the Bible to the world; and

WHEREAS He commanded the Church to disciple all nations, incorporate them into the Church by the sacrament of baptism, and teach them to observe all His commandments.

THEREFORE BE IT RESOLVED, that the General Assembly of the Cumberland Presbyterian Church shall order its proper agencies to formulate appropriate responses to these issues based upon Christian compassion and Biblical morality," be referred to the Unified Committee on Theology and Social Concerns for response back to the 186th General Assembly.

RECOMMENDATION 11: That the Unified Committee on Theology and Social Concerns find a means to make all theological and social statements from General Assembly easily accessible for anyone to read.

Respectfully submitted,
Committee on Theology and Social Concerns

REPORT OF THE COMMITTEE ON HIGHER EDUCATION

(Appendix H)

I. REFERRALS

Referrals to this committee are as follows: The Report of the Board of Trustees of Memphis Theological Seminary and The Report of the Board of Trustees of Bethel University.

II. PERSONS OF COUNSEL

Appearing before this committee were: Reverend Jay Earheart-Brown, President Memphis Theological Seminary; Reverend Kevin Brantley, member of the Board of Trustees for Memphis Theological Seminary; and Reverend Michael Qualls, Director of Program of Alternate Studies; Dr. Walter Butler, President of Bethel University; Ms. Nancy Bean, Vice President of the College of Arts and Sciences of Bethel University, and Stated Clerk Reverend Michael Sharpe.

III. CONSIDERATION OF REPORTS

The committee gratefully acknowledges that the 185th General Assembly is conducting its work on the campus of the Colegio Americano, Cali, Colombia, a premier educational ministry of the Cumberland Presbyterian Church under the auspices of Cauca Valley Presbytery. From its beginnings in 1928, the school has made a major impact for Christ and in the professional lives of countless young people. Commendation is given to administrator Guillermo Arguello and director Gloria Adrianna Ordoñez.

A. BOARD OF TRUSTEES OF MEMPHIS THEOLOGICAL SEMINARY

The Board Report expressed appreciation to those members whose terms have been completed or who were unable to continue service. However, since the report was prepared, two additional members resigned due to poor health. For this reason the committee took the following actions:

RECOMMENDATION 1: That Recommendation 1 of the Report of the Board of Trustees of Memphis Theological Seminary, "that the General Assembly express its gratitude to Reverend Jody Hill, Mrs. Jan Holmes, and Mr. David Reed for their faithful service to Memphis Theological Seminary and the Cumberland Presbyterian Church," be denied.

RECOMMENDATION 2: That the General Assembly express its gratitude to Reverend Jody Hill, Mrs. Jan Holmes, Mr. David Reed, Mrs. Pat Meeks and Dr. Robert M. Shelton for their faithful service to Memphis Theological Seminary and the Cumberland Presbyterian Church.

Appreciation is expressed also to Mrs. Cathi Johnson for years of service to Memphis Theological Seminary. Dr. Keith Gaskin is welcomed as the Vice President for Advancement.

Members of the administration, faculty and staff of Memphis Theological Seminary are commended for their fine work. The committee notes with special appreciation that Dr. Earheart-Brown has marked his tenth anniversary as President of MTS. It further celebrates with the seminary community the 50th anniversary of the seminary's move to Memphis, Tennessee, from McKenzie, Tennessee.

The committee affirms the action of the 183rd General Assembly granting the Board of Trustees of Memphis Theological Seminary permission to engage in a capital campaign. Cumberland Presbyterians are urged to support this effort which will result in the construction of a new chapel and the expansion of endowments for the seminary.

Gratitude to God is expressed for the estate gifts from Reverend Dr. Virgil Todd and Reverend Walter (Pete) Palmer. The committee was informed that an endowment has been established in the name of Pete Palmer and that contributions are welcome. The endowment is for PAS scholarships. The committee also acknowledged with thanksgiving the publication this year of a new book by Dr. Clinton O. Buck, *Unity and Diversity in Theological Education*, a sequel to the previously published *A History of Memphis Theological Seminary*. Proceeds from the sale of this book are dedicated to help fund the Baird-Buck Chair of Cumberland Presbyterian Studies.

The Memphis Theological Seminary representatives emphasized to the committee the significance of Seminary/PAS Sunday. However, in Recommendation 2 of the report, PAS and the date for the observance were inadvertently not included. Therefore the committee took the following actions:

RECOMMENDATION 3: That Recommendation 2 of the Report of the Trustees of Memphis Theological Seminary, "that the General Assembly encourage all churches to recognize and support Seminary Sunday," be denied.

RECOMMENDATION 4: That the General Assembly encourage all churches to recognize and support MTS/PAS Sunday on the last Sunday in September, which next year is September 25, 2016, or another date of their choosing.

The committee is grateful for the Program of Alternate Studies, and commends the work of Director Dr. Michael Qualls, along with the administrative and teaching team. Since the General Assembly is meeting in Colombia this year, the committee was particularly gratified to hear of the growing work of PAS-Colombia under the administration of Dean Michele Gentry (Moderator of the 185th General Assembly).

RECOMMENDATION 5: That the General Assembly encourage churches and presbyteries to pray for and support PAS-Colombia and that, following the vote on this committee's report, GA recognize the outstanding progress of PAS-Colombia with standing applause.

The committee observed that several Cumberland Presbyterian work groups have done voluntary service at Mempis Theological Seminary in recent years, and we express appreciation to those congregations and work teams. We encourage other churches to become involved with the seminary in this way.

The committee commends Memphis Theological Seminary and the Ministry Council's Mission Ministry Team for the initiative in providing "*Advanced CP Studies*," [p. 43].

B. BOARD OF TRUSTEES OF BETHEL UNIVERSITY

The committee commends President Walter Butler, the faculty and staff of Bethel University which is completing its 172nd year of service. With strong historical and covenantal ties to the Cumberland Presbyterian Church, the university is experiencing significant growth, with a total enrollment last fall of 5,906 and more applications for the fall of 2015 than at this time last year.

The committee notes that since the publication of the Trustees Report in the Preliminary Minutes, Cumberland Presbyterian Trustee Reverend Eugene Leslie, a faithful servant of God and devoted supporter of Bethel, has passed away.

It is encouraging that the number of Cumberland Presbyterian students at Bethel has risen significantly since the hiring of a recruiter for Cumberland Presbyterian students. Those who have visited the McKenzie campus in recent years have been gratified to see the addition of new buildings, including dormitories, student center and gymnasium, and football arena. Currently the library is undergoing a $3.1 million renovation. The construction of The Cumberland Chapel awaits completion of fund raising, with about one-half the goal now raised or committed. A new football fieldhouse is also in the funding stage.

The committee commends Bethel University for its involvement internationally, and particularly with the Colegio Americano through mission work teams and student teachers.

RECOMMENDATION 6: That the General Assembly encourage congregations and individuals to pray and provide financial support for Bethel University, and that names of prospective students from the churches be supplied to the University.

Respectfully submitted,
Committee on Higher Education

CHURCH CALENDAR 2015-2016

JULY 2015

5-10	CPYC, Bethel University, McKenzie, TN
11	Program of Alternate Studies Graduation
11-25	PAS Summer Extension School, Bethel University, McKenzie, TN
18	Children's Fest, Bethel University, McKenzie, TN
22-26	Ministers Retreat, Bethel University, McKenzie, TN
25-28	Children's Fest On the Go, Casa de Fe, Malden, MA

AUGUST 2015

22	MTS Fall classes begin
30-Sept 27	Christian Education Season

SEPTEMBER 2015

2	MTS Opening Convocation
13	Senior Adult Sunday
20	Christian Service Recognition Sunday
20	International Day of Prayer and Action for Human Habitat

OCTOBER 2015

1-31	Clergy Appreciation Month
4	Worldwide Communion Day
11	Pastor Appreciation Sunday
25	Native American Sunday

NOVEMBER 2015

Any Sunday in November Loaves and Fishes Program

1	All Saints Day
1	Stewardship Sunday
6	World Community Day (Church Women United)
6	Day of Prayer for People with AIDS and Other Life-Threatening Illnesses
8-11	The Forum, Brenthaven CPC, Brentwood, TN
15	Bible Sunday
22	Christ the King Sunday
29-Dec 25	Advent in Church and Home

DECEMBER 2015

Any Sunday in December Gift to the King Offering

24	Christmas Eve
25	Christmas Day
27	Youth Evangelism Conference, Louisville, KY

JANUARY 2016

6	Epiphany
11	Human Trafficking Awareness Day
11	BU Spring Semester Begins
11-12	Stated Clerk's Conference
12-14	Ministers Conference, Brentwood CPC, Brentwood, TN
15	Deadline for receipt of 2015 Our United Outreach contributions

FEBRUARY 2016

1-28	Black History Month
1	Annual congregational reports due in GA office
7	Denomination Day
7	Historical Foundation Offering
7	Souper Bowl Sunday
10	Ash Wednesday, the beginning of Lent
10-Mar 27	Lent to Easter
14	Our United Outreach Sunday
21	Youth Sunday

MARCH 2016

1-31	Women's History Month (USA)
20	Palm/Passion Sunday
20	One Great Hour of Sharing
24	Maundy Thursday
25	Good Friday
27	Easter
27-April 1	National Farm Workers Awareness Week

APRIL 2016

3-9	Family Week
10	CP Children's Home Sunday
25-26	30-Hour Famine

MAY 2016

6	Friendship Day (Church Women United)
7	BU Commencement
14	MTS Closing Convocation & Graduation
15	Pentecost
15	Stott-Wallace Missionary Fund Offering
15	World Mission Sunday
30	Memorial Day Offering for Military Chaplains & Personnel for USA churches

JUNE 2016

20-24	General Assembly, Nashville, TN
20-24	CPWM Convention, Nashville, TN
26-July 1	CPYC, Bethel University, McKenzie, TN

www.ingramcontent.com/pod-product-compliance
Lightning Source LLC
Chambersburg PA
CBHW080532170426
43195CB00016B/2541